RETHINKING VIENNA 1900

AUSTRIAN HISTORY, CULTURE, AND SOCIETY
General Editor: Gary Cohen, Center for Austrian Studies,
University of Minnesota

RETHINKING VIENNA 1900

Edited by

Steven Beller

Berghahn Books
NEW YORK • OXFORD

Published in 2001 by

Berghahn Books

www.berghahnbooks.com

© 2001, 2012 Steven Beller
Reprinted in 2012

Library of Congress Cataloging-in-Publication Data

Rethinking Vienna 1900 / edited by Steven Beller.
 p. cm. – (Austrian history, culture, and society)
 Includes bibliographical references.
 ISBN 978-1-57181-139-4 (hbk) -- 978-1-57181-140-0 (pbk)
 1. Vienna (Austria)–Intellectual life. 2. Austrian literature–Austria–
Vienna–History and criticism. 3. Vienna (Austria)–Social life and customs.
4. Politics and literature–Austria–Vienna. I. Title: Rethinking Vienna
neunzehnhundert. II. Beller, Steven, 1958– III. Series.

DB851 .R43 2001
943.6'13—dc21   2001018446

British Library Cataloguing in Publication Data

A catalogue record for this book is available from
the British Library.

Printed in the United States on acid-free paper

CONTENTS

ILLUSTRATIONS

PREFACE

This volume has its origins in the conference "Beyond Vienna 1900: Rethinking Culture in Central Europe, 1867–1939" held under the auspices of the Center for Austrian Studies at the University of Minnesota in Minneapolis, and organized by myself and David Good. The conference took place in the belief that "Vienna 1900" is a field that remains of central interest to Austrian Studies, and continues to be the subject of the sort of scholarly controversies on which academic life thrives. This volume reflects those controversies and confirms "Vienna 1900" as a topic of lively historiographical debate. It aims to provide scholars, teachers, and their students with a selection of the most recent critical discussions of various aspects of the subject, with the thesis of Carl E. Schorske's *Fin-de-Siècle Vienna* at the center, and should be of great help in aiding discussion, both in and out of the classroom, about "what happened in Vienna 1900." If the book opens to readers new aspects of the intricate developments that made "Vienna 1900" such a significant cultural and intellectual center, and generally enables them to think about the subject in new and fruitful ways, it will have served its purpose.

Not only did David Good initiate and organize the conference, but he has also been of immeasurable help in bringing this book to publication. I would like to thank all those who helped and advised us in planning the conference, especially William M. Johnston. The participants at the original conference are to be thanked for providing the enthusiasm which made that meeting a success; those conferees whose papers are not included here may rest assured that their efforts and insights have greatly helped shape the resulting volume. The contributors are to be praised for their patience and their tolerance during the editorial process. Gerhard Weiss and the staff of the Center for Austrian Studies are to be warmly thanked for their help and financial assistance in enabling this volume to be published. I am grateful to the editorial staff of the Austrian History Yearbook for their close cooperation. I would also like to thank Marion Berghahn and the staff of Berghahn Books for taking on the book, and for shepherding it to completion. I would especially like to thank Shawn Kendrick and Jacqueline Brownstein for giving the book its finishing touches.

Finally, I would like to thank Carl E. Schorske. Many aspects of his thesis about "Vienna 1900," or "*fin-de-siècle* Vienna," come under quite strong criticism in the following pages. It is just as well to remember, therefore, that without his pioneering work in exploring—in some ways even creating—the field, this volume would not have been possible.

CONTRIBUTORS

Steven Beller is the author of *Vienna and the Jews, 1867–1938: A Cultural History* (Cambridge, 1989), *Herzl* (Halban, 1991), and *Francis Joseph* (Longman, 1996). He is currently working on *A Concise History of Austria*.

Michael Burri teaches on Central Europe at the University of Pennsylvania. He publishes regularly on Vienna and the Habsburg predicament in academic journals and in the Czech press.

Mary Gluck teaches European cultural and intellectual history at Brown University. She is the author of *Georg Lukács and His Generation* (Harvard, 1985), and is in the process of completing a book on typologies of the modernist artist in nineteenth-century Paris.

Malachi Haim Hacohen is associate professor of history at Duke University. He is the author of *Karl Popper—the Formative Years, 1902–1945: Politics and Philosophy in Interwar Vienna* (Cambridge, 2000). His current research focuses on enlightenment, emancipation, and the limits of the multicultural imagination, as well as on the Congress for Cultural Freedom and Cold War liberalism.

Allan Janik is research fellow of the Brenner Archives at the University of Innsbruck and adjunct professor of philosophy at the University of Vienna. He co-authored *Wittgenstein's Vienna* and has written and lectured extensively on philosophy and cultural history. His latest book is *Wittgenstein's Vienna Revisited* (Transaction, 2001).

Robert Jensen teaches at the University of Kentucky. He is the author of *Marketing Modernism in Fin-de-Siècle Europe* (Princeton, 1994), and is completing a book on Central European self-portraiture at the beginning of the twentieth century entitled *Narcissus and His Muse*. He is also involved in a collaborative project on quantitative analyses of artists' careers.

Pieter M. Judson is associate professor and chair of the History Department at Swarthmore College. His book *Exclusive Revolutionaries: Liberal Politics, Social Experience and National Identity in the Austrian Empire, 1848–1914* (Michigan, 1996) won the Herbert Baxter Adams prize of the American Historical Association in 1997 and the Austrian Cultural Institute's book prize for 1998. His most recent book is *Wien Brennt! Die Revolution von 1848 und ihr liberales Erbe* (1998).

Alfred Pfabigan teaches cultural studies at the Institute for Philosophy at the University of Vienna. He edited *Ornament und Askese* (Brandstätter, 1985) and is the author of many works relating to Vienna 1900. His recent books include *Thomas Bernhard—Ein österreichisches Weltexperiment* (Zsolnay, 1999), *Die Enttäuschung der Moderne* (Sonderzahl, 2000), and *Verbotene Worte Gottes* (Eichborn, 2000).

Ilona Sármány-Parsons is visiting professor in Cultural History at the Central European University Budapest College . She also lectures at the University of Vienna. She is the author of *Gustav Klimt* (Crown, 1987), *Viennese Painting at the Turn of the Century* (Corvina, 1991), and the catalogue of the Nagybánya exhibition (Vienna, 1999).

James Shedel is a member of the faculty in the Department of History at Georgetown University, where he specializes in Central Europe and the history of the Habsburg monarchy. He is the author of *Art and Society: The New Art Movement in Vienna, 1897–1914* (Palo Alto, 1981).

Scott Spector is an associate professor in the departments of History and Germanic Languages and Literatures at the University of Michigan. He is the author of *Prague Territories: National Conflict and Cultural Innovation in Kafka's Fin de Siècle* (Berkeley and Los Angeles, 2000) and has written as well on a range of topics relating to ideology and culture. He is currently at work on a study of figures of sexual identity and violence in high and popular culture around 1900 in Central Europe.

INTRODUCTION

Steven Beller

The Life and Times of Vienna 1900

It is a generally accepted fact that Vienna at the beginning of the twentieth century was the birthplace of a major part of the modern culture and thought which forms the basis of our consciousness to this day. While Vienna's importance is perhaps not seen as being as great as it appeared a decade or so ago, when it could be called "the birthplace of modernity," the Habsburg capital still remains as a central fixture in the conventional picture of the origins of modernism. What is interesting about this is that, for a very large part of this century, this was not so. If one had asked at the turn of the century which city was the most important center of modern culture, the obvious candidate would have been Paris. Between the world wars, Weimar Berlin might have been seen as a greater center of avant-gardism. After the Second World War, New York lorded it over all other centers of modernity, and only really started to falter when "modernism" itself was undermined by the advent of "postmodernism." There was no place in this succession for Vienna. Even thirty years ago, although there had begun a shift in the Habsburg capital's favor, one would have been hard-pressed to make a case for Vienna around 1900 as a true rival in the invention of the modern world for those other cultural capitals. Shortly thereafter, however, things changed.

There had been harbingers of Vienna's significance. One of the very first texts to put Vienna at the, albeit negative, center of the modern world, and one which was seminal for later thinking, was Hermann Broch's *Hofmannsthal and His Times*, written in the late 1940s and published in 1955.[1] A decade later Ilsa Barea's *Vienna*, Arthur J. May's *Vienna in the Age of Franz Josef* and Frank Field's *The Last Days of Mankind* pioneered many of the themes that would shape later study.[2] It was, however, with the work of Carl E. Schorske, starting in the early 1960s, that *fin-de-siècle* Vienna—as a subject of academic research and intellectual analysis—was given its shape and its rationale.[3] Interest in Vienna as such had survived, naturally enough, in Vienna itself. In 1971 a collection of essays, edited and largely written by Hilde Spiel, *Wien: Spektrum einer Stadt*, was evidence of home-grown interest in the Austrian capital, but this was a different type of Vienna, not the version which would come to have such a powerful hold over the Western imagination.[4] That was the product of the early 1970s, and was based on the publication of two major books, William M. Johnston's *The Austrian Mind* and Janik and Toulmin's *Wittgenstein's Vienna*, together with Schorske's regularly appearing essays on various aspects of Vienna, which were eventually published in book form as *Fin-de-Siècle Vienna: Politics and Culture*.[5] These three books have dominated our understanding of Vienna 1900 ever since.

Johnston's major contribution was to provide to the English-speaking public, within a quasi-encyclopedic framework, an overview of the immense contribution made to modern thought and culture by inhabitants of the Habsburg Monarchy in the late nineteenth and early twentieth centuries, and to set this in some sort of historical context. Johnston's book provided, and still provides, the ballast for any study or course on Vienna 1900, even if some of his thematic explanations, such as the concept of "therapeutic nihilism," have not had the success of other "paradigms." As one of its authors, Allan Janik, describes in this volume, *Wittgenstein's Vienna* had a double impact on the field. It popularized the Schorskean view of Vienna as a center of aestheticist modernism. Yet, in its more narrow account of the background to Wittgenstein's thought, it also outlined the other major paradigm that would come to rival that of Schorske's, the idea of Vienna as a cradle of what would later be labeled "critical modernism." It was, though, Schorske's work, culminating in his book, *Fin-de-Siècle Vienna*, which became the dominant means by which to understand what was happening in Vienna at the turn of the century.

Schorske's thesis, as it developed through his essays and book, had the great attraction of being elegantly straightforward, yet at the same time tinged with a deep irony and buttressed by an intellectual and aesthetic sophistication, especially in its interplay of external and internal analyses, which was further enhanced by an impressive and readable prose style. In a nutshell, Schorske appeared to explain the origins of the ahistorical modernist mentality in Vienna as the retreat by the heirs of Austrian liberalism, the children of the bourgeoisie, from the political realm—where various illiberal collectivisms threatened the liberal assumptions of historical, rational progress—and into the cultural temple of the aesthetic and psychological, where the external, historical world held no sway. Having been struck by the connection between political alienation and cultural innovation in American society in the 1950s, the shift from Marx to Freud, social to psychological explanation, and noting the renewed interest, already in the 1960s, in things Viennese, Schorske looked for a similar explanation of ahistorical modernism in turn-of-the-century Vienna, and found it. There as well, it seemed, the defeat of liberalism had led to the intellectuals' retreat from history into a world closed off from the historical, which used as its model *homo psychologicus* rather than *homo œconomicus*. The ironic equation of political defeat and cultural success, overlaid with the ironic task of historicizing the ahistorical, proved immensely convincing, not only to the academic community, but also to a large section of the reading public. Modernism now appeared as the product not of a self-confident bourgeoisie, but rather as the introspective response of artists and thinkers who, in Schorske's phrase, were not so much alienated *from* their (bourgeois) class as *with* it. This fitted in with the idea, emerging among German historians, of the *Sonderweg* of German—and by implication Central European—history, whereby the failure of the bourgeoisie to assert themselves successfully in the political realm had led to German (Central European) history's leaving the proper path of (liberal) modern history. On the academic level, Schorske thus appeared to have discovered the link by which the internalist and externalist approaches to cultural history could be harmoniously combined. More generally, however, this psychologized reversal of the dominant idea of modernism as the culture of a hegemonic bourgeoisie proved eminently suitable to a society which was less and less confident of what it stood for and where it was going. Vienna 1900 now seemed to be the presager, and hence even the source, of both the malaise of modernity and the cultural forms and insights of modernism.

While part of the success of *Fin-de-Siècle Vienna* might well have been Schorske's good timing in tapping into an interest in Vienna that was already there, as he himself suggests, the Schorskean thesis greatly added to the intellectual excitement in the subject, which now took off. Studies of various aspects and individuals within the universe of *fin-de-siècle* Vienna now appeared. One of the greatest monographic works on the subject, by a student of Schorske, William J. McGrath, had appeared as early as 1974. McGrath's *Dionysian Art and Populist Politics in Austria*, while not exactly mirroring the Schorskean framework, had nevertheless reflected similar themes of political alienation, the irrationalist challenge to rationalist liberalism and the refuge of the aesthetic world available to the sons of the bourgeoisie. On a quite different level, Frederic Morton's *A Nervous Splendor: Vienna 1888–1889*, from 1979, added to the aura of political decadence and cultural richness. In a different medium, Michael Frayn's *Vienna, the Mask of Gold*, broadcast on the BBC in 1977, introduced the new vision of Vienna 1900 to a still largely unsuspecting television-watching public. Meanwhile the various fields of Viennese cultural achievement were being rediscovered within the new "*fin de siècle*" category, whether it was the music of Mahler, so hauntingly used by Visconti in the film *Death in Venice*, or the art of Klimt, Schiele and others. Pictures such as *The Kiss* now seem an almost clichéd part of modern consciousness, but at the time of the publication of books such as Peter Vergo's *Art in Vienna 1898–1918* (1975), they appeared as fresh, new and little known. When Tom Stoppard's adaptation of an Arthur Schnitzler play, *Undiscovered Country*, was performed in London in 1979, it could be described as "one of the National Theatre's major forays into unknown European drama."[6]

By the early 1980s Vienna 1900 had become distinctly fashionable. Conferences multiplied, pop songs such as Ultravox's smash hit "Oh Vienna" were inspired by it, major feature films such as *Bad Timing* traded in the new decadent chic of Klimtian ornamental sensuality. Moreover, the enthusiasm for Vienna was boosting its status as a cultural capital. Johnston had wanted to stress the significance of Vienna and the Habsburg Monarchy as a major center of modern thought that had previously been overlooked. Janik and Toulmin had wanted to point out the neglected Central European origins of a certain aspect of the thought of one of the seminal thinkers of modern times, Ludwig Wittgenstein. Neither had made any imperial claims for the imperial capital as the birthplace of modernity, although they had at times come close. Schorske had been somewhat more ambivalent about this aspect, at times seeming to see in Vienna just one, albeit powerful, instance of the emergence of the modernist mentality, at others appearing to see Vienna, as Broch had done before, as the birthplace of such a mindset. Yet the subtleties of such considerations were swept aside in the avalanche of interest in Vienna, so that one of the most innovative and stimulating histories of turn-of-the-century Europe to appear in the early 1980s, Norman Stone's *Europe Transformed* (1983), could claim that "it was in Vienna that most of the twentieth-century intellectual world was invented."[7]

It was in the light of this discovery of Vienna as the birthplace of the modern world that the spate of exhibitions of Viennese art occurred. The triumphal march went from the Edinburgh Festival of 1983 to the Biennale in Venice in 1984, back home to Vienna as *Traum und Wirklichkeit* in 1985, and on to what in many ways was its high point, the exhibition at the Beaubourg in Paris, *Vienne 1880–1938: L'apocalypse joyeuse* in 1986, before culminating in New York in the same year with *Vienna 1900: Art, Architecture and Design*.[8] Meanwhile a couple of other developments had intervened both to complicate and enhance the interest in Vienna 1900, and also to leave their mark on the exhibitions and conferences through which the topic was presented to the academic community and the public at large. The disquiet with the development of modernist thought and culture of the 1970s had coagulated into a diffuse but nevertheless identifiable cultural and intellectual movement, the more enterprising members of which came to articulate their dissatisfaction as "post modernism." What Schorske had identified in *fin-de-siècle* Vienna as the roots of ahistorical modernism now seemed even better suited as a precursor to the similarly cast-adrift mood of postmodernism. As one might expect, and as the catalogue to the Paris exhibition indicates, this identification was strongest in France. Michael Pollak, building on a Schorskean model of liberal failure and artistic alienation, was the first there to emphasize the postmodern theme of fractured identity in turn-of-the-century Viennese culture, in his *Vienne 1900: une identité blessée* (1984).[9] After Pollak's premature death, the same themes were taken up and elaborated by Jacques Le Rider, whose *Modernité viennoise et crises de l'identité* (1990) took Pollak's ideas on identity crisis and tied them overtly into postmodern discourse.[10]

The other, related development which influenced the picture of Vienna 1900 in the 1980s was what turned out to be the ending of the Cold War. At the time it appeared more as the rediscovery of "Central Europe," which was, among other things, a metaphor for intellectuals stuck in the Soviet-dominated Warsaw Bloc of "Eastern Europe" to claim a *Western* European identity for themselves, and hence to persuade their Western counterparts, and sometimes themselves, that they deserved to be seen as separate from the Soviet leviathan, and indeed deserved separation from it.[11] In today's perspective this looks more like the onset of the ideological and systemic collapse of the Soviet empire than it does the re-emergence of a geographical entity, but it dovetailed nicely into the fashion for Vienna 1900.

If the Cold War, as Schorske claimed, had in its McCarthyite manifestation been one of the driving forces behind the retreat of intellectuals in 1950s America from social to psychological and ahistorical modes of thought, and hence an interest in things Viennese, the prominence of Vienna 1900 in Western consciousness could now, in the 1980s, be utilized in strategies to end the same Cold War, or at least extract East Central Europe from it. This was because Vienna 1900 could be latched onto as the spiritual capital and symbol not only of itself but of the whole region of which it had once been cultural—and political—head. It was not long before Kafka's Prague and Budapest 1900 were receiving some of Vienna's reflected glory, and this realization that a large part of the birthplace of modern thought lay behind the Iron Curtain did make the recognition in the West of the legitimacy of Hungarian, Czech and Polish efforts to escape Soviet domination that much easier. Moreover the self-image of Central European dissidents such as György Konrad found reinforcement in the Viennese model of a modernist culture that had succeeded by leaving behind the world of "progress" and "politics." The Schorskean vision of retreat from politics into culture was not all that dissimilar from the concept of an "antipolitics," which sought to escape the ideological politics of *both* East and West.

The one part of this "Habsburgocentric" Central Europe to have remained in the West, Austria, could also, through this connection between Vienna 1900 and the dissidents' "Central Europe" find a way back onto an intellectual and cultural bandwagon, which had started without it, and with which it had been struggling to catch up. Austrian national identity, still a somewhat fragile entity, could also get a boost, and an attractive redefinition, by adopting Vienna 1900 as its own. Interest in the topic thus grew exponentially in Vienna itself.[12] The Schorskean paradigm of Vienna 1900 could both now tie Vienna and Austria more firmly into Western Europe by its emphasis on Vienna as being the origin of so much of Western thought, and at the same time it could soften up the barriers to its Eastern European neighbors by stressing their common, Central European and modernist, heritage.

It did not take long for the postmodern and Central European aspects of Vienna 1900 to merge. In many ways this was, given the heterogeneity of the region, its polyglot nature, and the fact that, one way or the other, most of the nineteenth and twentieth centuries' ideologies of modernity had met their demise here, inevitable. Vienna could now become subsumed in a "Central Europe 1900" which stood for the realization of the shortcomings of an over-confident, Cartesian and progressivist modernity, and hence was not so much the origin of the thought of the twentieth century but rather its victim and its antidote. This view of the region was superbly rendered by Claudio Magris in his deeply evocative *Danube*, which encapsulates in a travelogue form much of the wisdom which both the Vienna 1900 and the postmodern version of "Central Europe" have to offer.[13]

This postmodern vision of Vienna and Central Europe, which remained an expanded and modified version of the Schorskean interpretation, did not go unchallenged. There were those, such as Peter Gay in his work on Freud, who continued to de-emphasize any special Viennese aspect, stressing instead the larger German cultural field.[14] There were others, who insisted on the more straightforwardly "modern" nature of Vienna's contribution. The collection *The Viennese Enlightenment*, as its title suggests, saw Vienna in a much more progressive light, in the spirit of Karl Popper. Hilde Spiel's *Vienna's Golden Autumn* (London, 1987), despite its title, also stressed the positive contribution to modern thought, playing down the sense of crisis and decadence which provided some of the spice to the dominant, Schorskean, now postmodern model.[15] David Luft had similarly emphasized the empiricist tradition within Austrian thought, in his account of *Robert Musil and the Crisis of European Culture*.[16] Meanwhile Austrian historians tried to bring some sobriety to the subject by pointing out that not all of those in Vienna 1900 had been caught up in the ethereal decadence of the *fin-de-siècle* garden of modernist culture, but rather, as in all European capitals of the time, had lived harsh lives of crushing and benighted poverty.[17] John Boyer was similarly continuing his researches into Viennese local politics, the results of which, as Allan Janik points out in his essay, did not fit at all well with the Schorskean model.[18]

There was one aspect of the debate about Vienna 1900 that both appeared to challenge some of the fundamental assumptions of the Schorskean paradigm, and also threatened to take on a life of its own. This was the question of the Jewish contribution to the modern culture which had by now made Vienna 1900 so famous. That Jews and individuals of Jewish descent had played a large role in Viennese modern cultural life was not something that anyone had seriously disputed. What had been at issue was quite how large the role had been, and whether there was anything "Jewish" about it. Johnston's work had emphasized the Jewish aspect, but it had not been integrated into a larger explanation. Janik and Toulmin had acknowledged the Jewish perspective of Wittgenstein's family and the milieu which they had described, but it had not played a central role. Schorske had also acknowledged the Jewish dimension, but had tended to neglect the implications of it for his own approach, claiming that the Jewishness of so many in the Viennese cultural elite was merely incidental to the culture which this elite produced.

This way of dealing with the issue had a venerable tradition, going back as far as many of the Jewish participants in the culture of the turn-of-the-century. Indeed it continues to this day, particularly among disciples, ironically, of many of the Central European émigrés who did so much to shape Anglo-American culture and thought in the second half of this century.[19] Other refugees from Central Europe held, and hold, the opposite view, attributing most if not all of Vienna 1900's cultural significance to the role played by Jews within the city's cultural elite, and indeed making the same argument for the modern culture of Central Europe as a whole. Thus it was that, at the height of Vienna 1900's fame, at the conference in Paris which preceded the exhibition *L'apocalypse joyeuse,* George Steiner could give a talk which, in so many words, claimed all that was important in Central European modern culture, especially the "language turn," as the product of Jewish tradition, experience, and crisis.[20]

Along with the identification of Vienna 1900 with postmodern themes, and the revival of a Central European identity based on the cultural golden age of the Vienna-Budapest-Prague triangle, this renewed "Jewish Question" about Viennese modernism became a major avenue of research into the topic in the second half of the 1980s. The relevance of such researches, at least for contemporary Austria, was greatly enhanced by the Waldheim Affair of 1986 onward, which opened up many aspects of the Austrian past, and not least the attitude of the Austrian populace to their Jewish "co-citizens." The result of all this was a wave of publications on Viennese Jewry at the end of the decade. There had been Marsha Rozenblit's *The Jews of Vienna* from 1983, which remains a standard work on the social history of Viennese Jewry, but by now the focus was much more on cultural and intellectual history.[21] Robert Wistrich's magnum opus, *The Jews of Vienna in the Age of Franz Joseph,* offered an account of the development of Vienna's Jewish community and of the ideological ins and outs of Jewish identity within that community, but it devoted a large part of its space to essays on the major cultural figures who had contributed to the culture of Vienna 1900. Indeed it offered itself in its preface as a means to fill in "one of the missing links" to our understanding of *fin-de-siècle* Vienna by describing the Jewish context from which so much of the culture was created.[22] What Wistrich's book still did not do, however, was to make clear the extent of Jewish involvement in the Habsburg capital's modern culture and society, and the links between Jewish tradition and the modern culture which had made Vienna 1900 so famous.

That line of enquiry was more evident in Ivar Oxaal's collection, *Jews, Antisemitism and Culture in Vienna,* from 1987, and it was the main thrust of my own contribution to the subject, *Vienna and the Jews, 1867–1938: A Cultural History* (1989).[23] This purported to show that the contribution of Jews and those of Jewish descent to the modern culture of Vienna 1900 had been so large as to be predominant. Further, the Jewish background of these individuals, whether in the form of secularized religious tradition, the ideology of emancipation, the very forms of assimilation themselves, or the existential problems of living in an antisemitic environment, had strongly influenced them, and that this had been reflected in their work. Through them, the Jewish background had thus had a large influence on Viennese modern culture generally, which was far more "ethical" and "critical" than the Schorskean paradigm had suggested. Whether or not one agrees with Allan Janik in claiming that this created a new paradigm in the field, the opening up of the Jewish dimension did complicate—and to some extent undermine—the original model of Vienna 1900. Instead of a process which looked as though it had universal application—ahistorical modernism as the product of the cultural elite of an alienated liberal bourgeoisie—Vienna 1900 now appeared as something more particular: the response of the cultural elite of an alienated *Jewish* liberal bourgeoisie. Moreover the extent of the pluralistic, "postmodern" Central Europe, which had been the regional link between the turn of the century and the end of the Cold War, now appeared far narrower, confined to the Jewish bourgeoisies of Vienna, Prague, and Budapest, and some of the smaller commercial and industrial centers, along with a relatively small contingent of non-Jewish ideological and cultural allies. This shift was particularly problematic for many Austrians: having just co-opted Vienna 1900 as part of a modern Austrian identity, they were now faced with the prospect that this culture had been produced by a group within the society which had, to all intents and purposes, been liquidated in 1938. Even outside Austria, though, emphasis on the Jewish aspect threatened to make Vienna 1900 only a special instance of a larger phenomenon: the Jewish contribution to modern culture and thought, and hence to sideline it.

By 1990 the Schorskean model of Vienna 1900 was in trouble. It was still being used as the explanatory base for important studies, Michael Steinberg's *The Meaning of the Salzburg Festival* among them.[24] Yet many of its theoretical assumptions were being questioned and found suspect. Comments were being made about the relative paucity of new developments in the field, and the assertion was already being made, by Schorske's supporters, that the Schorskean contribution had been misunderstood and was not responsible for the "aestheticized" image of Vienna 1900.[25] Moreover, the whole subject was losing its perceived relevance. While a veritable culture industry had developed around the idea of Vienna 1900, and many researchers were now delving into the intellectual and cultural world which Schorske had made so enticing, contemporary events conspired to take some of the shine off the subject's relevance. Once the Cold War had actually ended in 1989, and definitively in 1991, the need to lean on a regional "Central Europe" was shaken off remarkably quickly by the former Eastern European countries, whose clear wish was not to be penned into a Central European holding station, but rather to reclaim what they saw as their rightful place as *Western* Europeans, or at least Europeans without the modifier. The aim quickly became not an "antipolitical" resurrection of a sort of revived Habsburg Monarchy but rather membership in the European Union and NATO. Similarly, the gloom among liberal intellectuals in the West began to lift in the 1990s, with the end of the Cold War and the revival of left-of-center political parties. The sense of identification felt with the supposedly alienated cultural elite of Vienna 1900, which had made a great deal of sense in the Thatcher and Reagan years, did not seem as relevant with the success of Bill Clinton and, a few years later, Tony Blair. "Postmodernism" similarly has lost some of its cachet in academic circles. It was always difficult to see quite what was so different about the "postmodern" perspective from various varieties of modernism and modernity, and the mood of ironic pessimism, which encouraged the idea of living in a world without the heroic force of modernity, has begun to pass. Instead, in the new millennium, there is a new-found optimism about, whether due to the miracles of the Internet or simply the good feeling produced by sustained economic growth, so that one can talk of a "neo-modernity" to overcome the postmodern hiccough. Vienna remains a topic of extensive academic research and publication.[26] Yet the factors which ratcheted up interest in Vienna 1900 have faded, and it is not without some irony that the historical center which seems to be replacing it in the public eye is the once and future "other" capital of Central Europe, Berlin 1900.

The pendulum having swung one way, it now threatens to swing much too far the other. This volume has as its purpose not only to re-examine the Schorskean model or paradigm, to rethink Vienna 1900 in the light of the latest research, but also to ensure that the remarkable cultural and intellectual achievement of Vienna 1900 is given its due, and is not forgotten in the eddies and maelstroms of cultural and intellectual fashion. The two goals are potentially closely linked, for if it is the Schorskean paradigm which is obstructing our view of the greater significance of Vienna 1900, and hence now acting as a drag on interest in the subject, then a rethinking of the subject is imperative. Something happened in Vienna around the turn of the century, which has had, in various ways, a profound impact on the history of the last hundred years. Its significance might have been exaggerated at times in the last twenty years, but any city that could produce Freud, Wittgenstein, Mahler, Schoenberg, Herzl, Kelsen, Popper, Hayek, Klimt, Schnitzler, Musil, Loos, Kraus—and Hitler—clearly had something important going on in it. If, in order to find out what was happening in Vienna 1900, one particular explanation, a paradigm, has to be jettisoned, or radically transformed, so be it.

The Schorskean Paradigm and Its Discontents

The essays collected in this volume are the result of a conference which was held at the Center for Austrian Studies at the University of Minnesota in the fall of 1995. As the title of the conference suggests, *Beyond Vienna 1900: Rethinking Culture in Central Europe, 1867–1939*, it was already clear before 1995 that a re-evaluation and reconsideration of the theoretical underpinnings of Vienna 1900 was needed.[27] This meant a discussion of Schorske's work and a comparison with other views of the subject, while attempting to place these theoretical and interpretative questions in the context of the most recent results of research. These were the main aims of the conference, which was also intent on placing our knowledge of Vienna 1900 in the larger contexts of Central Europe then and the modern/postmodern world now. What the conference made clear above all was the need to rethink *fin-de-siècle* Vienna, and to try to move beyond the Schorskean model to a new, perhaps less elegant, but more differentiated way of looking at the subject. As the essays in this volume show, the Schorskean paradigm no longer offers a convincing picture of Vienna 1900. The question is, whether there is any alternative which does.

Allan Janik thinks there is such an alternative, and that some such paradigm is necessary to make Vienna 1900 cohere. His magisterial discussion of the various theoretical issues involved in studying the subject starts with the premise that there has been a dominant Schorskean paradigm within the subject, and points out that its central plank, the idea that Viennese modernism was the result of the cultural elite's reaction to the "failure of liberalism," has become ever flimsier the more we know about Viennese and Austrian liberalism. Several of Schorske's supporters have asserted that such criticism is misplaced, inasmuch as Schorske never intended his interpretative essays of the transition from historicism to ahistorical modernism in Vienna to be taken as a general, comprehensive explanation of the whole city's modern cultural production. They may have a point about Schorske's own intentions, as, among others, Scott Spector points out in this volume. Yet Schorske did not noticeably object to the use by others of his interpretation as an explanatory schema of Vienna 1900, and it was certainly taken as such by most of its readership. As Mary Gluck and Janik both state, Schorske's views became the Schorskean paradigm, whether he wanted it to or not. Moreover, it is not as if Schorske was making no claim to represent the political and cultural reality of *fin-de-siècle* Vienna. His honesty in pointing out how he came to the subject is admirable, but it does not mean, surely, that he was merely creating a history of the ahistorical in order to suit the moment. Even if he was, then he was still making claims about the nature of Austrian liberalism, the differences between the liberal, verbal, and rational culture of the bourgeoisie and the aesthetic, sensuous "culture of grace" of the Austrian aristocracy, and the defeat of "liberalism" by the irrationalist mass movements represented in his controversial triumvirate of Schönerer, Lueger and Herzl. Otherwise, none of his views on the connections between politics and culture in Vienna had any bearing on the actual past.

It was precisely in this area, though, that research has shown Schorske's assumptions to be weakest. Janik rightly points to the importance of John Boyer's work in showing that the supposed clash between rationalist liberalism and irrationalist anti-liberalism in the shape of Lueger's Christian Social Party is a distortion of what was actually happening. The Liberals in Vienna had not been defeated for their rationalism but rather for their exclusivist, anti-democratic stance which had, naturally, deeply alienated the now newly enfranchised lower-middle class. Their Christian Social opponents had succeeded not so much because of their irrationalist (antisemitic) rhetoric and the charisma of Lueger, but rather because of their astute handling of bread-and-butter issues and their presentation of themselves as the party that would restore, if not "bourgeois" then at least "*bürgerlich,*" unity.

This crack in the "failure of liberalism" thesis has been opened to the size of a chasm by the work of Pieter Judson on the history of the Austrian Liberals, which has shown, most notably in his book *Exclusive Revolutionaries*, a far more complex, and far less harmless picture of liberalism than has hitherto prevailed.[28] His essay in this volume concentrates on two points. First, once one looks at the fate of liberalism not only in Vienna but in the Habsburg Monarchy as a whole, it becomes surprisingly clear that Schorske's idea that Austrian liberalism had "failed" was far too pessimistic. In the capital such a collapse did occur, but not in the provinces. Outside of Vienna, liberalism as a political force, while not as dominant as formerly, survived quite handily. It adjusted to the new circumstances of mass politics, emphasizing a nationalist side which had always been there in order to co-opt the lower classes to support the bourgeois interests which liberal politics represented. At the same time Judson has shown that the Schorskean view of liberalism as a rationalist ideology of law and the rights of the individual does not square at all well with the actual behavior of German liberals, for instance in leading the nationalist opposition against the Badeni ordinances, and the way in which the liberal criteria of who was and who was not "rational" was easily translated into the nationalist, and ultimately racist, hierarchy of superior (rational and cultivated) and inferior (irrational and ignorant) groups, whether nations or races. At this point one might ask whether Judson's "liberalism" really has much to do with what Schorske meant by the term, but this, again, begs the question as to what Schorske actually meant, and where, if at all, his liberals are to be found.

If questions about the nature of Austrian liberalism have undermined the Schorskean paradigm from one side, questions about the nature of the aristocratic "culture of grace" have gnawed away from the other. James Shedel has contested many aspects of the Schorskean thesis for a long time. In his book *Art and Society: The New Art Movement in Vienna, 1897–1914* (1981), he stressed the ways in which the liberal bourgeoisie had not been alienated from power in Vienna in the way that Schorske assumed, but had rather, through their domination of the economy and their allies in the Habsburg bureaucracy, retained a great deal of influence in the Austrian state.[29] In his essay for this volume he builds on this insight by looking at how the Habsburg state, identified in the Schorskean paradigm with the aristocratic culture of grace, actually related to the supposedly "bourgeois" culture of Law and the Word. Unlike the Schorskean thesis, which he sees as an Austrian variant on the *Sonderweg* model of unsuccessful political modernization in late nineteenth century Germany, Shedel emphasizes the way in which the Habsburg variant of the *Rechtsstaat* successfully married the cultures of grace and law, by seeing them as mutually dependent. In his view of Vienna 1900 it is not so much the antagonism between the bourgeoisie and the state, nor even the surrender of the bourgeoisie to the aristocratic, aesthetic culture of the Habsburg establishment, which was significant, but rather the ways in which the Habsburg establishment itself, especially its bureaucracy, either accepted supposedly "bourgeois" values such as rationalism and the rule of law, or had itself been the source of such values. Far from Vienna 1900 being the aesthetic response to the death-throes of a decadent empire and the "failure of liberalism," he points out how so much of the impulse for modernization, and even for modernism, came from within the state apparatus itself. Vienna 1900 becomes thus the beginning of a new century rather than the final crisis of the old, and the relationship between politics and culture a far more positive one than that suggested by the ironic dialectic of the Schorskean model.

A key part of that ironic dialectic was the claim that the children of the bourgeoisie, as a result of their parents' desire to adopt Austrian aristocratic culture, were raised with a heavy emphasis on the aesthetic side of life, and that it was this acquisition of aristocratic culture which was the necessary precondition for their flight into the temple of art as a refuge from a hostile political world. The passive, decadent aestheticism of the Viennese modernists is thus seen as an heir of the sort of decadent, hedonistic "culture of grace" cultivated by the Austrian aristocracy, as represented most famously in Strauss and Hofmannsthal's *Der Rosenkavalier*. This is a charming picture, and it is what Hofmannsthal wanted, but, according to Michael Burri, it is not an accurate one of the actual development of the image of the aristocrat by the aestheticist generation of *fin-de-siècle* Vienna. Instead he shows, through the writings and personas of Richard von Schaukal and Theodor Herzl, each in their own way prominent "self-made aristocrats" of prewar Vienna, how the supposedly passive "dandy" model of the aristocrat remained intimately linked to the older, overtly aggressive tradition of the knight-at-arms. In Burri's view the aristocratic moment in Vienna 1900 was not one of aestheticist retreat, but rather of masculine assertion; the aristocrat offered a mode of action, in Herzl's case of political action, in Schaukal's case, ultimately, of military action. Reading Burri, one begins to think that Georg von Schönerer, the "Knight of Rosenau," and the leading figure in Austria's racially antisemitic German Nationalist movement, was not, in his militant interpretation of "aristocratic" identity, quite as anomalous as Schorske has painted him.[30] From this perspective, indeed, the figure of the aristocrat provides the culture of *fin-de-siècle* Vienna with one of its prime links to the militarization of prewar Europe.

What emerges from this first section of essays is a far more complex picture of the relationship between politics, class, and culture in Vienna 1900 than the Schorskean paradigm offered. Illiberal liberalism; pragmatic, bourgeois anti-liberals; a political liberalism that did not fail; a liberalism that spawned exclusivist nationalism; a Habsburg state, wedded to the culture of Law *and* Grace, as the major engine of modernization; an aestheticist cult of the aristocrat as man of (military) action: rather than a view from on high of the broad river of liberalism encountering the fertile valley of aristocratic grace, plunging over the precipice of political defeat and then issuing forth in the fertile delta of aestheticist modernism, we are left with a self-contradictory jumble of tributaries, which begin in remote mountain valleys and meander through swamps, crisscrossing in quite surprising combinations, until rushing on through the cataracts of the aggression of the First World War and beyond; and Vienna is only part of this landscape, not necessarily typical. If Schorske presented a map of Vienna 1900 akin to the Danubian valley after the river's regulation, its cultural geography now resembles far more the region's topography before it.

It is this sort of complex intellectual and cultural cartography that Scott Spector offers, in trying to place the Schorskean moment within a larger context, both in terms of space and time. Picking up on the significance of the essay form used by Schorske, Spector moves back and forth from before 1900 to after, from center to periphery, majority culture to minority literature, the introspective self to social transformation, from Lukacsian Life to life—and back—and shows, embracing Lukacs's dialectical approach, that each was intimately linked to the other, so much so that each became its opposite. Suspending the clear divisions in Schorske's schema between politics and culture, or political activism and psychological retreat, Spector shows that, once one looks beyond the "thin ridge" of Schorske's Viennese *fin de siècle*, one can see that politics and culture were not the mutually exclusive worlds which liberal ideology, specifically in Viennese high culture, imagined. On the one hand, claims to "culture" were central to German nationalist political strategies in, for instance, Bohemia in the 1880s; on the other, a German-Jewish writer from Prague, such as Franz Werfel, could, by 1910, see his role as artist as an assertive one, challenging the supposed primacy of the political world in a way reminiscent of the Romantics. Spector, in a very respectful way, shows—in these and other examples—that the Schorskean paradigm, if it has validity for a certain time and place, does not work beyond that rather narrow purview. Even in Vienna itself, indeed at the center of Schorske's own book, his essay on Freud, what Schorske sees as a retreat into the psyche, becomes, once one looks beyond this moment, an extremely activist attempt to remold vast swathes of human thought—and behavior. If there was retreat this was only the dialectical prelude for a frontal assault.

If Spector's aim is to view *fin-de-siècle* Vienna from the margins, Alfred Pfabigan's purpose is to describe Vienna 1900 from the center, from the middle. What Pfabigan thus emphasizes is Vienna's function as a mediator between the worlds of the nineteenth and twentieth centuries, before and after Nietzsche, between the historicist, evolutionary model of a progressive modernity, and the revolutionary, ahistoricist modernism which Schorske sees as typifying the incoherent cultural landscape of the twentieth century. Pfabigan breaks away from the Schorskean paradigm in pointing out, through the example of Freud, how in Vienna the nineteenth century vision of a historically evolved modern civilization, encapsulated in the word *Bildung*, was not thrown over by the Nietzschean insights of ahistorical modernism, but rather responded to it, and, in Pfabigan's phrase, "tamed" it. The powerful attraction of what Pfabigan calls the "subtext" of Freudian psychoanalytic theory resides precisely in its ability to offer a way of absorbing the insights of Nietzsche about the irrational aspects of mankind without overturning the rich heritage of Western civilization, without doing away with history in the way Schorske seemed to suggest. Again, as in Spector's view, this is not retreat before the forces of irrationalism. Rather Freud is shown as evolving, hidden from others and almost from himself, a strong, indeed brilliant strategy to bring under the control of reason and civilization the instinctual drives unleashed by Nietzsche and his Viennese followers, so well documented by William McGrath.

Themes of centrality and marginality are also at the heart of Malachi Hacohen's discussion of another major intellectual figure who emerged from Vienna 1900, albeit from its later, interwar phase—Karl Popper. In Popper, Hacohen sees the representative of yet another current in Viennese intellectual life, that of "late-enlightenment" progressivism. From this movement's perspective, Vienna 1900 was about campaigning for social and educational reform from a left-liberal position, with some members embracing truly supranational, cosmopolitan ideals. This picture of a positive, optimistic, and activist intelligentsia flies in the face of the idea of a passive, retreating, aestheticist cultural elite as portrayed in the Schorskean paradigm. Yet appearances can be deceptive, for it all depends on how representative any of the figures or groups are of the cultural and social phenomena we choose to label as Vienna 1900. Hacohen is quite comfortable with the idea that Popper and his group are no more indicative of the general situation in Vienna at the turn of the century than the aestheticist group described by Schorske. Indeed it is one of Hacohen's main purposes to show just how *marginal* the cosmopolitan progressives were to developments in Central Europe, no matter how *central* they are to that region's perceived cosmopolitan character. Hacohen identifies in the network of progressive intellectuals which extended over Central Europe in the last decades of the Habsburg Monarchy and then again in the interwar years, the main embodiment of cosmopolitanism in Central Europe. His point, however, is that this group was numerically insignificant, and socially marginal, with its members either being exceptional individuals from majority national groups, which were anything but "cosmopolitan" in their ethnonational value systems, or coming from a group which was itself marginal in Central European society: assimilated Jews.

Hacohen goes on to discuss the intricate ways in which Popper's background in this progressive movement, composed largely of assimilated Jews such as himself, interacted with the political crises of the interwar years and the disastrous success of racial antisemitism, to shape Popper's views on nationalism, cosmopolitanism, and the question of Jewish identity. It is an often discouraging story, for it shows Popper, one of the great thinkers of this century, as not able to shake off his own personal experiences in the Central Europe of his youth and the resulting traumatic fears of antisemitism, which made him incapable of approaching the question of Jewish identity in the modern world in a truly cosmopolitan manner. Hence he was unable to negotiate successfully what Hacohen rightly sees as the crucial dilemma of cosmopolitanism—a balance between universality and particularity. What Hacohen also shows, however, when looked at in the context of the other contributions to this volume, is how diverse a social and cultural phenomenon Vienna 1900 was, and yet how inter-related many of its aspects were. Moreover, these linkages rescue many aspects of the Schorskean paradigm, which had been endangered by the other perspectives in this volume, although they do so in ways which profoundly alter the general Schorskean view.

The progressive liberalism of the circle from which Popper sprang, for instance, looks much more like the liberalism of the Schorskean paradigm than the political liberalism which both Boyer and Judson have uncovered, although it too, as Hacohen points out, demanded far more dispensing with particular (ethnic) identity than our pluralist liberalism now expects. Cosmopolitan progressivism's rationalism and optimism also confirm Shedel's picture of a forward-looking state, society and culture, rather than the decaying, crisis-ridden picture seen by Schorske. The group's political engagement and its enthusiasm for reform efforts also belie the Schorskean picture of aestheticist retreat, much in the way that Burri's analysis of the image of the aristocrat does. There were far more active and activist elements in the cultural elite than the usual view of Vienna 1900 depicts. As Spector is suggesting, there were not the sharp divisions between ahistorical and historical approaches implied in the Schorskean model, but rather there was much—often deliberate—"confusion" of elements, a concept which is strikingly similar to Pfabigan's idea of Vienna's being a center of cultural and intellectual mediation, of negotiation, compromise, of "well-tempered dissatisfaction" and "muddling through." Yet, to borrow another image from Spector, much of this view depends on the particular "valley" of Vienna 1900 in which one finds oneself.

Take Popper's case: once one looks over the protective "thin ridge," which a close-knit social and familial network, financial security and a functioning rule of law provided, then the picture of a Zweigian "world of security," progress, and optimism, rapidly makes way for some stark facts, which, no matter the flaws in the Schorskean paradigm, must remain a central part of our view of Vienna 1900: progressive cosmopolitanism was supported by only a small group of intellectuals and their allies—as a political movement its left-liberalism never reached beyond a few of the more liberal districts in Vienna; and its influence in the Habsburg state, which Popper was later to idealize, was minuscule compared to that of the conservative and antisemitic Christian Socials and the nationalist parties which Popper detested. Then there is a further crucial factor which cannot be ignored: while not all its members were Jewish or of Jewish descent, the large proportion who were meant that, given the antisemitism which riddled Austrian society in general and Viennese society in particular, the group, whether its members were willing to admit as much or not, was marginalized and alienated in almost precisely the way in which the Schorskean paradigm describes. They were, after all, for all their progressive optimism, living in a city run by Karl Lueger and his antisemitic Christian Social Party. Yet the Schorskean paradigm is right for the wrong reasons: the ground for their marginalization was not their being bourgeois, nor their being "liberal," especially in a Judsonian definition, but because they were identified as either belonging to, or being allies of, a particular ethnic group: the Jews.

Beyond the Schorskean Paradigm; beyond Vienna 1900?

If we now return to Janik's discussion of what alternative there is to the Schorskean paradigm in the light of this last insight, his suggestion that something like a synthesis of the Schorskean "failure of liberalism" model with the "critical modernism" model is the practical way forward, appears ever more cogent. The two increasingly appear as aspects of the same cultural developments, albeit in a much more complicated and self-contradictory set of processes than the received Schorskean model apparently allowed, and with less universal application than it supposed. That Schorske himself has reportedly mentioned a second volume that was planned but never realized on the ethical and rationalist side of Viennese turn-of-the-century culture is, apart from being deeply intriguing in itself, a fascinating confirmation of Janik's intuition. Yet, for any supporter of the Schorskean approach, there remains a catch. Janik calls this combined approach the "failure of Jewish liberalism" paradigm, and has accepted the shift of perspective from the more "universal" categories of "liberal" and "bourgeois" to the far more particular aspects of (Jewish) religious tradition, and ethnic identity. As I appear to have been largely responsible for this, let me explain briefly why I think Janik is right, and what such a shift does, and does not do, for our understanding of Vienna 1900.

To start with, it allows us to make sense of the Schorskean picture as the small part of a much larger landscape. The idea of an alienated cultural elite of an alienated liberal bourgeoisie makes perfect sense when we see that a large, indeed predominant part of the educated sector of such a class would have been Jewish—in Vienna. However the provincial liberals fared, and however much the "bourgeois" elements in Vienna felt comfortable with, and even supported, the Christian Socials, Viennese liberalism collapsed, and with it the hopes of one of its core group of supporters, the Jews, who could not, and did not, feel at all comfortable under Lueger's regime. The Habsburg state may have in many respects been modern, and Lueger a modern, pragmatic politician, and there was indeed much that was positive about life in Vienna 1900, but for the Jews modernity had taken a wrong turning with the success of antisemitism: this is the crisis against which so many figures in Schorske's *fin-de-siècle* Vienna were reacting. To that extent "Schorske's Vienna" is identical with "Schnitzler's Vienna," the world of anxiety-ridden Jewish individuals, whose lives have been cast adrift by the failure of liberalism to produce the enlightened society promised by the ideology of emancipation, and who are confronted with the need to respond to an antisemitic reality any way they can. The avenues of retreat into the temple of art, into the psyche, but also to the Promised Land of Zion, to socialism and social reform, and also the attempt at aristocratic "bearing," are all set out in Schnitzler's *Der Weg ins Freie* (*The Road to the Open*), published in 1908. Yet all these responses are understood within the specific context of the Jewish bourgeoisie, as a Jewish-centered problematic, with the non-Jewish aristocrat artist, Georg von Wergenthin, the supposed ally to this group, looking on, and in the end, not really understanding what was happening.[31] It is almost as if the Schorskean paradigm of Vienna 1900 described the crisis of the Viennese Jewish bourgeoisie, but without the ethnic markers.

Reinstating those ethnic markers not only explains the sense of crisis in Vienna, but it also goes a long way to explaining the nature of the response. The roots of Jewish attachment to "liberalism" in the movement for emancipation, and, before that, in the adaptation of Jewish tradition to modern Enlightenment undertaken by the *Haskalah*, are the clue to the immense resistance which many Jewish figures in Vienna 1900 showed to abandoning the Enlightenment principles of *Bildung*, Freud chief among them. Moreover, the way in which the Jewish adoption of liberal values stressed the continuation within this modern form of the ethical emphasis of traditional Jewish thought and practice explains much of the ethical spirit in the "critical modernism" which Janik sees as Vienna 1900's greatest contribution.

There are other ways in which the Jewish involvement allows insights into what was happening in Vienna and Central Europe. George Steiner, for all his rhetorical exaggeration, undoubtedly does have a point when he stresses the part played by the Jewish background in the "language turn" of Central European thought. Yet it is always important to remember that we are discussing here only a particular version of Vienna 1900, the part that has caught the public imagination, and that did indeed have a profound influence on Western culture and thought. What the "failure of Jewish liberalism" paradigm does not do is to provide a comprehensive explanation for everything happening in Viennese culture and thought around 1900. It might describe the main, broad valley of Viennese modern culture, but it is far from encompassing the whole of what remains a complicated terrain. On the other hand, how we understand, how we map the rest of that terrain relies to a certain extent on the vantage point gained from the recognition of the Jewish aspect, and vice-versa.

* * * *

The last two essays in this volume study a cultural field in which few Jews were involved as creative figures: painting. They discuss, centrally or tangentially, two of the "giants" in the world of Vienna 1900, Egon Schiele and Gustav Klimt, neither of whom was Jewish. Each essay, though, confirms in a different way the sort of landscape sketched out above. Robert Jensen's discussion of Schiele speaks not only to our view of Schiele, but also to our view of the Viennese art world generally. In the Schorskean paradigm, the art of the Secession is seen as both a rebellion against the liberal establishment, and yet, in the career of Klimt, a case study in the retreat from the public realm of art as statement into the private realm of art as ornament, in reaction to the alienation from, and rejection by, the political world. In the case of the "Klimt Affair," concerning the university ceiling paintings, Schorske's argument is fairly convincing. Yet, for the rest of the Secessionists, the argument does not seem at all convincing, for it was they and their architect allies, such as Otto Wagner and Josef Hoffmann, who quickly became the new art establishment in Vienna, acquiring the professorial appointments and commissions to go with this new status. The crisis for the Viennese artists, especially young up-and-coming talents such as Schiele, was, as Jensen points out, not caused by changes in the political realm, but rather by those in the art world. The shift from public patronage to a commercial marketplace centered on art dealers disrupted the relation of the artists to their public, while the revolution in painting stemming from Paris threatened to undermine the status of Central European—German—art, in particular the decorative arts, and hence to destroy the artists' livelihood. Klimt's response, in Jensen's interpretation, was to make the most of his "Viennese" particularity by re-emphasizing the decorative qualities of his earlier work; Schiele's response was to identify himself with Klimt and yet also to style himself as a stripper-away of the hypocrisies of conventional notions of beauty, to get at the "naked truth" of sexuality, also in his own self. Jensen presents a Schiele who is not so much driven by his psychological needs, as the expressionist cliché claims, as he is rather quite consciously creating an image of himself as the artist was supposed to be, in order to gain success and be chosen as the Viennese answer to Vincent van Gogh. He is, in Jensen's phrase, "marketing identity." He is also creating searing images of the human condition, but for Jensen those images remain essentially conservative in their representational nature, when compared to the truly radical departures taking place in Paris at the same time.

Viennese art remained, in Jensen's terminology, a minor, conservative art, attempting to survive in an art world increasingly dominated by French art and the commercial marketplace. The survey of Central European art at the turn of the century by Ilona Sármány-Parsons confirms this insight. It shows in a wealth of illustrative detail that the misogynistic image of woman, of the "femme fatale" so popular in Western modern art by the turn of the century, was very slow to establish itself in Central European art, even in Vienna. In other artistic centers of Habsburg Central Europe, such as Prague, Cracow, and Budapest, it hardly figured at all. Sármány-Parsons sees this fact as confirming the marginality of Central European art, its seclusion from many of the main currents of West European, metropolitan art, with Vienna being a partial exception. This is not to say that great art was not produced, as the illustrations show. What it does say, though, is something which goes far beyond questions of the image of women in art: it points out that Viennese art was not necessarily at all typical of art in the other "Central European" cultural centers, and that those other centers, Prague, Budapest, and Cracow, were so dominated by nationalist loyalties that even most of the "modern" artists were constrained by their ideological commitment to the nation to present positive images of the female, as symbol of the nation, something which the Viennese did not generally feel constrained to do.

We are again confronted with the fact that Vienna 1900 was not Central Europe 1900, and that not all aspects of Vienna 1900 were as important to twentieth century culture and thought as Freudian psychoanalytic theory or Wittgensteinian philosophy. As Kirk Varnedoe has written: "Klimt was not Freud, and Schiele was not Schoenberg."[32] One might be tempted to conclude from this that it was precisely the absence of the Jewish background in these artists which led to their lack of truly transformative power, or at least will. Yet this implication should be resisted. There were many key figures in Vienna 1900, who were not Jewish and who nevertheless transformed their fields: Adolf Loos comes immediately to mind. Admittedly, many of his key supporters and ideological allies were Jewish, but his example, along with those of many others, including Musil and Trakl, clearly shows that there were other sources of Vienna 1900 than the Jewish one, other important parts of the landscape. These other parts were, nevertheless, still linked in many ways with "Jewish Vienna," whether it was in the patrons of Klimt, Schiele, and Kokoschka, or the influence of Karl Kraus on a whole generation of writers, or, in Musil's case, on the myriad acquaintances with Jews, including his wife. If the Viennese landscape was a complicated, multifaceted one, at the center of the cultural and intellectual processes which make Vienna 1900 so important to us was the Jewish Vienna which the "failure of Jewish liberalism" paradigm attempts to describe.

But then again, who is to decide what is and what is not important about Vienna 1900's contribution to our modern culture? Ultimately, and obviously, "we" do, but such a subjective response leaves unanswered the question of Vienna 1900's real significance. Partly, also, this question has already been answered for us, by our parents, and our teachers, in the broadest sense. It has been remarked that no one would have been interested in the Jewish contribution to Vienna 1900 if Hitler had not happened. In one sense this is incorrect, for it presupposes that Jewish ethnicity and identity would have disappeared completely, in a "success-ful" assimilation, if only Nazism had not raised its ugly head—one unlikely counter-factual playing off another. In another sense, though, the comment is extremely perceptive, for our interest in Vienna 1900 is partly due to the fact that so many of the leading lights in the Western academy, as well as in Western literature and culture generally, were either émigrés—a predominantly Jewish group—or the offspring and students thereof. As Janik points out, we are in so many ways the chil-dren of the emigration, the great sea-change which profoundly altered American and British cultural and intellectual life in mid-century. Look-ing at Vienna 1900 is thus not so much looking at the origins of moder-nity as such, as at the origins of the particular modernity which came across the seas in the 1930s and 1940s and found extremely fertile soil. This is, perhaps, why Schorske could see in Vienna the origins of the ahistorical modernist thinking of American academia in the 1950s, because that, or somewhere like it, had been the place from which so many in that academic world had come. It was, after all, Karl Popper who wrote *The Poverty of Historicism.*

The emigration occurred half a century ago, and its direct impact is fading. Also, the model of an ahistorical modernity which Schorske per-ceived is neither as prevalent, nor even as attractive, as it once was. Vienna 1900 has waxed and waned in popularity with the public. "Modernity" has given way to "postmodernity," which is now challenged by "neo-modernity," or even "post-postmodernity." Yet the cultural and intellectual heritage, of which the émigrés were the heirs and then the representatives, the world of "Central Europe" and Vienna 1900, remains the source of many of the leading cultural and intellectual movements in the English-speaking world, more so, ironically, than in the current cultural and intellectual world of contemporary Central Europe. It is not as the "birthplace of modernity" or as "harbinger of postmodernity" that Vienna 1900 is best understood, but rather as one of the main sources of the intellectual building blocks which make up *our* modern world.

In this sense, then, Schorske was quite right to see that *fin-de-siècle* Vienna was as much about Western (American) modern culture as it was about Central Europe, for the two are inseparably linked through the fact of the emigration. In this sense, as well, the emergence of Vienna 1900 as a center of modern culture is explicable in terms of the ripening of the Central European influence in the English-speaking world, espe-cially the fact that this perception began there and then spread back to Central Europe. As the modern culture of the English-speaking world has come to dominate global concepts of modernity, it is understandable why "modernity" itself came to be seen as springing from Vienna. Yet the one is not identical with the other, and it is as well to recognize this. Vienna at the turn of the century was only one among many places where the modern world was taking shape. In Vienna the group most central to that endeavor was the cultural elite of its Jewish bourgeoisie. This was precisely the group, however, which was thrown out of its home city, and then did so much to reinvigorate modern culture and thought in the West. Its members brought with them a basic loyalty to liberal and Enlightenment values that was shared only by particular groups in Central Europe, but more or less universally in their new homes. They also brought with them, though, a sense of the fragility of this value system, and a sense of its flaws. They brought with them, in other words, a highly developed "critical modernism," which has stood the Western intellectual world in good stead ever since.

This, if nothing else, makes Vienna 1900 eminently worthy of our study.

Notes

1. In Hermann Broch, *Schriften zur Literatur 1*, ed. P. M. Lützeler (Frankfurt-on-Main, 1975), 111–284. In English as Broch, *Hofmannsthal and His Times*, trans. Michael Steinberg (Chicago, 1984).
2. Ilsa Barea, *Vienna* (London, 1966); Arthur J. May, *Vienna in the Age of Franz Josef* (Norman, 1966); Frank Field, *The Last Days of Mankind* (London, 1967).
3. Schorske's first article on Vienna was "Politics and the Psyche in *Fin-de-Siècle* Vienna: Schnitzler and Hofmannsthal," in *American Historical Review* 66 (July 1961): 930–946.
4. Hilde Spiel, ed., *Wien: Spektrum einer Stadt* (Munich, 1971).
5. William M. Johnston, *The Austrian Mind: An Intellectual and Social History 1848–1938* (Berkeley, 1972); Allan Janik and Stephen Toulmin, *Wittgenstein's Vienna* (New York, 1973); Carl E. Schorske, *Fin-de-Siècle Vienna: Politics and Culture* (London, 1980).
6. Arthur Schnitzler, *Undiscovered Country*, trans. Tom Stoppard (London, 1980), back cover.
7. Norman Stone, *Europe Transformed* (Glasgow, 1983), 407.
8. See the exhibition catalogues: Peter Vergo, *Vienna 1900: Vienna, Scotland and the European Avant-Garde* (Edinburgh, 1983); *Le Arti a Vienna* (Venice, 1984); *Traum und Wirklichkeit: Wien 1870–1930* (Vienna, 1985); *Vienne 1880–1938: L'apocalypse joyeuse* (Paris, 1986); Kirk Varnedoe, *Vienna 1900: Art, Architecture and Design* (New York, 1986).
9. Michael Pollak, *Vienne 1900: Une identité blessée* (Paris, 1984).

10. Jacques Le Rider, *Modernité viennoise et crises de l'identité* (Paris, 1990).

11. Cf. Milan Kundera, "The Tragedy of Central Europe," in *New York Review of Books,* April 26, 1984, 33–38.

12. See Alfred Pfabigan, ed., *Ornament und Askese im Zeitgeist des Wien der Jahrhundertwende* (Vienna, 1985); P. Berner et al., *Wien um 1900: Aufbruch in die Moderne* (Vienna 1986).

13. Claudio Magris, *Danube* (London, 1989).

14. Peter Gay, *Freud: A Life for Our Time* (New York, 1988).

15. Mark Francis, ed., *The Viennese Enlightenment* (Beckenham, 1985); Hilde Spiel, *Vienna's Golden Autumn* (London, 1987).

16. David Luft, *Robert Musil and the Crisis of European Culture* (Berkeley, 1980).

17. Hubert Ch. Ehalt et al., eds., *Glücklich ist, wer vergisst ...? Das andere Wien um 1900* (Vienna, 1986).

18. John W. Boyer, *Political Radicalism in Late Imperial Vienna* (Chicago, 1981).

19. See Francis, *The Viennese Enlightenment,* 8–9.

20. George Steiner, "Le langage et l'inhumain," *Revue d'esthétique,* new series, 9 (1985): 65–66. Original lecture given in Paris at the conference *Vienne 1880–1938: Fin de Siècle et Modernisme* on October 10, 1984.

21. Marsha Rozenblit, *The Jews of Vienna 1867–1914: Assimilation and Identity* (Albany, 1983).

22. Robert S. Wistrich, *The Jews of Vienna in the Age of Franz Joseph* (Oxford, 1989), vii.

23. Ivar Oxaal et al., eds. *Jews, Antisemitism and Culture in Vienna* (London, 1987); Steven Beller, *Vienna and the Jews, 1867–1938: A Cultural History* (Cambridge, 1989). Other books on the subject published at the same time include William O. McCagg, Jr., *A History of Habsburg Jews, 1670–1918* (Bloomington, 1989), and George E. Berkley, *Vienna and Its Jews: The Tragedy of Success, 1880–1980s* (Cambridge, Mass., 1988).

24. Michael Steinberg, *The Meaning of the Salzburg Festival: Austria as Theater and Ideology 1890–1938* (Ithaca, 1990).

25. Michael P. Steinberg, "'Fin-de-siècle Vienna' Ten Years Later: 'Viel Traum, Wenig Wirklichkeit,'" *Austrian History Yearbook* 22 (1991): 151–162.

26. For example, Stephen E. Broner and F. Peter Wagner, *Vienna: The World of Yesterday, 1889–1914* (Atlantic Highlands, N.J., 1997).

27. *Beyond Vienna 1900: Rethinking Culture in Central Europe, 1867–1939* at the Center for Austrian Studies, University of Minnesota, Minneapolis, October 12–14, 1995.

28. Pieter M. Judson, *Exclusive Revolutionaries: Liberal Politics, Social Experience and National Identity in the Austrian Empire, 1848–1914* (Ann Arbor, 1996).

29. James Shedel, *Art and Society: The New Art Movement in Vienna, 1897–1914* (Palo Alto, 1981), 60.

30. Cf. Schorske, *Fin-de-Siècle Vienna,* 132–133.

31. Arthur Schnitzler, *Der Weg ins Freie* (Frankfurt am Main, 1978), in English as *The Road to the Open,* trans. H. Samuel (Evanston, 1991).

32. Varnedoe, *Vienna 1900,* 220.

Chapter 1

VIENNA 1900 REVISITED

Paradigms and Problems

Allan Janik

Forty years ago Robert Kann published his penetrating *Study in Austrian Intellectual History*.[1] This book was a pioneering effort in a field, Austrian cultural history, which has subsequently burgeoned. Kann's legacy has been recognized and honored in many ways, not least being the annual Kann Memorial Lecture, but the full significance of his *Study in Austrian Intellectual History* for our understanding of Austrian cultural history has rarely been realized. It is the neglected contribution which Kann's book made to the discussion of *method* in Austrian cultural studies that interests me here.

My concern is with models of explanation, rather than the strictly empirical side of research—although the two can never be fully separated.[2] It would, indeed, be scarcely possible to survey the developments in the study of Austrian culture at the level of what I have termed, "monographic" studies of *fin-de-siècle* Vienna.[3] By monographic studies I understand what Thomas Kuhn might term "normal" historical research, such as documentation, which is carried on in the context of an established "paradigm," that is, with established hermeneutic procedures for identifying questions and producing explanations. Here, however, I am concerned with what I have termed "interpretive" history, that sort of "revolutionary" research that aims at challenging established explanatory models and developing new ones by uniting hitherto disparate levels of discourse—although, unlike Kuhn, I would not make the distinction between the two strictly dichotomous, especially as it applies to historical research.[4] If, in what follows, it should seem that I neglect my Austrian colleagues in favor of my Anglo-Saxon ones, it is because Austrian work in the field, for all its frequent achievements, has tended to be monographic rather than interpretive, to work within established paradigms rather than developing new hermeneutic strategies.

The questions I want to pose are these: What has happened in the last forty years? Where are we now? And where should we go next?

The first and most obvious point to be made here is that Vienna and Austria have emerged in that period as objects of systematic study in their own right. Since 1960, cities in general have become interesting as fields of historical research. Vienna specifically has tended to exert a fascination upon the intellectual world, which had so long neglected it. At the same time it became increasingly clear that Austrian culture could not simply be treated as a series of footnotes to German history, as it has often tended to be.

Among other significant developments in monographic studies in the last forty years—the sorts of things I shall *not* be talking about in what follows—we must include recognition of the role that feminists, and women generally, played in Viennese life, thanks to the painstaking research of Harriet Anderson, Lisa Fischer, and others. The study of Vienna's Jews has all but become a discipline in itself since the path-breaking work of Ivar Oxaal, Steven Beller, and Marsha Rozenblit. The last-named has called our attention to the role of the *family* in lending a collective identity to Jewish immigrants to Vienna that was not available to their Christian counterparts, who immigrated to the city as impoverished "singles," as it were. Monika Glettler has given us a rich picture of Vienna's Czech minority.[5] Art historians like Peter Vergo have given us superb accounts of the main developments in painting, while studies of individual figures such as those of Alessandra Comini on Gustav Klimt and Egon Schiele have similarly enriched our knowledge, as have a number of first-class memoirs and biographies, such as George Clare's *Last Waltz in Vienna* and Henry-Louis De La Grange's mammoth study of Gustav Mahler, respectively. In general the public imagination has been stimulated by captivating journalistic accounts of remarkable Viennese constellations of figures and events, such as Frederic Morton's *A Nervous Splendor*.[6] Finally, the opening of the East since 1989 has stimulated scholars there (with considerable support from Austrian sources) to reexamine their erstwhile ties to the Habsburg monarchy with the hope of finding an important part of a lost identity.[7] In short, whereas it was frequently difficult to find material on many of the figures I wanted to write about twenty-five years ago—Klimt and Schiele, as well as Adolf Loos and Robert Musil, come to mind at once—the wealth of material on them today is becoming as much a burden as it is a help to scholarship. This mountain of literature attests to the way that the story of Vienna has expanded in all sorts of directions.

How that story was understood, the "interpretive" side of our Kuhnian model, has also shown many developments over the last forty years. Over a long period the research of individual scholars was loosely guided by theses that were would-be paradigms, such as Hermann Broch's notion of the Viennese "value vacuum," William Johnston's notion of "therapeutic nihilism," Ilsa Barea's view emphasizing the consequences of the Counter-Reformation in shaping the Viennese mentality and the city's image, and last but not least, Robert Kann's cyclical model (to be discussed later).[8] Finally, Carl Schorske's "failure of liberalism" thesis succeeded in providing a pattern around which a research field could crystallize. He established a model that became the basis for the work of other scholars, such as William McGrath and Michael Steinberg, to mention but two of the best-known "Schorskeans."[9]

However, the publication of John Boyer's *Political Radicalism in Late Imperial Vienna* in 1981, when Schorske's book was still hot off the press, provided a covert challenge to the "failure of liberalism" hypothesis by altering our picture of Karl Lueger dramatically, whereas the first *overt* challenge to the adequacy of the "failure of liberalism" paradigm came from Steven Beller in his *Vienna and the Jews* of 1989.[10] Beller argued convincingly that the mainstream of Vienna's so-called assimilated Jewry (1) was in fact the "soul" of Vienna's liberal intelligentsia and (2) deserted neither liberalism nor morality, even if it did not attain political power. Alleging that Schorske neglected the enlightened-Jewish character of Viennese culture and the powerful stream of opposition to Viennese aestheticism and "the politics of fantasy" that aestheticism encouraged—that is, what I have called "critical modernism"—Beller claimed to offer a more satisfactory paradigm for grasping the most important achievements of the Viennese *fin de siècle* in terms of precisely that attachment to moral values whose demise Schorske laments. Here we seem to have a clash of paradigms in the classical sense. I believe that much future research on the interpretive level will have to preoccupy itself with the relative merits of these two positions, as well as the question of whether they are reconcilable.

What is it to have a paradigm in the first place? Despite considerable confusion in Kuhn's classical study of the development of scientific ideas, to have a paradigm seems to mean at least three things.[11] First, it means that we are in possession of a *hypothesis* that allows—or, better, requires—us to see things together that we previously only could perceive disparately. Second, a paradigm is itself an example to be imitated and further elucidated. Finally, a paradigm incorporates a bold conjecture that *provokes* criticism and thereby creates a common "field" of research by challenging its readers to enter into a systematic discussion. Briefly, our third point refers to nothing more than the fact that research within a paradigm is the activity of a community of scholars rather than isolated individuals. Where there were previously solitary scholars such as, say, Arthur May, who produced a highly informative and frequently insightful overview in *Vienna in the Age of Franz Joseph*,[12] it is with "the failure of liberalism" that we first have a matrix adequate to the interdisciplinary task of systematically identifying problems for research comprehensive enough at once to stimulate further research at the interpretive level and to evoke criticism of the paradigmatic interpretation itself.

As the creator of a new discussion about Vienna 1900 that brilliantly unified turn-of-the-century political and artistic discourse, Schorske is the father of all who work in the field of Viennese cultural studies. His poignant exposition of politics and culture turned Vienna 1900 from a local phenomenon into something crucial for the whole of Western culture, with his twofold allegation that both modern mass politics *and* the rejection of the bond between art and society simultaneously had their origins there. Like Plato, however, who found it necessary "to lay unfilial hands" upon the thesis of "father" Parmenides,[13] our very commitment to the enterprise that we inherited from Schorske—that of determining the causes and reasons which brought about the extraordinary hothouse of culture that was Vienna at the turn of the century—would seem to impel us to criticize him roundly.

I have until now refrained from mentioning the contribution that Stephen Toulmin and I made to the discussion of Vienna at the turn of the century, because I believe it must be located in the context of the development of such systematic research programs for understanding culture and society in Vienna 1900 as are here under discussion. Briefly, the problem with *Wittgenstein's Vienna* is that it fits into both the "failure of liberalism" and the "critical modernist" paradigms.[14]

History often has a way of being stunningly implausible: it is, for example, not always "historical," if one means by that simple chronological narrative. So "the failure of liberalism" thesis, and the paradigm that developed around it, was known long before Schorske published his book in 1980, because he had been publishing parts of it as articles as early as 1961. The result was that the broader reading public first encountered the thesis as part of *Wittgenstein's Vienna* in 1973. Thus, Herbert Marcuse greeted Stephen Toulmin shortly after our book was published with the words: "So you have written Schorske's book for him!"[15] In that book, we took what I have subsequently termed the "critical modernism" of Karl Kraus and company to be the reaction of what might be called the second generation of postliberal Viennese intellectuals to the first.[16] As far as Toulmin and I were concerned, Schorske's three essays "Politics and the Psyche," "Politics in a New Key," and "The Transformation of the Garden" told the first part of a story whose second part we told.[17] We saw ourselves clearly as working within the "failure of liberalism" paradigm. It is important that despite the title *Wittgenstein's Vienna*, which was a compromise from the start, we did not see our book as being about Vienna except secondarily. In the first instance it was a study of the social and intellectual origins of Wittgenstein's injunction to silence at the end of the *Tractatus.* The point is that Schorske's public had to be different from what he might originally have imagined, because the publication of *Wittgenstein's Vienna,* seven years before his book, had altered the terms of the discussion (at least as concerns the broader public).

All this would merely be an exercise in vanity on my part were it not for the fact that Schorske's work, too, has been subject to considerable misunderstanding, at least from his point of view, inasmuch as it has been read as a definitive, comprehensive study of the relation between politics and culture in Old Vienna as opposed to a case study in the origins of antihistorical thinking, which he claims it is in his preface.[18]

The upshot is that neither of the two best-known books about Vienna at the turn of the century claims to be principally a book about Vienna at the turn of the century. One is an account of the background to a very curious philosopher's efforts to "show," that is, to gesture in words at, something that cannot be said in words, and the other is about the Viennese origins of (1) the twentieth-century retreat from history and (2) the McCarthyite mentality.

Clearly enough each of these first-person views is *absurd,* even if it is true. In the end, the intention implicit in a work itself is more important than the subjective intentions of the author, as has been clearly demonstrated in the case of painters and painting (although these intentions need not be mutually exclusive).[19] Schorske and Toulmin and I have written books about Vienna, whatever we may say.

But the paradoxes do not end there, for *Wittgenstein's Vienna* is an important source of arguments for the "critical modernist" thesis that came to challenge the "failure of liberalism" paradigm. For this reason I am more than a little interested in the question of whether there is actually a "revolutionary" clash of paradigms here or merely a dramatic instance of "normal" criticism.

While there is certainly no need to belabor the details of the model that is at the heart of the Schorske paradigm here, nevertheless I wish to review its main lines.

The "failure of liberalism" thesis is first and foremost a thesis about the way in which the political frustrations of the Viennese upper middle class turned it from a patient, rational, "scientific-moral" attitude to life and society, embodied in the historicist architecture of the Ringstraße, to a decadent, narcissistic preoccupation with self-fulfillment. It explains, in short, how the pursuit of high culture became a surrogate for political engagement for the second generation of Viennese liberals, as racist demagogues undermined the nascent liberal political order at the same time that Nietzsche's "Dionysian," ecstatic ideal of self-fulfillment poisoned the minds of a youth who could no longer see any sense in political engagement—the parallels to Allan Bloom's subsequent thesis in *The Closing of the American Mind* are striking indeed.[20] In aesthetics this transition is marked by the rejection of the aesthetic ideal of naturalism—that is, Emile Zola's notion of a politically engaged, critical art working toward enlightenment in society—in favor of an impressionist or symbolist fascination with the poetic elucidation of subjective states—that is, what Hermann Bahr called a "Romanticism of nerves."[21] In this view, the work of Arthur Schnitzler is the nostalgic embodiment of the abandonment of "moral-scientific" culture for hedonism, whereas that of Hugo von Hofmannsthal epitomizes the growing fixation with the hedonist's self and comes to incorporate a kind of hedonist's bad conscience, which posits a surrogate society to give itself the very "social space" from which it has in actuality severed itself. Thus in Schnitzler's *The Green Cockatoo* a half-aestheticized relation to society expresses itself as self-alienation and a fatalistic defenselessness before the politically inevitable, whereas in Hofmannsthal it becomes the effort to move the populace to fellow feeling by utilizing all of the forceful emotional effects of the Wagnerian *Gesamtkunstwerk*, as Hofmannsthal did in, say, *The Woman without a Shadow* or *The Tower*. Ultimately Austria itself becomes conflated narcissistically with its theatrical self-image as incorporated in the Salzburg Festival.[22]

The lower-middle-class version of this "politics of fantasy" is a demagogic exploitation of theatrical gesture for narrow political ends, or better, making theatrical effectiveness and the wishful thinking it entails, instead of rational decision-making based upon the greatest good for the greatest number, the basis of political life. Invented by the fanatical Pan-German racist Georg von Schönerer, this "politics of fantasy" is perfected in the opportunistic antisemitism that paved Karl Lueger's way to power as mayor of Vienna on the basis of a Romantic vision of a medieval corporate state—and, astonishing as it seems, in Theodor Herzl's Zionist utopia, which exploited Jewish messianism in just the same way that Lueger's Christian Social movement exploited ideologically the archaic image of medieval Catholicism, or Schönerer's Pan-German movement a mythical *Deutschtum.* Freud fits into the picture as providing, if not a fantastic ideological vision of utopia, a radical skepticism about rational motivation and moral values by producing an account of motivation entirely rooted in egoism. Like Schönerer, Lueger, and Herzl, Freud's personal frustrations with his father and the values of his father's generation provide the crucial clue about why he rejects liberal rationality. Gustav Klimt's withdrawal from being the public-spirited artist producing frescoes for the "Apollonian" embellishment of public life in the Burgtheater into an ever-deepening glorification of unbridled, "Dionysian" sexuality in the monumental paintings for the university *Aula* exemplifies the tendency of the society as a whole to withdraw from the public into the private, from society into the self, and ultimately from rationality to irrationality. So widespread was this withdrawal that not even the work of such Viennese giants as Arnold Schoenberg and Adolf Loos could escape its temptations entirely. Thus we should not be shocked when we find Hitler at once admiring Schönerer and Lueger, as well as referring to Vienna as the most difficult, most thorough school in his life.[23] Indeed, the "failure of liberalism" thesis would appear to be based to a great extent on Hitler's view of Vienna before the Great War.

The "failure of liberalism" model is, then, a thesis about the inability of liberal high culture to respond rationally to failure in the political arena, and its withdrawal, at worst, into complete hedonism; at best, into a nostalgic, mystical concept of public life that was completely incapable of facing the challenges presented by rapidly modernizing Viennese society. Its three pillars are an analysis of the Viennese "politics of fantasy," an account of the Viennese rejection of literary naturalism, and the conceptual apparatus of psychoanalysis, which supplies simultaneously the conceptual basis of the rejection of delayed gratification in politics and the substitution of an aesthetics of wish fulfillment for engagement in the arena of actual political conflict.

The result of such bold moves as associating the founder of modern Zionism with antisemitic demagogues or interweaving an analysis of the external disorder of the brawls in the Viennese parliament with the internal disorders in the psyches of Nietzschean decadents, as well as Schorske's graphic portrayal of the way that the cultural burden on the liberals' sons often evoked self-destructive tendencies to cultural patricide in them, is simply dazzling—so much so that on first glance we are easily tempted to accept uncritically the magnificent set of portraits that he presents.

Because many readers failed to pay attention to the claim that the real theme of Schorske's work was how we could find striking examples of the retreat from history that was ubiquitous in Viennese society, they posed a number of questions about the incompleteness of Schorske's work, which Schorske himself does not seem to consider relevant to *his* work, but which remain, nevertheless, crucial to the "failure of liberalism" paradigm. Above all, for anyone with the slightest tinge of historical materialism in his consciousness, the question, "Who were these liberals, after all?" jumps out of the book. Schorske himself offers us no answer. Apart from the names of two of the liberal mayors of Vienna, liberalism was little more than the set of values that informed the writings of Stifter and Saar but that found their most perfect realization in the decoration of—and the debates surrounding—the buildings on the Ringstraße. In fact, John Boyer would tell us who they were.

Just at the point when *Fin-de-Siècle Vienna: Politics and Culture* began to circulate, a powerful challenge to its main thesis was issued so quietly in Boyer's work that scholars for the most part have failed to this day to notice the vast implications of his brilliant researches into Viennese politics for the study of Viennese *culture*.[24] In showing us exactly wherein Karl Lueger's political achievements lie, Boyer also explained what political liberalism in Vienna was really all about, that is, what liberals aspired to and why fundamental contradictions in their program determined that they *had* to fail. I refer to the antidemocratic stance of the Viennese liberals' efforts to maintain the franchise exclusively for those who paid ten florins tax—that is, at about 5 percent of the population—which was wholly incompatible with their cultural "mission" of uniting the *Bürgertum* and thus could only be regarded as a provocation to the excluded "little men," who were, after all, the vast majority. In effect the liberals of the 1870s betrayed the cause of the liberals of 1848, namely the political unification of the middle classes.[25] To put it glibly, the liberals were not very liberal and in their own illiberalism provoked an even more dangerous illiberalism that destroyed them politically.

Moreover, Boyer's analysis deftly demonstrates that Lueger, far from being a fanatic, was in fact Vienna's first professional politician,[26] something best illustrated by his refusal to settle political debates in duels. In bringing disparate, indeed conflicting, economic groups such as artisans and their landlords into one party, Lueger in fact realized the highest aspiration of Viennese liberals of an earlier generation. Boyer argues—actually less convincingly than he might have done if he had given us some examples of comparative rhetorical tactics—that Lueger's type of political leadership actually had more in common with the Baroque notion of the ruler as "father" than with that of the totalitarian "leader," that is, that Lueger was paternalist rather than "protofascist."

In creating a successful political party out of conflicting interest groups, Lueger was wholly sensitive, as the genuinely fanatical and self-destructive Schönerer was *not*, to the dual dimension of Viennese political life. From the Baroque onward its *public* face had been profoundly *theatrical*.[27] Think of how the emperor would wash the feet of twelve poor men and wait upon them in the imperial palace on Holy Thursday,[28] or the ceremony of the burial of an emperor in which the grand master of the court would stand before the door of the Capuchin church in the first district asking three times for admittance, being refused first as emperor and king, and then as "Apostolic King of Hungary, King of Bohemia, Dalmatia, Croatia, Slavonia, Galicia, Lodomeria, Illyria, Jerusalem [!], Archduke of Austria, Grand Prince of Transylvania, Grand Duke of Tuscany and Cracow, Duke of Lorraine, Salzburg, Styria, Carinthia, and Carniola," only to be admitted at the moment that the deceased emperor was identified as a man begging God's mercy.[29] So Lueger knew that theatricality was necessary to success in public life. To that end he espoused antisemitic rhetoric as "spice" for the public's taste for entertainment (in direct imitation of the way that liberals used anticlerical rhetoric).[30] But he well knew that this was only the public side of Viennese politics; in *private* there was in fact very little elbow room for maneuvering: *compromise* reigned supreme. In short, Boyer's Lueger has very little to do with the merely charismatic Lueger of the "failure of liberalism" thesis—even if he presents as many problems as he illuminates—but Boyer's treatment of Lueger does draw our attention to aspects of Viennese *tradition*, especially the Viennese tolerance for *ambiguity* with respect to the difference between the public and private meanings of words and events that are crucial for understanding Viennese culture.[31] In a nutshell, Boyer's research shows clearly that we cannot begin to understand the relationship of culture to politics until we raise the question of the nature of Viennese *society* and its values. Without a social history of Vienna, the relation between politics and culture is a purely hypothetical one.

After Boyer's work, the "failure of liberalism" thesis had begun to limp badly, for it was no longer possible to lump together the immensely successful, if vulgarly, even dangerously, opportunistic, Lueger with the fanatic, ne'er-do-well Schönerer, whose main achievement was to get himself banned from Austrian public life. Subsequent work by Klaus Dethloff shows that the picture of Herzl presented in the "failure of liberalism" thesis was equally one-sided. To be sure Herzl did, like Lueger, have a marked flair for the dramatic, with his deep debt to Wagner and the concept of the *Gesamtkunstwerk*,[32] both of whose importance for Vienna 1900 is immeasurable. Consider, for example, his plan for a baptism *en masse* for the Viennese Jews or a duel to the death with a leading antisemite. However the principle behind Herzl's thinking was eminently rational, namely legal recognition of the Jews as a "nation"—the only move that, as we now know, could really have undercut the evil thrust of political antisemitism. Indeed, Dethloff argues convincingly that Herzl, an educated lawyer, in fact was entirely realistic in his efforts, first, to achieve recognition for the Jews as a *"Volk,"* second, to establish a state for that *"Volk"* on the basis of the principle *negotiorum gestio* drawn from Roman Law.[33] That principle permits a person to act on behalf of another when the latter's property is endangered. As a precedent it could be appealed to in order to make a *"Volk"* out of Central European Jewry.

Reading Dethloff carefully, it is clear that Herzl was fully conscious of the dual aspects of Viennese politics, the theatrical and the pragmatic, to which Boyer has called our attention, and was prepared to act strategically, both histrionically in the theater of public politics and with sober legal acumen behind the scenes. If this is true, the "politics of fantasy" involved in winning recognition for his people in a duel or through mass conversion in Saint Stephen's Cathedral is but the Romantic political husk of a politics whose rational kernel is to be found in its attachment to legality—something very Jewish. However, that would imply, as does Boyer's revised portrait of Lueger, that the concepts and strategy that have given us the "failure of liberalism" hypothesis hardly do justice to the complexities of Viennese political culture.

These are just some of the problems that have led scholars to seek an alternative that would be able to accommodate the main points in the "failure of liberalism" thesis but at the same time tell a more comprehensive story.

At this point I want to introduce Robert Kann into the picture. Kann's thesis, which to my knowledge has never really been explored, is that there is a cyclical pattern in Austrian intellectual life, inasmuch as two alternating constellations of values dominate within Austrian society in succeeding generations. In short, there are not one, but two "Austrian minds," between which the country vacillates—*roughly* corresponding to the theatrical and the pragmatic sides of political life.[34] One of these mentalities is at once sentimentally nostalgic and highly moralistic in the spirit of Counter-Reformation Catholicism: eloquence and wit are its earmarks. The other is more dryly reformist and rationalistic, seeking to introduce the "values of the Enlightenment" into a country to which they are basically foreign.[35] Kann made his thesis come to life by illustrating it vividly in the persons of the antisemitic Baroque court preacher Abraham a Santa Clara, who ultimately represents entertainment and the culture of the picture, and the assimilated Jewish professor of "Polizei- und Kameralwissenschaft," later president of the Academy of Fine Arts, Josef von Sonnenfels, the leading representative of the Enlightenment, who represents the critical culture of the word. These two were important to Kann as much for what they symbolize as for what they actually did, or failed to do: the one for his dazzlingly witty mixture of moralizing entertainment, the other for his Promethean, if frustrated, effort to introduce the values and practices of secular "civil society" into Austria.[36] They were "type-forming characters" who were the key to understanding the dominant mentality in successive generations.

The speculative character of Kann's thesis doubtlessly accounts for its neglect by historians of Austrian culture. This mode of attacking the problem of understanding Austrian intellectual history would seem to be indebted in some loose sense to Giambattista Vico's view of history as a spiral process of *corsi* and *recorsi*.[37] It is hardly a secret that such cyclical views of history are neither particularly easy to grasp nor easy to reconcile with empirical detail. Moreover, the idea of a "type-forming pattern" is not particularly easy to fathom: is he giving us criteria for the *explanation* of Austrian cultural development over generations, *or* heuristic hints about what to look for in the "mentality" of succeeding generations? There is a big difference here. The former is hard to swallow; the latter is, however, highly suggestive with respect to the hermeneutic possibilities it offers, both with respect to the peculiarities of Austrian Catholicism and the situation of "assimilated" Jewish "enlighteners," neither of whose importance can be exaggerated.

Be that as it may, Kann had very specific ideas about the way these alternating periods would illuminate one another. Thus he insists that we shall only understand developments in one generation by looking carefully into developments *in the last generation but one*. But is this not exactly what Boyer suggests we must do if we want to see Lueger rightly? For readers of Kann, Boyer's account of Lueger contains no surprises. So, even if we are suspicious of sweeping generalizations, we disregard Kann at our peril. Kann's model can usefully guide us by reminding us of the need to think of the long term when we are trying to get hold of the basic values of specific individuals in specific epochs.

That brings us to Ilsa Barea. In her superb *Vienna: Legend and Reality*, she employs just such a long-term perspective to explain how Vienna came to have a carefree image, "cheerful Vienna," which has precious little to do with life there. With an irony seldom surpassed in Austrian cultural historiography she relates how even figures who contributed significantly to that image were in fact victims of harsh Viennese realities. Mozart is perhaps the most dramatic case in point. Always happier in Prague, he lies buried ignominiously in a common grave, whose whereabouts will probably always remain unknown, while his music has become the very symbol of a city that for the most part rejected him in life, only to celebrate him after his death by erecting a lovely memorial to him in a cemetery where he does not lie—and, finally, to name the national bonbon, the *Mozartkugel*, after him. This is not an atypical Viennese destiny.

Barea's explanation for this attitude takes us all the way back to the Counter-Reformation, which imposed Catholicism on a city that had gone overwhelmingly over to Protestantism almost as soon as Luther nailed his theses to the door of the Wittenberg Cathedral.[38] While it took a century to do so, the Catholic Habsburgs wiped out Protestantism by forcing emigration or reconversion. The implications of Barea's position, which she does not herself elicit from her position as I do here, are as deep as they are wide for our understanding of Viennese culture. Thus the effects of this forced conformity go a long way to explaining the most prominent characteristics of the Viennese popular mentality in comparison with, say, the Berliner mentality circa 1900: obsequiousness, melancholy, and irony (the phrase "assimilated self-haters" suggests itself). In effect the forcible re-Catholicization of Vienna and much of eastern Austria produced a quasi secularization of society, as people were forced to pay lip service to a set of values in which they had ceased to believe. Think of the situation of former inner-directed Protestants, who had to observe Catholic ritual despite their consciences. The only possible result would have been cynicism with respect to both religion and politics, as well as an inner emptiness that often prompted them to seek theatrical surrogates for the missing self-fulfillment. If this is true, we should find Viennese hedonism and escapism linked to a peculiar set of "alienated" *religious* values—and, indeed, we do. Boyer, for example, calls attention to the fact that underneath the surface glitter of Viennese Catholicism there lurks another religion, that of the Biedermeier "Herrgott," which at best employs certain Catholic symbols and expressions, but is really a kind of sentimentalized, fatalistic theism:[39] "Wenn der Herrgott nicht will, nützt es gar nix" (which might be loosely translated, "if the Good Lord ain't willin', fergit it"), runs a well-known *Wienerlied* that captures perfectly the popular Viennese concept of Providence.[40] Thus the Viennese disposition, which extends into the political sphere, to melancholy, and the tendency to escape into an operetta-like fantasy world, is part of a long story that takes us back to Luther's time.

This thesis, like Kann's, has not yet been put to the test, but it certainly should be. Doing so would raise the kind of questions—about the *transmission* of Baroque values from the seventeenth century—that are typical of French, anthropologically oriented history and that have yet to be applied in the Austrian context. The work of R. J. W. Evans on the transition from Renaissance to Baroque (although not in the French tradition) marks a serious move in this direction.[41] Considerations of space allow me to do little more than hint at its importance. Evans has tried to specify how the Austrian variant of the Baroque only half succeeded in producing absolute monarchy but ended up "a complex and subtly balanced organism, not a 'state' but a mildly centripetal agglutination of bewilderingly heterogeneous elements" linked by a common mentality,[42] which was too traditional to accept modernization but too modern to be content with tradition. The result was that by the turn of the century Austria held fast to all sorts of colorful traditions officially, while ignoring them in practice, or worse, exploiting them for commercial purposes, as has been the practice in Salzburg.[43] It is crucial to fill in the outline he has sketched from the end of the Counter-Reformation to the *fin de siècle*, for example, to see how magic and superstition have been transmitted from the Baroque to the *fin de siècle* (and farther). More important, the half-completed centralization process would seem to account for the curious sort of "melting pot" that Vienna 1900 would become. Evans's work suggests at once certain comparisons with centralized capitals such as Paris or Stockholm and with American cities such as New York or Chicago. Finally, it goes a long way to explaining the half-heartedness of the Viennese use of language, that is, more as ornament to social life than as a vehicle for conveying literal significance.

If Boyer has emphasized the distance between the public and the private in nineteenth-century Viennese politics, Barea and Evans have offered us an explanation of how that gap came into existence. In doing so, both of them have given us an explanation of what is perhaps the major difference between a typically Austrian and a typically German mentality, for, as Ralf Dahrendorf has emphasized, Germans are only able to cope with conflict so long as they believe that a solution at some "higher level" is possible.[44] This is exactly the opposite of the Austrian—especially east Austrian, as opposed to the Alpine—and, above all, the Viennese mentality, which has no problems with conflicts but skeptically and even cynically considers all *solutions* to pressing conflicts absurdly utopian, while accepting, and almost masochistically glorying in, the resultant ambiguity. Thus it could be that, as Kraus put it, in Berlin a situation could be serious but not desperate, while in Vienna it could be desperate but not serious.

And this brings us—finally—to our second paradigm. Where the devil is abroad, the Holy Ghost cannot be far away, to paraphrase Ferdinand Ebner.

It is precisely because the "value vacuum" of which Broch speaks, that obsession with novelty that arises as one set of values becomes passé without yet being replaced by another, evoked a far deeper response than the "mysticism of nerves" that gave us the avant-gardism of "Young Vienna," Jugendstil, and the Secession, as well as Lueger and company, that the "failure of liberalism" thesis has been challenged by what I have termed the "critical modernism" thesis. I have coined the term "critical modernism" in explicit contrast to superficial postmodernism, which has sometimes wanted to claim *fin-de-siècle* Viennese "decadence" as an anticipation of certain crucial aspects of "postmodernity." The "critical modernist" paradigm, on the contrary, turns on the hypothesis that the most important contribution of *fin-de-siècle* Vienna to our culture is a peculiarly skeptical healthy reaction against the spellbinding power that modernity exerts upon us. Its Viennese representatives, who were by no means its only representatives and were never particularly popular in Austria down to our own day, are distinguished by the power of a critique of modernity that, nevertheless, was not a rejection of modernity pure and simple, but an immanent critique of its limits.

"Critical modernism,"[45] then, is a label that I have invented after the fact to describe a cast of mind, not a conscious movement or even all of the works of the figures that I use to designate it; rather critical modernism as the property of their foremost achievements. It has two aspects: critical modernism refers, first, to a *scathing diagnosis* of that attitude to culture that considers art's power to move us emotionally by being bigger than life as a drug to get "high" on; second, it is a *strategy* for combating the narcissistic, theatrical solipsism that was part and parcel of both the Viennese religion of art and its "politics of fantasy," which was the correlative of that narcissism. The figures whom this term designates[46] were for the most part influenced by the critique of *fin-de-siècle* Viennese mores inspired by Karl Kraus, Adolf Loos, and the much misunderstood Otto Weininger, whose work we have only recently begun to comprehend, thanks to the researches of Hannelore Rodlauer, Waltraud Hirsch, and Steven Beller.[47] They include, for example, Arnold Schoenberg, Egon Schiele in the last years of his lamentably short life, Ludwig Wittgenstein, Georg Trakl (a figure who has hardly even been mentioned in connection with *fin-de-siècle* Vienna), Hermann Broch, and later the Theodor Adorno of the "Meditations on Metaphysics," and Erwin Chargaff, to mention but a few.[48] However, I would also insist upon including any number of figures outside the sphere of Kraus's influence and even some of his antagonists, such as Freud, Schnitzler in some of his moods (for example, *The Far Country*), Robert Musil, and Rosa Mayreder, among the critical modernists.[49] Mayreder's feminism, with its skeptical attitude to many feminist clichés, such as the universal enemy "man" or the "sacrificing" woman,[50] for example, is exactly the sort of thing I want to call attention to under the rubric "critical modernism."

Inasmuch as they concentrated upon art, critical modernists were all concerned in one way or another with extricating Viennese aesthetes from their cultural daydreaming, that is, what the *Brenner* philosopher Ferdinand Ebner called *Traum vom Geist*, or "intellectual fantasizing."[51] The critical modernists press crucial questions about the aims and goals of artistic activity based upon profound medium-immanent reflections in their creative work itself, as Kraus does by making texts out of the texts of others. Thus, explicitly or not, they rejected with Nietzsche the monumentality of the Wagnerian *Gesamtkunstwerk* for a minimalist *Gesamtkunstwerk* that found the message in the medium itself. Thereby they could build a pregnant Wittgensteinian "silence" into the very structure of, say, their music, in the case of a Schoenberg or a Webern, or their poetry, in the case of a Trakl.

Indeed, it was Trakl who produced the most devastating critique of Viennese aestheticism, because his critique of aestheticism was entirely *immanent*. Long confused with "primitives" and expressionists, careful study has shown that Trakl was an absolute perfectionist whose art was directed against the "value vacuum" in a "cursed, godless century."[52] Master of all the avant-garde techniques for writing poetry that Symbolist poets had inherited from Rimbaud and Baudelaire, Trakl turned those techniques against avant-garde art, as he did the symbols of Baroque Catholicism or German Romanticism, to *show*, in Wittgenstein's sense, the emptiness of an art that poisoned itself in its own beauty. In the very structure of his poems, Trakl contrasted the Symbolists' narcissistic obsessions with the personalism of Dostoyevskian Christianity, with all its sensitivity to the lot of the helpless and the downtrodden. It is a mark of his success that this poetic critique of the spiritual barrenness of his age remained powerful enough to inspire the likes of Ingeborg Bachmann, Paul Celan, Christine Levant, Thomas Bernhard, and many others decades after his death. Trakl is particularly important as a contrasting figure to the Schorske thesis because his poetry contains probably the most scathing critique of Nietzsche ever written.[53]

Kraus set the tone for this group by providing a critique at once of the "politics of fantasy" and the "Romanticism of nerves," not to mention the hypocrisy of an authoritarian church, precisely by refusing to tolerate a situation in which words did not mean what they said. His campaign against Austrian slovenliness (*Schlamperei*) took the twofold form of an assault upon the Austrian public's tolerance for ambiguity and artistic cultivation of it. Although he would increasingly, after World War I, assume the role of an Old Testament prophet in ways that became problematic, Kraus, as Harry Zohn and Reinhard Merkel emphasize,[54] began his career as a sort of casuist critic of the misuse of language in public life. His first polemics were directed in good liberal fashion at the collusion of public officials, priests, and journalists who allowed the moral and the criminal, the private and the public aspects of conduct to become fatally confused, but worse than that exploited that very confusion for profit. In a society in which such confusions were possible, rational intercourse between citizens was impossible. In fact Kraus was among other things protesting that the kind of gap that existed in Vienna between what people said and what they meant made "civil society" (what Jürgen Habermas calls "Öffentlichkeit") impossible.[55] The assumption behind his early polemics is that without integrity there could be no public life. Without the integrity of language there could be no personal integrity. If we start by debasing language, we end up debasing people. From his early campaigns for the rights of prostitutes and homosexuals to his attacks on Lueger and later Imre Bekessy and Johannes Schober, and, above all, in his commentary upon the sort of "doublethink" that lay behind the rhetoric of the Central Powers' leadership in World War I, expressed in his monumental play *The Last Days of Mankind*, Kraus was doing nothing more than objecting violently to Viennese and Austrian tolerance toward the very sort of ambiguity in public life that made Lueger possible. This is not to say that Kraus was always right in his judgments, but that the target of his polemics, lack of integrity in the use of language, was precisely what was separating Austria increasingly from the mainstream of Western liberalism. If liberalism failed in Vienna, it was not the fault of Karl Kraus.[56]

Be that as it may, the most exciting development in Austrian studies recently has been the recognition of the "Jewish" character of critical modernism. It is the merit of Steven Beller to have done so (before the concept existed as such). This is particularly impressive because once upon a time it seemed that it would be impossible to prove that the achievements of the Viennese Jews, of which everybody had always been conscious, were due to their Jewishness rather than their liberalism. On the basis of an astute statistical analysis, Beller shows us how Jewish overrepresentation within the educated class (that is, Gymnasium graduates) put them in a position to dominate Vienna's intellectual life from 1867 to 1938,[57] in much the same way that Jews have come to dominate, say, that of New York for most of this century—that is, by "setting a tone" to intellectual life so as, for example, to draw a young Catholic philosopher like me to finish his education at a Jewish university. Beller emphasizes that before and after these dates Vienna has been a relatively uninteresting place. Moreover, on the basis of an even more astute analysis of the moral values of so-called assimilated Jewry, he demonstrates why it was imperative for them actively to "Judaize" Austrian society,[58] and exactly what it meant to do so. In stark contrast to Catholicism, whose hierarchical structure has made acceptance of Enlightenment highly problematic, if not outright impossible, to this day, the Jewish Enlightenment (*Haskalah*) was able to produce a secular synthesis of traditional Judaism and Kantian moral philosophy, which turns upon the absolute duty of rational beings to act rationally. Classical German culture took on virtual religious significance as the German classics, first in connection with natural science, later literary and aesthetic culture generally, replaced the Talmud.

Thus from 1848 onward, as "assimilating" Jews gravitated in increasing numbers toward the Habsburg capital, they came with the idealistic (both in the philosophical and the colloquial sense) project of becoming Germans. When they arrived in Vienna they discovered to their dismay that before they could do that, they had to liberate Austrians from the fetters of ignorance bound up with superstitious Baroque Catholic values, to replace an ornamental pictorial culture with a critical culture of the word.[59] "Assimilation," therefore, was anything but a passive process of adaptation to their new environment. Rather it was a *project*, not unlike Habermas's project to become modern,[60] to introduce the culture of Kant, Beethoven, Goethe, and, above all, Schiller to a deprived people raised on Abraham a Santa Clara. However, it is important to emphasize that this critical spirit viewed "unenlightened," Orthodox Jewry as every bit as deprived and thus criticized its shortcomings roundly. This Jewish self-critique is often confused with another very different, very real phenomenon, self-hatred.[61] Nevertheless, it was paradoxically a strongly *Protestant* value system that assimilating Jews imparted to Vienna's liberal intelligentsia (and supported financially), both by their example and in their salons. So it should not be particularly surprising that the crypto-Protestant "critical Catholicism" (sadly neglected by cultural historians) that emerged in Innsbruck after World War I in and around Ludwig von Ficker's *Der Brenner*, which bitterly and unqualifiedly condemned the Salzburg Festival as idolatrous, should have at once developed out of, and in reaction to, Karl Kraus in exactly the same way that, for example, the thought of Elias Canetti did.[62] Both grew out of a secularized Jewish passion for truth in their very different ways.

I suspect that the achievement involved in laying bare the Jewish foundations of Enlightenment in Vienna 1900 would have pleased Robert Kann *very* much. When one reads his account of Josef von Sonnenfels in his *Study in Austrian Intellectual History* closely and carefully after Beller, and in connection with, for example, the penetrating studies of Bruce Pauley on the antisemitism of the interwar years,[63] one senses movingly the agony that the Jewish "enlighteners" of Austrian society were to experience "between the lines," as it were, in Kann's exposé. Kann's translator, Inge Lehne, told me that the book that became *Kanzel und Katheder* in German was far and away the most difficult she had ever undertaken and seriously entertained my suggestion that her practical difficulties were connected with the fact that Kann could not really bring himself to express all of the hard truths about the Viennese rejection of assimilated Jews and Enlightenment that he wanted to enunciate.[64] I have certainly been shaken, reading Kann again after Beller.

Be that as it may, we have our second paradigm. But do we have one, or two, paradigms here? We certainly have two very different, opposed *theses* about Vienna 1900. Both "the failure of liberalism" and "critical modernism" fill the three criteria for being a paradigm: they allow us to see things together that we could only previously see separately, both are exemplars that are being imitated in current research, and both have provoked an exciting and illuminating discussion. But are they "incommensurable and incompatible," as different paradigms must be, according to Kuhn? The answer would seem to be: yes and no. They are certainly incompatible with respect to certain specific points, for example, in classifying Viennese upper-middle-class culture as a culture of "grace," which developed in imitation of aristocratic sensuousness. In fact Beller has argued that there was precious little in aristocratic circles that would count as high culture for liberals to imitate. The predominant role of military virtue, so central to callous villainy in the works of Schnitzler, and its leisure-time equivalent, hunting in aristocratic life, were as foreign to the Viennese liberal intelligentsia as they were to Orthodox Jews. To the extent that there was culture at all—even when it was verbal—it was musical and pictorial; amusing, not challenging; in a word, not literary, as was liberal culture.[65] So there are clearly points of deep disagreement. On the other hand, there is also a high degree of *complementarity* between the two theses, as the argument of *Wittgenstein's Vienna* itself would attest. In this view, critical modernism came into existence as a response to "the failure of liberalism." So there is room for doubt about whether we really have a clash of paradigms here. Time will tell.

Perhaps we ought to be developing a synthesis in the form of a "failure of Jewish liberalism" thesis. The depth of Jewish commitment to liberalism, by the way, can be measured by the fact that the right to vote in the Israelitische Kultusgemeinde remained attached to the payment of ten florins tax until the end of the monarchy.[66] Consider briefly the following caricature of a sketch: if we read "Jewish liberalism" where Schorske has simply spoken of liberalism, if we further consider with Boyer that Viennese liberals were illiberal in fundamental respects and we go on to substitute the traditional Viennese values, nostalgically evoked in the phrase "Backhendlzeit," for the "aristocratic culture of grace," as Boyer and Barea suggest we should, we get a picture of a younger generation of Jewish liberals deserting the One True God, that is Kant's and Schiller's Rational Ideal, not for Catholicism itself, but for its debased, counterfeit, sentimental "Herrgott" mammonism, now in various secularized, aestheticized guises. That desertion then provokes a reaction on the part of equally dissatisfied contemporaries who insist that it is not "Jewish liberal values" that are at fault but the fact that the older generation failed often to live up to them. The resulting picture is one combining the corrected "failure of liberalism" thesis with the "critical modernism" thesis in a long-term story, which loses none of its poignancy for being in a very deep sense an internal "Jewish" debate. The result of such a thought experiment leaves us remarkably, even disquietingly, close to the argument of chapters 13 and 14 of part II in Otto Weininger's *Sex and Character*.[67]

Perhaps the future lies in that direction, which of course is not without its thorny problems. Such an approach would have to "square the circle" by doing justice both to Kraus and to Lueger, to morality and to politics. That in turn would involve little more than analyzing the deepest problems in our own culture.[68] But then, is not all history contemporary history, as Benedetto Croce suggested? And is it not precisely this aspect of Schorske's work that has made Vienna so important in the first place? Be that as it may, since squaring the circle is a good seventeenth-century Austrian preoccupation, as Evans points out, we should not shy away from it.[69]

Problems for Future Research

I would like to conclude by enumerating a list of problems for future research (not all arising from the perspective of critical modernism), which I take to be particularly pressing. Most of them turn in one way or another upon the importance of social history for understanding the link between politics and culture. In doing so I in no way want to imply that my list is exclusive; it only claims to emphasize areas that are particularly neglected. Thus I have not mentioned such areas as women's studies, philosophy, the social sciences, and so on, because considerable work is being done in those areas, even if its implications for our paradigms of Vienna 1900 have not become clear.

Analytic philosophy has taught us that we are in a position to understand the meaning of a word, sentence, sign, or symbol only to the extent that we know how it was used normally at the time it was uttered or written. Moreover, usage changes over time. Thus the history of the reasons for and causes of such changes in rhetoric will be crucial to the project of cultural history.

First, social history is also the key to the dynamics of the *transmission* of values. We desperately need a comparative study of the Viennese cultural elite such as Peter Burke's *Venice and Amsterdam*, which reconstructs the political, economic, and cultural values of the respective elites of those cities by contrast to a similarly situated city.[70] We need to understand, for example, the genesis and development of the "Herrgott" religion, but we also need to know in *detail* how the north German ideal of *Haskalah* spread *to* and *in* Vienna. To that end, we need to cultivate the sort of social history that has been so highly developed in France, that is, history with a long-term perspective concentrating upon "those who have suffered, worked, declined and died without being able to describe their sufferings."[71] Moreover, the sort of history of "moeurs" that Emanuel LeRoy Ladurie has brought to perfection in works like *Montaillou* and *Carnival* is wholly lacking in the area of Austrian studies. As a result we have had more or less to take Baroque Catholicism at its own word with respect to the significance of any number of beliefs and practices.

Another value constellation that has gone all but unresearched is the Neo-Stoic *ethos* of the civil service as it developed out of the political philosophy of Justus Lipsius into the Enlightenment through the nineteenth century and down to Kafka.[72]

To understand the significance of many social phenomena in literature we need to know what the social reality was. For example, to understand the role of the ubiquitous prostitute in literature we must know what prostitution was like in practice in Old Vienna, a theme that has only of late been investigated for the first time, significantly by a scholar working in the Netherlands. Similarly, we shall certainly not be in a position to understand the world of Schnitzler's *Anatol* until we have an accurate picture of what it was to be independently wealthy around 1900. The question of just who got rich and just how rich they got in the "Gründerzeit" remains to be posed, not in the context of industry but in the context of understanding how both Jugendstil art *and* a decadent lifestyle were financed.

Second, equally important and equally dependent upon the creation of a social history of Austria would be an Austrian equivalent of the project in civil courage that issued in Ralf Dahrendorf's redoubtable *Society and Democracy in Germany*. Austrian history and social science will not come of age until an Austrian is *brave* enough to raise the question of why it took two world wars to achieve a semblance of Western "civil society" and *learned* enough to answer it plausibly. That person will have to explore notions of equality as they relate to the process of industrialization and economic modernization, the traditional elites and education, the development of law and the legal profession, attitudes to authority, modes of distinguishing between public and private, et cetera, et cetera. That person will, like Dahrendorf, probably have to be a member of the House of Lords and vice-chancellor of an English university as well as an Austrian.

Third, since most of the "big" questions that we want to raise about Viennese and Austrian culture in one way or another turn upon that question of just how "rational" developments there have been, one important desideratum concerns the history of natural science, which is perhaps our most important measure of "rational" activity. In this area there has been practically no research whatsoever. The sheer number of first-rate scientists that came from *fin-de-siècle* Vienna is astounding. Four Nobel prize winners attended the same Gymnasium there at the same time. Erna Lesky has given us a comprehensive picture of the state of medical research in Vienna 1900 but has really only scratched the surface, so rich was Vienna's medical science at the turn of the century.[73] All of this needs to be integrated into our discussions of culture. If we want to learn about the mental habits of Viennese intellectuals before World War I, for whom natural science was a vitally important part of culture, we shall need to know more about the history of science.

Further, since the nature, importance, and social role of science is central to debates about Enlightenment, it is crucial when we are evaluating figures of the *fin de siècle* to establish how the opinions of philosophers, social critics, and literati along a broad spectrum, from racists to feminists, stood in relation to "best knowledge" in the natural sciences. For example, the number of "Monists" among Viennese intellectuals was simply huge. To evaluate their opinions, that is, to distinguish science from speculation in their thought, we need to know how they understood, say, Darwin and how that understanding relates to developments in zoology at a specified time.

In more remote periods, such as the seventeenth century, the Habsburg monarchy produced relatively few first-rate scientists, but what passed for science is highly revealing of the intellectual values of the society. I refer to the preoccupation with the "squaring of the circle." Now that reputable historians of science have taught us that it is not only legitimate but absolutely necessary to the enterprise of the history of science to concern ourselves with "false" ideas—which they assure us are usually less "false" than we think—we ought to start taking a serious look at the development of natural science and medicine in Vienna.

Fourth, another very different sort of study that we ought to be concerning ourselves with is making comparisons with the other great urban centers in Europe and America. To understand the role of Vienna in the monarchy with respect to Prague or Czernowitz, for example, we should be looking into, say, the relationship between London and Edinburgh, or Dublin, or Manchester. To some extent this sort of comparative perspective has begun to be employed as scholars from Prague, Budapest, and Zagreb explore their historical relations with the Habsburg capital. But we need yet other types of social comparative studies, too. Since there is absolutely no question that Vienna, like New York, Chicago, or London, was a magnet for immigrants, we ought to be seeking to determine what was unique about Vienna by comparing it with other "melting pots." The point of these comparisons is as much to clarify just what a "melting pot" is as it is to clarify an issue like the role of immigration in Viennese politics. While the comparisons of Vienna with other centers within the monarchy are interesting and important, this theme is crucial if we are to understand the politics of "the little man" that, we should remember, was displacing liberalism in the great U.S. industrial cities increasingly after the Civil War.

Fifth and finally, the question that Robert Kann posed about explanations of Viennese culture in terms of alternating cycles of rational and irrational dominance within public life remains. If Kann's approach seems too speculative and abstract, I would remind skeptics that the best account we have of irrationalism in the United States, that of Kann's brilliant contemporary Richard Hofstadter, takes exactly that form by tracing the roots of American anti-intellectualism back to the "Great Awakening" in 1740.[74] As for the question of his use of ideal types, do we not in fact recognize them when we take a close look at today's Austria? Does not the demagogic voice of Abraham a Santa Clara, albeit in an institutionalized form and lacking the stylistic brilliance, resonate through the pages of the *Kronenzeitung*? Have not today's "enlighteners," such as Simon Wiesenthal, shared Sonnenfels's fate of ultimate rejection despite limited superficial success? There are indeed reasons for taking Kann seriously today. These issues and many more need to be reconsidered.

Notes

This is an amended version of the Kann Lecture, delivered at the Center for Austrian Studies, University of Minnesota, Minneapolis, Minnesota, on 12 October 1995, which appeared in the *Austrian History Yearbook*, Vol. 28 (1997): 1–27.

1. Robert A. Kann, *A Study in Austrian Intellectual History: From Late Baroque to Romanticism* (New York, 1960).

2. Here we might paraphrase Kant and suggest that criticism of sources is blind in the absence of models of explanation that allow us to identify just what is worth researching in the first place, whereas models that are applied without mastery of sources are empty. The systematic study of sources, that is, documentation, yields a discourse for dealing with a particular set of "facts." However, to consider such research history is to confuse history with chronicle. It is in fact but the philological prolegomenon to history. Models, on the other hand, offer *perspectives* on those facts that can be seen as relevant to other groups of facts, that is, they are devices for unifying the various levels of discourse that have emerged from the study of sources. However, we often forget that we need models to do any research at all, that is, relatively simple "Vorbilder" of what the results of our study of sources should be like.

Nevertheless, the insight that perspectives provide will lack convincing power if they are not developed from a close study of sources into a rich hermeneutic narrative yielding "thick" descriptions of *significant* facts.

3. Two problems crop up immediately as soon as one mentions "*fin-de-siècle* Vienna": what do we mean by "turn-of-the-century," and what is the relation between Vienna and Austria? "*Fin de siècle*" can refer to any period from the two to three years before and after 1900 to the whole period from 1867 to 1938. My own preference is for the period roughly from 1890 to 1914 (or 1918). Similarly, "Vienna" can refer to the city, or "Austria," or eastern Austria. Normally these designations are not problematic. When they become so, the crucial questions are "As opposed to what?" And "For what purpose?"

4. On the notions of "paradigm," "normal science," and "revolutionary science," the *locus classicus* is Thomas S. Kuhn, *The Structure of Scientific Revolutions*, 2nd ed. (Chicago, 1970). For critical estimates of Kuhn, see the essays in the volume *Criticism and the Growth of Knowledge*, ed. Imre Lakatos and Alan Musgrave (Cambridge, 1970); cf. Martin Brody and Allan Janik, "Paradigms, Politics and Persuasion: Sociological Aspects of Musical Controversy," in Janik, *Style, Politics and the Future of Philosophy* (Dordrecht, 1989), 225–231. For a fuller account of my views on the problem of method in cultural history, see Janik, *How Not to Interpret a Culture: Essays on the Problem of Method in the Geisteswissenschaften* (University of Bergen Philosophy Department Stencil Series, no. 73; Bergen, 1986).

5. Harriet Anderson, *Utopian Feminism: Women's Movements in Fin-de-Siècle Vienna* (New Haven, 1992); Lisa Fischer, *Lina Loos oder wenn die Muse sich selbst küßt* (Vienna, 1994); Ivar Oxaal, *The Jews of Pre-1914 Vienna: Two Working Papers* (Hull, 1981); Steven Beller, *Vienna and the Jews, 1867–1938: A Cultural History* (Cambridge, 1989); Marsha Rozenblit, *The Jews of Vienna, 1867–1914: Assimilation and Identity* (Albany, 1983); Monika Glettler, *Die Wiener Tschechen um 1900* (Munich, 1972).

6. Peter Vergo, *Art in Vienna, 1898–1918* (London, 1975); Alessandra Comini, *Egon Schiele's Portraits* (Berkeley, 1974); idem, *Gustav Klimt* (New York, 1975); George Clare, *Last Waltz in Vienna* (London, 1983); Henry-Louis De La Grange, *Mahler*, 3 vols. (Paris, 1979–84); Frederic Morton, *A Nervous Splendor* (New York, 1980).

7. For a typical example, see the report of the research project *Ambivalenz des Fin de Siècle. Wien-Zagreb*, ed. Damir Barbari and Michael Benedikt, research report, Ministry of Science, Research, and Art (Vienna, 1995).

8. Hermann Broch, *Hofmannsthal and His Time*, trans. Michael Steinberg (Chicago, 1984); William Johnston, *The Austrian Mind: An Intellectual and Social History, 1848–1938* (Berkeley, 1972); Ilsa Barea, *Vienna: Legend and Reality* (New York, 1966); Kann, *A Study in Austrian Intellectual History*.

9. Carl E. Schorske, *Fin-de-Siècle Vienna: Politics and Culture* (New York, 1980). Since most of the French literature on Vienna descends from Schorske, it can be considered as part of the "Schorskean paradigm"; see Michael Pollak, *Vienne 1900: Une identité blessé* (Paris, 1986), 10; cf. Jacques Le Rider, *Modernité viennoise et crises de l'identité* (Paris, 1989) (the recent symposium on women at the turn of the century, "Wien um 1900. 'Such-Bewegungen,'" indicates that much of current feminist thinking about Vienna 1900 proceeds from Le Rider). William McGrath, *Dionysian Art and Populist Politics in Austria* (New Haven, 1974); Michael Steinberg, *The Meaning of the Salzburg Festival: Austria as Theater and Ideology, 1890–1938* (Ithaca, 1990).

10. John W. Boyer, *Political Radicalism in Late Imperial Vienna: Origins of the Christian Social Movement, 1848–1897* (Chicago, 1981) (the second volume of Boyer's study, *Culture and Political Crisis: Christian Socialism in Power, 1897–1918* [Chicago, 1994] was not available to me at the time of writing this essay); Beller, *Vienna and the Jews;* cf. Janik, "Neuerscheinungen über die Kultur der Jahrhundertwende," *Mitteilungen aus dem Brenner Archiv,* 1990, 101–102.

11. For a full account of the conundrums surrounding the nature of a Kuhnian paradigm, see Margaret Masterman's "The Nature of a Paradigm," in *Criticism and the Growth of Knowledge,* ed. Lakatos and Musgrave.

12. Arthur May, *Vienna in the Age of Franz Josef* (Norman, Okla., 1966).

13. "Τολμητέον ἐπιτίθεσθαι τῷ πατρικῷ λόγῳ," *Sophist,* 242.

14. Allan Janik and Stephen Toulmin, *Wittgenstein's Vienna* (New York, 1973).

15. Personal communication from Stephen Toulmin. Neither he nor I take this story as more than an amusing anecdote. For an account of what he and I saw ourselves as doing in writing that book, see Janik, "In Place of an Introduction: Writing *Wittgenstein's Vienna,*" in *Essays on Wittgenstein and Weininger* (Amsterdam, 1985), 5–25. I have never been happy with the title of our book. The words "ethics" or "ethics of silence" should have appeared, but they made the title too unwieldy. It was only around 1988 that I realized that the book should have been called "Cordelia's Silence," alluding to the inappropriateness of demanding that a supreme moral value (in her case, love) be put into words.

16. This has nothing to do with generations as they are conceived in political or military history, for intellectuals can be the same age and represent different constellations of values whereby one reacts upon the other, as did Hugo von Hofmannsthal and Karl Kraus, who were both born in 1874.

17. The first and third appeared originally in the *American Historical Review* 68 (July 1961): 930–946 and *American Historical Review* 72 (July 1967): 1283–1320, respectively, whereas the second was first printed in the *Journal of Modern History* 39 (Dec. 1967): 343–386.

18. Schorske, *Fin-de-Siècle Vienna,* xii–xxii; cf. Michael Roth, "Performing History: Modernist Contextualism in Carl Schorske's *Fin-de-Siècle Vienna,*" *American Historical Review* 94 (June 1994): 729–745.

19. On the important distinction between the intentions of the artist and the intentions immanent in the work of art, see Tore Nordenstam, "Intention in Art," in *Wittgenstein, Aesthetics and Transcendental Philosophy,* ed. Kjell S. Johannessen and Tore Nordenstam (Vienna, 1981), 127–135.

20. Allan Bloom, *The Closing of the American Mind* (London, 1988).

21. Hermann Bahr, "Die Überwindung des Naturalismus," reprinted in *Die Wiener Moderne: Literatur, Kunst und Musik zwischen 1890 und 1910,* ed. Gotthart Wunberg (Stuttgart, 1980), 202.

22. The last point is Michael Steinberg's extension of Schorske's thesis in *Fin-de-Siècle Vienna.*

23. "Vienna was a hard school for me, but it taught me the most profound lessons of my life" (Hitler, cited in Alan Bullock, *Hitler: A Study in Tyranny* [New York, 1961], 13).

24. Boyer's work is a good example of work that is conceived and presented as "normal" or "monographic" history in the sense used here but is in fact "revolutionary," that is, "interpretive." This is possible in history, where, unlike the situation in natural sciences, the models that inform research are often largely unarticulated and are never formal.

25. Boyer, *Political Radicalism*, 26, 37.
26. Ibid., 411–421.
27. Ibid.
28. Arthur May, *The Habsburg Monarchy, 1867–1914* (New York, 1968), 147.
29. Johnston, *The Austrian Mind*, 58.
30. Boyer, *Political Radicalism*, 210 passim.
31. Ibid., 414. It is important to emphasize that Boyer's picture of Lueger in no sense absolves Lueger from responsibility for the spread of rabid antisemitism in Vienna, for, as Boyer emphasizes, Lueger certainly tolerated real fanatics in his entourage. However, Boyer's position does falsify Schorske's picture of Lueger as merely a charismatic figure whose political practices were somehow less realistic than those of his predecessors. The question of responsibility thus turns out to be more complicated than a thesis like Schorske's would suggest. But then responsibility in these matters is a highly complex matter, as Karl Jaspers insisted in his classic *The Question of German Guilt*, trans. E. B. Ashton (New York, 1947), 31–46.
32. The concept of *Gesamtkunstwerk* is a murky one, inasmuch as Richard Wagner developed a notion for the cooperation between artists under that rubric that does not in fact apply to his work. The term later came to be applied to his music dramas with respect to the way in which they captivate and overpower the audience with a view to moving the audience to see the world differently. In effect, the Wagnerian *Gesamtkunstwerk* aims at something akin to a religious conversion (see Peter Revers, "'Erlösung dem Erlöser—Wer Erlöst uns von dieser Erlösung.' Zur Rezeption des Erlösungsgedankens bei Wagner und Nietzsche," in *Der Fall Wagner*, ed. Thomas Steiert [Laaber, Ger., 1991], 137–146). For an example of the importance of this concept, see James Shedel, *Art and Society: The New Art Movement in Vienna, 1897–1914* (Palo Alto, Calif., 1981), 29–30.
33. Such recognition was the only move that would have undermined *political* antisemitism; that is, the concept of Jews as "parasites" in German culture (Klaus Dethloff, *Theodor Herzl oder Der Moses des Fin de Siècle* [Vienna, 1986], 36 passim).
34. Kann, *A Study in Austrian Intellectual History*, xiii.
35. Here it is worth quoting Kann at length: "The genuine Liberal in German Austria does not occupy a firm middle ground between the party ideologies of political Catholicism, integral nationalism, and Socialism. He is at times—more often than not erroneously—to some extent associated with one of them, but generally attacked by all of them.... The liberal position is even more seriously jeopardized by its later failure to cope with social, national, and historical traditional problems. Above all, it has never had a social group support equal in strength to that of any of the other groups mentioned" (255).
36. On civil society, see the contributions of Edward Shils and Charles Taylor in *Europa und die Civil Society*, ed. Krzysztof Michalski (Stuttgart, 1991), 13–51, 52–84.
37. On Vico, see Isaiah Berlin, *Vico and Herder* (London, 1976), 64 passim.
38. Barea, *Vienna: Legend and Reality*, 45ff.
39. Boyer, *Political Radicalism*, 117.
40. Thus Hitler's fanatical fatalism—which was the other side of the coin of his fanatical belief in his own will—can be taken to be continuous with Viennese sentimental fatalism even if it is not identical with it. On Hitler's fatalism, see J. P. Stern, *Hitler: The Führer and the People* (Berkeley, 1975), 61, 222, passim; cf. Sebastian Haffner, *Anmerkungen zu Hitler* (Munich, 1983), 153 passim.
41. R. J. W. Evans, *The Making of the Habsburg Monarchy, 1550–1700* (Oxford, 1979).

42. Ibid., 447.
43. On "Modernisierung via Fremdenverkehr," see Ernst Hanisch and Ulrike Fleischer, *Im Schatten berühmter Zeiten. Salzburg in den Jahren Georg Trakls (1887–1914)* (Salzburg, 1986), 51–54. The little-discussed notion of modernizing through tourism is of the utmost importance for understanding the Alpine regions of Austria from the turn of the century, as well as the rest of Austria, including Vienna, which became "provincialized" in this respect as capital of rump Austria. Modernization via tourism helps to explain Austrian reluctance to come to grips with the shadier aspects of the Austrian past, such as antisemitism, in the great international exhibitions, which are principally conceived as tourist attractions.
44. Ralf Dahrendorf, *Society and Democracy in Germany* (New York, 1967), 129–155.
45. Here we must distinguish at the philosophical level between *modernism* understood as the view that there are true-for-all-time criteria of rationality that can be comprehensively represented in a single theory (the "verificationism" of the Vienna Circle, Lenin's "dialectical materialism," and Habermas's "theory of communicative action" would be three examples); *antimodernism* (the wholesale rejection of everything that has to do with industrialized society in favor of some romantic ideal of lost communitarian values); *postmodernism* ("anything goes": the simple negation of the modernist monolithic account of rationality); and *critical modernism* (the pluralistic, because practice-immanent, search for the criteria that make it possible to carry on particular activities based upon the analysis of specific cases, that is, for criteria that do not prejudge the normative issues by imposing a universally valid scheme, rather than giving up in despair at ever arriving at any criteria for evaluating anything). Popper's "falsificationism" is a step in the direction of critical modernism that finds its full expression in Wittgenstein's differentiating efforts to base reflection upon the nuances of particular cases. Martin Seel has made an eloquent case for a "second modernism"—free of the abuses of the first, corresponding to what I understand under "critical modernism"—in his "Plädoyer für eine zweite Moderne," in *Die Aktualität der "Dialektik der Aufklärung." Zwischen Moderne und Postmoderne*, ed. Harry Kunneman et al. (Frankfurt, 1989), 36–60. In the critical modernist view, Enlightenment is more a matter of establishing the limits of reason than it is of improving society through the application of scientific knowledge. Here Diderot's dialogue *Rameau's Nephew* is perhaps the crucial text. In aesthetics, the critical modernist approach is heralded in Nietzsche's critique of Wagner (see n. 31). Nearly everything of interest in the postmodernist conception of culture is anticipated in one way or another by Egon Friedell, who has been all but completely neglected in discussions of Vienna 1900 both in Austria and in France. In his *Kulturgeschichte der Neuzeit* (Munich, 1927), we find clear anticipation, for example, of the rejection of any hard and fast distinction between truth and falsity, Derrida's "pharmakon," the rejection of the notion of the "author" (in the defense of plagiarism), an emphasis upon the importance of the fragmentary and the will to incompleteness, a love of paradox, the notion of the social construction of disease (Foucault) and "illness as metaphor" (Sontag), and a conception of a "laughing" philosophizing.
46. It should be pointed out that critical modernism is first and foremost an attitude to culture. None of the figures in question incorporated this attitude in all of their work—let alone their personal lives, as Lisa Fischer's *Lina Loos* clearly indicates with respect to Adolf Loos. Many of the designs of Adolf Loos, for example, are clearly products of classical modernist megalomania, such as his sketches for his Chicago

skyscraper or his plans for the restructuring of Vienna. The point is that his most important achievements are precisely those that call the assumptions of classical modernism into question. I have profited from conversations with Hans Veigl concerning the ambiguities of Viennese "modernism."

47. See Rodlauer's introduction to Otto Weininger, *Eros und Psyche: Studien und Briefe*, ed. Hannelore Rodlauer (Vienna, 1990), 11–51; Waltraud Hirsch, *Eine unbescheidene Charakterologie: Geistige Differenz vom Judentum und Christentum als Lehre vom bestimmten Charakter bei Otto Weininger* (D.Phil. diss., University of Tübingen, 1995); Beller, *Vienna and the Jews*, 221–236; and Janik, "Weininger's Vienna: The Sex-Ridden Society," in *Vienna: The World of Yesterday, 1889–1914*, ed. Steven E. Bronner (New York, 1996).

48. On Schoenberg's critical modernism, see Janik, "Schoenberg's Vienna: The Critical Modernism of a Viennese Composer" (in Dutch), *Nexus* 12 (1995): 43–68. On Schiele, see Leon Botstein, "Egon Schiele and Arnold Schoenberg: The Cultural Politics of Aesthetic Innovation in Vienna, 1890–1918," in *Egon Schiele: Art, Sexuality, and Viennese Modernism*, ed. Patrick Werkner (Palo Alto, Calif., 1994), 101–118. On Wittgenstein, see Janik and Toulmin, *Wittgenstein's Vienna*, and Janik, "Nyíri on the Conservatism of Wittgenstein's Later Philosophy" and "Wittgenstein, Marx and Sociology," in Janik, *Style, Politics and the Future of Philosophy*. On Trakl, see Janik, "Georg Trakl und die Zerstörung des habsburgischen Mythos," in *Studia Trakliana*, ed. Fausto Cercignani (Milan, 1989), 51–62; cf. Walter Methlagl, "Der schlafende Sohn des Pans," in *Studia Trakliana*, ed. Cercignani, 63–80, and Methlagl, "Nietzsche und Trakl," in *Frühling der Seele*, ed. Gerald Stieg and Remy Colombat (Innsbruck, 1995), 83–123. One of the few scholars to follow my usage is Christian-Paul Berger in his unpublished study "Georg Trakls Begegnung mit Ludwig Wittgenstein. Eine Kulturtheorie der österreichischen Moderne" (Innsbruck). Broch practically defined the aesthetic position that I refer to as critical modernism in an early essay, "Notizen zu einer systematischen Ästhetik," which was rejected for publication in *Der Brenner* by Ludwig von Ficker in 1913 (typescript, Brenner Archives); cf. Walter Methlagl "'*Der Brenner*'—Beispiel eines Durchbruchs zur Moderne!" *Mitteilungen aus dem Brenner Archiv* 2 (1983): 11–12. Theodor W. Adorno, "Meditationen zur Metaphysik," *Negative Dialektik* (Frankfurt, 1990), 354–400. On Chargaff, see Walter Methlagl, "Von Wright, Chargaff och *Heraclitus's Fire*," *Dialoger* (Stockholm) 26 (1992): 32–38.

49. Arthur Schnitzler, *Das weite Land*, in *Das dramatische Werk*, 2 vols. (Frankfurt, 1962), 2:217–320. Musil's extended meditation on both "Genauigkeit" and "Seele"—on both natural science and what he called "the other condition," intense feeling or the state of being enraptured—is a case in point; see Robert Musil, "The German Personality as Symptom," in *Austrian Philosophy*, ed. J. C. Nyíri (Munich, 1981), 173–200.

50. Anderson, *Utopian Feminism*, 52.

51. Ebner's campaign against *Traum vom Geist* is a paradigm case for defining critical modernism. On Ebner, see Janik, "Offenbach—konsten mellan monolog och dialog," *Cordelias tysnad* (Stockholm), 1991, 45–63, and "Ebner contra Wagner. Erkenntnistheorie, Ästhetik und Erlösung in Wien um 1900," in *Kreatives Milieu Wien um 1900*, ed. Emil Brix and Allan Janik (Vienna, 1993), 224–241.

52. Georg Trakl, Letter to Ludwig von Ficker, 26 June 1913, *Historisch-kritische Ausgabe*, ed. Walther Killy and Hans Szklenar, 2 vols. (Salzburg, 1969), 2:519.

53. See Methlagl, "Nietzsche und Trakl."

54. Harry Zohn, *Karl Kraus* (New York, 1972), 42; Reinhard Merkel, *Strafrecht und Satire im Werk von Karl Kraus* (Baden-Baden, 1994).

55. See Jürgen Habermas, *Strukturwandel der Öffentlichkeit* (Neuwied, 1962).

56. See Merkel, *Strafrecht und Satire*, 154–155.

57. Beller, *Vienna and the Jews*, 33–70.

58. Ibid., 153.

59. For a trenchant comparative analysis of the impact of the Enlightenment upon Judaism and Catholicism, see David Sorkin, "From Context to Comparison: The German Haskalah and Reform Catholicism," *Tel Aviver Jahrbuch für deutsche Geschichte* 22 (1991): 23–58.

60. The difference is that Habermas is not "idealistic," in the colloquial sense, in the way that Viennese liberal Jews were. In a sense the ideal was more real than the world before them. The difference between them is the latter's belief in the ideology of "progress," which was extinguished by World War I.

61. On the problems surrounding the notion of "self-hatred," see Janik, "Viennese Culture and the Jewish Self-Hatred Hypothesis: A Critique," in *Jews, Antisemitism and Culture in Vienna*, ed. Ivar Oxaal, Michael Pollak, and Gerhard Botz (London, 1987), 75–88.

62. See Gerald Stieg, "Ferdinand Ebners Kulturkritik. Am Beispiel der Salzburger Festspiele," in *Gegen den Traum vom Geist*, ed. Christoph König et al. (Salzburg, 1985), 243; and Christian-Paul Berger, "Kritischer Katholizismus versus kritische Theorie. Der Brennerkreis und die ältere Frankfurter Schule," *Mitteilungen aus dem Brenner Archiv* 10 (1991): 72–92. I am grateful to Gerald Stieg for information about Canetti; see Stieg, "Ebners Kulturkritik," 241. On Kraus and *Der Brenner*, see Stieg's seminal study, *Der Brenner und Die Fackel* (Salzburg, 1977). For an overview of the history of *Der Brenner*, the only periodical to survive both world wars, see Walter Methlagl and Allan Janik, "*Der Brenner*," in *Major Figures of Austrian Literature: The Interwar Years, 1918–1936*, ed. Donald G. Daviau (Riverside, 1995), 83–106.

63. See Bruce Pauley, "Political Antisemitism in Interwar Vienna," in *Jews, Antisemitism and Culture*, ed. Oxaal, Pollak, and Botz, 152–173, and Pauley, *From Prejudice to Persecution: A History of Austrian Antisemitism* (Chapel Hill, 1992).

64. Personal communication from Inge Lehne regarding Robert A. Kann, *Kanzel und Katheder*, trans. Inge Lehne (Vienna, 1985).

65. In this connection it is worth quoting Hilde Spiel quoting Madame de Staël: "Few books were read in the great houses to which she was invited and no writers were received. 'It results from that separation of classes that the literary people lack grace and the fashionable people rarely receive instruction'" (*Vienna's Golden Autumn* [London, 1987], 38). There is little reason to think that this changed much.

66. Robert Wistrich, *The Jews of Vienna in the Age of Franz Josef* (Oxford, 1989), 90–91.

67. Otto Weininger, *Geschlecht und Charakter* (Vienna, 1903).

68. This claim should be compared with the provocative thesis of Isaiah Berlin in his "Political Ideas in the Twentieth Century," in *Four Essays on Liberty* (Oxford, 1969), 1–40, arguably the most trenchant study in twentieth-century Western political ideas yet to appear.

69. On this "problema Austriacum," see Evans, *The Making of the Habsburg Monarchy*, 335. On Croce, see R. G. Collingwood, *The Idea of History* (New York, 1956), 202.

70. Peter Burke, *Venice and Amsterdam* (Cambridge, 1994).

71. Jules Michelet cited by Peter Burke, *The French Historical Revolution* (Cambridge, 1990), 8.

72. Gerhard Östreich has laid the foundations of such a study in the essays collected in *Geist und Gestalt des frühmodernen Staats* (Berlin, 1969) and *Strukturprobleme der Neuzeit*, ed. G. Östreich (Berlin, 1980). I have benefited from conversations with Raoul Kneucker and Waltraud Heindl on this subject.

73. Erna Lesky, *The Vienna Medical School of the Nineteenth Century*, trans. J. Levij (Baltimore, 1976).

74. Richard Hofstadter, *Anti-Intellectualism in American Life* (New York, 1967). Like Dahrendorf's study of society and democracy in Germany, Hofstadter's well-documented book claims to be an exercise in civil courage more than an academic study. If they are accurate in describing their work, the importance of both of these books ought to tell us something about standard "academic" priorities. One important reminder to American students of Austrian culture implicit in Hofstadter's work is the closeness of American and Austrian forms of political fundamentalism. Schorske himself has pointed out how the Chinese Exclusion Act of 1882 was a model to Schönerer (Schorske, *Fin-de-Siècle Vienna*, 129), whereas Pauley has indicated that the quotas on Jewish students that Viennese antisemites demanded in the 1930s were already in effect at American elite institutions like Harvard (Pauley, *From Prejudice to Persecution*, 94, 128).

Chapter 2

RETHINKING THE LIBERAL LEGACY

Pieter M. Judson

In a review of Carl Schorske's influential *Fin-de-Siècle Vienna: Politics and Culture* two decades ago, John Boyer noted the "uneven monographic base" from which Schorske had drawn his portrayal of Austria's liberals.[1] At that time the study of imperial Austrian politics and culture around 1900 relied on a tentative, preliminary, and often inadequate reading of a few limited sources on liberalism. This was highly problematic in Boyer's view because much of the Schorske thesis and many of its later variants relied on important, if unexamined, assumptions about the nature of liberal influence on Austrian society. These assumptions cast liberalism as the philosophy of the nineteenth-century fathers against which the early twentieth-century sons rebelled. In political terms, this thesis depicted liberalism as a rootless elitist movement against which defiant populists established a new mass-based politics. The ease with which rabid nationalists, antisemites, and Christian Socials routed the Viennese liberals confirmed for many observers that such a Western phenomenon as liberalism was ill suited to conditions in Central Europe. According to this story, the normalization of radical nationalism and antisemitism in Austrian political culture around 1900 marked a simultaneous rejection of all things liberal and a decisive middle class retreat from politics. At the same time, disillusioned artists, writers, and philosophers moved well beyond liberalism's empirical-rational norms to establish radical new cultural values. This supposed cultural, social, and political defeat destroyed any potential legacy liberalism might have left to Central European society.[2]

As this early reading of the origins of twentieth-century politics and culture gained increasing authority, historians remained surprisingly silent on the subject of liberalism. In a perceptive essay published in 1984, Harry Ritter lamented the tendency among contemporary scholars to accept those unexamined assumptions about liberalism which its nineteenth-century critics and supporters had bequeathed them. Ritter drew attention to the ways in which a "figurative language of pathology invented in some cases … by insecure or disillusioned turn-of-the-century liberals themselves" had shaped the terms in which later generations conceived of Austrian liberalism. He also placed this issue squarely in the context of larger debates over the viability of the Habsburg Monarchy itself, cautioning that "ideas of what was possible for nineteenth-century liberalism are colored by conventional ideas about what was possible for the old empire. If we believe the empire was "destined" to collapse, this is likely to affect our approach to liberalism and its *fate.*"[3]

Nevertheless, in the two decades since the appearance of Schorske's book precious little attention has been afforded the liberalism that preceded the movements of the *fin de siècle*. Although a few scholars published valuable work on specific aspects of liberalism, they have not yet managed to make a dent in the paradigm that continues to structure the study of late nineteenth-century politics and culture in Central Europe. Political liberalism is still assumed to have been a weak import, popular among a tiny upper bourgeoisie, and cultural-philosophical liberalism remains the strawman against which the aggressive new political and cultural movements of the *fin de siècle* defined themselves.[4]

Yet for liberalism's collapse to have constituted an event of tragic, or at least theatrical proportions, liberalism must have achieved considerable prominence of its own prior to the *fin de siècle*. One critical assumption about liberalism, therefore, is that it somehow dominated the world of the 1860s and 1870s. It was the creed of the professional, business, industrial and bureaucratic classes who worked to remake public life in their own image. Liberalism supplied the rhetoric which shaped most political and social debate from 1848 to 1900. Its values were made visible in the historicist style of the *Ringstrasse*, a project designed to celebrate in concrete terms the victory of liberal virtues in the public sphere. And yet, according to the very same story, liberalism's hegemony was as short-lived as Austria's attenuated *Gründerzeit*, over before it had truly established itself, perhaps never really there in the first place. In hindsight, liberalism's victories turned out to have been ephemeral, its successes fleeting. Its optimistic proponents failed to establish liberalism's tenets as the basis for popular attitudes or academic social thought. This emphasis on its collapse forced Austrian liberalism, unlike its *Reich* German cousin, (which was always assumed to have failed), to bear a paradoxical double burden. Austrian liberalism had both to succeed and to fail. If liberalism had not truly established its cultural values in the middle decades of the nineteenth century, then the cultural explosions of the *fin de siècle* would appear less pronounced and far less coherent to us a century later.

The liberal failure was most often explained in instrumental terms. Contemporaries and later scholars attributed the apparent fragility of liberal politics to its status as a foreign ideological import which never took root in the monarchy. In other words, the social power of those groups whose interests liberal ideology is thought to have represented, never amounted to much. The bourgeoisie was too socially insignificant, the aristocracy too powerful, the state too overbearing, and capitalist forms of production too embryonic for liberalism to flourish. All these reasons for liberalism's easy demise relied on a deeply ingrained and familiar narrative about Central Europe: a weak bourgeoisie failed to establish the kind of liberal political institutions that characterize the West, and Austria fell prey to the emotional power of twentieth-century mass movements organized around nationalist and racial hatred. These movements in turn contributed to a tragic modern legacy of dictatorship, cultural conflict, and political violence. In the case of the German *Reich* this compelling and, for the West, reassuring narrative has long been controversial.[5] Yet for Austria, the story has raised few objections. This is due partly to the state of historical work on Austria, but also to the overwhelming influence of Vienna 1900 as a paradigm for understanding the cultural history of twentieth-century Central Europe. This paradigm requires the self-conscious renunciation of liberalism as a condition for the birth of the modern.

What are we to make of theories about the *fin de siècle* that are founded so completely on this paradox of a simultaneously hegemonic and enfeebled liberalism? And what are we to make of a liberalism which was at once everywhere and nowhere, dominant and tentative, overbearing and fragile? Some of the difficulty in providing answers to these questions originates in the tendency by those who study this period to treat municipal Vienna as if it were the Habsburg Monarchy. Vienna, after all, was hardly typical even of other cities in the monarchy, and it existed within several larger political, cultural and social contexts. Much of the Viennese experience around 1900 may well embody important trends in Central European history but other apparently key elements of the paradigm may derive from Viennese peculiarities. I can't help wondering whether their fascination with Vienna 1900 makes historians read the local political downfall of Vienna's liberals in 1895 as somehow emblematic of an entire epoch in European history. Do historians equate the emerging political culture of the European *fin de siècle* with the decisive rejection of liberalism, simply because of an accident of local history? How, for example, would historians explain the relationship between liberalism and an emerging *fin-de-siècle* political culture if Brünn (Czech: Brno) or Graz or Prague or Budweis (Czech: Cesky Budjeovice) were under their lens? What then would they conclude about the relation of liberalism to *fin-de-siècle* society, to the "politics in a new key," or even to the birth of modernism? They might even see *fin-de-siècle* culture, the birth of the modern, as a fulfillment of liberalism's promise, at least in its Central European context.[6] It is this last possibility that I wish to address more fully.

Where It Was to Be Found and How It Got There: Associational Life and the Public Sphere

In an 1861 speech to the voters of Brünn on the eve of the new constitutional era, Carl Giskra observed with some irony that everyone suddenly seemed to be calling himself liberal and that from these claims, "one might assume that the reactionaries [of the 1850s] had simply disappeared over night." Where, Giskra wondered, "had these millions of liberals been hiding themselves during the past [decade]" of absolutist rule?[7] It was not simply that liberal parties dominated the Austrian *Reichsrat* and most of the provincial diets and city councils in the 1860s and 1870s, nor even that the powerful voices of a liberal press helped shape the terms of most public debate, that fostered an impression of overwhelming liberal dominance in the public sphere. The hegemonic liberal public culture based its success on a far more personal sense of involvement than anything the voting habits of the small number of enfranchised men (and women), or the reading habits of a much larger number of Austrian *Bürger* might inspire. The most influential and yet oddly underrated contribution of liberalism to Austrian social life is the way in which its values and its internal logic shaped popular perceptions of how the world ought to function. Here I do not mean the popularity at any given moment of any particular liberal issue like low tariffs or education reform. Rather, I refer to the ways in which liberal conceptions of how the world should be ordered had long ago become the often unacknowledged ideal toward which those in public life strove to move society.

These common if rarely acknowledged norms provide a useful point of connection for studying the seemingly disparate manifestations of liberalism in Austrian society: liberal political parties, liberal cultural values, liberal social theories, liberal philosophies. They all emerged from particular types of social experience in Austria. They were not imposed through the import of foreign occidental ideologies to Austrian soil, as some scholars have claimed.[8] Their liberalism expressed the powerful yearnings of Austrian *Bürger* for institutional legitimation of their contributions to society, for control over their local polity and for the security necessary to pursue their economic goals. If the *Bürger* spouted a free trade or civil rights rhetoric, these abstract concepts only gained meaning in the context of particular forms of social experience. The most important experience for liberals in Austria was gained in the institutions like the voluntary association that underlay the new civil society, institutions separate from both bureaucratic state and traditional *ständisch* corporations. An examination of the political culture which emerged from the associational life of the *Vormärz* demonstrates the ways in which the liberals' world view originated and spread largely through a particular kind of organizational experience.

Liberal ideas were understood and shaped at the local level through the mediation of the voluntary association. In an era of absolutism, associations had provided a public forum for the expression of social values often at odds with those propagated by the government. Non-political associations (that is, with the brief exception of 1848–49, all associations before 1867) adopted *both* moral and political goals, since *Bürger* society viewed associations as central to the enlightenment and reform of society. The importance of these twin purposes gave even the most avowedly unpolitical association a real moral, and thus a political potential. Associations that viewed their task as the spread of progressive ideas also undermined the legitimacy of religion and traditional social hierarchy. They engaged in quasi-political activities both explicitly in their discussion circles and implicitly through the repetitive invocation of symbols and rituals that celebrated their autonomy from the state. By the mid-nineteenth century, voluntary associations helped middle-class Austrians to formulate and disseminate common cultural norms in disparate regions of the monarchy, from Dornbirn in the west to Czernowitz (Ukrainian: Cernwici) in the east. The associations constituted a public space where interregional issues could be recast and understood in terms of local identities and struggles. Growing communications and railway networks at mid-century also contributed to the interpenetration of shared values and political identities in several regions. This development would have an enormous importance for the rise of mass politics in the 1880s, creating a sense of common values, norms, identities and issues among far-flung *Bürger* social groups across the empire.[9]

So much for the means by which liberal ideas circulated in Austrian society. My argument goes much further, however, into the matter of ideology itself. For the associations did not simply promote already current liberal ideas: liberal assumptions about society were embedded in their very organizing structures. Membership in an association was conceived in terms highly reminiscent of the models of active citizenship promoted by liberal activists both in 1848 and again in the 1860s (and which themselves originated in what Isabel Hull so aptly calls the Enlightenment *practice* of civil society).[10] Once an individual became a member, he or she exercised certain rights, including the liberty to elect club officers, to negotiate club agendas and to determine financial outlays. Membership implied responsibility, and its privileges were not wantonly conferred (although club practices varied in their requirements for membership). Once this little society had deemed an individual acceptable, he or she gained the privilege to participate in all its aspects. Membership gave those individuals who passed certain threshold requirements equal rights in the public sphere of the association. It embodied the same distinctive combination of invisible hierarchy with proclaimed democracy which underlay the liberal concept of citizenship in the state.

The loose networks of these organizations created, in aggregate, a kind of generalized political culture based on the way in which liberal values synthesized hierarchic beliefs about an individual's particular quality with abstract universalist beliefs in fundamental equality. It is in terms of this political culture and its distinctive norms that I examine the unacknowledged legacies of liberalism to *fin-de-siècle* political culture. I want to stress the ways in which liberalism too may have been responsible for the foundation of the so-called irrational politics which supposedly repudiated it. In this way I also question the implicit notion of an Austrian *Sonderweg* that underlies most theories about Vienna 1900. The belief in a *fin-de-siècle* rejection of liberalism in Central Europe not only serves conveniently to explain Georg von Schönerer and Karl Lueger, but also implicitly to absolve Western liberal ideals and culture of any responsibility for the horrors perpetrated by the legacies of *fin-de-siècle* nationalism, racism, and "irrational" mass politics.

Liberal Ideologies

The liberal epistemological legacy to politics in the *fin de siècle* was considerable. Once we scratch the surface of liberal philosophies, we find an understanding of citizenship and a public sphere which is not all that different in its basic structures from that adopted by radical nationalists or even some antisemites in the 1890s. Similarly, we can see that not all forms of political nationalism and antisemitism rejected the liberal legacy so completely as they may have claimed to do. A close examination of liberal nationalist political rhetoric in the 1880s reveals an important genealogy, showing how certain liberal ideological structures, when recast in the rhetoric of nationalism, became encoded in the new racialized politics of the *fin de siècle*.[11]

European liberals as diverse as John Locke, Mary Wollstonecraft, John Stuart Mill and the Slovenian archeologist Dragotin Dezman all noted that in the abstract, the global everyperson enjoys one trait in common which is essential to the formation of civil society: the ability to reason. Reason, according to Locke, was "that law which teaches all mankind who will but consult it, that being all equal and independent, no one ought to harm another in his life, health, liberty or possessions."[12] In targeting the potential to reason as the foundation for a common human identity, however, the same liberal thinkers implicitly posited the existence of a potentially darker side to human existence, a realm of *unreason*. Liberals painted a disturbing picture of those who do not make reason the guide of their existence, those who have not used their reason to gain property (Locke), or those who allow "deeply rooted prejudices" to "cloud reason" (Wollstonecraft).[13] But they also included others among the marginalized exceptions to the human rule: those who have not attained "the maturity of their faculties, such as children, dependents and backward states of society in which the race itself may be considered in its nonage" (Mill).[14] For Mill as for most liberals, "Liberty, as a principle, [can have] no application to any state of things *anterior to the time when mankind have become capable of being improved by free and equal discussion*" (my italics).[15]

Although Mill went on to assure the reader that such a time had indeed been reached in all of the nations with which his readers might possibly be concerned, many liberals after 1848 betrayed ambivalence on precisely this point. The universal concept of the reasonable individual provided a foundation for all kinds of liberal political theory, from the writings of Locke to the journalistic urgings of local village activists in nineteenth-century Central Europe. Behind its optimistic façade, however, nineteenth-century liberalism implicitly harbored the growing fear that there exist individuals in all nations who, on whatever grounds, do not make reason the guide of their existence. And if we move from their universalist rhetoric to examine specific liberal attitudes toward citizenship, we find that these invisible, unreasoning beings actually constitute a majority of the world's inhabitants.

Liberal confidence in the globally "reasonable individual" as well as fear of his unreasoning counterpart, profoundly shaped access to the rights of citizenship in the Habsburg Monarchy. For nineteenth-century European liberals, rights of active citizenship belonged to individuals who demonstrated reasonable behavior in distinctive social situations. Only those who passed certain tests of reasonableness earned full personhood and the attendant rights and opportunities which attached to it. Similarly, those who gained membership in voluntary associations had to have passed a threshold test to demonstrate they had the requisite qualities. Failing any of these tests indicated one's inability or unwillingness to use reason. Among Austrian liberals, reasonableness came to mean the rejection of particularist forms of social difference as the basis for community identity. Those who insisted on the primacy of family, class, regional, religious, ethnic national, or any comparable form of identity in the public sphere, it was believed, could never reach beyond their parochial interests to comprehend the larger common good of society. They could not be trusted to exercise the rights of citizenship properly.

It is not my intention here to analyze the twisted inconsistencies of nineteenth-century liberal thought regarding questions of social difference. Rather, I want to lay bare liberal arguments about community membership to show how the nationalist and racialist ideologies of the turn of the century emerged from and transformed this hierarchic vision. The liberals made two demands on Austrian citizens which betray the hierarchic nature of their vision: first, that in public, individuals abandon the particularist loyalties which kept them in thrall to local interests, and second, that they embrace a global model of the reasoning citizen. These twin demands allowed the liberals to struggle visibly for the universal emancipation of humanity, while simultaneously limiting the access to liberty of those who had not yet become reasoning persons.

Austrian liberal assumptions about the human condition derived largely from observation and experience, but were usually expressed in terms of human nature and abstraction. Debates about the franchise in 1848 illustrate how liberals cast their particular social experience in terms of universal principles. In that year, liberals in provincial diets and city councils across the monarchy defined the vote as a political function to be exercised only by those capable of contributing to the community and thereby capable of perceiving its best interests. Liberals claimed that the independence of mind so necessary to citizenship was reflected in the degree to which an individual had achieved financial independence. Just where individual liberals located the theoretical boundary dividing the reasonable citizen from the unreasonable non-citizen constituted grounds for debate, but no liberal would have questioned that such a boundary did exist.

In the Upper Austrian Diet of 1848 liberals denied the vote to those "who live from a daily wage or who enjoy charitable contributions, in short, those who are not independent." In Styria, liberal members of the diet distinguished mere inhabitants of a community from tax-paying members or true participants with the phrase, "whoever does not share in the burdens of the community should have no voice in the administration of community funds." In barring non-tax-paying residents from access to the decision-making process liberals not only imposed an implicit hierarchy on humanity, they also connected the trait of reasonableness to income level. However, one should not conclude that they viewed property ownership as an end in itself. Rather, it constituted for them one of the few reliable indicators that a person was capable of exercising reason. When, for example, the Vienna City Council imposed a minimum tax payment as the qualification for the right to vote, it added "degree of education" as a recognized alternative sign of reasonableness to property ownership.[16]

Liberals created other unspoken barriers to citizenship. No matter how high a degree of education they attained or how much property they might own themselves, bourgeois women, for example, had no formal access to citizenship. In those same 1848 debates we find both the Upper Austrian and Styrian liberals stymied by cases in which a woman's ownership of a local business technically gave her the right to vote. In such cases, the fact that women were defined in the abstract as dependent beings made real life situations that suggested otherwise appear as bizarre and exceptional cases. By the 1880s, the middle-class assumption of women's permanent dependent status had become so ingrained that liberals in Lower Austria banned those women from voting whose exceptional economic status had enfranchised them, arguing that a woman's natural modesty required that she be protected from such a brutal public ritual as voting. In this case no amount of education, acquisition of property, or social status outweighed nature's decree.[17]

When they gained the opportunity to redraw the constitutional boundaries of citizenship on the national level in 1867, liberals continued to value the social contributions of some groups above others, while professing universalist motives in the abstract. Wherever possible during this period, for example, liberals used their powers to limit workers' abilities to constitute themselves as a class through social organization and political representation.[18] Through the 1870s liberals continued to maintain that workers were far too immature to enter the political community as full citizens. The proof of this immaturity lay in the workers' stubborn insistence on defining their interests using a particularist rhetoric of class difference. Arguments based on class subverted the liberal claim that use of reason, through education, would eventually help everyone in this classless society to adopt sensible bourgeois values and thereby to prosper. Most liberals rejected even a moderate reform idea like the establishment of Chambers of Labor (*Arbeiterkammer*) because, as one *Reichsrat* deputy explained, it would give "legal expression to the concept of a separate working class," and the state would for the first time "formally recognize the existence of a class conflict separating labor from capital."[19]

It is important to note that this liberalism did leave a theoretical back door open for some workers, peasants, Slavs (if not women) to gain reason and thus the full rights of citizenship. As long as education offered an alternate route to reasonableness, it would technically be possible for even the poorest worker or the most ignorant Slav to gain full rights of citizenship. "To be free is to make reason the constituting principle in one's life," wrote Johann N. Berger, a student activist in 1848 and later minister in the *Bürgerministerium*, the first Liberal cabinet. Noting that "People are not free in one blow, they become free, they develop and educate themselves to freedom," Berger argued against giving the masses complete liberty and citizenship until they had received enough education to make proper use of it. Another commentator noted of the workers, "they can not be transformed overnight into a nation of sober housekeepers. They must be educated to ... delay gratification for a safer future."[20] These examples reveal both the liberal belief in the workers' present inherent unreasonableness (hierarchy) as well as their potential to become citizens through a long process of education (equality).

The liberals applied the same reasoning to the issue of national identity, as I have argued elsewhere.[21] In 1848 the liberals assumed that those who wished to advance socially would educate themselves, and thereby gain a German national identity. German identity was understood largely in terms of cultural values and not, as we know it today, in terms of ethnic identity. One did not have to descend from a German family to be a German. One had to adopt the cultural values which signified Germanness to these early liberal nationalists. Thus, most liberals considered both national and class identities to be theoretically contingent, since education could eventually remedy shortcomings in either.[22] Here let me note by way of example, the ways in which these concerns shaped liberal attitudes toward the emancipation of the Jews. Liberals defended citizenship rights for Jews not only for humanitarian reasons, but also because of the visible efforts made by urban middle-class Jews to adopt German bourgeois cultural norms. Liberal leader Ernst von Plener commented approvingly in his memoirs that as a group, the Jews had come to "possess certain bourgeois virtues to an unusual degree." This Jewish affirmation of German culture was understood and rewarded as a substantial attempt to overcome social difference, since as Plener added, centuries of oppression and living apart from society had also developed "some unpleasant characteristics among the Jews."[23]

The belief in the theoretical ability of individuals to improve themselves gave liberalism its emancipatory flavor. The efforts of the first liberal government, the short lived *Bürgerministerium*, to institutionalize liberal theory as policy primarily through education, religious, and administrative reform, made it the most radical government in Austria's history. Yet the confidence that when given the opportunity, humans will choose to improve themselves, was increasingly outweighed in the nineteenth century by the growing fear that some individuals might not choose to do so. While liberal theory continued to celebrate the strengths which a diverse citizenry contributed to society as a whole, the liberal conceptualization of citizenship in fact narrowed, as liberal practice worked to erase diversity in the public sphere. Conceptions of difference among various groups in the monarchy had to be decreased, if not erased, for the liberal order to take root. Linguistic, religious, regional, ethnic and even class differences might season private life, they might be displayed in parades and in museums, but they would only be salutary in a society of people who shared the same fundamental loyalties to a particular social vision of progress and civilization. For this very reason it would be misleading and unfair to accuse the liberals of somehow betraying their ideals when they resorted to apparently illiberal measures, a point many twentieth-century liberals are often inclined to make. To the contrary, that very liberal world view that insisted both on universal citizenship and on distinguishing between the enlightened and dependent being, helped liberals to make sense of the social conflict they experienced in everyday life. If liberals became illiberal, the seeds of their illiberal behavior could be found in liberalism itself.

Liberal Legacies

By the mid-1880s it was apparent that, despite the best efforts of the new liberal school system, the politicization of local class and nationalist identities had far outpaced the spread of reason. The liberals gradually adopted new tactics to accomplish the goal of uniting diverse peoples under a common identity which might transcend localist concerns. They turned to a rhetoric of German nationalism to accomplish what their rhetoric of universal humanism had, up until then, failed to achieve. The German liberals created a powerful new politics organized around nationalist community identity in order to pursue their traditional program more effectively and to repulse several growing threats to their local hegemony, threats which were increasingly couched in nation-, class-, or race-based discourse. Yet it is important to understand that the liberals did not simply abandon liberalism for nationalism. Rather, they adopted a particular version of nationalism organized around the same concerns for diminishing intra-community differences which had dominated their liberalism.

The historiographies of nationalist, of racial and political antisemitic politics in the monarchy at the *fin de siècle* have for years rested on the notion that collectively, this new politics constituted a fundamental rejection of liberalism. And yet those phenomena shared with liberalism its original intent to build political community by enfranchising a group of basically similar people, erasing their internal differences, and highlighting their differences with external others. In addition, most German nationalists tended to maintain the liberal commitment to the values of progress, science, and education. Where self-defined radical nationalists or antisemites often battled the liberals, it was over the particulars of nation, and later race, and rarely over the legitimacy of those concepts in defining community. Many political and social conflicts of the 1880s and 1890s may have been articulated in terms that contested one or another parameter of the German national community, but never the centrality of that national community in the first place.[24] This observation should not, however, detract from the importance of those battles. Many German nationalists continued to argue for an inclusive vision of the nation. At the same time, their commitment to such inclusiveness meant including the antisemites along with the Jews. Ironically, this commitment to inclusion often helped to normalize antisemitism within the nationalist community.[25]

Liberal ideas about society provided a fertile ideological foundation for the explosion of German nationalist politics at the end of the nineteenth century. The liberal belief in hierarchic spheres of active and passive citizenship was transformed by 1900 into a discourse about cultural and later, occasionally racial difference, as activists recast ideas about *social* differences into beliefs about *national* differences. The ideological similarities between liberalism and its radical nationalist progeny go well beyond the nationalist translation of liberal concern with social difference into a rhetoric of national difference. The early liberal nationalists of the 1880s had treated national identity not as an inborn quality, but much as their liberal progenitors had treated reason: as something to be unfolded through a process of education. If reasonableness had to be nurtured in people, so now did consciousness of Germanness. Specific examples of what could be defined as particularly German behavior in this transitional period (1880–1900) resembled earlier liberal markers of what had constituted reasonableness. The attainment of property, education, the proper management of land or capital, good manners, upright behavior, respect for property, these virtues became reinscribed as specifically German virtues.[26]

This ideological transformation took place largely within the voluntary association. Local bourgeois activists in the 1880s spearheaded the efforts to revive the flagging liberal movement through the organization of clubs for nationalist defense. They argued that particularly in ethnically mixed regions of the monarchy, the German liberal inattentiveness to national issues had both ceded political initiative to their Slavic rivals and had let down community defenses. Using a rhetoric that mixed geography and history with identity politics, German nationalists claimed that German territory was being lost and German communities subverted. Their energies created mass associations like the German School Association (110,000 members in 1885), the *Böhmerwaldbund* (34,000 members in 1900), and the *Südmark* (over 50,000 members after 1905), organizations that demonstrated a strong degree of liberal influence in both their social composition and their programs. If historians have ignored the significance of these mass organizations in reviving bourgeois liberal influence at the level of local politics, the antisemitic populists of the 1880s and 1890s certainly did not do so. They did their best to challenge liberal dominance in several of these organizations because they understood how much power these groups wielded within the German nationalist community. When the antisemitic challengers failed in their attempts to wrest complete control from the liberals, as they did in the case of the School Association in 1885, they subsequently denounced these organizations as elitist, un-German, and worst of all, as liberal.

While the liberal nationalists succeeded in transforming their movement along nationalist lines, often staving off populist, antisemitic challenges in the 1880s and 1890s, the antisemites did not completely lose the battle to define membership in the German community. Liberal nationalists may have expelled antisemites from some of the largest associations, but a glance at nationalist ideology around 1900 suggests that liberal nationalists also came to tolerate and even accommodate racial arguments about identity (if not always comfortably). By 1900, the ideology propagated by the large progressive or liberal nationalist associations had changed in content. The School Association leadership easily rebuffed annual challenges by antisemites to its policy that anyone, without regard to religion (or race), might join its local branches. Yet in 1899, after the retirement of its long time liberal leader Moritz Weitlof, the leadership offered a compromise to the antisemites: each locality would have the option to found more than one branch. Although Jews were not mentioned explicitly, the reform allowed for the creation of both liberal and antisemitic branches of the same organization in any given locality.

This School Association compromise, which tacitly enabled some local branches to practice a policy of antisemitic exclusion, shows the degree to which antisemitic rhetoric had infiltrated the broader nationalist lexical repertoire by 1900. Still, we should not necessarily view this change as a victory for radical antisemites over liberal nationalists. The compromise reflected a growing toleration that saw antisemitism as one legitimate point of view on a larger spectrum of views, all of which should be accommodated within the German national community. The compromise did not reflect a wholehearted adoption of an antisemitic world view by German nationalists. The right of local branches to exclude Jewish members, for example, did not lead to any new and overt antisemitic practices in the School Association, nor did it result in a reduction of contributions made by the organization to Jewish-run schools. In specific localities it may have contributed to a reconsideration by Jews of their national loyalties and options, but in the long run, it did not mark a break in the association's development. And yet, the new policy did not please the antisemites themselves who rejected the notion that their ideology could be accommodated within a "big tent" pluralist German liberal nationalism.

The fact that nationalist associations continued to position themselves within the liberal nationalist tradition, while tolerating antisemites at the local level, suggests that by 1900 antisemitism had somehow become normalized in Austrian *Bürger* culture. Neither support for it nor opposition to it constituted a critical division between liberals and *völkisch* radicals any longer. Ironically, the antisemites understood this best. They continued to boycott or protest festivals, conferences, or other undertakings which included the still suspect, but highly successful School Association. One antisemitic historian noted with contempt that the internal reform of 1899 had not amounted to a true refounding of the School Association "on the basis of national purity (*Volksreinheit*)," and this made any serious collaboration with it quite impossible.[27]

Some readers may object that my argument about the normalization of racial rhetoric ignores the profound abhorrence of antisemitism expressed by several highly articulate liberals in the last decades of the nineteenth century. It is certainly true that liberal nationalists like Joseph Kopp, Max Menger, Gustav Gross or Moritz Weitlof fought hard at certain moments for a non-racialized vision of German community. However, their principled rejection of antisemitism should not divert our attention from either the ideological or organizational legacies of liberalism. Nor should we take their highly visible positions as necessarily typical of local German liberal and nationalist activism in the monarchy, just as we should avoid imagining that Schönerer's radical positions were in any way typical of German nationalists. Mainstream German nationalist discourse as evidenced in the popular press was increasingly racialist in tone after 1900, even as it maintained highly progressive positions on issues such as secular education.

In the 1880s, liberal nationalist activists had worked to awaken an awareness of national identity among those Germans who were ignorant of it. Nationalists had focused on defining Germanness for the individual as a means of bringing him or her into a larger community. By 1900 German nationalist publications and organizations (like those of their Slavic or Italian opponents) had shifted their focus to underscore the need to maintain stricter boundaries between German and Czechs, Germans and Slovenes, Germans and Italians, in the ethnically mixed regions. In Bohemia this new concern for separation resulted in part from the German strategy of defining a purely German-speaking territory (the so-called *Deutschböhmen*) which might someday achieve administrative autonomy from the rest of the province. Every Czech incursion in ethnically mixed borderlands diminished the degree to which this national delineation could reasonably be made. But at least in part, the heightened concern about national mixing reflected the degree to which racial theories had also come to influence beliefs about nationality. The figure of the racially other Jew differed formally from the figure of the nationally other Czech in German antisemitic rhetoric.

The former had no legitimate home, no authentic *Nationalbesitzstand* (except what he could steal), while the latter had a legitimate *Nationalbesitzstand* of his own which he aggressively sought to increase at the expense of his German neighbors. Of course such differences in individual stereotyping ultimately paled beside the growing tendency to understand all national differences in biological terms, using a rhetoric of science borrowed both from antisemitic and from British and French colonialist discourse.

Liberal nationalists had worried publicly about how to keep German property in German hands for some twenty years; now with an increasingly racialized understanding of national differences they warned against the dangers of intermarriage. "To prevent our enemies from making further progress we must practice a personal national separation to the extreme," explained one progressive leader, "starting from the endeavor to encourage and support everything that helps us to maintain every possible opposition between the German population and the Czech." The "Ten Commandments of the German Farmer," first published in the 1880s, were recast as the "Ten Commandments of the German People" in 1898. Where the former had stressed self-help, independence, and capitalist virtue, the latter warned against "social contact with strangers" or "succumbing to alien customs and beliefs," while commanding pride in "German descent." In the story "Eine Mischheirat" by radical nationalist and antisemitic *Reichsrat* deputy Karl Türk, a young man ignores the warnings of his parents and, on the advice of a local Jew, he marries a Czech woman from another village. The result is catastrophic. He loses his fortune, his national identity and eventually his life, while his wife raises his children as Czechs.[28]

Although extremely at odds with earlier liberal concepts of national identity, these newer beliefs carried with them important cultural legacies of liberalism. Where they differed was in the way they made visible the kinds of hierarchy which for liberals had remained hidden and subject to potential change in the distant future. Liberals had denied the full rights of citizenship to racial inferiors, to workers, most peasants, and to women since all were deemed dependents incapable of using reason. Liberal rhetoric had lingered far more on the promise of universal citizenship and progress than on the specifics of who remained unenfranchised, but as we have seen, its revolutionary potential was matched by its hierarchic commitment to the status quo. Radical nationalist rhetoric in turn focused far more pessimistically on the outsiders, seeing them often as biologically different, and using them just as the liberals had, to distinguish one population from another.

Whose Mass Politics?

Traditionally, historians have argued that liberalism's inability to survive in an era of mass politics had as much to do with its rigidly unimaginative ideologies as with its organizational culture of elitism. A decade of harsh economic depression after 1873 and the growing perceptions of corruption within the liberal parties weakened popular belief in liberalism's utopian promises and suggested that liberal rhetoric did not always match liberal actions. By the 1880s liberalism appeared to favor the social status quo at every level of society. At the same time, however, historians, have generally ignored alternate evidence of liberalism's underlying vitality, particularly at the local level, preferring to focus on its parliamentary decline. That decline, however, is only a small part of a larger story played out within several influential associations and municipal governments, and not primarily in the imperial metropole Vienna.[29]

Certainly the centrality even of local politics in Vienna to our understanding of the dimensions of social and cultural change in Central Europe has blinded some historians to precisely the critical connections between liberalism and the political radicalism of the *fin de siècle*. And if most historians don't directly refer to the practice of politics in the Austrian *fin de siècle* in exactly the terms invoked by Schorske two decades ago, (the return of the repressed, the revolt of the sons, and most importantly, the rise of a politics of irrationalism, emotion, or manipulation) they are nevertheless hard pressed to find the internal logic or rationality in Austrian parliamentary politics as practiced after the excesses of the late 1890s. The image of politicians hurling harsh invective (and sometimes inkwells) at each other and provoking police intervention, seems at first glance irrational. Yet if we examine the history of the obstruction surrounding the Badeni ordinances, from which the worst examples are always drawn, we would see that it was as often the more progressive nationalists (liberals like Otto Lecher or even Josef Kopp) who led the nationalist charge, becoming heroes of the hour, while antisemitic populists like Steinwender and Lueger held back, behaving as the liberals might have behaved twenty-five years before.[30]

I don't want to confuse the issue here, but I do want to suggest that the degree of demagoguery practiced by an individual movement depended largely on the particular context of a given issue. Despite their populist careers, neither Lueger nor Steinwender, for example, had an interest in fomenting mass opposition to the government over this particular issue. And both Lueger and Steinwender were trumped, in this case, by the progressive nationalists who were clearly not beyond using such modern tactics themselves. While their nationalist strategy never restored them to their former position in Austrian politics, it kept the liberal nationalists a force to be reckoned with until the end of the monarchy.[31]

If one approaches liberalism from the perspective of the local associational and regional political cultures it created, particularly in those crucial and well populated regions that were separated from Austria after 1918 (Bohemia, Moravia, and Silesia), the narrative looks different from the more familiar experience of Vienna and Lower Austria. The years after 1895 did witness the fragmentation of liberal parties according to regional and social interests, but traditional liberals often maintained their political voice in local associations and in municipal politics. Liberal political culture seems to have reinvented itself frequently, adapting its influential rhetoric and organizational practices to dramatically changing circumstances as it tried to maintain its power to order local society. This was particularly the case in ethnically mixed regions where, unlike the case in Vienna, national identity remained at the center of political, social, and cultural struggle. Almost every important issue had to be expressed in terms of the struggle to define and unite a German community. And contrary to received opinion, that community had constantly to be made and remade. From this viewpoint, the central drama of Austrian liberalism becomes the challenge to alter its practices in order to maintain its social hegemony, and not its defeat in the Vienna *Rathaus* by Lueger's Christian Social party.

Outside Vienna it was often the liberals, and not their populist opponents, who politicized ethnic and gender differences most successfully in the 1880s. In Austria, German nationalism came to serve a political function closely resembling that of early liberalism, namely to consolidate *Bürger* hegemony in local politics by demanding social unity at all costs. Nationalism outside of Vienna helped to mediate an attempted *trasformismo* from traditionally elite liberal politics to a controlled form of mass politics under the watchful eye of *Bürger* elites (just as John Boyer's work has stressed the way Lueger's Christian Social movement fulfilled a comparable function for the Vienna *Bürgertum*). By the late nineteenth century, German nationalism often augmented liberalism as a world view which promoted social harmony and the protection of property among a *Bürgertum* whose social and cultural parameters were becoming more broadly defined. And more often than not, the bourgeois liberal voluntary association remained the site where German identity was constructed and elaborated for the larger communities down to the collapse of the monarchy in 1918.

Conclusions: Liberalism and Vienna 1900

The experience of parliamentary political decline in the 1880s ultimately strengthened the long-term ability of the German-speaking middle classes to maintain their considerable local political influence and privilege. By translating their traditional principles into a universalist rhetoric of German nationalism, liberals outside of Vienna found a way to restate the visions of 1848 and 1867 in more effective political terms for the Austria of the 1890s. What was different by 1900 was that German speakers focused more on defining their differences with other groups than on encouraging others to join them. Nationalists produced a culture that made visible their traditional liberal hierarchies, some even using a new language of race to characterize social difference. German national identity, which had previously been understood as something contingent and at least potentially universally applicable, was increasingly imagined by many German liberal nationalists in the 1890s as something fixed, inborn, transhistorical, and limited. This should not surprise us. After all, the Austrian liberal vision of a pluralist yet homogenous bourgeois world had emerged from the narrow civic culture of bourgeois association in the early nineteenth century. Its social practice and assumptions about people were based on limited experience of social difference within a bourgeois milieu, yet understood as natural and universally applicable. The rights and responsibilities of citizenship modeled on the rules of club membership could only be extended to those people who implicitly accepted those rules or fit those norms. In the same way, experience within the voluntary association shaped the ideological conflicts which defined the nationalist community in the 1880s and 1890s.

If the liberals lost several battles to preserve their political predominance, they may have won the war in their efforts to maintain a political culture based on much of their world view. Almost every group which challenged the liberals in the nineteenth century made the same universalist claims for itself, and each built on rules of engagement established by the liberals themselves. Liberal freedoms became understood as the *natural* rights of human beings. Other legacies of liberalism such as anti-clericalism, education as the premier site for citizenship training, and the rhetorical link connecting the individual citizen to the state through ideas of cultural or national identity remain popular today.

Austro-German liberal visions of community, however pluralist, required at least a modicum of assimilation from the outsider before they could tolerate even limited forms of individual difference. The liberal tendency to find justifications for such exclusionary principles in a rhetoric of nature, calling on an emerging positivist natural science for proof, succeeded in placing basic liberal principles outside the realm of critical discussion to such an extent that their relatively recent invention was thereby more easily ignored. The implicit hierarchy within which forms of difference were understood by Austrian liberals remained at least as important as their liberal commitment to democratic pluralism.

If the study of Vienna 1900 is going to recover the intricate genealogies of political mobilization and cultural explosion of the Austrian *fin de siècle*, it must be informed by a greater recognition of the complex and influential liberal legacy to Central European politics and culture. The compelling but ultimately ahistoric paradigm that has dominated most discussions of Vienna 1900 must be replaced by approaches that rest on a greater appreciation for historical, geographic, and social context. I have suggested two ways in particular that this might be accomplished: one by locating liberalism's influence in organizing the structures of political institutions and popular discourse, and the other, by recognizing and subjecting the hierarchic elements of liberal ideology to greater scrutiny. In both cases it seems clear that local social experience constitutes a far better indicator of how liberalism informed the movements of the *fin de siècle* than does parliamentary politics alone.

Notes

1. *Journal of Modern History* 52 (1980): 725–730.
2. Schorske believed that the Social Democrats were the inheritors of the liberals' rationalist/empirical tradition, but more recent work on late nineteenth-century Austrian socialism suggests that socialists too engaged in a cultural politics similar to that of Christian Socials and nationalists. John Boyer, *Culture and Political Crisis in Vienna: Christian Socialism in Power, 1897–1918* (Chicago, 1995); William McGrath, *Dionysian Art and Populist Politics in Austria* (New Haven, 1974).
3. Harry Ritter, "Austro-German Liberalism and the Modern Liberal Tradition," in *German Studies Review 7* (1984): 227–247.
4. Scholarship on Austro-German Liberalism from the last decade is unremarkable, for example, *Studien zum Deutschliberalismus in Zisleithanien 1873–1879*, ed. Leopold Kammerhofer (Vienna, 1992). Interesting exceptions based on local studies are: Peter Vodopivec, "Die sozialen und wirtschaftlichen Ansichten des deutschen Bürgertums in Krain vom Ende des sechziger bis zum Beginn der achtziger Jahre des 19. Jahrhunderts," in *Geschichte der Deutschen im Bereich des heutigen Slowenien 1848–1941*, ed. H. Rumpler and A. Suppan (Vienna, 1988); also articles by Hanns Haas, Robert Hoffmann, Peter Urbanitsch, and Peter Vodopivec in the first two *Bürgertum in der*

Habsburger Monarchie volumes, and Lothar Höbelt's political history of the German Nationalist parties, *Kornblume und Kaiseradler: Die deutschfreiheitlichen Parteien Altösterreichs 1882–1918* (Vienna, 1993). For the period before 1848, Waltraud Heindl's *Gehorsame Rebellen: Bürokratie und Beamte in Österreich 1780 bis 1848* (Vienna, 1991) provides superb insights on the increasing influence of liberal cultural values within the imperial bureaucracy.

5. See Robert G. Moeller, "The Kaiserreich Recast?" in *Journal of Social History*, 1984.

6. See, for example, the work of Gary Cohen, Cate Giustino, and Scott Spector on Prague; Lothar Höbelt on Reichenberg; Heidemarie Uhl on Graz; Peter Vodopivec on Laibach (Ljubljana).

7. *Wahlrede des Dr. C. Giskra für die Landtagscandidaten des II. Bezirks in Brünn* (Brünn, 1861). Giskra's 1848 activities in the Frankfurt Parliament had earned for him police surveillance and a ban on practicing law in Vienna. His successful law practice in Brünn brought him popular recognition and political success in the 1860s, culminating with his appointment as Minister of the Interior in the radical *Bürgerministerium* of 1868–1870.

8. See, for example, Georg Franz, *Liberalismus: Die deutschliberale Bewegung in der habsburgischen Monarchie* (Munich, 1955).

9. David Blackbourn, "The Discreet Charm of the German Bourgeoisie," in *Populists and Patricians: Essays in Modern German History* (London, 1987); Robert Hoffmann, "Bürgerliche Kommunikationsstrategien zu Beginn der liberalen Ära: Das Beispiel Salzburg," in *"Durch Arbeit, Besitz, Wissen und Gerechtigkeit:" Bürgertum in der Habsburgermonarchie II*, ed. Hannes Stekl et al. (Vienna, 1992); Rudy Koshar, *Social Life, Local Politics and Nazism* (Chapel Hill, 1986); Thomas Nipperdey, "Verein als soziale Struktur in Deutschland im späten 18. und frühen 19. Jahrhundert: Eine Fallstudie zur Modernisierung," in *Gesellschaft, Kultur, Theorie: Gesammelte Aufsätze zur neueren Geschichte* (Göttingen, 1976).

10. Isabel V. Hull, *Sexuality, State, and Civil Society in Germany, 1700–1815* (Ithaca, N.Y., 1996), especially 199–228.

11. I am not arguing that nationalists and antisemites were in fact liberals, nor that liberals were in fact closeted nationalists or antisemites (some were, some were not). Rather, that in ideological terms it is far more difficult to draw a line separating these tendencies from each other than has previously been asserted. Ernst Hanisch, for example, has on many occasions voiced to me his belief that it was precisely their antisemitism that for him separated the later German nationalists from the earlier German liberals. This may be true. But if we draw the line here, how do we treat these antisemitic non-liberals' ongoing struggle to realize other elements of the traditional liberal political vision?

12. John Locke, *Two Treatises of Government* (New York, 1965), 311.

13. Mary Wollstonecraft, *A Vindication of the Rights of Woman* (New York, 1975), 12.

14. John Stuart Mill, *On Liberty* (Garden City, N.Y., 1973), 484.

15. Mill, *On Liberty*, 485.

16. "Protokoll nr. 1 über die am 24. Juli 1848 von den gesammten Herrn Ständen des Landes ob der Ems mit Zuziehung aller Herren Mitglieder des provisorischen Landes Aussschusses zu Linz gepflogene Verhandlung," in *Oberösterreichische Landesarchiv, Flugschriftenversammlung* B, vol. 5; *Verhandlung des Landtages Steiermark* (16 June 1848), 28–30.

17. See Pieter M. Judson, "Deutschnationale Politik und Geschlecht in Österreich 1880–1900," in David F. Good, Margarethe Grandner, and Mary Jo Maynes, eds., *Frauen in Österreich* (Vienna, 1994).

18. Bourgeois memories of the 1848–49 revolutions colored liberal attitudes well into the 1860s. The liberals' references to that year praised their own orderly reform of the old regime while strongly criticizing the "visions that [working-class] malcontents and utopian dreamers sought to realize through political and social upheaval." Yet in fact it was that very social upheaval which had given the liberals their brief opportunity to reform society in 1848. Still, they were determined to prevent anyone else from using their revolutionary example to establish an alternate order to their own, and they were quick to characterize working-class tactics as selfish, irrational, and even primitive. See Ernst Schwarzer, *Geld und Gut in Neuösterreich* (Vienna, 1857), 6–8.

19. As liberal deputy and later leader Ernst von Plener declared in 1873, the vote was merely "a function which the state might give to those who offer a guarantee that they [would] exercise it properly," and "not a natural right" of human beings. See Wilhelm Wadl, *Liberalismus und soziale Frage in Österreich* (Vienna, 1987), 233; Karl Ucakar, "Demokratie und Wahlrecht in Österreich: Zur Entwicklung von politischer Partizipation und staatliche Legitimationspolitik" (Habilitationsschrift, University of Vienna, 1984), 245.

20. Johann N. Berger, "Die Pressefreiheit und das Pressegesetz" (Vienna, 1848), 1., in *Oberösterreichische Landesarchiv, Flugschriftenversammlung*, A, Vol. 24; B. Friedmann, *Die Wohnungsnot in Wien* (Vienna, 1857), 6.

21. Pieter M. Judson, "'Not Another Square Foot!': German Liberalism and the Rhetoric of National Ownership in 19th-Century Austria," *Austrian History Yearbook* 26 (1995).

22. See, for example, "Das Deutschtum in Krain: Ein Wort zur Aufklärung," Graz, 1862.

23. Ernst von Plener, *Erinnerungen* (Stuttgart/Leipzig, 1911–1921), 2: 233–234. This approving, if somewhat ambivalent, attitude toward Jews meant that like other party leaders, Plener responded to antisemitic politics in the 1880s and 1890s with great difficulty. While he sympathized with the sensibilities of the Jews under attack, he believed that their active defense against antisemitism would only make things worse.

24. Pieter M. Judson, "'Whether Race or Conviction Should Be the Standard': National Identity and Liberal Politics in Nineteenth-Century Austria," in *Austrian History Yearbook* 22, 1991.

25. Antisemites of course opposed the idea of an inclusive community, and fought its proponents. Yet in the long run they clearly benefited from their inclusion in larger German nationalist organizations which often treated them as one among many important directions in German public life.

26. Nationalist activism thus became a useful tool for extending the hegemony of the liberal classes, especially at the municipal level. See Pieter M. Judson, "Inventing Germans: Class, Nationality and Colonial Fantasy at the Margins of the Hapsburg Monarchy," in *Nations, Metropoles, Colonies*, ed. Daniel Segal and Richard Handler, *Social Analysis* 33 (1993).

27. Friedrich Pock, *Grenzwacht im Südosten, ein halbes Jahrhundert Südmark* (Graz, 1940), 21.

28. "Die zehn Gebote des deutschen Bauern," in *Deutscher Volkskalender für die Iglauer Sprachinsel* (Iglau, 1887), 156; "Die zehn Gebote des deutschen Volkes," in *Deutscher*

Volks-Kalender für Schlesien 1898, 115; "Die Aufgaben der nationalen Schutzvere-
inen," in *Deutsche Rundschau* 1 (1895), 5; *Deutscher Volks-Kalender für Schlesien
1898* (Troppau, 1898), 92–96; "Szenen aus der Tragödie Ferdinand Bernts '*Zwischen zwei Sprachen*," in *Deutsche Arbeit* 8 (1905), 505–514; "Von unseren Gegnern"
Deutsche Volkszeitung (Reichenberg) 4 October 1895. The latter article warned
against the dangers for German men of marrying Czech women.

29. This is one problem, for example, with John Boyer's observations about liberalism
in his important *Political Radicalism in Late Imperial Vienna* (Chicago, 1979).

30. Höbelt has suggested in particular some excellent ways of seeing the "rationality"
behind the practice of radical nationalist politics at the turn of the century. See
Lothar Höbelt, *Kornblume und Kaiseradler* (Vienna, 1993), 150–186.

31. Memories of the Badeni crisis ensured the liberal (Progressive) nationalists in parliament a voice larger than their twenty to forty deputies (out of 516) ought to have
given them. It was the progressives who led two important coalitions of German
Bürger parties on the left, the *deutsch nationaler Verband*, in 1907, and its successor,
the *Nationalverband der deutschfreiheitlichen Abgeordneten* in 1908. While the populists hoped to defuse nationalism by focusing on social and economic issues, the
liberal or progressive nationalists pinned their hopes for survival precisely on the
exploitation of nationalist fears.

Chapter 3

FIN DE SIÈCLE OR *JAHRHUNDERTWENDE*

The Question of an Austrian *Sonderweg*

James Shedel

Prominent in our current vision of Vienna 1900 is the image of the *Secessionsgebäude* and the famous inscription above its portal, "Der Zeit ihre Kunst, der Kunst ihre Freiheit" (To the time its art, to art its freedom). Less prominent, indeed almost vanished from our line of sight, however, is another coeval fixture of Vienna's landscape, the *Burgtor*. It too carries an inscription above its entrance, "Justitia Regnorum Fundamentum" (Justice is the foundation of kingdoms). Two more contrasting structures and sentiments are hard to imagine; one a pioneer of geometric art nouveau, the other a prudent example of neo-classicism; the former announcing a vernacular declaration for the era, the latter proclaiming a Latin verity for the ages. Of course, unlike the *Secessionsgebäude*, the *Burgtor* was not a product of the 1890s; completed in 1824, it appears distant in time and alien in its spirit to the phenomenon of Vienna 1900. Therefore, it seems only natural that we should focus on what members and friends of the Secession, such as Gustav Klimt or Hermann Bahr, were thinking rather than be concerned with the words Kaiser Franz I chose to signify his philosophy of government.

Yet, was the symbolism of the *Burgtor* and its inscription really so out of step with an Austria on the threshold of the twentieth century? After

FIGURE 1 *The Burgtor at Night,* c. 1930. Courtesy of Bildarchiv der Österreichischen Nationalbibliothek.

all, in 1900 the state and dynasty that built this ceremonial gate were still very much in evidence, so much so that the Secession actively courted their patronage and even Bahr, the titular head of the literary Jung Wien movement, proclaimed his "schwarz-gelb" patriotism.[1] The answer to this question depends very much on whether we interpret that moment in time as a *fin de siècle* or a *Jahrhundertwende*; that is to say, as a caesura that underlines the historical abnormality of a *Sonderweg*, or as a transitional moment that points to a unique but hardly deviant continuity of historical development. In the historiography of nineteenth and early twentieth century Austria, the former interpretation with its connotation of modernity gone awry has tended to dominate, but it is the intention here to suggest a revision of that view by arguing for an Austrian version of modernization that can be seen as a separate and valid model of this historical process.

At the center of this alternative version is the Austrian manifestation of the *Rechtsstaat*. Like the *Burgtor* which linked the urban modernity of the Ringstraße with the city's old imperial core, the *Rechtsstaat* served as a bridge between change and continuity, the modern and the traditional in Austrian state and society, while at the same time firmly linking these factors to the Habsburg dynasty. "Justitia Regnorum Fundamentum" expressed both the Enlightenment idea of the rule of law and the European reality of its monarchic foundation. That even an emperor as conservative as Franz I saw no contradiction between his traditional authority and the limits to it implied by his motto indicates the unique flexibility represented by this Austrian version of the *Rechtsstaat*. Thus, in the Vienna of 1900 movements like the Secession and Jung Wien could proclaim sentiments that suggested a critical break with the dominant culture while at the same time function firmly within the established order precisely because that order was stable yet dynamic enough to accommodate them.

This proposition, as much as it distances itself from the interpretation it seeks to challenge, has in common with that interpretation a fundamental recognition of an Austrian exceptionalism. What separates the rhetorical characterizations of Vienna 1900 as either a *fin de siècle* or a *Jahrhundertwende* is the type of exceptionalism each connotes. It has already been stated that the term *fin de siècle* rests on a basically negative view of this exceptionalism, a historical *Sonderweg*, while the alternative offers a more positive and less prescriptive approach in its expectations of what constitutes a viable form of historical development. Both positions, however, play off of the same definition of what constitutes the normative development of modern states and societies, the difference between them in this regard being that the interpretation based upon the phenomenon of the *Rechtsstaat* modifies this definition in significant ways. Before the "*Rechtsstaat* interpretation" outlined above can be elaborated upon, however, the normative definition and its characteristics need to be identified and their connection to the notion of an Austrian exceptionalism made specific. Accordingly, that process has to begin with an examination of the normative implications of the *fin-de-siècle* concept and the "*Sonderweg* interpretation" it stands for.

The origin of "*fin-de-siècle* Vienna" as a historical phenomenon in Austrian studies dates back to 1961 and the appearance of Carl Schorske's article on "Politics and Psyche in *fin-de-siècle* Vienna: Schnitzler and Hofmannsthal."[2] Against the backdrop of a skillfully rendered prose description of the frenetically decaying melody in Ravel's "La Valse," Schorske depicted late nineteenth century Austria as a society in crisis due to the decline of liberalism and the ascent of its Christian Socialist, antisemitic, social democratic, and nationalist enemies who were making it impossible for the rational culture of law favored by the upper bourgeoisie to flourish. In this atmosphere, he argued, the crisis of liberal culture forced the children of liberal fathers into the cultural escapism offered by the traditional sensual, Catholic culture of the aristocracy thereby giving up the productive political pursuits innate to liberalism. This led, however, from political frustration directly to intellectual inspiration, the discovery of "psychological man" and the construction of modern culture around him and his needs. With turn-of-the-century Vienna as the location of this entire process, Schorske focused on two prominent scions of the declining liberal bourgeoisie, Arthur Schnitzler and Hugo von Hofmannsthal, each of whom in his own way mirrored the crisis of Austrian liberalism and the search for a way out of a disintegrating society through aesthetics. Yet there was a crucial difference between the two. Schnitzler became a critical observer of the breakup of liberalism's "moral and scientific" heritage, evincing a lingering, if pessimistic, attachment to it, while Hofmannsthal, as an admirer of "Habsburg traditionalism," embraced an irrationalist conception that fused art and politics in an unrealistic unity. Schorske concludes with Hofmannsthal, and in so doing underscores not only the hopelessness of the poet's politics of the aesthetic, but also the doomed nature of his faith in Habsburg tradition as a source of anything constructively positive.[3] The article left little room for doubt that substituting an aristocratically based *Gefühlskultur* for the liberal culture of reason and law was a decisive symptom of Austrian society's sickness unto death. Thus was born the persona of Vienna's *fin de siècle*.

Although in subsequent essays Schorske elaborated on the various aspects and figures of Viennese culture in the *fin de siècle*, when these essays were brought together in a single volume in 1980 it was clear that they were essentially only more detailed variations on the original theme. Still, taken together, these well written and original analyses of Viennese art, architecture, literature, and music have been immensely influential, such that no one has had a greater impact on how we have looked at late nineteenth and early twentieth century Austria than Carl Schorske. His interpretations and the work inspired by them, have helped not only to associate a movement like the Secession with our vision of Vienna 1900, but also to place it in a nexus of other creative developments that symbolize the ironic birth of cultural modernism in conditions dominated by the social and political anachronisms of a dying state. Its irony not withstanding, this image of efflorescent creativity has served to add an element of elegant justification to the hard-edged earlier interpretations of such historians as Oscar Jaszi, A. J. P. Taylor, and Robert Kann, for whom the entire edifice of Habsburg Austria was either doomed or seriously crippled long before 1900.

Schorske's interpretation internationalized this decadent vision of Austrian history by wedding Habsburg decay to a European-wide phenomenon of late nineteenth century world-weariness. The feeling that the end of the nineteenth century somehow presaged an unhappy conclusion to man and his aspirations was, of course, present in the musings and forebodings of many of Europe's intellectuals at the time and has been a favorite topic of many historians besides Schorske.[4] What he accomplished, however, was to describe the Austrian version as more creative, more filled with the spiritual uncertainties of modern life because it was born of circumstances more the result of historical development gone wrong than could be found in most countries at the time. As Steven Beller has put it, Schorske sees "modern culture" as hinging "on the idea that Vienna was the first place in Europe where bourgeois rationalism met its demise, and that therefore the figures of that culture were in a better position to express the problems of the forthcoming age."[5] Along with that failure of bourgeois rationalism, however, went the failure of bourgeois political and social values. This is the *fin de siècle* as the *fin d'un monde* for the Austrian bourgeoisie and it is at this level that Schorske connects with his predecessors in the historiography to form a powerful *Sonderweg* interpretation of Austrian history. To understand the significance of such an interpretation we need to look at the context in which this term has taken on interpretive meaning.

In Central European history the term *Sonderweg* is normally used in connection with German, not Austrian, history, and it represents an interpretive school that seeks to explain German responsibility for two world wars, the rise of Hitler, and the Holocaust as the result of a fundamental deviation from the norms of historical development that have characterized modern European history since the French Revolution.[6] At the core of this explanation is the belief that the histories of France, Britain, and the United States represent normative models of development, and the degree to which the histories of other countries have managed to duplicate the essential features of these models, preferably as nation-states, indicates how successful they are as modern societies. Within this pattern of normative development, participation in the Industrial Revolution or its successor forms of technological change is a necessary but not sufficient condition of being modern. Far more important in this model of historical development is that positive political, social, and technological change must be carried forward by the bourgeoisie who are historical agents of progress. In the Marxist view, they are the historical instrument necessary to create conditions for the ultimate class revolution that will lead to the establishment of an earthly utopia, while in the non-Marxist argument they are the permanent carriers of human progress and liberty as defined in the world view of the Enlightenment. Without the triumph of this class, usually through an armed revolution that displaces the old agrarian-based feudal elites, there is no real modernity and, therefore, no normal historical development. Such a deviant scenario must sooner or later result in a social and/or political disaster of some kind that clears the way for normative development. In Germany's case that disaster became the crisis of the century. With no revolution in 1789 that paralleled the French or even the American Revolution, not to mention no history in the early modern period of a gradual shift in power as in the British model, on top of which 1848 appeared to be a disappointing failure, Germany was doomed to pursue an aberrant form of development, a *Sonderweg*, made fatefully dangerous by German power. Only with its total defeat in 1945 and subsequent reconstruction under the guidance of the West's normative states did Germany's *Sonderweg* come to an end. This is, of course, a very simplified account of the *Sonderweg* interpretation and its major application, but it has the virtue of highlighting its uncompromisingly normative stance when it comes to how we define what is modern and therefore positive in historical development, and the penalties every society must suffer for significant deviation from this model.

Happily for Austria, no one has sought to rank it with Germany in the rogues' gallery of history's deviants, but a deviant it is nonetheless, for it has failed in key ways to follow the course of normative development along the road to modernity. As with Germany, its penalty was the destruction of the Empire, a sojourn in the wilderness of interwar Europe, and a time in purgatory with the Third Reich, all of which was ultimately followed by normative reconstruction under its "liberators." But unlike Germany, no stigma as the enemy of humanity has been attached to Austria for its historical failures, even if those failures may have meant it was the real cause of World War I. Officially classed by the Allies as the first victim of fascism in World War II, the period of Austria's *Sonderweg* has been limited to its pre-1918 incarnation as the Habsburg Monarchy. Its historical sins did not extend beyond the Monarchy's collapse, which was itself the punishment and one that has since come to serve as a kind of historical object lesson for revolutionary failure, an unsuccessful bourgeoisie, multinationalism, and a dynastic/aristocratic order that outlived its usefulness.

The elements of this Austrian *Sonderweg* can be seen in most of the major general treatments of the Monarchy written since World War I. Prior to the war, views of the Monarchy, like that written by Henry Wickham Steed in 1913, had often been critical, but conceded the presence of strengths and the probability of its survival.[7] In the wake of World War I, Austria-Hungary's demise appeared to be proof of its unsuitability to exist; and voices from historians on the Allied side, some of whom like R. W. Seton-Watson had championed the cause of the

Monarchy's so-called "subject peoples" even before the war,[8] pointed to the supposed triumph of the principles of nationality and Western democracy or parliamentarism in the successor states as a sign that normal development had finally come to this part of Europe. Even truncated Austria itself became a republic. This transformation also represented the triumph of America's Wilsonian values and, by extension, those of its compatible allies, Britain and France. Victory carried with it Clio's seal of approval and the elevation of the histories of "the big three" to normative status. Like that of Germany, the history of Austria was now to be placed *de facto* into the category of a *Sonderweg*.

Interestingly, in the effort to delineate the traits that made the Monarchy's demise inevitable, the focus was largely on the Austrian half of the Monarchy, the common institutions between Austria and Hungary created by the *Ausgleich*, and the policies and personalities of the Habsburg dynasty. Until recently, Hungary occupied a subordinate position in the historiography, being cast in the role of a chauvinistic villain whose overweening nationalism oppressed the non-Magyar majority within its borders and made the *Ausgleich* system highly problematic as the basis for a workable state. In the interwar years, treatments of Hungary in histories of the Monarchy were within the context of the nationality problem, which became the major explanatory factor for the Monarchy's collapse. From multinationalism in an age of nation-states, combined with Austria's other historical transgressions, flowed a pattern of interpretation that would change very little until the 1980s.

Two principal historians who helped lay the foundation for this pattern between the wars were themselves products of the Monarchy. One was the Austrian jurist and sometime politician, Josef Redlich. In 1926 Redlich published the second and last volume of his massive narrative-based analysis of nineteenth century Austria,[9] and in 1928 his highly perceptive biography of Franz Joseph appeared.[10] Both books emphasized the centrality of the nationality problem and the lost opportunity to solve it by instituting the federalist and liberal Kremsier constitution, following the failure of the revolution in 1848. Hungary's dark role in the nationality difficulties and the creation of the problematic character of the *Ausgleich*, as well as the inherent weaknesses of the dynastic state, were also cited as obstacles to the Monarchy's viability. Echoing this list of problems in his 1929 book on the collapse of the Monarchy, the émigré Hungarian politician-turned-historian Oscar Jászi added the political incapacity of the Monarchy's bourgeoisie and the connected weakness of their liberal ideology as reasons why this class was never "capable as in the great Western states of directing the evolution of the state."[11] Out of Jászi's analysis emerges the classic *Sonderweg* factor of a missing bourgeoisie. When this is added to the opinion held by both him and Redlich, that 1848 was a lost opportunity to create a healthy federal state based on liberal principles of government, the essential ingredients of 1848 as a turning point that failed to turn, thereby preventing a Western style development for the Monarchy, factors that had supposedly been so telling in creating Germany's *Sonderweg*, were all in place for an Austrian version.

The emphasis placed on the nationality problem as the central cause of the Monarchy's demise remained a constant in the subsequent histories, but with the difference that the experience of World War II resulted—with one notable exception—in a more favorable view of the Monarchy as a multinational great power that, had it survived, might have prevented the rise of the Third Reich and the war itself. Especially in light of the Cold War fate of its successor states, Habsburg hegemony appeared infinitely more benign than that of Soviet Russia. Of course, this nostalgia for the positive traits of the Monarchy's multinational structure had been voiced even between the wars, but the post-1945 variety was less wistful and more careful to point out why only the supranational *ideal* was attractive as opposed to the reality of its flawed application.

The notable exception to this tendency was expressed by A. J. P. Taylor in his influential history of the nineteenth century Monarchy. He was convinced that the post-Napoleonic Empire never had a chance of surviving and that "The national principle, once launched, had to work itself out to its conclusion."[12] Taylor's history paints an almost unrelieved picture of *ancien régime* anachronism, failed bourgeois liberalism, and an inevitably triumphant nationalism. Only his more detailed treatment of Austrian foreign policy as a factor in her fall added something new to the list of negatives that had doomed the Monarchy. In its uncompromisingly negative evaluation of the Monarchy it is one of the strongest supports of an Austrian *Sonderweg*.

* * * *

More typical of the general post-war historiography and its less strident *Sonderweg* tendency is the equally influential, but more scholarly work of Robert A. Kann. Especially in his two-volume work on the nationalities of the Empire,[13] Kann made what is probably the most persuasive case for seeing 1848 and the rejection of the Kremsier constitution as the decisive lost opportunity for saving the Monarchy. Published in four editions between 1950 and 1977, it became the standard work in English on the nationality problem and its potential solutions, but in its lack of analysis concerning social forces it cannot be claimed as a full-fledged advocate of the *Sonderweg* interpretation. Indeed, even in Kann's 1974 general history of the Empire, while he ascribes the collapse of the Monarchy primarily to internal causes, he made no unequivocal judgements about the role of the bourgeoisie and liberalism. Rather, it is nationalism that remains his consistent leitmotif for the modern period and he even denies that the collapse of the Monarchy was inevitable.[14] Still, the effect of Kann's work with its emphasis on the unrealized Kremsier constitution makes the Revolution of 1848 and its bourgeois liberal aspirations toward an imperial federalism the unexperienced turning point necessary to the *Sonderweg* argument.

The *Sonderweg* tendency is also discernible in the two main German language histories of Austria. The conservative historian Hugo Hantsch in the 1968 fourth edition of his general history laments the unrealized constitutional solution of 1848–49 and the unsuitability of the Hungarian dominated *Ausgleich*, while the more liberal Erich Zöllner in the 1979 edition of his survey considers the federal constitutionalism of Kremsier a victim of autocracy and he sees the *Ausgleich* as raising questions about the unity of the state, the well-being of Hungary's non-Magyar peoples, and also as subjecting the Monarchy to periodic crises.[15] Additionally, Hantsch in discussing the situation at the time when the introduction of universal manhood suffrage was being debated makes a judgement about the demise of bourgeois liberalism in which he says, "Der bürgerliche Liberalismus war keine entwicklungsfähige Substanz mehr."[16] Although the period 1905–07 is rather late for bourgeois liberalism to go missing, it still points to the less than dominant role played by this modernizing force in the Monarchy. While neither of these historians consciously sought to argue a *Sonderweg* position, key parts of their explanations for why the Monarchy was beset with problems involves failure of popularly based constitutionalism in the fateful year of 1848, an ultimate inability to adequately address the force of nationalism, and, in one case, the weakness of bourgeois liberalism, all of which are factors outside the mainstream of "normative" development.

The impact of these points in the literature is cumulative and suggestive. Even as judicious and thorough a historian as C. A. Macartney writing in 1969 implied in his massive work on the Habsburg Empire that the start of its problems began when Joseph II retracted his centralizing reforms for Hungary in 1790 signaling a long retreat before "the new forces of nationalism and democracy, until at last the peoples of the Monarchy, allied with its foreign enemies, repudiate not only the character of the Monarch's rule, but the rule itself."[17] Of course, in the more than 800 pages that comprise the narrative Macartney presents the pros and cons of the Empire in great detail and even debunks the significance placed on 1848 and Kremsier, while at the same time finding positive things to say about the *Ausgleich*, yet as the quote above indicates, there is a strong suggestion that the Monarchy succumbed ultimately because it was out of step with key elements of modern history. If such an impression can come from a work as generally favorable to the Monarchy as Macartney's we need only to set it along side that conveyed by the interpretations already discussed to see how the idea of an Austrian *Sonderweg* can find resonance within the historiography. It is not surprising then that by 1980 Carl Schorske's interpretation should find an audience already prepared to receive it.

The Schorskean concept of an Austrian *fin de siècle* represents the capstone of an Austrian *Sonderweg* interpretation. With 1848, Kremsier, the *Ausgleich*, an anachronistic supranational dynastic state, and proto-*Sonderweg* arguments like that of Oscar Jászi standing behind it, Schorske's depiction of the final act of the Monarchy's history in terms of the failure of the bourgeoisie and liberalism makes the *Sonderweg* complete. But unlike its German counterpart, Schorske is able to add a positive coda to Austria's *Sonderweg*. In his interpretation failure to be socially and politically normative resulted in Austria's ironic success as the normative source of modern culture. Thus Schorske unites historical irony to the attractive simplicity of the *Sonderweg*, but is this an enduring union? Most of the recent historiography suggests it is not.

Since the early 1980s a substantive revision has been underway in our understanding of the Habsburg Monarchy. In English some of the more notable contributions have been by John Boyer, David Good, and Steven Beller, while in German the *Habsburgermonarchie Bürgertum* project with contributions by, among others, Peter Urbanitsch, Hannes Stekel, and Ernst Bruckmüller are all providing a much more variegated and nuanced picture than was previously available.[18] With respect to the specific issue of an Austrian *Sonderweg*, this work has raised points that bring it into question. In Boyer's examination of the origins of Christian Socialism the Viennese bourgeois liberals emerge as a far more complicated group than conceived of by Schorske and their support for Lueger's party raises fundamental questions about the nature of Austrian liberalism in the first place. The analysis of the Monarchy's economic development by Good suggests that it was more economically normative than previously thought. Beller's work on Vienna's Jews in the nineteenth and early twentieth centuries demonstrates their role as the core of the city's liberal bourgeoisie and the main force behind Austria's version of modernity. This argument when combined with his view that Vienna must share the origins of modern culture with such normative centers as London, Paris, and New York forms a persuasive corrective to Schorske's thesis. Finally, the *Bürgertum* project, though lacking any overall conclusions is also showing an image of the Monarchy's bourgeoisie that is too complex to be contained any longer within the assumptions of a *de facto Sonderweg*.

Although these works represent only the tip of the iceberg in current Habsburg studies, they demonstrate that the central issues concerning the roles of the bourgeoisie and liberalism in Austrian society are in considerable flux. Especially now that recent scholarship has demonstrated a more or less "normal" course of economic development in the Monarchy replete with *Bürger* involvement, it suggests that a more fundamental form of bourgeois success occurred than Schorske's model can account for. Evidently, all sons of the bourgeoisie did not become aesthetes. What all this revisionism points to is the need for a new interpretive framework that drops the biased idea of a *fin de siècle* and its *Sonderweg* baggage. This brings us back to the concept proposed earlier, of Vienna 1900 more appropriately being considered a *Jahrhundertwende* and as the product of a developmental continuity defined by the concept of the *Rechtsstaat*.

It needs to be reemphasized that what is being argued here is an interpretive model that retains the concept of an Austrian exceptionalism. It is, however, Austrian only in recognition of the Habsburg Monarchy's "Cisleithanian" roots and represents an exceptionalism only in so far as the Monarchy's historical development is no more abnormal, but also no less different, one from the other, than that of any European or Western country. Rather, that it is simply a variant of a general process that in the case of the Habsburg Monarchy allowed it to acquire the necessary elements of a modern state and society within an institutional structure that in a normative theory of development is considered after 1789 to be pre-modern and anachronistic. While the impact of the French Revolution certainly brought changes to the then Austrian Empire, these changes were imbedded in a continuity based on the rule of law as understood in both rational and traditional terms such that up to 1914 a basic positive stability was maintained that allowed for the accommodation of change. Thus, the phenomenon known as Vienna 1900 cannot be viewed as a caesura that must be explained as the culmination of a long process of historical failures, but as a transitional event that does not negatively prejudice our understanding either of what went before or came after. It is to be understood simply as a turn of the century, a *Jahrhundertwende*, and on its own terms within this overall continuity.[19]

Therefore, our discussion will begin at the point chronologically opposite to it when the Austrian *Rechtsstaat* took on its basic form.

While the idea of the *Rechtsstaat* did not originate in Austria, in the late eighteenth century the rule of law came to occupy pride of place in the dynastic state as its *raison d'être* and chief means of achieving, accommodating, and influencing change and modernization. As Mark Raeff has pointed out, by 1700 the German states, including Habsburg Austria, had become the focal points of instituting positive change from above through the law. By means of ordinances and regulations it was thought that the commonweal, "der gemeine Beste," could be served and the ruler carry out his or her duty toward guarding the well-being of the subject. Of course, this process was also aimed at increasing the power of the state through the control of its subjects and regulation of the country's economic resources. The result was the *Polizeistaat*, that is, the well-policed (i.e., well-regulated) state. With the spread of the Enlightenment, this concept of rational utilitarian administration was transformed into an ideology of human improvement through rational progress which in Central Europe took on the form of so-called Enlightened Despotism.[20] Beginning with Maria Theresa's reluctant rationalization of the state into a more centralized monarchy, and reaching fruition in the self-conscious policy of officially sponsored Enlightenment for the benefit of mankind and the state under Joseph II, the Habsburg Monarchy became one of the leading examples of state-led modernization.

This process was profoundly secular and could be used, as it was under Joseph, to bring even the Catholic Church and the practice of religion under state control. Joseph's 6,000 decrees on everything from religious toleration to the size of coffins constructed an edifice of law to support a machine for progress and state power. As is well known, however, Joseph went too far and by 1790 much of his work was undone, but the basic legacy of Josephism, including the Habsburg dynastic state as a *Rechtsstaat*, remained. In the dynasty itself the role of the monarch was consciously reconstructed after the Frederickian model as "first servant of the state" who, as the executor of a social contract without the escape clause of revolution, was bound to be both creator and guarantor of the law as the subject's basic source of security. This rational image of the ruler as both above and under the law was part of the internalized self-image of all Habsburgs through Franz Joseph.[21] As Waltraud Heindl has demonstrated, the Josephist spirit of the *Rechtsstaat* and the state as responsible for a progressively regulated social order was reified in the bureaucracy from Joseph onwards[22] so that both the master and servants of the dynastic state were bound by law. Finally, a dynasty that so closely identified itself with the rational and legalistic spirit of the Enlightenment could also acquire a new source of legitimation to augment that bestowed by God and traditional right. Indeed, this combination of modern and traditional sources of legitimation became the nexus that defined the Austrian *Rechtsstaat*.

Even Joseph II never disavowed the Catholic and Christian character of the dynasty that was so much a part of the post-Reformation Monarchy. The heritage of "Pietas Austriaca" that claimed a special divine sanction for Habsburg imperium was tacitly recognized by Joseph in his preservation of the official Corpus Christi procession despite his abolition of so many other similar religious events. The Eucharist as the symbol of his family's fortunate connection to God could not be dispensed with.[23] Similarly, Joseph appreciated the utility of religion as a form of social control to maintain order through a divinely ordained morality. In his world rationalism did not equal atheism. As far as the authority of the emperor and the dynasty were concerned, Joseph's policies had the effect of maintaining side by side both the old and the new sources of legitimacy. Divine selection and earthly reason served to keep the dynasty with a foot in both the new and the old worlds, with the intention of benefiting from both. In terms of the *Rechtsstaat*, this meant that the dynastic state became an expression of both divine and earthly law through the agency of government. The emperor followed divine law by acting as a traditional Christian shepherd to his worldly flock, protecting their souls by upholding the church and controlling their sinful bodies by the power of the secular sword. By the same token, when the emperor acted through the persona of reason as law, he could claim to exercise power for the common good, whether to control the actions of his subjects or to encourage their participation in some enlightened scheme for their benefit. This combination of the new and the old under the aegis of the *Rechtsstaat* would prove a powerful asset to the Monarchy, for it could now simultaneously maintain its ties to its traditional allies in the church and aristocracy, while finding new ones in the people and assure its authority by acting as the balancing point between them.

Through Josephism, the Monarchy claimed the high ground in the process of change. By connecting change from above with improvement, the dynastic state identified itself with the cause of the Enlightenment and, therefore, with modernization. From 1780 to 1914 it provided either the direct or indirect incentives for economic development, the growth of the bourgeoisie, virtually all major cultural changes, and, ironically, even the early growth of national consciousness. Additionally, by setting the example of the rule of law as a source for and a structure within which positive social development could occur it arguably provided the intellectual basis for Austrian liberalism, just as the Josephian bureaucracy provided most of that movement's initial followers. In essentials, the developmental process in the Habsburg Monarchy followed a scenario that, except for the more prominent role played by the dynastic state and the special difficulties of multinationalism, resulted in outcomes that were not significantly different from those of the so-called normative countries of Europe.

In its economic policy the Monarchy went from mercantilist to physiocratic/cameralist, and ultimately to the classical economics of laissez-faire; that is to say, from interventionist to non-interventionist policies culminating in a legal framework that guaranteed the rights of private entrepreneurial activity for the benefit of the individual and society alike. The Monarchy chose a well trodden European path of economic development that even during the conservative period of 1815–1848 laid the groundwork for industrial development in the Austrian and Bohemian crown lands.[24] After 1848 and the end of manorialism, as Good has demonstrated, the Monarchy followed a reasonably successful course of economic development, the extent of which was geographically based on the varying levels of regional receptivity. In this regard, except for a somewhat slower pace in its traditionally more agrarian areas, by 1914 Austria-Hungary had a modern mix of industrial and non-industrial economic activity. With this modern economy a modern bourgeoisie was not lacking.

In the *Sonderweg* interpretation a successful bourgeoisie is indispensable. Certainly even Schorske acknowledged that the Habsburg Monarchy possessed a bourgeoisie, but the problem, of course, was whether it was the right kind of bourgeoisie with the right kind of influence in the society. Schorske answered this in the negative, as did others. But was this the right answer? Like its German counterpart, the Austrian bourgeoisie evolved out of the early-modern *Mittelstand* of artisans, merchants, professionals, and functionaries with the addition, in the eighteenth and early nineteenth centuries, of the newly created bureaucrats. Indeed, it can be argued that this is the same, with variations, everywhere in Europe. Moreover, except primarily in France and England, this social grouping related to the state as either the protective shell in which it existed or as the source of its livelihood through service to it. Grievances and projects for reform were habitually directed to it following the pattern established under Josephist and traditional paternalistic models of government. Discontent became insurrectionary or revolutionary only when the state's response was perceived as inadequate or out of keeping with its established role of positive leadership. In its broadest terms, a surfeit of negative action and a consequent lack of Josephinian initiative on the part of the Habsburg Monarchy is what made the Revolution of 1848 possible. But if inaction by the state caused the Revolution, the state's actions created the class from which the revolutionaries came and its subsequent response to the Revolution would ultimately bring them back into the state's orbit.

Nowhere in 1848 did the revolt happen because of a conscious bourgeois liberal plan of action and nowhere was this more true than in Austria. To be sure, once under way the bourgeoisie and their liberal ideology became active in promoting modified French and English models of constitutional monarchy such as that represented in the Kremsier and Stadion constitutions of 1849, but, aside from their federalist provisions, these were basically constitutional *Rechtsstaat* models for enhanced bourgeois participation. After 1850 and the institution of neo-absolutism that participation in the state remained the goal of this group, and they showed themselves willing to realize it within the structure of a *Rechtsstaat* that was heavily defined by its monarchic base. As for the dynastic state, it was willing to reform that *Rechtsstaat* to accommodate and coopt the participation of its bourgeois subjects.

What caused the state to lose control in the Monarchy in the period leading to 1848 can be seen as an imbalance in the relationship between the rational and traditional aspects of the Austrian *Rechtsstaat* as expressed by government policy. The existence of a traditional divinely sanctioned concept of the just ruler as part of the Habsburg embodiment of the *Rechtsstaat* reflects the underlying dynastic character of the state and its power. It was willing to be progressive, but not at the cost of its existence. Even Joseph accepted this premise, and therefore, when forced to it, he retreated from his reform posture after 1788. He had allowed the rational, enlightened, modernizing side of the *Rechtsstaat* to become excessive. Joseph's retreat, however, was tactical and pragmatic, as were the measures taken by his brother Leopold. When reason proved excessive, tradition was called in to strike a balance and reestablish order, but key elements of the rationally based reforms remained, including the legal base of the *Rechtsstaat* itself.[25] Under Franz fear of revolutionary change led to stasis and only sporadic intervention by the state in either a rational or traditional mode. Franz's motto, however, emphasized that the *Rechtsstaat* was still at the heart of the Monarchy, but no longer as a transforming agent.[26] Under the less-than-capable rule of Ferdinand, it continued to slumber with the state, only occasionally either encouraging positive change in an area such as industry or using its traditional persona in a defensive manner, as in the raising of the Ruthenian peasantry against their revolutionary Polish overlords. These, however, were more like the inept stumblings of a sleepwalker than the actions of government as the embodiment of divine and rational justice. With 1848 as an object lesson, the state returned in neo-absolutism to a more Josephist stance that coopted liberals, such as Alexander Bach, into the government, and consciously sought to put the state once again at the forefront of progressive, modernizing change from above, whether in the economy or in education. Additionally, this kind of aggressive enlightened policy could appeal to the progressivist sympathies of the liberal bourgeoisie.[27] This was clearly the modernizing, interventionist *Rechtsstaat* in action supported by both rational and traditional justifications of state power. Why did it not work?

The answer to that question is the combination of financial weakness and a failure to recognize initially the need for more active cooperation from the liberal bourgeoisie. On top of these factors, military defeat in 1859 and 1866 damaged both the credit and prestige of the state to the point where it was forced to make concessions to the constitutional variant of the *Rechtsstaat*. While Franz Joseph would clearly have preferred the continuation of the neo-absolutist version, he accepted the final constitutional reform of 1867 as an act of pragmatism not unlike those carried out by his great uncle and grandfather.[28] The document that embodied the new liberal parliamentary system with its guarantee of individual rights also made it clear that the source of all sovereign authority came from a "sanctified" emperor, not from the people, and that he retained direct control over the bureaucracy, selection of the government, foreign affairs, the military, and the powers of war and peace. Moreover, no law could be enacted without his signature. The December Constitution was therefore a document well within the parameters of the *Rechtsstaat* that originated with Joseph II, since it combined the rational modern side of progress with the divine, traditional side of the dynasty's authority. From 1867 until the end of his life Franz Joseph punctiliously observed his constitutional status as the monarch of what was now generally described as a *Rechtsstaat*.[29] While the establishment of this updated version of the *Rechtsstaat* was far from perfect and would not banish all further problems for the Monarchy, it did succeed in remaining in place until 1918.[30]

Of course, 1867 was also one year after the other great change in the Monarchy, the *Ausgleich* with Hungary. It too became a kind of adjunct to the *Rechtsstaat* since it provided an update to the rational authority of the state by creating the quasi-federal structure of dualism while preserving the traditional power of the dynasty. Accompanying it was a constitutional *Rechtsstaat* for Hungary. The *Ausgleich*, however, pointed to the nagging problem of nationalism that, with the defeat of imperial centralism after 1866, now became manifest in the popular political life of the state. Still, it was a problem that was innate to the dynastic supranational character of the Monarchy and one the state had nurtured early on by encouraging nationalism's cultural variety as a substitute for political activity. True to the liberal conception of rights, the new constitution in Article 19 even specifically recognized the rights of all nationalities in the Cisleithanian half of the Monarchy including that of equal treatment for their languages in public and private life. Under these circumstances the constitution and the parliament itself would become important legal forums for dealing with the gradual exacerbation of national animosities, especially those between Czechs and Germans. Indeed, until the Badeni crisis, the liberals, now influenced by theories of a very statist-oriented liberalism developed in the 1860s,[31] could be used, along with the constitutional order they had called into being, as allies in the state's struggle to maintain the equilibrium of the *Rechtsstaat*. From 1867 on, nothing was so central to the continuing existence of the Monarchy from the Cisleithanian side as the reality of the *Rechtsstaat*, in both its constitutional and Josephist forms. It acted as a kind of legal containment field for a struggle that would otherwise have become endemically violent rather than only sporadically.

Because of these nationality problems, Austrian political life in the constitutional era saw the *Rechtsstaat* under its greatest threat, but in its response at its most resilient. While the bourgeois, liberal elements of all national groups could be said to have benefited from both the pre- and post-1867 *Rechtsstaat*, it had been the Germans among them who, because of their more advanced position as the erstwhile *Herrenvolk* of the Monarchy, had formed the main stream of the bourgeoisie and liberals. With the advent of parliamentary politics and the spread of economic development, their dominance was gradually threatened by their nationalist counterparts among the non-German, mostly Slavic, peoples of the Monarchy's Austrian half. This threat played itself out in the central parliament and the legislatures of the crown lands. The political decline of this group was recognized by the state as early as 1879, when the emperor chose to form a more conservative government, not with the German liberals, but with their conservative and Slav opponents instead. The creation of Minister-President Taaffe's "iron ring" of political support, that lasted until 1893, was the first of many occasions when the rational, constitutional side of the *Rechtsstaat* would be subject to its traditional side, to maintain what were perceived as the state's vital interests.

With the onset of obstructionism from both the German liberals and their Czech counterparts after 1897, the *Rechtsstaat* was maintained not only by forming shifting alliances among parties for the sake of viable ministries, but also by the use of the infamous Article 14 that gave the government (i.e., the emperor, his ministers, and bureaucracy) the right to rule while parliament was not functioning. Its frequent invocation and the willingness of the parties to allow its use rather than act to resolve their differences showed that they recognized the traditional aspect of the *Rechtsstaat* as a valid, useful, and still powerful force even in the constitutional era.[32] Moreover, parliament's consistent acceptance of all measures taken during its use demonstrated the degree to which imperial power, as such, was seen as legitimate.[33] It is not surprising, then, that the rational, constitutional side of the *Rechtsstaat* was being supported in this period by its traditional alter ego precisely because of the latter's ability to invoke a legitimacy that transcended purely rational authority. Thus, in an effort to bolster the parliamentary system, it was the emperor who insisted on introducing universal manhood suffrage in 1907 and it was his agents who facilitated and approved the regional compromises between national groups in Moravia in 1905–06, the Bukovina in 1909–10, and Galicia in 1913–14. It was also with imperial assistance that the efforts to bring the Czechs and Germans together over the issue of Bohemia were tried before 1914. Indeed, the rule of law had become such an indispensable tool to the dynasty in regulating the affairs of the Monarchy that the aversion felt by Franz Joseph toward his heir, Franz Ferdinand, could be interpreted, in part, as stemming from the latter's willingness to solve the Monarchy's problems through extra-legal means that would nullify the *Rechtsstaat*. But perhaps an even more telling fact regarding the centrality of the *Rechtsstaat* in maintaining the continuity of peaceful change is that all the main schemes advanced for resolving Austria's nationality problem were couched entirely as a matter for constitutional adjustment.[34]

Clearly, by 1914 the Habsburg Monarchy and its *Rechtsstaat* were confronting significant problems, but being a modern state is no guarantee against even the life-threatening variety. As serious as its nationality problems were, before World War I there was no sign of the state's imminent collapse and nothing suggesting a revolutionary situation. Even the ostensibly revolutionary social democrats were among the constitutional monarchy's strongest supporters.[35] All this suggests that the Austrian *Rechtsstaat* not only served to facilitate the Monarchy's transition to the basic forms of modern economic, social, cultural, and political life, but that it also provided an element of stabilizing continuity for the change this process involved. If this is the dominant context within which developments in nineteenth century Austria are to be viewed then we must place the phenomenon of Vienna 1900 in that context as well.

In the Schorskean model, the cultures of law and grace are opposites. The supposed triumph of the latter over the former is part of a major crisis in which the liberal German bourgeoisie, as Austria's principal bearers of modern, rational, Weberian social and political values have been rendered tragically ineffective by the rise of mass socialist and conservative parties, not to mention by the nationality conflicts. Their sons then created modern culture in reaction to, and as an escape from, a situation that prevents them from engaging in the constructive political and, presumably, commercial pursuits of their liberal fathers. If we look at this scenario in light of the *Rechtsstaat* interpretation it becomes far less dramatic and critical.

It is true that the German bourgeois liberals were in political decline and being replaced in the public sphere by the forces Schorske identifies, but it was a decline that had begun in 1879. Where they lost power in the public sphere they were arguably gaining it in the less public administrative one, not to mention exercising influence as the leaders of industry and finance.[36] They still retained a considerable and vital role within the society. But the point also has to be made that the bourgeoisie, both German and non-German, in their origins and political orientation were heavily beholden to the Josephinian source of the modern Habsburg Monarchy. When they gained the right of participation in it, they did so as collaborators and beneficiaries in its *Rechtsstaat*, not as outsiders. While this is in no way meant to diminish the importance of the bourgeois achievement in Austria, it is meant to see it in a less Weberian light. Vienna's liberal elites were so well integrated into the structure of the state that it is difficult to take seriously the kind of crisis Schorske posits. So long as the *Rechtsstaat* continued, their influence did as well. Moreover, the forces that threatened to displace them were themselves operating in the context of that *Rechtsstaat*: the social democrats could not exist without it and Christian Socialism, for all its antisemitic and seemingly anti-liberal characteristics, was actually working to maintain the continuity of the *Rechtsstaat* by both strengthening its traditional dynastic character and pressing for ministerial government in its modern constitutional persona.[37]

Yet what of the cultural dimension of Austria's *fin de siècle*? Undoubtedly, Schnitzler and Hofmannsthal were sons of the liberal bourgeoisie, as were other cultural figures such as Stefan Zweig and Hermann Bahr; but while all of these men may have been representatives of the avantgarde, they were not all agonizing over questions of decline nor seeking to escape it through the creation of a new culture. Certainly, as Schorske points out, they were all raised in an atmosphere saturated with the cultural inheritance of the Habsburgs,[38] but is this really as significant as he maintains, given that high culture in nineteenth century Europe was fairly similar everywhere? The question also needs to be asked as to whether the sons of other wealthy bourgeoisie in the "normative" countries of England and France were not also pursuing careers in culture and if so, is this a sign of crisis or simply a case of enjoying the fruits of a previous generation's labor? The cultural dimension of Schorske's argument loses its significance if the kind of bourgeois liberal crisis he describes did not occur. Without it, the dominant cultural context in which Schnitzler and Hofmannsthal functioned comes to be of greater significance than their individual experiences.

It was in fact a context that in the fine and musical arts was heavily influenced by the Habsburg dynasty and state.[39] It was also, however, a context that most creative figures wished to be a part of. This was true for the Secession, for Loos (despite his independence), for Zweig, Bahr, and for Gustav Mahler, who was quite happy to be conducting at the *Hofoper.* Even radical expressionists like Schiele and Kokoschka were at most detached from the establishment rather than alienated from it, with Schiele before his death actually planning to become an active part of it.[40] As for Schnitzler and Hofmannsthal, the traditions, orderliness, and façades of the Habsburg Monarchy were the indispensable means to Hofmannsthal's end of creating a new Austrian *Gemeinschaft,* while to Schnitzler they were simply the structures of a flawed reality, neither good nor bad, but susceptible to delineation and criticism like any others. Indeed, in Schnitzler's case it is difficult to reconcile his capacity to write a critical work like *Der Weg ins Freie* with his composition of the patriotic *Der junge Medardus* unless he is viewed as the self-conscious fellow-traveler of an ongoing social and political enterprise. Indeed, the variety and creative vitality manifested in the Vienna of 1900 can as easily be ascribed to the underlying, if imperfect, stability of the Austrian *Rechtsstaat* as to any notion of its impending dissolution. A few well-known scandals notwithstanding, like Schiele's brief incarceration for "pornography," in Austria the rule of law tended overwhelmingly to guarantee freedom of expression rather than to suppress it. Thus when Otto Wagner was once asked if he feared for his teaching position because of his association with the controversial Secession, he could reply, "Das könnte man unter einem autokratischen Regime. Aber Kaiser Franz Joseph—ich bin deshalb Anhänger der Monarchie—hält sich starr und anständig an die Konstitution."[41]

The social and political hierarchy of the Habsburg Monarchy displayed broad tolerance in cultural matters, and its not infrequent patronage of the avant-garde, as in the case of the Secession, was more typical of the Austrian establishment than were the hostile opinions of Franz Ferdinand.[42] Unlike imperial Germany to the north, the Habsburg Monarchy was more willing to coopt creative change than to fear it.[43] Certainly, this was not a less healthy reaction to cultural modernism than could be found among the establishments of Great Britain, France, and the United States; "normative" countries where one would be hard pressed to find models of Weberian behavior among the bourgeois sons and daughters attracted to the Bloomsbury Group, the circles of post-impressionism, and the "ashcan" school. As in these other " modern" societies, Austrian civic life could not be threatened by modern culture while the *Rechtsstaat* was still an effective institution.

Finally, where does this leave the concept of a Viennese *fin de siècle*? Hermann Bahr, who is often cited as a bellwether of cultural matters around 1900, admitted to using the term in 1891, but only because of its topicality and three years later "admitted that he had no clear idea of its meaning."[44] In the *Neue Freie Presse*'s editorial for 31 December 1899 the writer was critical of those who placed too much significance on a mere change of numbers and noted that there would still be a continuity between the centuries with much of the old one still in the new. Like most of the other major Viennese papers on the eve of the new century, the *Presse* acknowledged the seriousness of the lingering political crisis caused by the Badeni language ordinances, but professed to optimism about its solution in the near term.[45] Even when three days later the *Presse* published a long, rather world-weary feuilleton by the Danish philosopher Georg Brandes entitled, "Zur Wende des Jahrhunderts," his pessimism about the new century was directed at Europe's general bellicosity and the disappointment he felt over France's deplorable behavior during the Dreyfus affair, and not at Austria. For him, Austria was a positive spot in his recollections from the century just ended, and he declared himself pleased with the scholars, ministers, and poets he had met there, including the young Schnitzler and Hofmannsthal, but with no suggestion whatsoever of their representing the dying spirit of their class or country.[46] If any of this is at all indicative of the atmosphere in Austria, and Vienna in particular, at the end of the century, then the Schorskean *fin de siècle* is a less than useful concept for understanding it.

The image of "*fin-de-siècle* Vienna" and the *Sonderweg* concept it feeds into are dubious constructs, at best. Rather, we should look on the phenomenon of Vienna 1900 as a transitional period within a modern culture and society, one that had its own developmental "peculiarities,"[47] but none that were setting it on the road of ineluctable crisis. It is the image of the *Burgtor* with its inscription, "Justitia Regnorum Fundamentum," that offers a more accurate picture of an Austrian society based on a functionally unique version of the *Rechtsstaat* in which there could be change with continuity. Once the period 1890–1914 is freed of its *fin-de-siècle* label in favor of the less deterministic *Jahrhundertwende* image, so too will our understanding of Austrian history be freed of an intellectually inhibiting interpretation. Certainly Vienna 1900 deserves to be seen as a time of historical significance, but not on the basis of representing the culturally rich death of one of history's notorious non-conformists.

Notes

1. See James Shedel, *Art and Society: The New Art Movement in Vienna 1897–1914* (Palo Alto, 1981), 75–76; on Bahr's conversion in the late 1880s from pan-Germanist to Austrian patriot, see Donald G. Daviau, *Der Mann von Übermorgen: Hermann Bahr 1863–1934* (Vienna, 1984), 61–62; and on his perception of the Secession and its art as Austrian, see Hermann Bahr, *Secession* (Vienna, 1900), 257–259.
2. See Carl Schorske, "Politics and Psyche in *Fin-de-Siècle* Vienna: Schnitzler and Hofmannsthal," in *The American Historical Review* 66 (July 1961): 930–946.
3. Schorske, in *Fin-de-Siècle Vienna* (New York, 1980), quotes Hofmannsthal's observation that modern poets seemed to stand "'under the decree of necessity, as though they were all building on a pyramid, the monstrous residence of a dead king or an unborn god.' Hofmannsthal, with his Habsburg traditionalism and his daring quest for a new politics of sublimation, seemed to be at work on both" (22).
4. See Mikuláš Teich and Roy Porter, *Fin de Siècle and Its Legacy* (Cambridge, 1990), 1.
5. Steven Beller, *Vienna and the Jews 1867–1938: A Cultural History* (Cambridge, 1989), 3.
6. For a complete presentation of the *Sonderweg*'s normative implications and the role played by this concept in the historiography of modern German history, see David Blackbourn and Geoff Eley, *The Peculiarities of German History: Bourgeois Society and Politics in Nineteenth-Century Germany* (Oxford, 1984).
7. See Henry Wickham Steed, *The Hapsburg Monarchy* (New York, 1969); this is a reprint of the 1914 second edition.
8. See the discussion of their father's activities before, during, and after the war as they relate to the destruction of Austria-Hungary and the Slav successor states in Hugh and Christopher Seton-Watson, *The Making of a New Europe: R. W. Seton-Watson and the Last Years of Austria-Hungary* (Seattle, 1981); in particular, pages 433–436 present a useful summary of his responsibility and sometimes conflicted reaction to political developments within the successor states.

9. Josef Redlich, *Das österreichische Staats- und Reichsproblem: Geschichtliche Darstellung der inneren Politik der Habsburgischen Monarchie 1848 bis zum Untergang des Reiches*, 2 vols. (Leipzig, 1926), 2.

10. See Josef Redlich, *Emperor Francis Joseph of Austria* (New York, 1929).

11. Oscar Jászi, *The Dissolution of the Habsburg Monarchy* (Chicago, 1966), 171.

12. A. J. P. Taylor, *The Habsburg Monarchy, 1809–1918: A History of the Austrian Empire and Austria Hungary* (Chicago, 1976), 7.

13. See Robert A. Kann, *The Multinational Empire: Nationalism and National Reform in the Habsburg Monarchy 1848–1918*, 2 vols. (New York, 1977).

14. Robert A. Kann, *A History of the Habsburg Empire 1526–1918* (Berkeley, 1977); see the summation on 518–520.

15. See Hugo Hantsch, *Geschichte Österreichs 1648–1918*, 2 vols. (Graz, 1968), 2; and Erich Zöllner, *Geschichte Österreichs:Von den Anfängen bis zur Gegenwart* (Munich, 1979).

16. Hantsch, *Geschichte Österreichs*, 458.

17. C. A. Macartney, *The Habsburg Empire, 1790–1918* (New York,1969), 1.

18. See John Boyer, *Political Radicalism in Late Imperial Vienna: The Origins of the Christian Social Movement, 1848–1897* (Chicago, 1981) and *Culture and Political Crisis in Vienna: Christian Socialism in Power* (Chicago, 1995); David F. Good, *The Economic Rise of the Habsburg Empire, 1750–1914* (Berkeley, 1984); also the previous citation of Beller's work; and Ernst Bruckmüller, Ulrike Döcker, Hans Heiss, Hannes Stekl, and Peter Urbanitsch (Hg.), *Bürgertum in der Habsbugermonarchie*, 2 vols. (Vienna, 1990 and 1992, respectively).

19. See Beller, *Vienna and the Jews*, 4, where he points out Carl Schorske's projection of the United States in 1950 as the model for Vienna 1900.

20. For a full exposition of the argument, see Mark Raeff, *The Well-Ordered Police State: Social and Institutional Change through Law in the Germanies and Russia, 1600–1800* (New Haven, 1983).

21. Joseph, Leopold, and Franz all accepted this by virtue of their education and personal conviction. Ferdinand undoubtedly had this communicated to him at the behest of his father, but whether he understood it is open to question. Franz Joseph, whose punctiliousness in observing the law as both an absolute and constitutional ruler is well known, clearly reflected this principle as Kaiser. For a discussion of how the ruler could be both above and under the law see Leonard Krieger, *The German Idea of Freedom* (Chicago, 1972).

22. Waltraud Heindl, *Gehorsame Rebellen: Bürokratie und Beamte in Österreich 1780 bis 1848* (Vienna, 1991), 327–333.

23. See Anna Coreth, "'Pietas Austriaca': Wesen und Bedeutung habsburgischer Frömmigkeit der Barockzeit," *Mitteilungen des Österreichischen Staatsarchivs* 7 (Offprint, 1954); and James Shedel, "Emperor, Church, and People: Religion and Dynastic Loyalty During the Golden Jubilee of Franz Joseph," *The Catholic Historical Review* 76 (January 1990).

24. See the argument in John Komlos, *Nutrition and Economic Development in the Eighteenth Century Habsburg Monarchy: An Anthropometric History* (Princeton, 1989), in which he maintains that the Habsburg state under Maria Theresa and Joseph II may have encouraged an early onset of the Industrial Revolution in Austria through their policy of improved nutrition among the peasantry to provide the country with a more productive population and healthier recruits for the army. In this way a population explosion was stimulated that in turn stimulated increased economic demand.

25. The *Bürgerliches Gesetzbuch*, the reform of the penal code, of court procedure, the application of the common law to virtually all regardless of Stand, not to mention the legal procedures regulating the actions of the bureaucracy survived and were augmented after the reign of Joseph II. For a brief discussion of his legal reforms, see Macartney, *The Habsburg Empire*, 126.
26. See Boyer, *Political Radicalism*, 4–7.
27. Ibid., 18–19.
28. Redlich, *Francis Joseph*, 344–345.
29. In both popular and scholarly expositions on the constitutional character of the state after 1867, the nature of the Monarchy as a balance between the power of the crown and of the people is emphasized. In doing so it is described as a constitutional monarchy, but also with equal frequency as a *Rechtsstaat* whose legal origins begin with the Pragmatic Sanction and run through the December Constitution of 1867. Thus, the historical/traditional as well as the rational/constitutional character of the *Rechtsstaat* as a kind of legal duality is recognized. An example of a popular exposition of the constitution that ran into multiple editions is that of the anonymously edited *Katechismus der österreichischen Staatsverfassung*, 4th ed. (Vienna, 1884), which on page 2 compared the constitution favorably to those of any other state, saying that in many instances only that of Britain was comparable. That Austria was a *Rechtsstaat* was also specifically stressed as something teachers should impart to their students; see the oft-reprinted handbook for *Bürgerschule* teachers by Ludwig Fleischer, *Österreichischer Bürgerkunde: Ein Lehr- und Hilfsbuch für Bürgerschulen und die mit denselben verbundenen Einjährigen Lehrkurse*, 4th ed. (Vienna, 1908), 13–14. For the more scholarly view of the Monarchy as a historically and constitutionally based *Rechtsstaat*, see the work of the jurist Friedrich Tezner, especially *Der Kaiser* (Vienna, 1909).
30. For a very interesting and persuasive argument about the ability of the Monarchy to remain fundamentally viable until military defeat caused its collapse, see Alan Sked, *The Decline and Fall of the Habsburg Empire, 1815–1918* (London, 1989).
31. Boyer, *Political Radicalism*, 23.
32. See Tezner, *Der Kaiser*, 4; Tezner saw the emperor's power as partly analogous to that of the English crown in a historical/constitutional sense and cites the strong position of that power within the constitutional system as a partial explanation for why the parties are willing to obstruct the business of the Reichsrat and Landtage; i.e., they can be irresponsible because the crown is not and has the legal power to govern when necessary. While he sees the positive side of the imperial authority, he suggests that if it were less strong, the parties would be forced to accept more political responsibility for their actions.
33. For a complete discussion of the origin, use, and significance of Article 14, see Gernot D. Hasiba, *Das Notverordnungsrecht in Österreich (1848–1917): Notwendigkeit und Mißbrauch eines Staatserhaltenden Instrumentes* (Vienna, 1985).
34. In surveying the contemporary literature on the nature of the post-1897 nationality conflicts, their origins and potential solutions, it is striking to note the degree to which it is taken for granted that these conflicts are primarily legal/constitutional in character and can therefore be solved within the fundamental framework of the existing Austrian *Rechtsstaat*. As examples of this approach, see D—s [full name not given in original], "Die Lösung der Nationalitäten- und Autonomiefrage in Österreich auf historischer und verfassungsmäßiger Grundlage," *Österreichisch-Ungarische Revue* 25 (1899); and Alfred Freiherr von Offermann, *Die Bedingungen des constitutionellen Österreichs* (Vienna, 1900).

35. The social democrats supported the multinational state from a mixture of political legalism and a feeling that it was a historically valid source of economic rationalization and internationalism that could pave the way for the eventual advent of socialism.

36. Shedel, *Art and Society*, 60–61.

37. See Boyer, *Culture and Political Crisis in Vienna*, chaps. 2–3.

38. Schorske, *Fin-de-Siècle Vienna*, 298.

39. For an excellent study of state influence in the arts at the turn of the century and earlier, see Jeroen Bastiaan van Heerde, *Staat und Kunst: Staatliche Kunstförderung 1895 bis 1918* (Vienna, 1993).

40. For a discussion of how Schiele and Kokoschka related to the official artistic establishment, see Shedel, *Art and Society*, 151–197.

41. See n. 47 in van Heerde, *Staat und Kunst*, 271.

42. See van Heerde, *Staat und Kunst*, 271–273.

43. See Peter Paret, *The Berlin Secession: Modernism and Its Enemies in Imperial Germany* (Cambridge, Mass., 1980).

44. Donald G. Daviau, *Hermann Bahr* (Boston, 1985), 31.

45. *Neue Freie Presse*, 31 December 1899 (morning edition). For a digest of the views expressed in other major Viennese dailies on Austria's nationality problem and the future, see the survey entitled "Zeitungsschau," *Wiener Abendpost;* Supplement to *Wiener Zeitung*, 2 January 1900.

46. *Neue Freie Presse*, 3 January 1900.

47. See Blackbourn and Eley; the use of this term to describe unusual, but not abnormal, historical development originates with their characterization of nineteenth-century German history and their critique of the *Sonderweg* interpretation.

Chapter 4

THEODOR HERZL AND RICHARD VON SCHAUKAL

Self-Styled Nobility and the Sources of
Bourgeois Belligerence in Prewar Vienna

Michael Burri

The years following the deaths of Theodor Herzl and Richard von Schaukal have added to the distance that already separated the two during their lifetime. At the turn of the century in Vienna, neither writer could be said to have been close to the other, personally or creatively. Herzl, after a brief term as Paris correspondent of the *Neue Freie Presse*, had become its feuilleton editor. An author of short stories, dramas, and novels, he was also the renowned leader of the Zionist movement. Younger and less accomplished, Schaukal was an Austrian civil servant with great expectations, a writer known for his early success as a poet, and a contributor to the leading literary journals. Today, even these connections seem trivial. The legacy of the Burgtheater playwright Herzl is as clear as that of the "new Hofmannsthal" Schaukal. Herzl is the founder of political Zionism, a man with a flair for the theatrical, a dramatist who, like Václav Havel or Pope John Paul II, found a second career in public life, while Schaukal is regarded as a minor figure in what might be called "Austrian decadence," a conservative whose bloody-minded verses during

World War I both earned him a place in the *Literarisches Verbrecher-album* published in 1918 and sent an already fading literary reputation into near eclipse.[1]

Theodor Herzl and Richard von Schaukal were outwardly successful men of their time, men whose personal and professional identities were traversed by a variety of endowments, accomplishments, and ambitions. To describe in their work an exchange between the roles of "insider" and "outsider" would surely be one means of closing the distance between them. Herzl was an insider insofar as he worked for an audience in Vienna, yet an outsider by virtue of having been born in Budapest; insider as feuilleton editor of the *Neue Freie Presse*, outsider as the leader of a movement never mentioned in its pages; insider as an assimilated Jew, outsider as a Jew, and so forth. Schaukal might be thought of as the quintessential Viennese insider, but like Adolf Loos he too was from Brünn. An insider as a successful writer, he felt keenly and even overestimated his exclusion from the elect; insider as a Catholic, outsider in a predominantly Jewish literary milieu; and so on. Such an account of the relations between center and periphery would indicate a common problematic for the two writers and underscores the insider-outsider dynamic that has been so productive for critical writing on Austrian literature. Yet an account drawn along these lines would also be misleading. For in quite significant ways, both Herzl and Schaukal expressed a close and positive identification with the social elite. Far from being concerned with the fluid contours of their own identities, both men sought an assured place in this elite. Far from opposing the established institutions of culture and politics, they remained resolutely committed to them. A sense of exclusion would not have meant being an outsider, but quite simply being a failure.

"Without my newspaper, obviously, I could do nothing. Where would I get the authority?" wrote Herzl in his diary in 1895, and despite regular frustration with it, he never gave up his position with the *Neue Freie Presse*.[2] By most accounts, after all, this Viennese daily was one of the most important newspapers in Europe. With an appointment in 1891 as its Paris correspondent, then a transfer to Vienna as its feuilleton editor in 1895, Herzl moved through what was one of the most prestigious careers possible in Vienna. And the rewards were not only symbolic: according to Alex Bein, Herzl drew the highest salary at the *Neue Freie Presse*.[3] "It was as if Napoleon had pinned the Knight's Cross of the Legion of Honor upon a young sergeant on the battlefield," Stefan Zweig wrote of the significance of having his first article accepted by Herzl. "In my nineteenth year I had suddenly achieved a prominent position overnight."[4]

In similar ways, Schaukal was also able to find a continuity between his own interests and those of the high establishment. Indeed, from early on, Schaukal felt pressed to succeed. "I became a law student not out of any inclination, but only out of the ambition that had already beset me in childhood," as he recalled later.[5] And in the extraliterary career he fashioned for himself, Schaukal prospered at nearly every step. A *k.u.k.* civil servant, he quickly advanced from his post with the district administration at Mährisch-Weißkirchen to an appointment as department head (*Ministerialrat*) with the Ministry of Public Works in Vienna *(Ministerium für öffentliche Arbeiten)*. Upward bound, Schaukal moved on the fast career track that led to the highest offices of state, a track ultimately derailed, in his own account, by the machinations of a "hostilely disposed minister."[6]

Self-Made Aristocrats

The idealization of the social elite and the desire of those in a low place to move to a higher one, as Erving Goffman has pointed out, reflects a wish for not only a prestigious place but also one close to the sacred values of society.[7] The elite, who are stationed at the top of the social pyramid and who embody its finest ideals, as Goffman has it, mark their distinction in accent, carriage and demeanor, etiquette, dress, and lifestyle. To acquire this sign-equipment for oneself and to maintain the front of a person of high status is then possible through performance proper to such a person. And yet, the very notion that one can manage a self-presentation or "make" oneself suggests a certain attitude about the prospect of individual transcendence. Both Herzl and Schaukal had deeply internalized an ethic of self-realization. Each proceeded from the liberal principle that the self could be overcome and remade. Herzl presented the fruits of such self-realization in his own person, even as the Jewish figures of his literary and political imagination remained half-formed and thwarted; for Schaukal, too, the essence of social distinction seemed to be realized in himself, and in his texts he mythologized a self-presentation that was both his own and close to the "sacred values" of Austria.

From Budapest to Brünn, Austria itself was a relic of the European dynastic tradition. An empire in an age of the nation, a state marked by pre-democratic authority systems, pre-bourgeois elites, and "archaic" mentalities, Austria entered the modern age in the firm grip of its past.[8] Certainly, this does not mean that the empire was destined to "decline and fall." The years prior to World War I were in fact a time of accelerated economic growth and integration in the monarchy; had the Central Powers won the war, the Habsburg Monarchy would have not merely survived, but quite likely expanded.[9] What it does suggest, however, is that Austria could with some confidence turn to its own history and traditions in an encounter with modernity. With a feudal past far less interrupted than that of either England or France, with many of its borders set historically since the Middle Ages, Austria may have approached the *fin de siècle* with a mixture of dread and uncertainty, but in this there was also a profound faith. The historical continuity of Austria would prevail; the symbolic resources of pre-modernity—the forms, dispositions, and identities of the feudal tradition—would, as they always had, serve as its bearers.

Herzl and Schaukal would hardly have described their situation in such abstract terms. The natural superiority, sovereign right, and easy eminence of the would-be elite individual of the *fin de siècle* was grounded in the logic of demonstration, not explanation.[10] Their performance could not be said to have been regulated by a given set of formalizable propositions, anyway. In the figure of the self-styled aristocrat that both men presented to their turn-of-the-century publics, each simply complied with his own best instincts; in the "aristocrat," these two bourgeois men merged with themselves—what they had always been and what they were to become. Around 1900, Herzl and Schaukal each brought forward a claim to "nobility," a claim expressed in the form of a "noble ethos" or "aristocratic disposition" that was no less than a second nature enacted as if primordial.

In Vienna, to be sure, a personal self-presentation defined as "aristocratic" drew upon a certain historical prototype. The traditional role of Vienna, for example, as a bulwark against the outsider—whether against the non-Christian Muslim from the southeast or the non-Christian Jew from the east, the Slavic horde or the "oriental" Hungarian, or later, the worker from the *Vorstadt*—had already given a markedly Viennese urgency to personal bearing and comportment. In this city under siege, there emerged a historical imperative to "hold up," to maintain a posture of composed self-assurance, and to project the noble carriage of one who unquestionably "belonged."

That the aristocrat served as a kind of imaginary ideal for bourgeois artists and intellectuals around 1900 is, of course, a steady point of reference in much of the scholarship on *fin-de-siècle* Vienna. Yet while this scholarship generally sees the ambition to style oneself as an aristocrat as a withdrawal from social activism into a private aestheticism, I argue that the Viennese "aristocrat," as incarnated by Theodor Herzl and Richard von Schaukal, projects a slightly different intention. Alex Bein once remarked that in view of his overwrought sense of honor, Herzl would have been well suited to the career in the Austrian bureaucracy that he once envisioned for himself, and perhaps still better suited to a life in officers' circles.[11] In the ethos of the aristocrat, I contend, both Herzl and Schaukal found an attitudinal and aesthetic equivalent to the military man. Far from a solipsistic and enervated subjectivity, the aristocratic *habitus* offered a symbolic pose for the expression of belligerent impulses and combative attitudes. Although Herzl and Schaukal arrived at different materializations of this type, both felt themselves to be transformed by their noble self-fashioning, given over to a euphoric sense of gladiatorial strength, martial self-assuredness, and heroic inviolability. From this perspective, I suggest, the "aristocrat" represents a palpable link between what are often seen as two unrelated circumstances: the literary and social history of the *fin de siècle* and the outbreak of war—from Vienna—in 1914.

Richard von Schaukal: The Ultimate Knight

"There are only three respectable human beings," Charles Baudelaire wrote around 1860, "the priest, the warrior, the poet." To a striking extent, Richard von Schaukal represents a *fin-de-siècle* composite of these three types. A critic whose practice tended toward the programmatic and missionary, a man whose bearing in cultural matters was one of mighty conviction, a writer who never stopped writing, Schaukal radiated the very essence of a "respectable human being." If such an aura hardly distinguished him from Hugo von Hofmannsthal, Arthur Schnitzler, Stefan Zweig, or other of his more luminous contemporaries around 1900, his relentless and often brazen efforts to position himself among the social elite make him a remarkable figure. Indeed, it is the symptomatic excess of Schaukal that recommends him to attention. His exaggeration, an exaggeration that bordered on the grotesque, is suggestive, for here may be revealed something taken for granted, yet subdued, in the "restraint" of his peers.

From early childhood, Schaukal prepared for the role of elegant man and feudal heir. Although raised in "modest circumstances" (*einfache Verhältnisse*), he later recalled, his earliest impulse was "a clear sense for the well-to-do, an abhorrence of misery joined with a disgust at uncleanliness. Everything refined, light, and lavish [he] found agreeable."[12] In 1894, the year following his twelve-month service in the cavalry, he found himself under the influence of Baudelaire and his portrayal of the aristocratic dandy, an encounter that resounded throughout much of his later work By 1901 such experiences had been fictionalized. In *Intérieurs aus dem Leben der Zwanzigjährigen*, a collection of sketches, short stories, and diary entries that was clearly meant to be read as an autobiographical account, Schaukal told his own tale. Here were the trials and humiliations of a young bourgeois man cursed with an assertively elite nature, and here, for Schaukal, was his own break from the past. "Since I have fallen into the grand style," as the protagonist confesses, "I can no longer endure the scent of ordinary people."[13]

If *Interiéurs* reflected the early struggles of Schaukal, it also proposed a straightforward continuity between his fictional creations and his own person. Indeed, Schaukal made sure both to highlight any personal acquaintance with members of the high nobility in his literary work and, oddly enough, to use his literary work to support his own claim to nobility. His 1909 collection of critical essays, *Vom Geschmack* was thus dedicated to Andreas von Balthesser, the fictional dandy and would-be aristocrat of his 1907 novel.[14] To Arthur Schnitzler, on the other hand, he offered wisdom earned through experience. The Count in *Reigen*, he wrote to the Viennese dramatist, is "really the sole unsuccessful figure. Inasmuch as this type, 'Rittmeister Count X,' has always been my frequent companion and is now my sole intimate company in this dump, a district office in Mährisch-Weisskirchen, I know him like myself and can safely say that. Just an example...."[15] Schaukal knew counts well, and he knew them like himself. Whether as correspondent, colleague, or reader of his books, he made nearly everyone aware of this fact.

Although a dutiful and tireless self-chronicler, Schaukal was reticent about his own pedigree. Certainly around 1900, no one without a prophetic sense of irony, including the critic who described his appearance as one of "thoroughly well-groomed, aristocratically simple [*aristokratisch-einfachen*], tasteful, and solid elegance," would have thought to address him with the honorific "von."[16] True nobility, after all, came late to Schaukal. Thus with the *Allerhöchste Entschließung* of 18 May 1918, the last Habsburg monarch, Emperor Karl I, ennobled his last high civil servant, Richard von Schaukal.[17] By mid-November, Karl had relinquished his office and fled Vienna, while Schaukal witnessed the end of an institution to which he had just been admitted. Karl Kraus, who practiced a notable restraint in his criticism of Schaukal, alluded both to these circumstances and to the public perception of Schaukal as a feudal warrior when he renamed him "the ultimate knight" (*der allerletzte Ritter*) in *Die Fackel*.[18]

That he achieved noble status at all suggests the miraculous extent to which the claims of Schaukal as an "aristocrat" found a receptive audience.

To be sure, his service as a wartime propagandist, which encompassed not only "very worthy patriotic poems" but also editorship of the *Kriegs-Gedenkblatt*, clearly impressed the court as "truly inestimable services."[19] It might also be added that ennoblement often stood at the end of a career in the Ministerium für öffentliche Arbeiten.[20] Still, many equally "accomplished" wartime propagandists such as Hermann Bahr, Robert Michel, and Anton Wildgans were not so highly honored. Whatever the case, Schaukal prevailed. In spite of his enemies in the Ministerium, he managed a rare achievement: he styled himself as a noble and then became one. To what did Schaukal owe the recognition among both critics and admirers that his posturing expressed an ethos of nobility? What was it that suggested this agreement between the person and the ideal? How, in short, is it possible for a modern aristocrat to be taken for a feudal warrior—"the ultimate knight"?

Together with the more conventional decadent and symbolist motifs of the garden, dreams, and classical antiquity, a recurrent figure in the early poetry of Schaukal is the ancient knight. So pervasive is this figure, in fact, that Josef Nadler designates the type he represents as the primary trope in Schaukal's lyric writing.[21] And indeed, "der herrische Mann" or "das herrisch-heroische Wunschbild," as Nadler calls this trope, is an assertive symbolic presence here. In "Nacht-ritt" (Night-ride), the penultimate contribution to the 1897 volume of poetry *Meine Gärten*, for example, the clash of cavalry sabers sounds a fateful wake-up call in the garden:

> Über Wiesen und Nebeln
> Dämmert schläfrig der Tag.
> Kein grüssender Lerchenschlag,
> Nur Klirren von Reitersäbeln
> Und Lappern von müden Hufen
> Auf hartem, holprigem Weg.
> Beine und Träume träg ...
> Fernher ein Unkenrufen.[22]

The collection *Das Buch der Tage und Träume* that appeared two years later returned to the encounter between the garden and the call to heroic battle, but presented it in still more decisive terms: "Lebt wohl, ihr Gartenlüfte, / veilchendurchatmet und mild. / Unser Haar ist ohne Düfte, / wir haben ein Schwert an der Hüfte: / töne Schwert an den Schild."[23] The knight, with his identity fortified by a refusal of soft fragrance and mildness, bids farewell to the garden. Both his exit and the expectation of battle are motivated by the presence of a sword on his hip, rather than the urgency of any concrete event. Retreat to the garden, the garden as refuge, the transformed garden—in short, the broad register of themes advanced by scholars as characteristic of *fin-de-siècle* Vienna—finds no confirmation here.[24] This is a knight with will, purpose, and a high-pitched sense of heroism. He is leaving the garden and, put plainly, he is looking for a fight.

In "Das Lieblingsross" (The favorite horse), a poem reprinted in *Ausgewählte Gedichte* (1904)—the volume Rainer Maria Rilke considered to be Schaukal's best to date—the figure of the aggressive knight-aristocrat emerges in the course of the narration.[25] The speaker of the poem begins by describing the pleasure he takes in riding his favorite horse around his estate: "Sitz auf mein Pferd auf probe seinen / Gang / die Wandelbahn im Park das Schloß / ent- / lang…."[26] Consistent with his emphasis on self-presentation, he is pleased to call attention to his performance. Of the horse, he notes, "Sieh es gibt acht: / das Tier weiss wohl dass ich es nun be- / rede."[27] And yet, the closing lines underscore just how close this stylized portrait of noble rider, horse, and park is to an outburst of violence: "Sieh wie es stolz und glücklich lacht, / ich ritt das Ross zu mancher Jagd zu / mancher Fehde."[28]

Around 1900, there is little doubt that such a knight would scarcely have found himself alone in the Austrian poetic landscape.[29] "Die Weise von Liebe und Tod des Cornets Christoph Rilke" (1899, 1904, 1906), for example, recreated the heroic adventures of a certain Cornet Rilke, the recently "discovered" aristocratic forebear of Rainer Maria Rilke.[30] Indeed, as set in verse by the latter Rilke, this young Cornet moved through a world of chivalry and mortal struggle that the knights of Schaukal might well have recognized. And like Schaukal, Rilke steered his knight toward action, rejecting a medievalism of art objects and relics in favor of a poetics of anger and the deed.

In the Vienna-based journal *Der Gral: Monatschrift für schöne Literatur*, it was a cultural program far greater in scope and ambition that launched the knight into battle. Founded in 1906 by Franz Eichert, with the support of Richard von Kralik, *Der Gral* spoke with the voice of a muscular conservative Catholicism and set a romantic ideal of the grail together with a vaguely defined Middle Ages against the intolerable materialism, Nietzscheanism, and Social Democratic tendencies of the present.[31] To express their vision of cultural and spiritual regeneration, Kralik and his younger associate Eichert drew upon the religious tradition of the crusading knight. Around 1880, as William McGrath has shown, Kralik began his final break from the Pernerstorfer circle with his belief in artistic or religious redemption through the strong individual, a belief "dominated by the vision of the heroic brother-band who would do battle for the ideal reality after the manner of medieval knights."[32] Next to Kralik, Eichert demonstrated, if anything, more spleen. Already at the turn of the century, his aggressive lyrics had projected fantasies of a bloody crusade against liberalism. Comparing these verses with the occasional poems both Eichert and Kralik wrote during World War I, Bernhard Doppler has justifiably remarked that "the aggressivity of these crusade fantasies is not surpassed even by their fantasies of war."[33]

Although Schaukal became an occasional contributor to *Der Gral* from 1910 onward, his knight-aristocrat shared little with that of Kralik and Eichert. The knight of Schaukal, after all, was never intended to be the agent of a new cultural or religious order. His own program of self-realization, moreover, ensured that Schaukal would be accountable to himself, not God. In fact, a critical absence in the knight poetry of Schaukal is the lack of a religious context: the noble rider belongs to no Kralik-Eichert brotherhood and holds no place at the Round Table of the Pre-Raphaelites. Less a Christian knight than a battle-ready warrior, the knight embodied in his manner, movement, and bearing the essence of a noble man. This is a figure whose appearance projects an expectation of respect, as in "Ritterlicher Spruch" (Knightly adage):

> Höherm Walten stumm geneigt
> Feinden frank die Farb gezeigt
> hehres Ziel im Fernen.
>
> Halt mir offen Aug und Herz
> Herr mein Gott und lass von Schmerz
> wie von Lust mich lernen![34]

In this knight reside both the imaginary honor of ancient warrior-noble and the *Haltung* of the self-styled aristocrat of the *fin de siècle*. Pierre Bourdieu has described very well the agreement between bodily bearing and "manliness," in contrast to the "femininity" of the indecisive, non-noble man: "The manly man who goes straight to his target, without detours, is also a man who refuses twisted and devious looks, words, gestures and blows. He stands up straight and looks straight into the face of the person he wishes to welcome."[35] Like the knight, the "man" is always alert, holding his goal, whether near or far, in his line of sight. Pain or pleasure are inconsequential relative to the nobility of the task at hand; for the resolute and rigid knight, "manliness" is a *habitus,* a presence before the battle that anticipates the enemy as well as heroic action in battle.

Around 1900, as George Mosse has argued, codes of manners and morals, together with particular modes of self-presentation, acquired a new and powerful importance in Europe.[36] The knight of Schaukal who makes himself understood in his "air," his "attitude," and his "look" may be seen within this trend of individual socialization. Yet if Mosse finds in the new social and behavioral imperatives of the turn of the century a largely non-confrontational ethos of "respectability" or "masculinity," the knight of Schaukal indicates a far more menacing realization of correct demeanor, self-composure, and upright mental hygiene. Well dressed and well horsed, this knight moves in step with his knightly code of conduct, a code of conduct that expresses his own fierce nature and temperament. An invisible hand appears to guide him; when he acts, it is often, paradoxically, "to prevent" conflict. With such an imprimatur, the knight will always be busy, and when he rides, he will kill for the good of everyone.

"For Schaukal, life is not straightforward pleasure and intoxication," wrote the Czech critic and admirer of Schaukal, Arnošt Procházka.[37] It is an observation that also captures the predicament of the knight. The knight encounters the field not only as an open ground where his rivals wait; the field itself is malign. In the 1899 poem "Ritt ins Leben" (Ride into life), the speaker anticipates life as a form of combat: "Geharnischt geh ich von euch, verschliesset hinter mir / die Thore, / der Morgen kündet seine rote Wiederkehr. / Blickt mir nach von weithin schauender Empore, / erste Sonnenpfeile treffen meine blanke Wehr."[38] To an even greater extent than the speaker of "Das Lieblingsross," this rider does not find leisure or the glories of chivalry on the back of a horse. For here is a rider who must don armor and become a knight simply to enter life. Once outside familiar confines, the attack begins: the arrows of the sun begin to strike his armor.

Life for the speaker of "Ritt ins Leben," as for the other *fin-de-siècle* knights of Schaukal, is a series of battles. To grow up and enter the world means a constant struggle of all against all. One must be as hard and polished as steel armor to succeed against the others, and only the few who behave as warriors will rise to the top. For the bourgeois Schaukal, the noble knight provided a model for living. Like many other of the knight poems, "Ritt ins Leben" is narrated in the first person; the experience is, after all, meant to appear as a personal one. Physical violence, brutality, and self-fashioned hardness were qualities of mind and body that Schaukal clearly savored. The armor of the knight expressed these qualities. It is, indeed, a rare knight-poem that does not register the impact of this material that gives the body of the knight its shape. In "Der schwarze Ritter"

(The black knight), he writes of the protagonist: "Sein Helm trägt eine glatte Schiene / sein Harnisch ist von schwarzem Stahl / sein Ross hat Augen wie Rubine / sein Wink durchfuhr mich wie ein Strahl."[39]

The field serves as a polishing school for knights; they learn to repel the arrows of the world or they perish. Such an experience poses hazards, but it also excites. In the 1899 poem "Sehnsucht des Knappen" (Yearning of the squire), the equestrian dreams of a young squire, first-person narration, and armor are brought to the forefront: "O ritt ich schon im Waffenkleide aus / meine süsse Frau mir zu erringen!"[40] Battle vestments (*Waffenkleide*), the only description provided, hold the rider rigid and upright, as a man of respect, worthy of battle or of a woman.

Such a knight would make quick work of Perseus, the vegetal knight of the English Pre-Raphaelite painter Edward Burne-Jones, whose armor of leaves suitably conveys his pulpy disposition. Schaukal's knight triumphs through iron hardness, an outer finish that confirms his ideological rapport with Andreas von Balthesser, Schaukal's *fin-de-siècle* aristocrat-dandy. "Politeness," as Balthesser declares, "is smoother than polished steel." And so the incalculable daily provocations of ill breeding, bad taste, and stupidity strike the courtly social armor of Balthesser. Meanwhile, the modern unpolished man (*der Ungeschliffene*) is both resourceful and unrelenting. Against his heroic ignorance, it may even be that politeness is no match. "He has absolutely no shame," sighs Balthesser, "nor can anything stop him [*ihm kann nichts geschehen*]; one would simply have to shoot him down."[41]

In Andreas von Balthesser—or, as one reviewer called him, "Andreas von Schaukal"—fantasies of omnipotence, pathologies of social humiliation, and aristocratic self-presentation recombine.[42] Whereas the combative knight traveled in a fairly delimited realm of threats and adversaries, this new aristocrat-dandy rides boldly onto the wide-open field of culture. *Leben und Meinungen des Herrn Andreas von Balthesser* records his triumphs. The book, which takes shape in the fragmentary form of dialogues, short sketches, and aphorisms, thus reports on the self-assertive mastery of Balthesser in matters ranging from how to iron clothing to city planning to literary verse. It is the report of a man in whom the desire for strength, battle, and victory creates a sense of euphoria and intoxication, a man for whom all resistance must be crushed with merciless force. With Andreas von Balthesser, as the perceptive German critic Felix Poppenberg noted, "we are always on the warpath."[43]

A physiognomic and dispositional descendant of the knight, Andreas von Balthesser also bears the characteristic features of a *fin-de-siècle* aesthete. His acute sense of detail, nuance, and the beautiful, his discriminating aesthetic taste, and his refined nerves are attributes that he shares with this figure. That he should be so irritable does not speak against such an identification. Irritability is, after all, a logical consequence of the much celebrated sensitivity of the aesthete. It is simply that the sensitivity Balthesser displays is not attuned to such familiar decadent stimuli as decline, death, and melancholy, but rather to offense and insult. As a self-styled aristocrat, moreover, Balthesser knows why, how, and for what he should respond when his rivals violate his sense of propriety. Incited to battle, he dies in the third round of a pistol duel with Count Serges Wartburg.

The noble front of superiority, self-assuredness, and indifference will not withstand every assault. Nor was it ever meant to. Not only because honor, as Hegel famously concluded, turns upon individual sensitivity and "is the extreme embodiment of *vulnerability*,"[44] but also because the aristocratic ideal of Schaukal entails cruelty and steeliness—as well as good manners—from the outset. In the skillful exposé of the Balthesser-Schaukal plan of action that he published in 1907, Franz Blei revealed, in the form of advice, how this functioned. As Blei writes to his "imaginary" correspondent:

> Don't forget, you are still the pure amateur, although with a silently asserted suggestion of he who has been called. Something in you, in your way of walking, in your manner [*Haltung*], in your necktie must render this confession. You must discreetly let it be noticed how violently you continue to struggle against the poetic in you. How it is yet truly stronger than your principled will, how it is simply an elemental power, against which nothing can be done, how, indeed, it imposes itself upon you as an inborn genius that leaves you nothing but to observe the correctness of good manners and composure. Fake your struggle now, in order to be able to fake victory later.[45]

Schaukal's performance is correct, upright, and possessed of a duplicitous composure. His self-control would appear to underscore his dignity, and yet, there is something in the way he walks, his manner, his necktie that makes an intention manifest. Conduct and carriage, demeanor, etiquette, and comportment, as Blei knows, are themselves a means of settling disputes. Or, in the words of Andreas von Balthesser, "The person who can move is not obliged to refute arguments."[46] With such a full-fledged active and noble body, Balthesser-Schaukal might well disagree with scholarly claims concerning "the mental aristocratism which so appealed to *fin-de-siècle* man."[47] Certainly, Franz Blei would not have found a benign and incorporeal "aristocracy of the spirit" in his young and ambitious correspondent. In fact, he underscores precisely the blending of hostile intent and movement that marks the noble knight Balthesser-Schaukal. "Fake your struggle now," Blei reminds him, "in order to be able to fake victory later."[48] For Schaukal, it was no joke; victory was always his.

Theodor Herzl: Aristocratic Assimilation?

Nearly everyone who met Theodor Herzl commented in some way on his physical presence. His tutor claimed that young women, taken with his charm, stopped him on the street to engage him in conversation.[49] His cousin, Raoul Auernheimer, "never encountered a person of greater magic" than this self-possessed darling of the gods, whose features "impressed themselves upon all who met him as the most beautiful portrait in an art gallery does."[50] To Sigmund Freud, his neighbor in the Berggasse, he appeared in a dream as himself—as a "majestic figure."[51] And certainly no biographer of Herzl has ever withheld a glimpse of this picture-perfect man. Presented detail by detail—the beard, the cut of the suit, the look of contempt—or presented as a complete figure, handsome, polished, a man beloved among "the entire bourgeoisie—and also the aristocracy—of old Austria," Herzl projects a visual ideal, an ideal that few of his contemporaries could deny and even fewer could equal.[52]

"If only his personality were less fascinating! Elegance is the very breath of his life," the would-be critic of Herzl, Arnold Zweig, once sighed.[53] The frustration of Zweig provides an eloquent restatement of the problem. An opponent could not prevail simply by refuting Herzl's words and argument; one had to engage a man, in the recent words of Michael Berkowitz, whose "physiognomy to most Zionists was the purest symbol of Zionism's aspirations."[54] For Herzl, on the other hand, the ability to convey a physical presence that commanded assent was a political strength. In a Zionist movement marked by bitter factional divisions and widely divergent, idiosyncratic ideologies, the image of "Herzl" served as a cohesive force. For both men and women, moreover, Herzl's personality could provide the decisive factor in support of Zionism. On these grounds, for example, Emma Gottheil and Rebecca Kohut (the latter the president of the World Association of Jewish Women) overcame their original skepticism toward the idea of a Jewish state and added their voices to the movement.[55]

Herzl was a giant. The searching eyes of the flock converged on him and believed what they saw. But is this not a story already told too well and too often by his biographers?[56] The story of an incorrigible dandy, a man of the world who wrote for the theater, an actor in the world of great men, a near aristocrat who used dramatic means to engineer his political program? Perhaps. Yet because of their familiarity, these details have also acquired an undeserved reputation for being cut from the whole cloth of Herzlean myth-making. Thus scholars have conceded that "Baron Ritterhausen," as Herzl was once introduced in public, may have betrayed a certain obsession with the figure of the nobleman.[57] At the same time, they argue, this is not only self-evident, it is also so general a phenomenon as to be insignificant. Steven Beller expresses this view rather succinctly. "Herzl was also plainly a dandy, an aesthete and a snob, fascinated by aristocrats and ideas of chivalry," he writes, "but then so were many of the sons of parvenus all over Europe."[58]

Such assessments, while expressing a justifiable impatience with the clichés of Herzl biography, hardly begin to address the manifest phenomenon of Herzl as a dandy, an aesthete, and a snob. Meanwhile, the argument of *Vienna and the Jews*, that Jews did not "[share] the same set of values" of either *hofrätlich* or aristocratic culture, is problematic.[59] That Jewish girls at the *Beamtentöchterschule* read Schnitzler and Wilde, as reported in the memoirs of Käthe Leichter, while the daughters of gentile officials read "girls' books" opens a significant explanatory gap. Why were young Viennese Jews, who as Leichter suggests were concerned to act beyond their years, reading the works of the gentile Irish dandy Oscar Wilde?[60] The seemingly obvious choice of Schnitzler, the local and Jewish author, adds urgency to the question. What does it mean in Vienna to read about the dandies, aesthetes, and snobs of Oscar Wilde? And what might it mean for Theodor Herzl to style himself in this mold? How does one achieve the appearance of a noble? And in what ways does this become incorporated into Jewish experience?

Although he made creative use of its symbolic resources, Herzl by no means "invented" an aristocratic identity or a Jewish noble posture. On the one hand, there had existed an established tradition of Jewish ennoblement in Austria since the late eighteenth century. Thus prominent families such as Arnstein, Eskeles, Rothschild, and Wertheimstein, among others, received patents of nobility for their service at a time when Jews themselves enjoyed no civil or legal rights in the Habsburg Empire. Intermarriage between Jews and their gentile partners from aristocratic houses also worked to solidify a Jewish presence in the Austrian social elite.[61] In Hungary, moreover, Jewish ennoblement occurred on an unparalleled scale, and, although it is rarely treated in his biographies, this could hardly have been lost on the Budapest-born Herzl.[62]

A trend toward elite socialization of more direct relevance for the present context, however, is that around the turn of the century a group of Viennese Jews acquired visibility as high bourgeoisie and pretenders to nobility.[63] It was this feature and its palpably physical mode of expression that so affected the German-Jewish writer Jakob Wasserman during his long stay in Vienna. "That the Jews, as the most mobile group, kept all the others in continuous motion is, on the whole, not surprising," he wrote in his memoirs.

> Yet I was amazed at the hosts of Jewish physicians, attorneys, clubmen, snobs, dandies, proletarians, actors, newspapermen, and poets. From the very beginning my inner and outer relations with them were full of conflict. Truth to tell, among them I sometimes felt as if I were in exile. The German Jews among whom I had lived had accustomed me to a more polished bourgeois finish, a less conspicuous demeanor. Here I could never lose a certain sense of shame. I was ashamed of their conduct and of their whole attitude.[64]

Like Wassermann, the young Karl Kraus found in Jewish elite self-identification a reference to himself. And as he frequently did in his early work, he focused on its social display. More than a highly mobile group of individual "snobs" and "dandies" in Vienna, however, it was the assertive presence of a new Jewish nobility that Kraus registered. In "A Crown for Zion," the pamphlet he wrote against Herzl and the Zionist movement following the First Zionist Congress in Basel, he characterized the sons of wealthy Jewish bourgeoisie:

> The sons with their Aryan teammates have perfected a moral emptiness and an aristocracy of the fingertips, and distinguish themselves from the latter only by the plucky overenthusiasm with which they stress their similarity to them. They represent the perfected type of the feudal Jew, who is separated by infinite distances of rank from bourgeois society and the plebeian in caftan. I know one who only appears in his regular [*Stamm-*], or more precisely inherited [*angestammten*], coffeehouse wearing his steel-tipped shoes because he wants to summon a suggestion of the equestrian. The matching horse is no doubt stuck somewhere in the Middle Ages.[65]

A new generation of Jews claimed the feudal ideal as its own. In so doing, it positioned itself between both bourgeois society and the unassimilated caftan Jew. Riding with a greater sense of mission than his gentile counterpart, the new Jewish knight identified by Kraus sought integration via the Middle Ages. For Kraus, who is remembered today for his strident assimilationism and his argument that Zionist-sponsored emigration would suit the antisemites only too well, Jewish aspirations to nobility presented a limited case for integration.[66] And as a laudatory review of "A Crown for Zion" reprinted in *Die Fackel* noted, "The

Israelite Young Aristocracy" (*die israelitische Jung-Aristokratie*) could not help but fare poorly under the fire of the satirist.[67]

Such attacks extended a tradition. As Karlheinz Rossbacher has observed, a stream of criticism, satire, and prejudice that cut across all social and political barriers met newly wealthy Jews in nineteenth-century Vienna, even as poor or ill-fated Jews often found a sympathetic response.[68] Still, Viennese Jews who adopted a visibly "noble" conduct, carriage, and lifestyle emerged with a strikingly high profile. For their critics around 1900, they became a collective target—a "Young Aristocracy." One context in which to see the choice for noble self-styling is the conversion from Judaism to Catholicism that many Jews found it necessary to undergo for careers in the army and bureaucracy. Here, the Jew of aristocratic aspiration might be seen as a particular case. For if conversion implied a problematic relationship to religious ties, elite self-identification implied a sharp break with class ties; if conversion transformed the attachment to the religious community, elite self-identification transformed the connection to the social one.

In practice, of course, these distinctions were often blurred. *Der Weg ins Freie*, the remarkable novel of Arthur Schnitzler published in 1908, for example, unfolds in a milieu of Jewish high-bourgeois elegance in which the desire to assert oneself as an aristocrat clashes tragically with the struggle to remain Jewish in thought and feeling.[69] For although none of the Jewish figures in this book have converted in the form of being baptized as either a Catholic or a Protestant, they do pursue a variety of affiliations with aristocracy. The character most identified with "feudal exertions" is Oskar Ehrenberg, the son of the successful Jewish capitalist Salomon Ehrenberg. Already at the age of fifteen, the younger Ehrenberg had begun to "play the lord," wearing monocle, dinner jacket, and black gloves. Others "play the lord," as well. Leo Golowski becomes involved in a duel over honor in the army, and the "*Künstler*" Willy Eisler has remade himself in the image of a "born cavalier."[70] That aristocratic and Jewish ideals will not be so easily harmonized, however, is dramatically underscored in front of the Michaelerkirche in Vienna. Here, by chance, the elder, Zionist-leaning Ehrenberg observes his son piously raising his hat to the church. Enraged, he confronts him and delivers a sharp, punitive slap to his face. The younger Ehrenberg, who perhaps only greeted two aristocrats emerging from the church, is humiliated. In keeping with his code of honor, the young man of noble ambition shoots himself. The suicide attempt fails, but he is left with the use of only one eye.

The reputation of Theodor Herzl, to be sure, does not lie in his success in the role of "aristocrat." And yet, I have argued here, it is hardly a simple matter to separate Herzl's aristocratic performance from his accomplishments. What the name Herzl represents, quite correctly, is a visionary proposal for a state for Jews outside Europe. Of course, as Herzl acknowledged on the opening page of *Judenstaat*, he had not invented this idea himself.[71] This notion—the return of the Jews to Jerusalem—is as old as the expulsion. The proposal of a Jewish home-land, if bold and creative in itself, is not Herzl's most distinctive accomplishment. To put it in blunt terms, his permanent achievement is to have suggested a behavioral transformation, a restyling, of the Jewish individual. At the turn of the century, Herzl pursued what was a new idea—namely, that Jews could fight back.

The twentieth century has witnessed a dramatic change in the Jewish character, as a new ethos of militant resistance has developed out of the Holocaust. This was the value system and set of emotional responses to antisemitism first codified in modern times by Theodor Herzl. Herzl foresaw changes in Jews that would take place in the Jewish state of the future as changes in behavior, and it is as a maker of new Jewish values that he can be appreciated as a creative shaper of ideology. Much as Herzl had remade himself in the person of an aristocrat, Jews would be remade more "nobly," more "honorably," more "regally" in their future state. "Every great human being," as Herzl once wrote, "will be able to become an aristocrat among us."[72]

The Zionist public recognized the concrete ideal for self-transforma-tion envisioned by their leader, but such recognition did not necessarily entail rhetorical emulation. In the visual and gestural code by which Herzl also conveyed his Zionist ambitions, "impersonation" acquired the force of a political and cultural imperative. In his funeral oration, Adolf Kurrein expressed very well how the conduct and carriage, the manner, etiquette, and lifestyle of the noble Herzl were to be silently reembodied in his followers. "This highly capable, majestic 'I' is no longer among us," he declared, "so we must ourselves become this pow-erful 'I'.... If until now, Dr. Herzl was the Jewish people, so from now on, the Jewish people must be Dr. Herzl."[73]

Both the text of *Der Judenstaat* and, still more, Herzl's diaries repre-sent not only an imaginative program of how to set up a Jewish state—mechanics of property transfer, working conditions, administration, and so forth—but also a clear picture of how people will be expected to act there. Herzl describes the precise way in which the self is to be overcome. To find and apply a mode of behavior that would serve this land is a cen-tral task of his novels and diaries. Indeed, Herzl wrote a virtual *Sit-tenkodex:* "All officials uniformed, smart, upright, but not laughable."

The Jewish state would, however, be a place where stereotypical Jewish traits would be tolerated. As Herzl described it, "The promised land, where we can have our hooked noses or red beards and bowed-legs without being held in contempt."[74] This would be a nation, in other words, where behavior and only behavior would be modified.

In the Jewish state, Jews would be able to retain their physical features, yet they would be compelled to change their manner of self-presentation. Here, it should be evident that although Herzl may have directed his scorn equally toward Jews and antisemites, his critical frame of reference was not primarily linguistic. Thus although Sander Gilman cites Herzl's virulently anti-Jew essay "Mauschel" as evidence for his general thesis that "Herzl uses the image of Jews who speak with an accent as the icon of the 'bad' Jews," it would be a mistake to generalize about Herzl from this example. Rarely did Herzl connect language and character traits or use "mauscheln" as an index of stigmatized features; his concerns were not language-based. The more primary issue of "honor," and with it "nobility" expressed as a bodily projection, is apparent even at the conclusion of the passage Gilman quotes: "In times of antisemitism *Mauschel* shrugs his shoulders. Honor? Who needs it, if business is good?"[75]

In Herzl the self-fashioned presence of an aristocrat was de facto a kind of self-situation as a writer and political leader. That his own bearing, conduct, and manner had always been invested with such significance meant in part that although he respected great thinkers, he found closer affinity with those personalities of history who behaved nobly and honorably in public situations. Moses, Napoleon, and Bismarck were his own models, rather than Mendelssohn, Goethe, or even Heine.

If the land Herzl envisioned was to be outside the continent, much that was European would come with it. Herzl's thinking remained fairly consistent on this: the "Promised Land" would be a place of technological wonder, freedom from labor, and liberal tolerance. This place was, in many respects, the ideal of much of the *fin de siècle*. More than that, it was a continuation of European culture. Viennese cafés were to be transplanted: "Dig up the centers and take them over there. Transplant whole milieus in which the Jews feel comfortable."[76] The breadth of the work indicates not only a diagnosis of the *fin de siècle*, but also a project of what the European state would look like transplanted as an old-new utopia.

It would be, however, a utopia that envisioned the remaking of the Jewish individual as a behavioral imperative of noble honor. This new Jewish honor, the honor of the officer, would proceed through the medium of the duel. Although popular enough at the turn of the century, the duel here cannot be considered an inevitable product of Herzl's "time." Karl Lueger, for example, categorically rejected the "subjective and individualistic behavior" of the duel as "unacceptable for a modern political movement."[77] In fact, the new Jewish state, as Herzl imagined it, would not only make the duel legal—in contrast to Europe, where the duel was illegal—but would also feature a code written partly by Herzl. And the program he envisioned was not simply to "reform" the Jews in a new state, as many commentators have pointed out;[78] it was more. Herzl envisioned the duel as a kind of socializing process.

While working as a correspondent for the *Neue Freie Presse* in France, Herzl once famously claimed that antisemitism could be dealt a severe blow if six Jews would challenge six antisemites to a duel. Such strategizing reflected the Zionism of Herzl, a Zionism less confident in revitalizing the spiritual bases of Judaism than in taking on the antisemites. In Europe, action would lead to respect and self-respect. And yet, the situation Herzl projects in the future state of the Jews is different. This will not be a case of Jews dueling antisemites, but of Jews dueling Jews: a self-conscious toughening, even militarizing. Such behavior did indeed reflect an "honor" worthy of a *fin-de-siècle* aristocrat, but the Jewish man of tomorrow was more than an "aristocrat of the spirit."[79] The aristocratic *habitus* of Herzl, like that of Schaukal and other Viennese, was designed to act with his body, to assert himself, and to fight.

As Herzl saw it, there was indeed a "Jewish" behavior that would have to be restyled in the new Jewish nation. In general, scholars have argued that such an emphasis in Herzl not only demonstrated his own "Jewish self-hatred" but also gave support to antisemites.[80] This point need not be contested here. For what Herzl presented as a response to his critics was his own self, an aristocratic self-styling that predated his Zionism. Finally, although body reform movements around the turn of the century are not my principal interest, it should be recalled that Herzl was not the only one who envisioned individual Jewish self-overcoming through *Haltung*, bearing, and physical presence. These were the objectives of Jewish *Turnvereine* and sport movements, as well. "Our youth," wrote a Jewish student newspaper in 1896,

> have to be able to use their physical strength and to stand their man against the enemy, to possess courage, fearlessness, and practical training in order to wage with honor the fight that has been forced upon them. Therefore, Jewish parents, you must fortify your sons. Devote your special care and attention … to the cultivation of their physical strength and force. Let your sons be cultivated and schooled by capable teachers in gymnastics, fencing, and boxing.[81]

The Idol and the Ideal

In taking the measure of individuals and situations in Vienna, as the keen observer of the Viennese, Heimito von Doderer, knew, those who attend solely to the kinds of things that are "said" will be at a disadvantage. What is required, as his own work attests, is a perceptual apparatus capable of registering the kinds of things that are "done"—the purpose revealed in body hexis, the intention expressed by a demeanor, the ambition disclosed in a posture. Thus the possession of a certain kind of Viennese neck, Doderer noted in *Die Strudlhofstiege*, describes the mind-set of its bearer: "They have something very forceful, these necks whose shaved polish recalls a knee, a knee in its function not unlike a deliberate elbow." True, he conceded, one could guard oneself against such neck-elbows in the moment one recognized them: "Now and then, however, this happens only when they turn their back on one (which they know very well how to do), and only there does one really recognize with whom one is dealing—when one sees their neck: oh, I see, aha." For Doderer, the Viennese character brought together an angle of the body and an aggressive idea. The problem was that one could not see it: "But just in this lies the prank and trick of these neck-types: one sees their true face only when they have turned away, that is, too late, in any case upon first acquaintance much too late. It is already over; they carry their face backward."[82]

In some sense, this essay is an attempt to recognize the backward-turned face of the "aristocrat" around 1900. This self-styled figure, I contend, effortlessly combined good looks, elegance, and refinement with a self-assured posture that expressed the certainty of limitless power, a composure that visibly concealed rage, and an intolerant bearing that suggested aggressivity. Such traits were more than skin-deep; for Herzl and Schaukal, they were what distinguished them to their publics. To trade on manner and style, carriage, appearance, and comportment was self-evident, despite the difficulties and ambivalences that we may now see in them. Of course, Schaukal would never have attended the First Zionist conference in Basel in 1897, but he would have grasped only too well the sources of Herzl's insistence that all delegates dress in white tie, because, as Herzl later explained, "festive clothing makes most people stiff. From this stiffness a respectful tone emerged."[83] Herzl would never have joined Schaukal and his aristocratic circle on a hunting trip, but he surely would have understood the impulse behind Schaukal's claim that "features stamp one. In gesture and display resides the entire man."[84]

At the same time, this essay does not present a 360-degree perspective. What I have argued here is simply that for both Jews and gentiles in *fin-de-siècle* Vienna, elite self-fashioning was not only a significant and visible practice, but a problematic one, as well. By appropriating an aristocratic ethos, Theodor Herzl and Richard von Schaukal invested themselves with a range of possibilities unavailable to them as bourgeois men of their time. For both, it opened a not-so-imaginary realm of unrestricted movement. It implied a sovereignty of will in action, permitted an identification with the ruling elite, and even suggested a place in the world of great men.

And yet, this was not an aristocratizing process that brought either man to "aesthetic culture." The ideal represented by the Austrian aristocrat, as I have argued, is an ambivalent one: for Herzl, as for Schaukal and other Viennese writers, it was not marked by an aesthetic disposition, if by that one means a kind of non-aggressive refinement.[85] Nor did the social codes, conventions, and manners adopted by the self-styled aristocrat suggest either a dematerialized "aristocracy of the spirit" or an innocuous staging of an operetta-like society. An aristocratic ethos remade an individual entirely; once enacted, it surmounted all resistance, no matter the cost. The examples of Herzl and Schaukal should be retained even against the more skeptical accounts concerning the reputation of the (authentic) Viennese nobility. For if, as Ilsa Barea in her history of Vienna recalls, "it was generally held that aristocrats were all but morons," the vigor, resolve, and ferocity of Herzl and Schaukal in pursuing recognition as aristocrats is a salutary corrective.[86]

Despite their common ground, Theodor Herzl and Richard von Schaukal did not share a single model for their self-styled aristocrat. For Schaukal, the aristocrat exemplified the virtues of land, tradition, and rule. These ideals quickly transformed for him into fantasies of greatness, invincibility, and omnipotence. In Schaukal, as the historian and member of parliament Josef Redlich once wrote, the dream of a European warrior was arrested: "Spent last night with Schaukal, who still clings to his fantasy of the Austrian Napoleon hiding in himself and becomes angry when he notices my slight irony."[87] Meanwhile, such identifications were not accessible to the Jewish Herzl. If Schaukal's noble was a cavalier and knight, Herzl's aristocrat aspired to a model of charisma, an idol of the people.[88]

What both Herzl and Schaukal found so attractive in the aristocrat, and what they shared in their appropriation of this figure, was an emphasis on outward appearance, the lure of the heroic, and a self-authorized sanction for aggression. If in the comedy by the young Herzl,

Compagniearbeit (1880), the dramatic climax could be reached in the choice of the protagonist Boll either to marry or to duel (he chooses marriage), by the early 1890s there could no longer be any choice. Jacob Samuel in *Das neue Ghetto* thus emerges in the "new ghetto" of Vienna, but cannot live fully in this "wall-less enclosure" and dies in a duel with an aristocrat.[89] Nineteenth-century stage tradition called for Jewish cowardice and for comic avoidance of the duel.[90] For Herzl, the Jewish individual of the future would be able to answer all such challenges.

To the old joke, "How does someone get worked up Secession-style?" neither Schaukal nor Herzl would have quipped, "By turning green and yellow." Both men had more suitable replies to this question, and they knew how to demonstrate it. Although scholars have been correct to stress the light, fragmented, and neurotic colors of the turn of the century, they have been less persistent in exploring its other shades. Herzl and Schaukal—socialized as aristocrats in temperament and inclination, carriage, comportment, and etiquette—saw red. Stiff-necked and locked in a *fin-de-siècle* noble pose, they anticipated an Austrian posture of the near future, an impatient Austria of superior, elegant, and brutal warriors ready to assert themselves. The self-styled aristocrat of 1900 looked backward toward a glorious imperial past and forward toward 1914.

Notes

A version of this article was originally published in *Austrian History Yearbook*, Vol. 28 (1997): 223–246.

1. Fritz Karpfen, *Literarisches Verbrecheralbum* (Vienna, 1918), 14–15; Johann Sonnleitner, "Eherne Sonette 1914. Richard von Schaukal und der Erste Weltkrieg," in *Österreich und der große Krieg, 1914–1918*, ed. Klaus Amann and Hubert Lengauer (Vienna, 1989), 152–158. In addition to the much discussed work of Havel, see also Karol Wojtyła, *The Collected Plays and Writings on Theater*, trans. Boleslaw Taborski (Berkeley, 1987).
2. Theodor Herzl, *Briefe und Tagebücher*, ed. Alex Bein, Hermann Greive, Moshe Schaerf, and Julius H. Schoeps, 5 vols. (Berlin, 1983), 2:48.
3. Alex Bein, *Theodore Herzl*, trans. Maurice Samuel (Philadelphia, 1941), 335.
4. Stefan Zweig, *The World of Yesterday* (New York, 1943), 106.
5. Richard von Schaukal, "Herkunft und Anfänge. Kennzeichen," in *Beiträge zu einer Selbstdarstellung* (1929; reprint Vienna, 1934), 45.
6. Richard von Schaukal, "Selbstdarstellung," in *Um die Jahrhundertwende* (1928/29; reprint, Munich, 1966), 14–15.
7. Erving Goffman, *The Presentation of Self in Everyday Life* (New York, 1959), 36.

8. See Arno J. Mayer, *The Persistence of the Old Regime* (New York, 1981).

9. Alan Sked, *The Decline and Fall of the Habsburg Empire* (London, 1989), 187. Sked makes the case against the thesis of the decline and "inevitable" fall of the Habsburg order. Despite its well-known weaknesses, he concludes, the empire dissolved because it lost World War I.

10. Frank Trommler, "The Creation of a Culture of *Sachlichkeit*," in *Society, Culture, and the State in Germany, 1870–1930*, ed. Geoff Eley (Ann Arbor, 1996), 465–485; idem, "Sachlichkeit statt Bürgerlichkeit," in *Von der Aufgabe der Freiheit: Politische Verantwortung und bürgerliche Gesellschaft im 19. und 20. Jahrhundert*, ed. Christian Jansen, Lutz Niethammer, and Bernd Weisbrod (Berlin, 1995), 635–646.

11. Alex Bein, *Theodor Herzl* (Vienna, 1934), 81.

12. Schaukal, *Beiträge zu einer Selbstdarstellung*, 18. See also n. 59.

13. Richard Schaukal, *Intérieurs aus dem Leben der Zwanzigjährigen* (Leipzig, 1901), 102.

14. Richard Schaukal, *Vom Geschmack: Zeitgemässe Laienpredigten über das Thema Kultur* (Munich, 1910).

15. Richard Schaukal and Arthur Schnitzler, *Briefwechsel* (1900–1902), ed. Reinhard Urbach, *Modern Austrian Literature* 8, no. 3/4 (1975): 31.

16. Hanns Martin Elster, "Richard Schaukal," *Xenien* 11 (1909): 299.

17. The official proclamation for the ennoblement of Schaukal appeared in *Wiener Zeitung*, 28 May 1918, 1. For Schaukal as the last high civil servant, consult Viktor Suchy, "Die 'österreichische Idee' als konservative Staatsidee bei Hugo von Hofmannsthal, Richard von Schaukal und Anton Wildgans," in *Staat und Gesellschaft in der modernen österreichischen Literatur*, ed. Friedbert Aspetsberger (Vienna, 1977), 29.

18. Karl Kraus, *Die Fackel* 521–530 (1920): 69.

19. "Allerhöchste Entschließung," 18 May 1918 (Priora: 3934/ K.U.M.) Staatsarchiv (Vienna). The case of Schaukal numbered among the 712 elevations in rank performed during the two-year reign of Emperor Karl. For noble promotion during this period, see Peter Wiesflecker, "Nobilitierungen Kaiser Karls I von Österreich. Studien zum österreichischen Adel am Ende der Donaumonarchie" (D.Phil. diss., University of Vienna, 1992).

20. Walter Goldinger, "Geschichte der Organisation des Handelsministeriums," in *100 Jahre im Dienste der Wirtschaft*, ed. Bundesministerium für Handel und Wiederaufbau (Vienna, 1961), 361.

21. Josef Nadler, *Literaturgeschichte Österreichs* (Linz, 1948), 448.

22. Richard Schaukal, *Meine Gärten* (Berlin, 1897), 123: "Above meadows and fog / Breaks sleepily the day. / No welcoming larksong, / Only the clashing of cavalry sabers / And the dragging of tired hooves / On a hard and broken road. / Legs and dreams sluggish … / Out of the distance, a prophecy of doom."

23. Richard Schaukal, "Ausfahrt," in *Das Buch der Tage und Träume*, rev. ed. (1899; Leipzig, 1902), 7: "Farewell, you garden breezes, / suffused with the scent of violet and mild. / Our hair is without fragrance, / we have a sword on our hips: / sound the sword on the shield."

24. Although his sample reaches beyond 1908—the year that brought the Expressionist breakthrough and, for most scholars, the close of the "*fin de siècle*"—Armin A. Wallas responds to some now conventional readings of the garden in "Ort des paradiesischen Lebens und Ort der Verwüstung. Das Bild des Gartens in der österreichischen Literatur der Jahrhundertwende," *Protokolle* 1 (1991): 73–94.

25. Rainer Maria Rilke, review of *Ausgewählte Gedichte*, by Richard Schaukal, *Die Zukunft* 51 (1905): 39–40.

26. Richard Schaukal, *Ausgewählte Gedichte* (Leipzig, 1904), 93: "Mount my horse, test his / stride / along the covered path in the park next to the castle rid- / ing." Some editions of Schaukal's poetry use a dot stop, rather than a comma, to indicate a clausal break. This practice has been reproduced here.

27. Ibid.: "Look, it pays attention / the animal knows that I am talking about it."

28. Ibid.: "Look how proudly and happily it laughs / I rode the horse to much hunting / to many feuds."

29. Jost Hermand, "Gralsmotive um die Jahrhundertwende," in *Von Mainz nach Weimar (1793–1919)* (Stuttgart, 1969), 269–297.

30. For the genesis of this work, see the three versions and documentation collected in Walter Simon, *Rainer Maria Rilke: Die Weise von Liebe und Tod. Texte und Dokumente* (Frankfurt, 1974). On Rilke's noble self-understanding, see Erich Simenauer, *Rainer Maria Rilke: Legende und Mythos* (Frankfurt, 1953), 383–414.

31. For the literary and cultural context of *Der Gral*, see Robert Leroy, "*Der Gral*. Aus den Anfängen einer katholischen Literaturzeitschrift," *Tijdschrift voor Levende Talen/Revue des Langues Vivantes* 25, no. 1 (1979): 29–53.

32. William J. McGrath, *Dionysian Art and Populist Politics in Austria* (New Haven, 1974), 98–99.

33. Bernhard Doppler, "'Ich habe diesen Krieg immer sozusagen als meinen Krieg angesehen.' Der katholische Kulturkritiker Richard von Kralik (1852–1934)," in *Österreich und der große Krieg*, ed. Amann and Lengauer, 97.

34. Schaukal, *Ausgewählte Gedichte*, 40: "Higher workings silently disposed / Enemies frankly shown the colors / Noble goal in the distance. / Hold my eyes and heart open, / Lord, my God, and let me learn / From pain as from pleasure!"

35. Pierre Bourdieu, *The Logic of Practice*, trans. Richard Nice (Cambridge, 1990), 70.

36. See George L. Mosse, *Nationalism and Sexuality: Respectability and Abnormal Sexuality in Modern Europe* (Madison, 1985), and idem, *The Image of Man: The Creation of Modern Masculinity*, Studies in the History of Sexuality Series (New York, 1996).

37. Arnošt Procházka, *Literární siluety a studie* (1905; reprint, Prague, 1912), 93.

38. Richard Schaukal, *Sehnsucht* (Munich, 1900), 17: "Armored I ride from you, locking behind me / the gates, / the morning heralds its red return. / Watches me from its distant gazing gallery, / the first arrows of the sun hit my naked shield."

39. Schaukal, *Ausgewählte Gedichte*, 83: "His helmet bears a smooth edge / his armor is of black steel / his horse has eyes like rubies / his look shot through me like a ray."

40. Ibid., 80: "Oh, if only I were already riding in battle vestments / to win for myself a fair wife."

41. Richard Schaukal, *Leben und Meinungen des Herrn Andreas von Balthesser eines Dandy und Dilettanten* (Munich, 1907), 25, 98.

42. Wilhelm Herzog, review of *Leben und Meinungen des Herrn Andreas von Balthesser*, by Richard Schaukal, *Neue Revue* 1 (1908): 839–844.

43. Felix Poppenberg, review of *Leben und Meinungen des Herrn Andreas von Balthesser*, by Richard Schaukal, *Neue Deutsche Rundschau* 18 (1907): 1015.

44. G. W. F. Hegel, *The Philosophy of Fine Art*, trans. F. P. B. Osmaston, 4 vols. (1920; reprint, New York, 1975), 2:335; emphasis in original.

45. Franz Blei, "Drei Briefe an einen jungen Mann," *Hyperion* 1 (2 vols.) (1907), 2:88.

46. Schaukal, *Leben und Meinungen des Herrn Andreas von Balthesser*, 143.

47. Robert B. Pynsent, *Questions of Identity: Czech and Slovak Ideas of Nationality and Personality* (London, 1994), 108.

48. Blei, "Drei Briefe," 88.

49. Quoted in Andrew Handler, *Dori: The Life and Times of Theodor Herzl in Budapest (1860–1878)* (University, Ala., 1983), 42. For a study of Herzl suggesting that those talks on the street did not last long and that the sexuality of Herzl, in fact, had something in common with that of the woman-hating dandy, see Peter Loewenberg, "Theodor Herzl: Nationalism and Politics," in *Decoding the Past* (New York, 1983), 101–135.

50. Raoul Auernheimer, "Beard of the Prophet," *Herzl Year Book* 6 (1964–65): 76.

51. Leo Goldhammer, "Theodor Herzl and Sigmund Freud," *Theodor Herzl Jahrbuch* (Vienna, 1937), 268. For a more recent perspective, see Avner Falk, "Freud and Herzl," *Midstream* 23, no. 1 (1977): 3–24.

52. Stefan Zweig, "King of the Jews," *Herzl Year Book* 3 (1960): 110.

53. Arnold Zweig, "The Emergence of Theodor Herzl," in *Theodor Herzl: A Memorial*, ed. Meyer W. Weisgal (New York, 1929), 298.

54. See Michael Berkowitz, *Zionist Culture and West European Jewry before the First World War* (Cambridge, 1993), 135.

55. Claudia T. Prestel, "Frauen und die Zionistische Bewegung (1897–1933). Tradition oder Revolution?" *Historische Zeitschrift* 258 (1994): 68.

56. Amos Elon, *Herzl* (New York, 1975); Ernst Pawel, *The Labyrinth of Exile: A Life of Theodor Herzl* (New York, 1989); Desmond Stewart, *Theodor Herzl: Artist and Politician* (New York, 1974).

57. Herzl, *Briefe und Tagebücher*, 1:159.

58. Steven Beller, *Herzl*, Jewish Thinkers Series (New York, 1991), 10. See also 71–74.

59. Steven Beller, *Vienna and the Jews, 1867–1938: A Cultural History* (Cambridge, 1989), 185–186.

60. The reception of Oscar Wilde in Austria is a complex one. For a view of "Wilde's iconographic role among the German-Jewish avant-garde as the essential outsider," read Sander Gilman, "Opera, Homosexuality, and Models of Disease: Richard Strauss's *Salome* in the Context of Images of Disease in the Fin de Siècle," in *Disease and Representation: Images of Illness from Madness to AIDS* (Ithaca 1988), 155–181.

61. On the "neglected facet of the Jewish experience: assimilation with the upper classes, particularly the nobility," see William D. Godsey, Jr., "The Nobility, Jewish Assimilation, and the Austro-Hungarian Foreign Service in the Late Imperial Era," *Austrian History Yearbook* 27 (1996): 155–180.

62. See William O. McCagg, Jr., *Jewish Nobles and Geniuses in Modern Hungary* (Boulder, Colo., 1972).

63. Recent research has credited the significant Jewish engagement in the uprisings of 1848 with the later rapid assimilation of Jews to Viennese modes of behavior; see William O. McCagg, Jr., *A History of Habsburg Jews, 1670–1918* (Bloomington, 1989), 96–97; and Robert Wistrich, *The Jews of Vienna in the Age of Franz Joseph* (Oxford, 1989), 29–37.

64. Jakob Wassermann, *Mein Weg als Deutscher und Jude* (Berlin, 1921), 102–103. The translation is based on that of S. N. Brainin (*My Life as a German and Jew* [New York, 1933], 186–187).

65. Karl Kraus, "Eine Krone für Zion," *Frühe Schriften*, ed. Joh. J. Braakenburg, 2 vols. (Munich, 1979), 2:312.

66. On Kraus's "unconditional belief in assimilation," see Robert Wistrich, "Karl Kraus: Jewish Prophet or Renegade?" *European Judaism* 9, no. 2 (1975): 34. For a recent restatement, see Jacques Le Rider, *Modernity and Crises of Identity: Culture and Society in Fin-de-Siècle Vienna*, trans. Rosemary Morris (Cambridge, 1993), 254.

67. Karl Kraus, *Die Fackel* 1 (1899): 32.

68. Karlheinz Rossbacher, *Literatur und Liberalismus: Zur Kultur der Ringstraßenzeit in Wien* (Vienna, 1992), 135–136, 417–418.

69. On the role of the aristocracy in Schnitzler, see Egon Schwarz, "Arthur Schnitzler und die Aristokratie," in *Arthur Schnitzler in neuer Sicht*, ed. Hartmut Scheible (Munich, 1981), 54–70.

70. Arthur Schnitzler, *Der Weg ins Freie*, vol. 4 of *Das erzählerische Werk* (Frankfurt, 1978), 14–16.

71. Theodor Herzl, *Der Judenstaat: Theodor Herzl oder der Moses des Fin de Siècle*, ed. Klaus Dethloff (Vienna, 1986), 186–259.

72. Herzl, *Briefe und Tagebücher*, 2:225.

73. Adolf Kurrein, *Dr. Herzl's Grab: Nachruf, gehalten von Dr. Ad. Kurrein* (Brünn, 1904?); emphasis in original.

74. Herzl, *Briefe und Tagebücher*, 2:70, 128.

75. Sander Gilman, *Jewish Self-Hatred* (Ithaca, 1986), 239.

76. Herzl, *Briefe und Tagebücher*, 2:77; see also 94.

77. John W. Boyer, *Political Radicalism in Late Imperial Vienna* (Chicago, 1981), 235.

78. Beller, *Herzl*, 36; see also Herzl, *Briefe und Tagebücher*, 2:92.

79. Carl E. Schorske, *Fin-de-Siècle Vienna: Politics and Culture* (New York, 1981), 148.

80. See Gilman, *Jewish Self-Hatred*; see also Ritchie Robertson, "The Problem of 'Jewish Self-Hatred' in Herzl, Kraus and Kafka," *Oxford German Studies* 16 (1985): 86–92.

81. Quoted in Adolf Gaisbauer, *Davidstern und Doppeladler: Zionismus und jüdischer Nationalismus in Österreich 1882–1918* (Vienna, 1988), 424–425.

82. Heimito von Doderer, *Die Strudlhofstiege oder Melzer und die Tiefe der Jahre* (1951; reprint, Vienna, 1993), 260–261: "Sie haben etwas sehr Stoßkräftiges, diese Genicke, sie erinnern durch ihre rasierte Glätte an ein Knie, in der Funktion dem bewußten Ellenbogen nicht unverwandt.… Mitunter geschieht das jedoch erst, wenn sie einem den Rücken drehen (was sie gut können), und da erkennt man's erst recht, mit wem man es zu tun hatte—wenn man das Genick sieht: ach so, aha.… Aber hierin liegt eben der Kniff und Trick jener Genickler: man sieht ihr eigentliches Gesicht erst, wenn sie sich abgewandt haben, also zu spät, jedenfalls beim ersten Zusammentreffen viel zu spät und wenn es schon vorbei ist. Sie tragen ihr Gesicht rückwärts."

83. Herzl, *Briefe und Tagebücher*, 2:539. For a perspective on this episode that emphasizes Herzl's state-building aspirations, see Steven Beller, "Herzl's Tannhäuser: The Redemption of the Artist as Politician," in *Austrians and Jews in the Twentieth Century: From Franz Joseph to Waldheim*, ed. Robert S. Wistrich (New York, 1992), 38–57.

84. Schaukal, *Vom Geschmack*, 171.

85. The relationship between the conceptual pair "aesthetic culture" and "aristocratic culture" is in dire need of mediation and investigation in the work of Carl Schorske. Aristocratic behavior seems to be synonymous with a mostly vague kind of aesthetic refinement, yet, in the case of Schaukal and Herzl here, refinement is precisely a violent response. See Schorske, *Fin-de-Siècle Vienna*.

86. Ilsa Barea, *Vienna* (New York, 1966), 321.

87. Josef Redlich, *Schicksalsjahre Österreichs 1908–1919: Das politische Tagebuch Josef Redlichs*, ed. Fritz Fellner, 2 vols. (Graz, 1953), 2:27.

88. For more on Herzl's understanding of the aristocrat, see the important recent work of Jacques Kornberg, *Theodor Herzl: From Assimilation to Zionism* (Bloomington, 1993).

89. Theodor Herzl, *Das neue Ghetto*, in *Der Judenstaat*, ed. Dethloff, 94–155. See also idem, "Compagniearbeit: Lustspiel in einem Act," *Wallishausser'scher Theater-Katalog* 10 (1880): 26.

90. Mosse, *The Image of Man*, 63.

Chapter 5

MARGINALIZATIONS

Politics and Culture beyond *Fin-de-Siècle Vienna*

Scott Spector

In assessing the legacy of Carl E. Schorske's seminal *Fin-de-Siècle Vienna: Politics and Culture*,[1] we come to the question of whether or not we can speak of a Schorskean "paradigm" of the relation of cultural products and political contexts, and whether that paradigm has become dominant in the historical study of culture. Since Schorske argued that the case of Vienna 1900 was exceptional, rather than exemplary, he seems not to have posited it as a "paradigm" in the narrow sense, and yet his book has without doubt influenced a whole range of culture-historical work beyond the study of turn-of-the-century Vienna. Schorske's argument is an apparently simple one, and it is reasserted in his essays on diverse areas of cultural activity in this period through the use of recurring metaphors. Schorske's famous thesis (modern culture as political surrogate for a marginalized liberal bourgeoisie) is represented through constantly resurfacing dichotomies: liberal political engagement and (vs.) the aesthetic "garden" of modern art; history and (vs.) desire and "the psyche"; politics and (vs.) culture. All of this is well known. If we focus merely on these oppositions, we might identify Schorske's paradigm as what might be called the "aestheticist hypothesis"—the notion that aesthetic modernism emerged in opposition to historical consciousness and to political engagement. Yet, as I hope to show, a reading of essays written in Central Europe at the turn of the century belies such a thesis. But Schorske's essays do not work merely within sets of binary oppositions. There is a third figure running throughout his analyses, and that is the self-conscious figure of the historian himself, aware of the political or ideological work of his own analysis. Taking this third figure into account allows us to see structural similarities between Schorske's histories and the cultural critiques of *fin-de-siècle* essayists such as Broch, Musil, and Lukács, even as they seem on the surface to contradict the aestheticist hypothesis in their hapless insistence on the worldly work of the work of art.

In this essay I want both to assess our necessary debt to Schorske's powerful work and to suggest what lies beyond it. If, at the end of our own century, we want to rethink Schorske's founding project of an interdisciplinary cultural history of Central Europe, we cannot limit this initiative to the obviously important question of extending the *contents* of cultural inquiry (from high culture to popular culture, from the hegemonic nationality to non-German-speaking cultures, from patriarchy to the voices of women). The *formal* question packed up in the image of refuge from the historico-political in the aesthetic garden or the fortress of the psyche may offer most productive access to a reinvigoration of the Schorskean paradigm, instead of merely expanding its scope. For these reasons I want to focus on the rhetorical structure of Schorske's essay collection against that of aesthetic and critical works from the Central European turn of the century, and to offer some ruminations on the essay form itself, in order to open a discussion on the role of the historian or critic in any usable "paradigm" of the relation of politics and culture.[2]

The question at hand is hence two-fold. First of all, what is ideologically at stake in a historiographical construction that identifies Central European modernist aesthetic innovation as an escape from history and politics? Schorske's interdisciplinary project of contextualization (his significant subtitle "Politics and Culture" has become an unshakeable legacy for cultural history) is peculiar insofar as his diagnosis is that culture became increasingly isolated from political life. I have chosen to focus on the rhetorical opposition of "center" and "margin" in this essay because of Schorske's implicit claim that the very class which was central to nineteenth-century Austrian liberalism—the German-speaking bourgeoisie —was "marginalized" by the rise of hostile anti-liberal ideologies (the "culture-makers" were "alienated along with their class in its extrusion from political power"[3]). Further, as I hope to show, this geometry of center and margins was at the heart of the most innovative and potentially explosive play within so-called aestheticist texts around 1900. This brings us to the second half of this two-fold question: how might the "aesthetic moment" of the Central European *fin de siècle* be seen if we wish to go beyond Schorske's diagnosis of a forced retreat into the temple of art, the fortress of the psyche, or the aesthetic garden? To get at both sides of this question—the ideological valence of the aesthetic moment and of its histories—I will focus on literary products, in particular on essays, for several reasons. One of these is that Schorske's great synthetic work, after all, is itself a collection of essays published over two decades.

The privileging of the essay genre in coming to terms with the problem of turn-of-the-century aestheticism was established long before Schorske's work. If we can find early examples of this generic strategy in *fin-de-siècle* authors such as Musil and Broch, the paradigmatic instance—and the place where the function of the essay-critique within aestheticist criticism is worked through—is the brilliant collection of Georg Lukács, *Soul and Forms*.[4] Several positions are taken in that work which may be useful to an understanding of Schorske's essay project: Lukács asserts the essay's fragmentary nature at the same time as he stresses its unique power to fuse the realms of the aesthetic and of life; related to this is the seemingly insoluble tension between the aesthetic moment of the work of art and its historical context; and, finally, he is explicit concerning the autographical quality of this form of criticism, as the "aestheticist crisis" he describes in the essays increasingly approaches a narration of self. Thomas Harrison has borrowed Musil's term "essayism" to explore the "conscious bearing toward experience" that the practice of essay-writing entails, and which is implied in the tension between the essay's positivist concentration on poetic form and its own overtly subjectivist and antigeneric condition.[5] The essay can appear, deceptively, as a descriptive and formalist project, when in fact it performs a dialectic of forms and the release from them. This becomes clearest in Lukács's reflections when he asserts that "the end-point of poetry" defined by the essay "can become a starting-point and a beginning."[6]

It seems to me that Lukács's essays and his thoughts about essays are at the crux of the critical questions about *fin-de-siècle* cultural and political engagement which we are reevaluating here, and so I will return to him at the end of this discussion. But I mention these points now because they begin to suggest why it is that Carl Schorske's essays have had and continue to have such power: why they continue to stand out among the many intensely researched and often highly intelligent works on culture and politics at the century's turn, and also among the inaugural works of German cultural history generally which appeared in North America in the same decades as Schorske's essays. The essay, it seems, encircles and frames the art-work; it disguises itself at least as secondary to its subject, an annotation at the bottom of the page or a comment in the margin. The outline of the material in question is sketched by the formal apparatus of the essay genre. In these senses the essay itself is represented as peripheral, even if, as Lukács claims, it ultimately seeks to create a unity of things inaccessible to the work of art itself.

In his very brief and remarkable introduction to *Fin-de-Siècle Vienna*, Schorske, too, is overtly self-referential in his retrospective representation of the essays. In it, a historical narrative of academic disciplinary cultures spanning the long period of Schorske's career and the development of his project closely parallels and yet more than once touches the transition from High Liberal historicism to fragmentary modernism which is the book's subject. Thus in this narration Schorske turns to the "whirl of innovation" of European high culture, "with each field proclaiming independence of the whole, each part in turn falling into parts," in a period in which the New Critics in literature, the behaviorists in political science, and mathematically oriented theorists in economics were pulling apart a once more-unified academy. In each of these cases, "falling into parts" was synonymous with a loss of a big picture and hence closely identified with ahistorical, intrinsic, and formal—let us say "aestheticist"—critical practices. Each of these ahistorical and anti-contextual scholarly movements is also clearly identified by Schorske as a departure from an earlier connection to liberalism: formalists displaced humanists, political science changed "as the New Deal receded," a "politically neutralizing" strain of economics overran Keynesians.[7]

Thus Schorske confesses an awareness of his own investment in "a multidisciplinary inquiry on a political ground," that the "fertile ground" on which he imagined relatively autonomous cultural products to be also available representations of shared social experience was "suggested to [him] by politics and cultural change in postwar America." In turn, the crisis of Enlightenment felt among the American intelligentsia was not only the result of understandable socio-political causes, but also had intellectual roots in the emergence of cultural modernism in Vienna 1900. The last *fin de siècle* circled around to inform the next. The unabashed self-reflexiveness of Schorske's book suggests a complicated subjectivity that is not consistent with a prosaic reading of the thesis of art as an escape from politics. Michael Steinberg's assessment of the legacy, or lack thereof, of Schorske's essays emphasizes their misappropriation and the emergence of a commodified and aestheticized "Vienna 1900" that is not useable for a critical cultural history of modernity.[8] Another article by Michael Roth has been particularly successful at tracing the ways in which each of Schorske's essays is engaged not merely with describing but with "performing" or "reenacting" the salient tension between modernist and historical consciousness.[9] To be sure, this tension is the explicit theme of Schorske's own most recent volume, a collection of essays representing a balance of work from the present decade and from the period in which he wrote *Fin-de-Siècle Vienna*. In *Thinking with History: Explorations in the Passage to Modernism* he confesses that the essays in this collection had not been written to explicate a theory of history, but may nonetheless manifest history-writing as a cultural practice, and one that is self-referential. The productive conflict between history and aesthetic modernity is the privileged theme of the pieces in this new volume, which themselves, he asserts, embody the same encounter.[10]

The move "beyond *fin-de-siècle* Vienna" was thus already anticipated in Schorske's original texts, again in a way which one could not find in the contemporary culture historical work of liberal cultural historians of his generation such as Peter Gay and George Mosse. Perhaps Schorske's subject matter gave him an unfair advantage in this particular respect. The studies of Claudio Magris and Jacques Le Rider suggest that the "crises" of the Vienna Modern were out of season both for their attachment to a past that the "Habsburg myth" was sustaining artificially, and for their unwitting kinship to hallmarks of the postmodern future in relation to radical refigurations of language, subjectivity, identity, and meaning.[11] In all events, it is undeniable that Schorske's fantasies of "disintegration" more closely resemble postmodern atomization than they do the "ascetic aestheticism" Lukács identified at the century's turn.

At the same time we find in Schorske an almost sentimental preoccupation with the Viennese center, the generation of high liberalism that would come under such attack in the course of his story. Here, too, is the barely disguised nostalgia that, if only the liberals could have had the generosity to appease the growing, sometimes "unreasonable" if not irrational demands of the margins of the Habsburg scene, something, perhaps even everything, could have been spared. The fantasy of the German Liberals to represent class and national interests that did not feel represented by them is thus reiterated, albeit in revised form, in the liberal historical reconstruction of Schorske. Certainly one useful project is to extend the inquiry beyond Schorske's center: to other national cultures, to popular culture, to the other gender and to other sexualities. Such work is important. But interesting as well is the way that a consciousness of the "beyond" was inherent *within aestheticism itself.* That is: even the emblematic artists and works of Vienna 1900 can only be understood historically, as Schorske has shown us, within a particular matrix of politics and culture in Central Europe between liberalism and the competition of post-liberal alternatives.

I would suggest that the idealized aesthetic moment of "Vienna 1900" is best conceived not as a realm unto itself, but rather as a thin ridge, like the ridge of a mountain range, which as soon as it is reached reveals a vast and radically different terrain before it. The ridge metaphor operates temporally ("beyond 1900") as well as geographically ("beyond Vienna"). The ridge of aestheticist culture is crossed as soon as it is reached in the sense that the "retreat into culture" was always already ideological, and instantly began to decay. Consciousness of the "explosive" potential beneath the decorated surface of the aesthetic became increasingly explicit, so that as in a kind of historical retrospect Kokoschka and especially Schiele would show what Klimt's frenetic ornament, like heavy armor, had protected and concealed.

The aestheticist center was the eye of a hurricane which it could not ignore; one step toward the margins, a moment later or a step further, and it would be swept away. It seems to me that the celebrated affinity of the Central European with what Le Rider refers to as the "(post)modern" condition is deeply linked to this consciousness of crisis, or to this strange overlay of centeredness and marginalization. Thus in the cultural circles at home (or "centered") on the margins, for instance among the Czechs, there arose at times a robust modernity which, even where it was marked by self-consciousness and irony, cannot be described in terms of prefiguration of the postmodern in this sense (hence a Janáček but not a Schoenberg, a Hašek but not a Kafka). For similar reasons, it may not be as fruitful to focus on the high aestheticism of Klimt and Hofmannsthal, where these tensions are latent, as on those marginal spheres of German-language Central European thought where the relationship to the center is nonetheless strongly felt.

In what follows I will offer some brief comments on the relationship of the figures of "culture" and "politics" in German-liberal discourse in the late nineteenth century. The profound mutual dependency of these figures as they spilled out into the *Jahrhundertwende* has important implications for Schorske's analysis. Specifically, I would like to return to some primary texts where the problem of politics and culture is directly addressed. In the earliest essay work of Georg Lukács, Franz Kafka, and Franz Werfel, three Jewish writers of the half-generation after that of Klimt and Hofmannsthal and from the two other cultural "centers" of the Habsburg realm, we can begin to trace the struggle between marginality and centeredness and its role in the fate of Schorske's aesthetic moment. An important contribution to this discussion is contained in the essayistic work of Robert Musil, another writer who was preoccupied with the idea of crossings over between marginal and central positions, where we will encounter an important way to read the play of *ideology* in these *fin-de-siècle* transpositions between center and periphery. These disparate points of reference are meant to define a margin of the Central European literary *fin de siècle*, to surround and frame the aesthetic moment in a way that will give it a historical shape.

* * * *

Chronologically, the presumed aestheticist moment "Vienna 1900" straddles two explicitly instrumentalized functions of culture: on the one side, the late nineteenth-century German-liberal enlistment of culture to authorize German hegemony in the multiethnic Habsburg state, and on the other the radical deployments of culture which would develop in Central Europe in the first third of the twentieth century. Already in memories of the *fin de siècle* recorded in Zweig's *The World of Yesterday* and in Kafka's school friend Felix Weltsch's description of "an idyllic time—for the Jews and also for the world in general," where the paterfamilias read at table from the cultural pages without reading the headlines,[12] we cannot help but notice an idealized image of German-Jewish cultural life which stands in marked contrast to historical representations of 1900 as the culmination of two decades of popular and political anti-semitism in Bohemia and the Monarchy in general.[13] Of course, one way to domesticate this inconsistency is within the framework of Schorske's thesis that culture functioned as a retreat from an untenable political world.[14] Yet, such a conclusion would assume that the cultural sphere was at least imagined to be separate from the sphere of political conflict, when in fact, especially in Weltsch's Prague, just the opposite was supposed. In this sense—and not only in this sense—culture in this central-marginal space of the Habsburg realm operated more as it does for Edward Said's British Empire: inseparable from national fantasies, as a combative site of identity construction and defense, and as an instrument of power over those outside of the privileged national/cultural circle.[15] In German-liberal Prague, the mechanisms connecting cultural to political projects were more exposed than they have been elsewhere, which makes it a privileged site in which to study these dynamics.

In the late nineteenth century, German-liberal ideologues such as the Charles University professor Philipp Knoll demonstrated the function of German culture in defending the status of Prague as a German cultural capital as that status was put into question by the advance of

Czech-national municipal and regional policy. Knoll's lectures and scholarly essays on the German art and architecture of the city, on its German historical roots and on the German origins [*sic*] of the Charles University did not fail to make explicit contrasts to the "cultureless" Czech people.[16] This conferment onto German culture of the status of the *unique* authentic Bohemian culture, as opposed to a claim of mere cultural superiority or greater maturity, had an urgent function. The "liberal" component of German liberalism, the commitment to liberal politics, had undermined the "German" component in late nineteenth-century Bohemia. If German hegemony was to be preserved in some form, the discourse which privileged the Germans as the unique Central European *Kulturnation* had to be recovered and reinforced. Further, there was a need to address the conflict between a German claim to power, legitimated by "culture," and the competing Czech claim, legitimated by liberal "politics." The establishment of the primacy of culture, then, became more important than ever. Knoll's account of the history of the Charles University, "the oldest university of Germany,"[17] calls upon the authority of a centuries-old German culture (he calls it, significantly, a longstanding "center" of German culture) to defend itself against "the changing circumstances of political life, and to return to it the peace and quiet which are essential to intellectual production."[18] Thus a familiar discourse setting culture against politics—as well as Schorske's picture of an aestheticized culture's insulation from politics—needs to be seen in a different light in this Habsburg context where "culture" became identified with the centered and stable Germans, in opposition to a capricious parliamentary "politics" identified with insurgent nationalities, such as the Czechs, producing instability from the margins. The protection of culture from politics had, in this case, very particular national (hence political) implications.

This is a single example of a pattern of the political valence of culture in this period which even a cursory study of both German-liberal and Czech-national newspapers and journals would reveal. Such a situation at the turn of the century—where culture was so closely identified with hegemony that the two figures virtually shared a single rhetorical space—taxes the ground of the aestheticist hypothesis. That shrinking ground is oppressed, too, by Bohemian constructs of politics and culture on the other side of the aestheticist ridge. In the expressionist decade, Franz Werfel's work is one place to seek the fate of the relation between Central European politics and culture that had been established in the previous century. If we wanted to look for a bridge from aestheticism to expressionism, the young Werfel's poetry would be a good place to begin. Yet, a clearer view of what the ornament of aestheticism concealed—or of the political program latent in aestheticism—is to be had from a vantage "beyond" the aestheticist ridge, as ornament was violently stripped away. The moment I mean is the outbreak of the First World War, when Werfel turned to the genre of the essay in a gesture which coincided with the turn to the problem of the artist and politics.

In direct opposition to Schorske's diagnosis of the alienated bourgeois artist's aestheticist disengagement, Werfel's essays figure a spiritual revolution against the material order in which the revolutionary vanguard is from the start the artist; the politician-bureaucrat was his arch-enemy. Thus, Werfel's stance in the wartime essays is difficult to locate within the political spectrum historians are comfortable to recognize, although his program was by its own definition political and even radical. His painful negotiation of how he could best engage that program, while still remaining just this side of the battlefront he had inscribed, is a story which is difficult to follow and easy to misread. In "Letter to a Statesman," Werfel spells it out: he attacks the idea of a politicized literature, "the establishment of a purpose for poetry within the State," an *action directe* of art which he judged "all too artificial, all too theoretical.... All poetry represents a transformation: the transformation of reality into truth, of sinfulness into redemption, of the world into ... Paradise.... Oh, how impossible it is for me to express to you clearly how contradictory these terms 'poetry' and 'politics' are for me!"[19] The extraordinarily consistent rhetorical strand which will run throughout his essays up to the fateful moment when he would be forced to "take a side" is the subtle reversal of valences of the art/life binarism. The political vision here, and not the artistic, is the one that seems to him to be "constructed," "theoretical," and above all "abstract." The politician, with his unfathomably abstract conceptions of society, is cripplingly deceived by them. The poet on the other hand is incapable of understanding these abstractions; he cannot see this atmospheric medium which is the foundation of the state, he can only see through it. The politician, then, is the one who conceives and constructs temporal and fictive moments, while the artist, the supreme realist, sees.

The same dichotomy is attacked in Werfel's confrontation with Kurt Hiller over the notion of politicized art called "Activism." Werfel's contempt for what he identifies with contempt as "the *politicization of literature*" comes from his faith in the only true revolutionary work that can be done, that of the spirit and of art. After Werfel's constellation, it is clear that the move toward faith and toward art, away from party politics and social engagement, was a political program. The cohabitation of

these revolutionary goals with an orthodox prohibition against the profanation of worldly "politics" reached a crisis in the 1919 Revolution,
when Werfel tried in vain to reconcile his radical vision of aesthetic politics with the class struggle taking place on the ground. To describe this
failed engagement as "aestheticist," though, would be a grave misreading
of a turn to art and to the spirit that had no other object than to transform the world.

Moving back to the prewar period, and from Werfel to his compatriot
Franz Kafka, we might see where this practice of politics and literature
was already articulated in a de-centering reflection on *language* which
also emanated from the peculiar central-marginal space of German-Jewish Prague. While there is not space to rehearse this complex play in
Kafka texts here, the theoretical work on Kafka by the psychoanalytic
critics Gilles Deleuze and Félix Guattari is too relevant to these questions
to overlook. The crucial feature of the dynamic at work in these readings
is not marginality as such, but rather the more complicated tension
between central and marginal identities, or as Deleuze and Guattari have
formulated it, between major language and minor literature.[20] While
this study appeared in French not long after Schorske's, and was a prime
source in the United States for the discussions on minority culture and
politics in the 1980s, there seems to have been a recent, deliberate turning away from Deleuze and Guattari's focus on literature and politics.
Their text is worth revisiting. A chief issue of contention has been found
in the definition of a minor literature the authors put forth:

> The problem of expression is staked out by Kafka not in an abstract and
> universal fashion but in relation to those literatures that are considered
> minor, for example, the Jewish literature of Warsaw and Prague. A minor lit-
> erature doesn't come from a minor language; it is rather that which a minor-
> ity constructs within a major language. But the first characteristic of minor
> literature in any case is that in it language is affected with a high coefficient
> of deterritorialization.[21]

More than one critic has noted that this definition, on which the thesis of *Kafka* largely depends, is grounded in a casually blatant elision in the
very first sentence.[22] For the "and" between Jewish Warsaw and Jewish
Prague links two utterly oppositional statuses of language. Kafka's five-
page diary essay on "small literatures" as well as his introductory talk on
the Yiddish language focus on the Yiddish spoken by Polish Jews, "minor"
or peripheral in relation to "major" or central languages, such as German.
Like Czech (and Kafka is explicit in this comparison), Yiddish can be
seen as a language centered on the margins in that it is the expression of

a unified *Volk* within the boundaries of an integral and organic territory. The language of Kafka's Jewish Prague, in contrast, is the "major" language German, decentered (or in Deleuze and Guattari's terms "deterritorialized") by the self-consciousness of marginality among its speakers. Yet, a possible justification for this move could be that the conflation of these oppositional statuses of language is already present within Kafka's essayistic fragments on Yiddish—is it centered or marginal, rooted in *terra firma* or an instrument of "deterritorialization"? Deleuze and Guattari argue the latter case, and a close reading of Kafka's speech on Yiddish can only support this position.[23]

Just two months before delivering the address on Yiddish, Kafka wrote the diary entry on the literature of minor peoples in which, as Deleuze and Guattari point out, Kafka makes clear the necessary connection of culture and politics in the "cramped space" of the national canon. Something like a flight into the aesthetic, if it were possible, would require the grand scale of a great literature, or a larger space still. Deleuze and Guattari target this passage as the construction site of a notion of liminal literature, where self-consciousness of liminality paradoxically claims a central place of self-empowerment in terms of political contestation. In his introductory lecture on Yiddish, Kafka openly identifies with the function of language he describes as "Yiddish." The talk deftly establishes an explicit opposition between the place of Yiddish (on the stage) and the placement of the assimilated audience, feeling centered within German language and culture and alien to the Polish Jewish language about to be performed. But this opposition can be further identified on the level of historiography: the "staged" position of the subversive, "minor" language of the Yiddish performer and his German-speaking Jewish double Kafka is in fact the position defended by Deleuze and Guattari; the talk on Yiddish suggests that this role trumps the passive and depoliticized role of the German-Jewish bourgeois audience (the position represented in retrospect by Schorske). One point still, and it is Stanley Corngold's, ought to be addressed: Kafka identified his own art within the context defined by the great *German* writers, especially Goethe. But as we learn from Kafka's later letter about *Mauschel* (the derogatory term for Yiddish-inflected German of one sort or another), this decentering gesture from within the German language is in that lineage—it is the only hope left for a culture that is so centered and stable that it will stagnate: "nothing but ashes that can be stirred up to a semblance of life only by the rummaging of surviving Jewish hands."[24] The universality of the great German literature is not accessible to a culture that could even think of the slogan "l'art pour l'art."

In the foreword to the English edition of Deleuze and Guattari's *Kafka*, Réda Bensmaïa makes clear the importance of their reading to a rethinking of Schorske's thesis:

> The new category of minor literature is also essential because it allows one to dispense with dualisms and rifts—whether linguistic, generic, or even political—that have ultimately constituted a sort of vulgate (a fortress, if you will) that, although not indisputable, has been at least sufficiently restricting to impede access to what has been characterized as Kafka's "epoch."[25]

Bensmaïa lists the 'decentered' figures of Einstein, Berg/Schoenberg/Webern, Robert Wiene/Fritz Lang/Paul Wegener, Freud, and the Prague Circle linguists—a list which pointedly favors the Habsburg cultural realm.

The dualism of center and periphery, the rift between politics and art, the garden-fortress of the aesthetic moment—each of these, we see now, is relentlessly fortified in Schorske's account. While this rhetorical strategy of Schorske's enables the emergence of a breathtaking master narrative, it also "impedes access" to the power of the texts themselves, or even their will to break down these enforced boundaries. Kafka's essays on Yiddish and small literatures offer a structural model quite opposed to fortress-building, aesthetic retreat, and linguistic passivity. The examples of Werfel and Kafka both demonstrate how the Central European *fin-de-siècle* segregation of art from life became the primary instrument of the deconstruction of that very rift: thus a vulgate which seems to be a fortress is in fact the source of an attack on dominant language paradigms, and Werfel's program for art is conflated with the language of revolution. This operation corresponds to Rainer Nägele's observation that "[t]he most powerful and consequential [disciplinary] transgressions and transformations seem to emerge from the most rigorous pursuits within the boundaries of a discipline."[26] For Nägele, it is not for nothing that Saussure's focused gaze on the purest linguistics and De Man's strict concentration on literary analysis produced practices which most forcefully drove through the boundaries of humanistic disciplines. In precisely this manner, the intensification of the category of the aesthetic which Schorske seemed to lament as a retreat would in fact have explosive potential.

* * * *

Schorske's treatment of the psyche as another kind of aesthetic refuge further illustrates the function of the imposition of forms within historiographical writing. Clearly there are available readings of *Die*

Traumdeutung that do not take as their organizing trope the "escape" from reality into dreams, the "counterpolitical ingredient in the origins of psychoanalysis," the "detachment" of psychic phenomena from the moorings of life on the ground.[27] Schorske's chapter on Freud is brilliantly "interdisciplinary" within the context of his book, as it describes Freud's scholarly-literary construction of the psyche in exactly the same terms as the painter Klimt's cultivation of the aesthetic garden. The strangeness of this move resides in the narrative twist that Freud's discovery of the unconscious is itself, according to Schorske, a form of Freudian "repression" of Freud's external political, professional, and personal conditions. It is as if Freud's "discovery of the secret of dreams" must itself become a dream with referents that are opaque until the analytical process is initiated by Schorske. In Dominick LaCapra's terms, Schorske's reading "threatens to present Freud as yet one more frustrated liberal and, in the process, to construe history in terms that eliminate or obscure signs of alternatives to the state of affairs Schorske explicitly deplores."[28] But looking at Freud's texts instead of Schorske's, we must admit that this reading is forced: the *discovery* of the *secret* of dreams (Freud's witty prospect for a future plaque on the Berggasse house) was not a retreat into them, but an uncovering, a disclosure, a bringing-to-the-surface of what had been submerged. In other words, by bringing desire out into the open, Freud obliterated the insulation of the deepest stratum of the private sphere from the public realm of history and politics. One only needs to look at the span of Freud's work—not even to mention the myriad intellectual fields his project laid ground for in the later twentieth century—to see how much more was at stake than the epiphenomena of the psyche.

So here as well we see the pattern at work which I attributed to Rainer Nägele above. While the sort of interdisciplinarity which historicizes Freudian psychoanalysis as a retreat from politics (e.g., Schorske) or one which on the other hand employs a parodically reduced and simplified model of psychoanalysis to diagnose history (e.g., the fiasco of "psycho-history") ironically move toward closure and delimitation, Freud's hyper-intensive focus on the psyche as the locus of meaning-production's moves in the opposite direction, opening an original set of critical criteria, sending "shock-waves through all the humanistic disciplines."[29]

There is nothing devious or irresponsible about a work of history-writing or criticism establishing boundaries such as those we have been discussing—those setting apart the realm of the aesthetic from "life" and those distancing others from the "self." To the contrary, that is what such literature does: it gives form to experience which is formless in and of itself. Another essayist, Robert Musil, names this play of forms "ideology." The imposition of form can be seen as the primary task an essayist (critic, historian) takes on herself, as we see from Lukács's *Soul and Forms*. Musil opens his fragments for an essay on the modern state of ideology entitled "The German as Symptom" with a rebuttal-in-advance to Schorske's counterposed figures of a contextually engaged historicism and a disengaged aestheticism:

> Recall one fact above all: around 1900 (the last spiritual and intellectual movement of great vital force in Germany), people believed in the future. In a social future. In a new art. The *fin de siècle* gave the period a veneer of morbidity and decadence: but both these negative definitions were only contingent expressions for the will to be different, to do things differently from the way people had done them in the past.[30]

The fact "above all" about the moment Schorske would also come to examine (a period summarized parenthetically not with an image of sensual indifference or exhausted decadence but of "great vital force") is not its disengagement from the past but its commitment to future. In two four-word sentence fragments Musil succinctly puts to rest the assumption already in currency forty years before Schorske, that this aesthetic moment wallowed in studied indifference to social reality: belief in "a social future" is reiterated as belief in "a new art." If the surface or "veneer" of the aesthetic could be subject to a superficial diagnosis of degeneration, the inner force of this project was the positive "will to be other and to do other than the man of the past." Thomas Harrison's analysis of "essayism" focuses on *fin-de-siècle* essayists' self-diagnosis of this moment when, in Heidegger's phrase, "prior values are deposed and new values not yet posited," and the status of the essay as "a solution to the absence of a solution."[31] For his own part, Musil is explicit in the opening lines of his important (significantly fragmentary, essayistic, and incomplete) "marginal notes" on this ideological crisis that the will toward the other, or the potentiality of difference, are elements the critic ignores at his or her peril. While a proliferation of contemporary reflections were saturated with a focus on the negativity of surfaces, "our soullessness, mechanization, calculatedness, lack of religion, and so on," these again were misreadings of a historicist break as "decadence," whereas the important critical project would be to recognize the futurity of the moment, or the kernel of radical possibility concealed beneath the surface.

Clearly these provocative thoughts could be brought productively to bear on (or in turn be expounded by) focused readings of Musil's *Young Törless*, where the narrator's hope for an ecstatic and revelatory moment is packed up in the possibility of projection into the consciousness of his feminized and abused classmate, and of the seemingly bizarre dynamics of Ulrich and his feminine double in the third (again, fragmentary and uncompleted) volume of *The Man without Qualities*. Again we are dealing with a peculiar figure of inversion here: an interrupted or not-yet-complete projection into a radical peripheral other constructed by the centered subject. This formal move, like the formal moves of historians and critics as they construct narratives, can be understood within Musil's idiosyncratic definition of ideology, which is deeply relevant to this analysis. Fusing two ends of a familiar gendered spectrum, Musil writes "Ideology is: intellectual ordering of the feelings; an objective connection among them that makes the subjective connection easier." A network of bonds supports the life of the individual, limiting its potential mobility, and therefore sparing it from the paralysis that would ironically be its unbound fate; they give life a shape. Later in this diffuse essay, Musil will develop a stock anti-essentialist position (perhaps even a stock cultural relativism) under the rubric "the theorem of shapelessness." At first we might make little of this attempt properly to assess cultural phenomena as environmentally determined ("a person exists only in forms given to him from the outside ... he pours himself into its mold").[32] But within the context of this unfinished essay, the theorem serves the double function of beginning to outline both the unfinished project of ideological innovation represented by the aesthetic moment and a critical project, also incapable of resolution, to come to terms with that historical moment. This dual openness is represented in the following fragmentary and parenthetical clause in the essay notes:

> (... If it is set in its real significance: What existed around 1900 was not
> ideology, but doubtless the beginning of one; contemporary situation
>   Ideological symptoms)[33]

Musil describes the breakdown of a governing form connecting subject to context and art to life ("No single ideology reigns.... One can call it an inexpressible multiplicity") as a *not-yet-completed transition* between discursive regimes. Thus in the long present embracing both the hopeful aesthetic play around 1900 and the despairing post-war period in which Musil shapes his fragmentary critical notes, this formlessness or openness of form has itself become an ideological regime. It is an ideology which however is not one, a mold which is broken, a form which is amorphous.

* * * *

What are we to make of all of these immensely varied and yet mutually reinforcing crossings-over from the center to the marginal, from subject to critical object, from the condensation of a "pure" aesthetic to its consumption of the world outside the art-work? The Schorskean paradigm identified a particularly salient formal relation of "politics" and "culture" out of which, and at the same time against which, these historical examples and our critical appraisal of them have been operating. In the decades since Schorske, the focal points of cultural history have shifted. There has been an intensification of Schorske's method of attending more closely to readings of cultural products themselves, and there is now a general acceptance and self-consciousness of the complex self-reflexivity of historiographical practice that he laid out so boldly in his introduction. At the same time, the bird's-eye-view grand narratives of cultural histories of Schorske's generation have become refracted in several ways: canons have been challenged not for their specific contents but for their organizational validity, and the activity of the socio-political margins now seems no less important than that of the self-perceived centers of power. Most significantly, though, straightforward readings of the reflection of ideology in culture have been shattered by readings which relentlessly point up the internal tensions and contradictions of ideology and of representation. Clear-cut boundaries between power and resistance, collusion and subversion, or discursive participation and refusal are more likely to be broken down than erected in a contemporary culture-critical treatment of the turn of the century. The remarkable aspect of the essays I have been considering is the degree to which the self-consciousness of these tensions is apparent in them, and the way they are able to instrumentalize the ideologically troubled status of the aesthetic. Their play is temptingly comparable to what Ihab Hassan, writing about the German-Jewish critic Hans Mayer, identifies as "the crux of our postmodernity." By this he means "that fierce dialectic of centers and margins, assimilation and rupture, master codes and idiolects," such as those we have been examining.[34] Yet we could more precisely approach the question of the work performed or potentially performed by self-reflexive works which intensify dialectical oppositions at the same time as they begin to transgress them.

The concept Lukács invokes to encompass this crossing is that of the *gesture*. It is in Lukács's essay on Søren Kierkegaard's broken engagement to Regine Olsen that the (after all, Kierkegaardian) notion of the gesture is defined in *Soul and Forms*.

Perhaps the gesture—to use Kierkegaard's dialectic—is the paradox, the point at which reality and possibility intersect, matter and air, the finite and the infinite, life and form. Or, more accurately still and even closer to Kierkegaard's terminology: the gesture is the leap by which the soul passes from one into the other, the leap by which it leaves the always relative facts of reality to reach the eternal certainty of forms. In a word, the gesture is that unique leap by which the absolute is transformed, in life, into the possible. The gesture is the great paradox of life, for only in its rigid permanence is there room for every evanescent moment of life, and only within it does every such moment become true reality.[35]

This is the gesture, the moment of crossing-over where form touches life, where self is also other. As in Franz Werfel's essays, the force of the argument depends on the assumption of a reversal of valences which is taken for granted: "absolute" and "rigid" is the side of his dichotomy which includes air and the infinite, the realm of the aesthetic and therefore of form. The gesture emanates from this masculine source, and with its rigid determination penetrates the other ("in das andere gelangt") and brings "certainty" to the otherwise "relative" realm of "reality." This thought protects itself from any pedestrian accusation that the writer is removed from what really matters by ascribing relativity to "matter."

The coital metaphor I have just mentioned must be linked to Lukács's choice of this essay to pin down the crucial and elusive notion of the gesture. Mary Gluck has given an absolutely convincing account of Lukács's investment in the essay, mirroring as it does his own pained renunciation of the love of Irma Seidler, to whom the collection is dedicated.[36] The erotics of this structure continue past penetration, as the "rigid permanence" of the gesture makes room for the possible and makes fertile the latent moment within life so that it may come into being as a "true reality." Certainly there is no defense against a feminist critique of this system of terms which genders as feminine the inert and pragmatic realm of daily life, waiting for this masculine gesture to impregnate it with authentic being; nor for the male fantasies of both Kierkegaard and Lukács (we may incidentally add to this list Franz Kafka, among others) that abstinence from the profanation of blissful union with these material partners would bear art. The projection from the masculine center into an image of the feminine may not ultimately do much for the latter. But for the masculine aesthetic subject, the figure outside is the point on which the gesture—the thing that takes the aesthetic beyond Schorske's garden—turns. And so it is in an essay about a relationship with a woman, rather than a literary corpus, that Lukács explains the term which holds the secret to how a turn *toward and at the same time away from* the world ("in einem Hinwenden, in einem Abwenden") is not to be understood as a "retreat."

The sacralization of art theorized and practiced by the Romantics is for Lukács also a fusion of the two realms rather than a retreat into art. Novalis and the Romantics wanted to "create a culture"—a "whole" culture, that is—which was as material as "an inalienable possession," the basis of which would be "an art born of technology and the spirit of matter."[37] The Romantic guild-like workmanship of words (not "a refuge in the past," warns Lukács!) is another instance of this welding of the material with the literary. Novalis's description of poetry as a "mode of action" recalls Werfel's position toward poesy and politics—"The Romantics' art of living was poetry as action; they transformed the deepest and most inward laws of poetic art into imperatives for life." The conception of art as action leads in this essay to the conclusion which says as much of Lukács's position as it does of Novalis's: "This is not art for art's sake, it is pan-poetism."

Poesy was the only possible "center" (Lukács's term) of the Romantics' world. At certain historical moments the radical turn to the aesthetic subject is not a symptom of alienation. The project, he is clear, was not a retreat: "it was not a renunciation of life.... The goal of the Romantics was a world in which men could lead real lives." But the possibility of building a world in which "real life" would be possible depended, they thought, upon the realization of the aesthetic self—the becoming-I (*das Ich-werden*) of the artist, which was being crafted slowly and carefully and was work which was not yet complete, according to Novalis. Thus the becoming-I was a process of turning the self into an aesthetic object; this move was integrally linked to changing the world, even, in a Kierkegaardian leap, to becoming the world. Nothing could be further from the "aestheticism" Lukács was commenting on, under the guise of writing an essay on the turn of the eighteenth century.

> They looked for order, but for an order that comprised everything, an order for the sake of which no renunciation was needed; they tried to embrace the whole world in such a way that out of the union of all dissonances might come a symphony.

The musical metaphor makes it hard to resist comparison to Schorske's Schoenberg. If Schorske sought the relations between dissonances within the art work and in the world outside it, Lukács persistently traces the line crossing over from world to work and back out; indeed, the border between the inside and outside is in question in each of his essays. The liberal view of such works is always linear, if not rectilinear:

as the dichotomy of the garden and the wilderness suggests, the postliberal explosion was for Schorske a turning back from the confident nineteenth century's forward march of reason and civilization. The pre-Marxist but avowed Hegelian Lukács is in contrast always dialectical: the intensification of the aesthetic is always at the same time a move toward possessing or changing the world. His critical text, dancing around the margins of aesthetic moments into which he projects his own aesthetic crisis and that of his time, produces an interlocking dialectic and with it multiple layers of aesthetic—and ideological—possibility.

* * * *

In their own ways, Lukács, Musil, and Schorske have each been highly self-conscious of the project of the essay to impose form on intrinsically formless material (or of the critic's inescapably ideological function). While they each were exceedingly aware of the fragmentary nature of the essay, they had different takes on the question as Lukács formulated it, "is one entitled to publish such works—can a new unity, a book emerge from them?"[38] For, as Lukács goes on to say, a central question is the possibility of such unity. The tension between the essay's project to "endow the work with the force necessary for a conceptual reordering of life"[39] and the impossibility of the closure that the attainment of such a goal would represent is the space in which Lukács's own critical essays on the aesthetic moment will take shape. Musil, too, was fascinated with the essay form as a means of mediation between the precision of the scientific gaze and the sensual moment of the aesthetic object, and aware of the *necessarily* always incomplete status of that mediary project.[40]

Hence the critical gesture toward a fusion which is necessarily impossible corresponds to the move I am identifying among "central" Central Europeans in relation to the margins: a studied fusion and jumbling of terms of relation among aesthetic work, artist/critic, and social place. The "fusion" mentioned above may be easily read as a confusion. If so, it was a self-conscious one which was meant to contain revolutionary force, and which was circumscribed—in the inclusive sense of embrace, rather than the exclusive sense of closing off—by the aesthetic moment.

Notes

This essay is a modified version of Spector, "Beyond the Aesthetic Garden: Politics and Culture on the Margins of *Fin-de-Siècle Vienna*," *Journal of the History of Ideas* 59, no. 4 (October 1998): 691–710.

1. Hereafter *Fin-de-Siècle Vienna* (New York, 1980).
2. A nexus of texts reflecting on the rhetoricity of history and the dialogue between past and present in intellectual history is formed by Schorske's book; Hayden White's roughly contemporary *Metahistory: The Historical Imagination in Nineteenth-Century Europe* (Baltimore, 1973) and then *Tropics of Discourse: Essays in Cultural Criticism* (Baltimore, 1978); and Dominick LaCapra, *Rethinking Intellectual History: Texts, Contexts, Language* (Ithaca, 1983).
3. *Fin-de-Siècle Vienna*, xxvii.
4. Georg von Lukács, *Die Seele und die Formen/Essays* (Berlin, 1911), reprinted as Georg Lukács, *Die Seele und die Formen* (Neuwied and Berlin, 1971), in English as *Soul and Form*, trans. Anna Bostock (London, 1974).
5. Thomas Harrison, *Essayism: Conrad, Musil, and Pirandello* (Baltimore, 1992), 1–18. See also Theodor W. Adorno, "The Essay as Form," trans. Bob Hullot-Kentor and Frederic Will, *New German Critique* 32 (1984): 151–171; John A. McCarthy, *Crossing Boundaries: A Theory and History of Essay Writing in German, 1680–1815* (Philadelphia, 1989); and Réda Bensmaïa, *The Barthes Effect: The Essay as Reflective Text* (Minneapolis, 1987).
6. Lukács, *Soul and Form*, 8, cited in Harrison, *Essayism*, 16.
7. Ibid., see xvii–xxix. In a letter to me, Professor Schorske suggests that the equation of "culture" with "aesthetic culture"—indeed the aestheticist hypothesis we have identified with his book—should have been complicated by a projected second volume of the Vienna project, where the modern Austrian ethicist and rationalist traditions would have been explored. Certainly the book's final essay, "Explosion in the Garden," posits a function of art that points beyond the aestheticist hypothesis. Yet, the paradigm (if it is one) we are discussing emerges from this very dichotomy of aestheticists and ethicists, along with the self-reflexive gestures of the essayist (historian, critic) drawing it.
8. Michael P. Steinberg, "'Fin-de-siècle Vienna' Ten Years Later: 'Viel Traum, Wenig Wirklichkeit,'" *Austrian History Yearbook* 22 (1991): 151–162.
9. Michael S. Roth, "Performing History: Modernist Contextualism in Carl E. Schorske's *Fin-de-Siècle Vienna*," *American Historical Review* 99 (June 1994): 729–745, reprinted in idem, *The Ironist's Cage: Memory, Trauma, and the Construction of History* (New York, 1995), 47–68.
10. Carl E. Schorske, *Thinking with History: Explorations in the Passage to Modernism* (Princeton, 1998), 3–34.
11. See Jacques Le Rider, *Modernity and Crises of Identity: Culture and Society in Fin-de-Siècle Vienna* (New York, 1993), and Claudio Magris, *Il mito absburgico nella letteratura austriaca moderna* (Turin, 1963).
12. Stefan Zweig, *The World of Yesterday* (New York, 1943), and Felix Weltsch, "The Rise and Fall of the Jewish-German Symbiosis: The Case of Franz Kafka," *Leo Baeck Institute Yearbook* 1 (1956): 257.

13. See for example Christoph Stölzl, "Aus dem jüdischen Mittelstand der antisemitischen Epoche 1883–1924," *Kafkas böses Böhmen* (Munich, 1975).

14. *Fin-de-Siècle Vienna*, 304.

15. See Edward Said, *Culture and Imperialism* (New York, 1993), xiii: "culture … comes to be associated, often aggressively, with the nation … this differentiates 'us' from 'them,' almost always with some degree of xenophobia. Culture in this sense is a source of identity, and a rather combative one at that."

16. Philipp Knoll, *Das Deutschthum in Böhmen* (Dresden, 1885), 7–8.

17. Ibid., 8.

18. Philipp Knoll, *Vortrag über die Prager Universitätsfrage* (Vienna, 1881), 16.

19. Franz Werfel, "Brief an einen Staatsmann," *Das Ziel* (1916), 91–98, reprinted in Werfel, ed. Adolf Klarmann, *Zwischen Oben und Unten: Prosa-Tagebücher-Aphorismen-Literarische Nachträge* (Munich, 1975), 210–215.

20. Gilles Deleuze and Félix Guattari, *Kafka: Pour une littérature mineure* (Paris, 1975), trans. Dana Polan, *Kafka: Toward a Minor Literature* [hereafter *Kafka*] (Minneapolis, 1986).

21. Deleuze and Guattari, *Kafka*, 16.

22. First noted by Walter Sokel, "Two Views of 'Minority' Literature: Deleuze, Kafka, and the German-Jewish Enclave of Prague," *Quarterly World Report* 6 (1983): 5–8, more recently by Stanley Corngold, "Kafka and the Dialect of Minor Literature," *College Literature* 21, no. 1 (1994): 89–101. Somehow most intriguing of all is Mark Anderson's description of the elision in *Kafka* as a "flagrant but insightful misreading": Mark Anderson, ed., *Reading Kafka: Prague, Politics, and the* Fin de Siècle (New York, 1989), 11.

23. See Scott Spector, *Prague Territories: National Conflict and Cultural Innovation in Franz Kafka's Fin de Siècle* (Berkeley, 2000), 85–92.

24. Franz Kafka to Max Brod, *Briefe*, 336–338, trans. Richard and Clara Winston in Max Brod, ed., *Letters to Friends, Family, and Editors* (New York, 1977), 286–289.

25. Deleuze and Guattari, *Kafka*, xv.

26. Rainer Nägele, *Theater, Theory, Speculation: Walter Benjamin and the Scenes of Modernity* (Baltimore, 1991), ix.

27. "Politics and Patricide in Freud's *Interpretation of Dreams*," *Fin-de-Siècle Vienna*, 181–207.

28. Dominick LaCapra, *Rethinking Intellectual History*, 96, cf. idem., "Is Everyone a Mentalité Case? Transference and the "Culture" Concept," in *History and Criticism* (Ithaca, 1985), 71–94, and Michael Roth's rebuttal in *The Ironist's Cage*, 62–63.

29. Nägele writing on Saussure, *Theater*, ix–x.

30. Robert Musil, "Der deutsche Mensch als Symptom" [1923], in Robert Musil, ed. Adolf Frisé, *Gesammelte Werke* 8 (Reinbek bei Hamburg, 1978), 1353–1400, see 1353. Translations adapted from Robert Musil, ed., and trans. Burton Pike and David S. Luft, *Precision and Soul* (Chicago, 1990), 150–192.

31. Harrison, *Essayism*, 2.

32. Musil, "Precision and Soul," 165.

33. Ibid., 173.

34. Ihab Hassan, Foreword, in Hans Mayer, *Outsiders: A Study in Life and Letters*, trans. Denis M. Sweet (Cambridge, Mass., 1982), ix.

35. Lukács, *Soul and Form*, 29.

36. Mary Gluck, *Georg Lukács and His Generation 1900–1918* (Cambridge, Mass., 1985), 118–126.

37. Lukács, *Soul and Form*, 42–53.

38. Lukács, *Die Seele und die Formen*, 7.

39. Lukács, *Soul and Form*, 1.

40. Beyond the best-known representation of this aspect of Musil's thought, the figuration of Ulrich as "essayist" in *The Man without Qualities*, see the untitled fragment "Über den Essay," [1914?] in *Gesammelte Werke* 8, 1334–1337.

Chapter 6

FREUD'S "VIENNA MIDDLE"

Alfred Pfabigan

Repression, the Oedipus complex, the Freudian slip—these concepts have become so embedded in the universal language of Western modernity, that it seems as though the immense success of Freud in sheer quantitative terms has bypassed any "resistance" there might be in principle to the psychoanalytic view of the world. The success of Freudian thought, indeed, has not come primarily in the scientific community to which Freud addressed his discoveries, but rather through a popularization process, which has given the Freudian contribution to our culture a multitude of meanings. Everyone has his or her own Freud: "sleek American psychoanalysis,"[1] advertising, journalism and film criticism, the Frankfurt School and other parts of the spectrum between left radicalism and Social Democratic reformism, Parisian existentialism and (post-)structuralism, even the theoreticians of the New Age.

Many have questioned the correctness of Freudian theory; others justifiably point to the tactical skill of Freud as a man with a mission and the way in which the expulsion of his followers mid-century helped to spread the word far and wide. The purpose of this paper, however, is to explore a different aspect, starting from the following observation: a way of thinking, which is able to be claimed by such different thought-systems, and thus gains a mass audience, cannot rely for its power on the "official text," which is a theoretical text far from easily accessible to the general public. There must be a "subtext." This "subtext," which belongs not so much in the field of "history of science" as in that of "history of *mentalité*," is rather more general than the central text of the theory. It is distinctly stamped with the author's personality, but has little to do with the actual achievement of that author; it is sometimes peripheral, yet nevertheless answers central questions of modernity. In this "subtext" there are other discourses which intersect underground, solutions to collective conflict situations are offered here, which satisfy fundamental needs and thus enable the mass-reception of the theory.

The characteristic of the Freudian "subtext" of particular significance here is its author's ability to provide what one might call "mediation" in numerous points of controversy between influential tendencies competing against each other within the modern world. Each of these tendencies was so successful as to be impossible to ignore, yet had any prevailed entirely, modernity would not have been viable. As I hope to show in the following examples, the Freudian "middle" avoids the one-sidedness of certain protagonists of modernity, thus providing that modernity the viability it might otherwise lack. The special formula of this "middle" points to its origin, turn-of-the-century Vienna. The question of "Viennese identity" is perhaps even more entangled than the much-discussed problem of "Austrian identity." "Vienna" is a symbol with an extremely uncertain content. There is room within it for the apparently almost irreconcilable worlds of "Wittgenstein's Vienna" and "Hitler's Vienna," on the one hand for a path to modernity full of contradictions, under conditions of co-existing native and imported backwardnesses, and on the other for a modernization which gradually picked up tempo. "Vienna" was in a way a battleground for various ways of life and thought. Its character has to be sought less in particular traits than in the synthesizing power which this "melting-pot-society" for a while possessed, and to which the Freudian "subtext" made an unintended contribution.

Freud's "more visionary style of practicing science"[2] and the aim of that work, which ultimately was for revolutionary innovation, are closely tied to an essentially universalistic attitude toward posterity. As with several other Viennese innovations, Freud's work aimed from early on at the social whole. "The Claims of Psycho-Analysis to Scientific Interest" already in 1913 posted the claim to be able to throw light on the origins of religion, morality, law and philosophy, and made the explanation of "the whole history of culture" its goal. Therapy, the collective explanation of meaning, and the opportunity for creating a future in the context of psychohygienic ideas for collective prevention are inseparably bound up in this concept. The Austrian version of the second influential attempt at the self-determination of modernity, Marxism, shows the same attitude. At almost exactly the same time as Freud's claim to an explanation of "the whole history of culture," the Austromarxist Max Adler explained to intellectuals the "cultural meaning of socialism" as follows: "The natural scientist, the engineer, the economist, the teacher, the physician, the lawyer, the pastor, the writer, the artist—they all ultimately, once they have begun to wonder about the purpose and effect of their work, arrive at the sort of problems, which only social science can solve theoretically, and for which only socialism has practical answers...."[3]

Freud and his followers have been accused by the American historian of science Frank J. Sulloway, among others,[4] of having created a "legend," even a "myth," around the origins of psychoanalysis and its subsequent development. According to this view, the originality of Freud was exaggerated, as was the resistance, with which he was confronted. In reality, the components of Freudian thought were known, in many instances they were even traditional. Freud's account of the relationship to his predecessors and of where the foundations of his thought are based is indeed often unclear, contradictory, or hard to follow. Freud did indeed occasionally deny an important side of himself as someone who read and inwardly digested a prodigious number of texts. Freud's critics often attempt to catch him out in the question of priority, about which he was so sensitive. It is more productive, though, to see such blind spots in Freud's self-image without malice, as the expression of a conflict situation, which transcends Freud's person—and in our context that means looking for the connection with the "subtext."

Freud's work is covered by a network of allusions and quotations that can be summed up in one word: *Bildung*, the culture of German humanism. *Bildung*, along with navigation of the sea of contradictions in which it found itself during Freud's lifetime, is a central component of the "text" and the "subtext" of psychoanalysis. Psychoanalysis inherited some things from *Bildung*, which were so self-evident to Freud, that he could hardly have said what they were. The *Bildung* which Freud, the star pupil, had acquired in the *Gymnasium* in the Taborstrasse as well as elsewhere, was definitely a major center of an enduring identity crisis, typical for Vienna, which arose from successful assimilation. *Bildung*, a concept, as with the English idea of the "gentleman," embracing one's whole existence, was what was "one's own," what one had acquired oneself and therefore something precious. It also meant the "home" of the cultural heritage and the admission ticket for what Peter Gay has called "the European family of high culture," whose values Freud cherished his whole life.[5]

This is not the place exhaustively to describe the concept of *Bildung* derived from German tradition. The contents of the *Bildung* with which Freud was made familiar at school anticipate in a fragmentary way a multitude of themes that we meet, directly or indirectly, within psychoanalysis. *Bildung* includes within it the Aristotelian concept of catharsis, which not only played a role in numerous approaches to psychiatric therapy at the time, but was also the subject to which the uncle of Freud's wife, Martha Bernays, devoted a study.[6] *Bildung* contains Plato's thoughts on the soul as two horses, only barely controlled by their driver, one a noble and beautiful being, the other a coarse and wild one.[7] It also includes the advice of the oracle of Delphi to know thyself, and the continuance of this thought in the work of Montaigne, Rousseau, and Schopenhauer. Within the purview of *Bildung* can be found the views of Schiller and Börne, which Freud knew, on how to become an original writer by following the free associations of one's mind.[8] Here as well were Lichtenberg's ideas about dreams as instruments of self-knowledge. Goethe, Schiller, Schopenhauer and Nietzsche had already marked the unconscious as a place of creative productivity. Indeed one can in general assume that, in the words of Lancelot Whyte, "the general conception of unconscious mental processes ... was *conceivable*... around 1700, *topical* around 1800, and *fashionable* around 1870–80."[9]

Freud's loyalty to the principle of *Bildung* put him in the middle of a complex web of tensions, and the viability of psychoanalysis is closely linked to his successful navigation of this network. *Bildung*, in its German-European orientation, assumes within itself first of all an element of the ignoring of the specifically Austrian. One of the roots of the still crisis-ridden question of Austrian self-identity stems from the fact that the cultural heritage of the nineteenth century has only a few things in common with Austrian tradition. The assimilant's opting for *Bildung* was effectively also a rejection of the specifically Austrian alternative. In this choice lie the origins of what is, in view of the result, the productive distancing of Freud from the oppressive events of his immediate circumstances: the decline of the Habsburg Monarchy and the perpetual crisis of the First Austrian Republic. Apart from an intense participation in domestic politics in the 1880s and 1890s, Freud rarely refers to Austrian matters. Freud has nothing to do with that particular, Austrian form of narcissism: the attempt to make observations of general validity about modernity based on local, Austrian phenomena, which we see in figures as different as Hermann Bahr and Karl Kraus. Freud talks of "our war loans" for only a short time; the leading figures of the First Republic, Otto Bauer, Engelbert Dollfuss, Johannes Schober and Ignaz Seipel, are hardly noticed.

Similarly, it is due to an aspect of *Bildung*—its Enlightenment orientation—that Freud hardly ever refers to Christian culture and its achievements. The cultural power springing from the Austrian Baroque, which Hermann Bahr among others attempted to revive, was as foreign to Freud as the deep-seated "open ledgers" from the time of the Counter-Reformation, whose continuing influence into the modern era has been so graphically described by Friedrich Heer. [10]

* * * *

The second conflict inherent in Freud's loyalty to *Bildung* arises from the clash with modernity's imperative of innovation. Can *Bildung*, with its allegiance to the Western tradition, serve as a motor of modernity, or is it something to be overcome? Moreover, for what kind of "modernity" is *Bildung* suitable? It is true that, through its adherence to the developmental approach of classical German philosophy, *Bildung* is open to "progress," understood as the achievement of classical values such as reason, freedom, and self-determination. In this view, however, "progress" develops gradually from the given. The champions of a radical modernity, whom we usually label modernists, thought this conception inadequate. In the view of Tommaso Filippo Marinetti and his Futurist followers, technology had taken civilization to a completely new level, where traditional ways of thought no longer worked. The fight against *passatismo* became the central mission of a self-confident modernity. [11]

A milder form of this conflict was also present in Austria. While in Berlin, Hermann Bahr had joined Eugen Wolff's modernist association, *Durch*. [12] Henceforth, Bahr was opposed to the enthusiasm of the nineteenth century for the past: "I am modern. That is why I am quite different from all others.... Modern—that means I hate everything that has been, every paragon, every emulation, and I recognize no other law in art than the commandments of my momentary, artistic sensation." [13] A self-referential modernism more or less presupposes itself into existence. The aesthetician Friedrich Jodl took the opposite position. In his inaugural address, given in the wake of the scandal over Klimt's paintings for the ceiling of the university's *Aula*, Jodl stated that the sole acceptable school for critics and artists alike, was the past. [14]

Freud's life in Vienna inevitably confronted him with the particular character of Viennese modernism. "Antiquity and vagueness" (Hugo von Hofmannsthal) are the watchwords of this epoch. In a small prose piece entitled "Die Moderne," the self-proclaimed prophet of that movement, Hermann Bahr, has a young woman make the following accusation: "You are always talking about it, night and day, but you never explain what it actually is ... the modern."[15] Whether defined or not, we can confirm one thing about Viennese modernism. The conflict there between both sides of modernity—the one side "enlightened," devoted to "Reason" and "Laws," ascetic-functional; the other side "critical of reason," doubting the sense of the social order, gratuitously oppositional, hedonistically aesthetic, ornamental, intoxicating, in a world of signs and symbols far from reality—was particularly pronounced (even when a few figures could be found, in their prophecies of doom and redemption, on both sides of the spectrum).

Adolf Loos, whose thoughts on the necessity of suppressing unbridled sexuality (in the form of ornament) as a precondition of the progress of civilization are not dissimilar to Freud's thinking, appealed in his rejection of function-restricting ornament to the "modern man" with "modern nerves."[16] Yet did Freud similarly ever consciously argue in the name of modernity? His way of life was certainly modern: telephone, automobile, and airplane, these symbols of modern life, were used by him, even with the occasional complaint.[17] Freud's life shows signs of both directions of modernity. Oliver Cromwell was one of the first figures with whom Freud identified, and Jones supports the ascetic image in his description of the Freudian lifestyle.[18] Freud's distancing himself from the confusions of the Austrian domestic scene was framed in objective, practical terms, the abstinence from politics coolly justified by the claim that mass psychoses were impervious to reason.[19] Also in line with the objective approach was the conception of the "disinterested" analyst, devoted only to research and medical assistance, as was the exhortation to the abstinence of the analyst with regard to his patients, and Freud's agreement with his daughter about his care.[20] The lack of sentimentality of Freud's choosing his own point of death, the ascetic decision of the married couple for sexual abstinence, also point in this direction.[21]

The "objective-ascetic" Viennese modernists were, to be sure, either "Americanists," like Adolf Loos, who was known as "the good American," or at least supporters of the dynamic Prussian metropolis when it came to the rivalry between Berlin and Vienna. Freud, on the other hand, was known for his excessive and irrational anti-Americanism, and his favoring Berlin is only occasionally alluded to. Indeed, starting with the furnishings of the apartment at Berggasse 19, which recall Egon Friedell's comment about the typical bourgeois apartments of Vienna, that they were "not living rooms, but rather pawnshops and antique stores,"[22] there were many anachronisms in Freud's lifestyle. Wittels thus described his as an "outdated" existence: the letters to the betrothed, the fervent male friendships, the circle of like-minded in the Wednesday Society, finally the secret committee, all this was seen by Wittels as pointing back to the time of Goethe.

Such "atavisms" were actually not that rare among even the explicit Viennese modernists: Adolf Loos looked to the design and the artisanal tradition of the Biedermeier era. Freud appears here as well to have achieved a productive synthesis between diverging currents. Freud, it is true, did not see his own discoveries as a digest of the time, but rather in terms of his own talent and his dedication to research. His main discoveries relate to a, as it were, "supratemporal" heuristic system—this released him from the need to tie them into "the modern" as such. Freud's intellectual strategy respected influential currents of thought, which, seen in the circumstances of the times, could be adapted, but which, at the same time, due to their inherent exaggeration, were not viable on their own.

His multifaceted work of mediation can be illustrated by the following example. As his use of Oedipus shows, Freud had no wish to give up the power of ancient myth to order existence. The first, private use of the Oedipus myth, the identification with the solver of riddles, remained within the bounds of nineteenth century conventions. The second use, the confirmation of universal oedipal drives, returned to the myth a lost validity, and gave to it a suprahistorical, and thus necessarily also a modern, heuristic relevance. The central idea in the Oedipus complex, what for the time was the scandalous claim that the male child directed his libido toward the mother, was a quite typical "modern provocation." Its provocation value was equal to that of the following passage from Marinetti's *Futurist Manifesto*: "We affirm that the world's magnificence has been enriched by a new beauty: the beauty of speed. A racing car whose hood is adorned by great pipes, like serpents of explosive breath … a roaring car that seems to ride on grapeshot is more beautiful than the *Victory of Samothrace*."[23] The Freudian subtext positions itself here, between the dogmatic and non-viable posturing of a self-referential modernism on the one hand, and a monolithic, traditional attitude, which ignores the modern impulse, on the other. The universality of the oedipal conflict combines, integrates modernity and tradition. The fact, indeed, that we still use the fable of Oedipus today as a means to interpreting existence, is the most significant justification for the claim which *Bildung* makes for the universal heuristic power of antiquity.

The field of *Bildung* intersects with the question of Freud's relation to poetry and poets. While Freud, as we shall see, was most chary in acknowledging the influence of philosophers, he was most generous in doing so when it came to poets and writers: Shakespeare, Lichtenberg, Schiller, Heine, Börne, Dostoyevsky. Each proved for Freud his view that writers are pioneers in the exploration of the psyche.[24] Arthur Schnitzler is presented to us by him as a sort of "double," of whose works he remarked: "I always seem to find behind their poetic sheen the same presuppositions, interests and conclusions as those familiar to me as my own."[25]

Freud's favoring of poetry ignores the immense potential for conflict between psychoanalysis and poetry that is made quite evident in many of the notorious aphorisms of Karl Kraus on psychoanalysis: "After mature consideration of the matter, I would rather find my path back to childhood with Jean Paul than S. Freud."[26] Freud's claiming of Schnitzler for the psychoanalytic world view is in any case hardly justified. Schnitzler attempted to distance himself, as witness his letter to Theodor Reik, responding to the latter's *Arthur Schnitzler as Psychologist*, in which he asserts that "more paths [lead] into the darkness of the soul ... than psychoanalysts can dream of (or interpret)."[27] Schnitzler's characters are akin to neurotics; they struggle with compulsions, phobias and excruciating ambivalence. Yet the law under which they act is not that of neurosis, and the writer hardly provides any causal explanations akin to those of Freud for the pathological behavior he describes. Above all, Schnitzler is not viewing his characters as a doctor. He finds value in the contemplation of what, to the enlightened medical mind, is merely sickness. The vision of the writer, which can find inspiration in a piece of carrion at the side of the road, constitutes in modernity its own relation to the world. Only in extreme cases and with much casuistry can aesthetic life strategies and scientific observation be made compatible. The seductive power of narcissists, the bizarre behavior of hysterics, the noble pallor of melancholy and the scurrility of compulsion-neurosis—all of these Freud carefully catalogued, but he completely ignored their aesthetic value. It is no coincidence that, when he came to catalogue his strategies of life management in the essay "Humor," Freud did not include the aestheticization of life.[28] The difference between their worldviews is made clear by an episode on 27 May 1907, when Fritz Wittels, a disciple of Freud and Kraus, praised in a lecture to the Psychoanalytic Society "the great courtesan," only for Freud to counter icily by calling her a "ragamuffin."[29]

Since "Black Romanticism," at the latest, we are confronted in the media of poetry and painting with a great number of modes of behavior that appear to be hostile to modern civilization. The artist is faced with coming to discursive terms with these modes of behavior—a challenge that many Viennese artists took up gladly. Freud's intellectually profitable readiness to work with such material destroys the self-proclaimed worth of the aesthetic realm, and is, in effect, an expropriation of the artist. Poetry is seen by him in the context of the overpowering drive of the unconscious to articulate itself; behind the many admiring declarations of Freud lurks the occupying and ultimately domesticating gambit of an objective modernity. This is not the enthusiasm of Jean Paul, alluded to by Kraus, for letting oneself be dazzled by the memories of childhood. None of Freud's works concerning literature expresses a readiness to put oneself in the shoes of the writer as he works, and to see literature as literature. Indeed, some of it reads like an anticipation of Soviet literary theory's concept of the "writer as engineer of the soul." However much Freud celebrated poets, when it comes to the question of whether the objective or the aesthetic approach is better at interpreting the psyche, we enter a field of ambivalence and conflict.

The same is true of Freud when it comes to philosophy and natural science. Odo Marquardt—in many ways the opposite of Holt and Sulloway and their idea of the "hidden biological assumptions" of psychoanalysis[30]—has suggested that psychoanalysis does not stand in opposition to (transcendental) philosophy, but rather is a "condition" of philosophy.[31] It is hard to think of any other area where Freud expressed himself as obfuscatingly as he did with regard to his relationship to philosophy. The list of analogies which have been noted between psychoanalysis and various philosophical systems is by now an almost infinite one, especially as regards the pessimistic-realistic thinkers who many view as the godfathers of *Civilization and its Discontents*, and those thinkers such as Nietzsche and Schopenhauer who warn us not to overestimate the conscious and rational element in our decision-making, offering us instead an "unmasking psychology."

When it comes to Schopenhauer and Nietzsche, two thinkers with a defining influence on the spirit of Vienna 1900, it has been much discussed that Freud persistently denied any such influence on himself. In his *Autobiographical Study* Freud discusses how concerned he was to abstain from Nietzsche in particular, for the sake of "keeping my mind unembarrassed": "Nietzsche, another philosopher whose guesses and intuitions often agree in the most astonishing way with the laborious findings of psycho-analysis, was for a long time avoided by me on that very account."[32] Into his old age, Freud denied having had any direct acquaintance with Nietzsche's work before he had formulated his psychoanalytic discoveries. Sometimes this denial was made with extremely abstruse reasoning. In 1931 Freud told Arnold Zweig that in his youth the philosopher had symbolized for him "a nobility to which I could not attain."[33] Only after Nietzsche's death (and after publication of *The Interpretation of Dreams*) does Freud report to his friend Wilhelm Fliess the purchase of a *Collected Works* of Nietzsche, in which he hopes "to find words for much that remains mute in me." Freud claims to be too lazy to read it—"for the time being."[34]

* * * *

The extent to which Freud could be thought to be a "follower" of Nietzsche is indeed very great, even though many of the instances identified by various authors of such indebtedness come from work published in Freud's maturity. For almost all his life, Freud found himself in the midst of Nietzscheans such as Paneth, Adler, Andreas-Salomé, Rank, and Jung. Here too he stands under suspicion of having denied an influence upon him in order to preserve the "legend" of his originality. I suggest that Freud's behavior in this case should be viewed as the result of a conflict whose solution includes important preconditions to the realization of his discoveries. We should also ask ourselves whether Freud's repeated avoidance of philosophy in general did not include a certain element of justified criticism of the same.

We know that Freud burned papers on at least two occasions. The famous letter of 28 April 1885 to his fiancée—"all my thoughts and feelings about the world in general and about myself in particular have been found unworthy of further existence. They will have to be thought all over again, and I certainly had accumulated some scribbling"—bears witness to Freud's pleasure at the cluelessness of future biographers trying to discover the influences to which his thought had been subject: "I am already looking forward to seeing them go astray."[35] At the same time, the burning of his papers brought an end to an active interest in philosophy in the widest sense, which apparently had begun in puberty, and which in his last decades of life was to be taken up once more. It was impossible, however, for Freud completely to destroy the traces of this engagement, and indeed his interest in denying this became ever less over the decades.

The distinctively "philosophical phase" in Freud's development is reckoned at about 15 months, ending in 1876.[36] Freud had already recorded his growing doubts about philosophy in a letter to Silberstein from the summer of 1875, during his formative stay in England.[37] From October of that year we find him working under the Prussian, Protestant, and ascetic Ernst von Brücke, according to Freud the figure with the greatest influence on him. This break does mark a turning away from philosophy, even if the letters to his fiancée often relate the field's attraction for him, and the hope that he will be able, at least in his old age, to return to it. Freud apparently opted, under the influence of the positivist tradition represented by Brücke, for a concept of science that excluded philosophy, and he did not accord it any priority as a theory of science or of knowledge.

The intellectual and, above all, the biographical motives for this decision cannot be exactly reconstructed. Freud was in close contact with Franz Brentano, and it was under his influence that Freud found himself confronted, as we know from his letters to Silberstein, with the question of the existence of God: "I am no longer a materialist, also not yet a theist."[38] His reading of Feuerbach at approximately the same time, a philosopher with an anti-philosophical attitude, helped Freud to overcome this oppressive influence of Brentano, which went against Freud's character, and irritated him. It was much harder to deal with the irritation caused by Nietzsche.

Freud was a member of the Leseverein der deutschen Studenten (German Student Reading Club). Founded in 1871 and dissolved in 1878, this was an organization, which can with full justification be called the primal cell of the student radicalism of the times. Freud was certainly not a prominent member, yet his membership occurred at a very critical time. The economic and moral crisis after the Stock Exchange Crash of 1873, in which the champions of Austrian liberalism, already under threat from the conservative opposition, lost a great deal of their remaining legitimacy through the revelations of rampant corruption in political and economic circles, provoked among the socially conscious students a sense of deep outrage. The Viennese students eagerly seized on Nietzsche's early writings as a means to articulate their feelings intellectually. Nietzsche was the man against whom Franz Brentano gave a lecture in the Leseverein with the title "What sort of philosopher creates epochs, sometimes?" Nietzsche was the recipient of letters, works and admiring addresses from the young Viennese; he was the man whom Freud's friend Josef Paneth visited.[39] He was so central to the interests of the students, that Freud's claims of ignorance about him are simply untenable.

* * * *

The texts of Nietzsche, which so impressed the young Viennese intelligentsia at the time of Freud's participation in their activities, were *The Birth of Tragedy* and, from *Untimely Meditations*, "Schopenhauer as Educator" and "On the Uses of History." Nietzsche's conflict with Wagner also caused a split among their followers in Vienna, and brought to an end the first stage of their mass reception.[40] Nietzsche, the man who diagnosed a cultural crisis, the enemy of the masses, the creator of a new sensibility, the aesthete and psychologist, the critic of an exaggerated reliance on science, the doubter of progress, justice and reason, figures less in this phase as a philologically definable representative of certain ideas, but much more as a symbol for a new style of life, based on social-philosophical principles, and as a symbol for a new approach, which revealed the sham of order, prized the solitude of the thinker, and held out the possibility of the ascent of the individual to a "higher level of existence." His critique of reason and of the sense of a bourgeois way of life (most broadly defined) had a strong influence on the lives of many of his Viennese disciples. Keen to emulate their spiritual leader, whom they associated with the idea of a Bohemian and libertine existence, they led lives of aestheticism, opposition, intoxication and speculation. Victor Adler, for a time one of Freud's heroes, voluntarily ceased to be fit for bourgeois existence during this period. The life of the polymath, Friedrich Eckstein, Emma's brother, can serve us as exemplary of this group, leading from the coffeehouse to Bayreuth, theosophy, vegetarianism, yoga and a host of other irrationalist movements. One of Eckstein's claims was that breathing exercises had led him along mystical paths into hitherto undiscovered recesses of the soul. At the end of the first part of *Civilization and its Discontents*, Freud responded to the career of his friend, in a spirit of friendly mockery, by citing Schiller: "Let him rejoice who breathes up here in the roseate light!"[41]

Even in the years of enthusiasm for Nietzsche as cultural hero, however, the young Freud was not that far gone. In any case, what Nietzsche stood for in the eyes of Freud or his Viennese contemporaries was not unique to them; rather he represents in his double existence, as source of strength and as endangerment of Western culture and politics in the twentieth century, a problem, which, in one form or another, every intellectual has to try to solve—even if not consciously. Freud's intellectual development compresses thus a conceivable and fruitful variant of the intellectual movement of our century into one existence. If we view the achievements of the twentieth century in light of the conflict about Nietzsche, then they are, taken together, as unthinkable without him as "pure Nietzsche" would be. The period when Freud was subjected to this conflict apparently lasted a long time, and the remark cited above, about the attempt to express silent aspects of his own being through Nietzsche, shows that he situated his relationship to this thought in an area where it also took him a long time to gain full control.

* * * *

If, according to the first discourse of Zarathustra, the human being is something that must be overcome, then we can legitimately view Freud's self-analysis as a Nietzschean project. Freud's project, which was to set aside all established values and allow all the repressed and violent drives in oneself to rise up, points to Nietzsche, as do the skeptical generalizations of the result of the self-analysis and numerous other analyses, which, despite all enlightenment, show themselves to have been ruled by self-deception and unconscious lies. Freud's intellectual movement with regard to Nietzsche is thus somewhat different from the picture painted of a crossing over from a philosophy hostile to rationality on the one side to positivism on the other.

Freud tamed the "Nietzschean share" (of himself) by the use of a strict, scientific methodology.[42] The "tamed Nietzscheans," who, despite the irrationalist philosophizing of their youth, engage in scientific and political pursuits, are actually not that rare a phenomenon. Victor Adler, another erstwhile rebel against rationalism and a later practitioner of a Marxism which thought of itself as scientific, also is to be counted among them. Just as Freud, he continued to show signs of his youthful commitments into his maturity. There was much in this attempt at taming which remained unfinished, and, despite his best efforts, Freud, frequently changing the meaning of his fundamental categories, never became the creator of a completely coherent system. In the process of this taming, however, he had put Nietzsche's playful, contradictory, and "dancing" ideas before the screen of a strictly described reality, and given them an element of plausibility that they do not have in their original form. Freud, as it were, took Nietzsche more seriously than Nietzsche had taken himself, in that he subjected the basic theories of the latter's "psychology" to what amounted to experimental research. Much of what the later Nietzsche represented is, admittedly, excluded. Freud was a man of "order," and he could not follow Nietzsche to where he produced "madness." The opposition Freud *versus* Nietzsche is also a conflict between the coherence and arbitrariness of ideas.

The famous "Carmen letter" to his fiancée (August 1883) bears witness to the fact that Freud knew equally well the destructive side to Dionysus and of his own particular vulnerability in this regard, seeing this as proof of his own superiority: "The mob gives vent to its appetites, and we deprive ourselves.... And this habit of constant suppression of natural instincts gives us the quality of refinement.... Why don't we fall in love with a different person every month? Because at each separation a part of our heart would be torn away.... In short, the people like the Asra who could love only once.... The poor are too helpless, too exposed, to behave like us."[43]

The jealous betrothed's comments about the universal key to women's hearts supposedly being possessed by poets show that Freud experienced his turning-away from the aestheticized world of his youth as a loss. His embrace of the strict methodology of the natural sciences gave him security, and enabled him to conduct his self-analysis, in which he used, after a fashion, Nietzsche. After this point Freud was superior to Nietzsche on Nietzsche's own territory, as is shown by his relaxed attitude to his own pathologies and those of others. Nietzsche had also been aware of the narcissistic humiliation that comes from the fact that the Ego is not "lord in his own house." Yet Nietzsche needs to prove this again and again; that the emperor has no clothes is alluded to repeatedly in a garish and coercive manner. Freud, by contrast, is, from the time of his self-analysis, very tactful about this affront to the self's worth. When an eminent judge is convinced that, for the sake of world order, God must regularly have sex with him, Freud does not use this to proclaim triumphantly something about the state of society.

Nevertheless, there remained something, which caused Freud to make the remark about Nietzsche as expressive "for much that remains mute in me."[44] This "silence" clearly is closely related to the "unanalyzed" remainder that Freud himself recognized on various occasions, one instance being the fainting fit in his legendary confrontation with Jung.[45] It is no coincidence that it was Jung who accused Freud of willfully hiding a part of his self in their relationship.[46] Freud did have something to hide from Jung when it came to his relation to Nietzsche, with his critique of rationality, and his imperative of truth at any cost, and what he had to hide went beyond any supposed failure of Freud to admit the German philosopher's influence. Moreover, as Fritz Wittels once expressed in a "shrewd suggestion" (Jones), Freud "was perhaps one of those whose bent towards speculative abstraction is so powerful that he is afraid of being mastered by it."[47] Freud himself speaks of his "phantastic self," and Jones calls it the "daemon of creative speculation."[48] The attraction of the mature Freud to telepathy, as well as speculations about the true identity of Moses and Shakespeare, and, finally, the years-long enthusiasm for the pathological numerologist Wilhelm Fliess, are all "untamed" survivals from the philosophical period of his youth.

All of these necessary "tamings" in the form of "syntheses" point to Freud's Vienna. They are quite a bit stronger than the traditional assumption that Vienna, as a city that was particularly hypocritical in sexual matters, provided Freud with an ideal proving ground for his researches.[49] The coexistence of lechery and hypocrisy, the phenomenon of "bourgeois double standards," was known in other cities as well. What made Vienna stand out was the high niveau of social criticism, the drive for truth, springing from the trauma of the 1873 crisis, which typified the champions of Nietzschean "unmasking psychology." What made the city special was the effort of this group to expose in their published work the contradictions between public and private morality—a collective approach, then, among the intelligentsia, which Freud shared. Added to this, the energy of self-observation, the readiness to take "the path inside," was more marked in Vienna than in other, comparable cities.[50]

In confronting the crisis, a special means of dealing with it had developed among Vienna's intelligentsia, ranging from prophecies of doom to projects of world rebirth. Sometimes we find the same person on both sides of the scale. Victor Adler, for instance, spoke at the Inaugural Congress of the Second International at Paris about the collapse of the capitalist social order "without our having to help out, as it were."[51] At the same time, we find him as the leader of a constructive, cultural-revolutionary movement, spreading the gospel of the "New Man."

Freud helps to mediate also within this spectrum. Both *Civilization and its Discontents* and *The Future of an Illusion* take the ideas of the Viennese prophets of doom as psychological and cultural givens, and reject the idea of the inherent perfectibility of human nature as illusory. They do this, however, without drawing the conclusion of an inevitable catastrophe, a conclusion, which is, for example in the Schreber analysis, clearly interpreted as a projection onto the cosmos of individual problems. What Freud was able to offer was in a certain sense the perspective of "muddling through," where, even in the best—post-analytic—case, neurotic misery is replaced by ordinary unhappiness. In this he shows some affinity to that other Austrian master of compromise, Count Taaffe, with his policy of "well-tempered dissatisfaction," but that is another story.

Notes

1. Russell Jacoby, *The Repression of Psychoanalysis* (New York, 1983), 6.
2. Frank L. Sulloway, *Freud—Biologist of the Mind: Beyond the Psychoanalytic Legend* (Cambridge, Mass., 1992), 86.
3. Max Adler, *Der Sozialismus und die Intellektuellen* (Vienna, 1910), 49.
4. Sulloway, *Biologist*, 86.
5. Peter Gay, *Freud: A Life for Our Time* (London, 1988), 348.
6. Jakob Bernays, *Zwei Abhandlungen über die Aristotelische Theorie des Drama* (Berlin, 1880).
7. Plato, *Phaedrus*, 34/35.
8. Ernest Jones, *The Life and Work of Sigmund Freud* (New York, 1953), vol. 1, 246; vol. 2, 42.
9. Quoted in Sulloway, *Biologist*, 468.
10. Friedrich Heer, *Der Kampf um die österreichische Identität* (Vienna, 1981).
11. Eva Hesse, *Die Achse Avantgarde—Faschismus: Reflexionen über Filipo Tommaso Marinetti und Ezra Pound* (Zürich, 1992), 9.
12. Cf. Comments of Reinhard Farkas, in Hermann Bahr, *Prophet der Moderne: Tagebücher, 1888–1904*, ed. Reinhard Farkas (Vienna, 1987), 12.
13. Ibid., 43.
14. Carl E. Schorske, *Fin-de-Siècle Vienna: Politics and Culture* (London, 1980), 230.
15. Bahr, *Tagebücher*, 41.
16. Alfred Pfabigan, "Urne und Nachttopf," in idem, *Geistesgegenwart: Essays zur österreichischen Moderne* (Vienna, 1991).
17. Jones, vol. 1, 328.
18. Ibid., 152, 179; vol. 2, 407.
19. Jones, vol. 3, 98.
20. Ibid., 96.
21. Gay, *Freud*, 73.
22. Egon Friedell, *Kulturgeschichte der Neuzeit* (Munich, 1979), 1301.
23. In U. Apollonio, ed., *Futurist Manifestos*, trans. R. Brain (New York, 1973), 21.
24. Sigmund Freud, *Der Wahn und die Träume in W. Jensens, "Gradiva,"* (Frankfurt, 1973), 12.
25. "Letter to Arthur Schnitzler," 14 May 1922, in Jones, vol. 3, 443.
26. Karl Kraus, *Nachts* (Vienna, 1924), 76.
27. Theodor Reik, *Arthur Schnitzler als Psycholog*, ed. Bernd Urban (Frankfurt, 1993), 12.
28. Freud listed as methods of avoiding suffering: neurosis, madness, intoxication, solipsism, ecstasy, and humor. Cf. *Der Humor*, in *Studienausgabe*, vol. 4 (Frankfurt, 1970), 279.
29. Edward Timms, ed., *Freud and the Child Woman: The Memoirs of Fritz Wittels* (New Haven, 1995), 62ff.
30. Sulloway, *Biologist*, 120.
31. Odo Marquard, *Schwierigkeiten mit der Geschichtsphilosophie* (Frankfurt, 1973), 87ff.
32. Sigmund Freud, *An Autobiographical Study*, trans. J. Strachey (London, 1935), 110.
33. Jones, vol. 3, 460.
34. Sigmund Freud, *The Complete Letters of Sigmund Freud to Wilhelm Fliess, 1887–1904*, ed. J. M. Masson (Cambridge, Mass., 1985), 398.

35. Sigmund Freud, *The Letters of Sigmund Freud,* ed. Ernst L. Freud, trans. T. and J. Stern (New York, 1975), 141.

36. Cf. Christfried Tögel, *"und gedenke die Wissenschaft auszubeuten." Sigmund Freuds Weg zur Psychoanalyse* (Tübingen, 1989).

37. Cf. Gay, *Freud,* 31.

38. Ibid., 29. Cf. also Patrizia Giampieri, "Freud und die österreichische Philosophie," in Nagl Vetter and Leupold Löwenthal, eds., *Philosophie und Psychoanalyse,* (Frankfurt, 1990), 41–54.

39 William McGrath, *Dionysian Art and Populist Politics in Austria* (New Haven, 1974), 62; Paul-Laurent Assoun, *Freud et Nietzsche* (Paris, 1980).

40. Cf. the autobiography of the "Wagnerian" Friedrich Eckstein, *Alte unnennbare Tage* (Vienna, 1988).

41. Sibylle Mulot-Déri, "Nachwort" to Eckstein, *Alte unnennbare Tage,* 302.

42. A second "taming" of Freud's thought, following Jacoby (see note 1), was the migration of analysis to the United States. On the regular role of anxiety in the decision for methodologically assured research strategies, cf. Georges Devereux, *From Anxiety to Method in the Behavioral Sciences* (The Hague, 1968).

43. Freud, *Letters,* 50–51.

44. Freud, *Complete Letters,* 398.

45. Cf. John Kerr, *A Most Dangerous Method: The Story of Freud, Jung und Sabina Spielrein* (New York, 1993), 429–430.

46. Kerr, *Method,* 266.

47. Jones, vol. 1, 29.

48. Jones, vol. 2, 431.

49. Cf. Gay, *Freud,* 10, 249.

50. Ibid., 129.

51. Quoted in Norbert Leser, *Zwischen Reformismus und Bolschewismus: Der Austromarxismus als politische Theorie und Praxis* (Vienna, 1968), 214.

Chapter 7

POPPER'S COSMOPOLITANISM

Culture Clash and Jewish Identity

Malachi Haim Hacohen

Karl Popper admired one nationalist statesman: the founder of Czechoslovakia, Thomas Masaryk. The Czechoslovak Republic, Popper thought, was exemplary for its humanity, democracy, and industry. But its achievement, he emphasized, had been dearly bought. "The dissolution of the Old Austrian Empire was partly Masaryk's work. [It] proved a disaster for Europe and the world."[1] "The old Austria" represented almost idyllic multiculturalism. It "was a reflection of Europe: it contained almost innumerable linguistic and cultural minorities. Many of these people who found it difficult to eke out an existence in the provinces came to Vienna."[2] This created "a permanent population-blend (*Mischung*)" in the capital.[3] Multicultural urban life promoted critical thinking and "extraordinary cultural and social activity and productivity."[4] This came to an end with World War I, and Masaryk was partially responsible. Not recognizing the incompatibility of his humanist and nationalist beliefs, he adhered to the "dreadful heresies" of national self-determination and "the national state," and led a pack of nationalist leaders, urging that Austria "be dismembered." It was. "The instability that followed this dissolution was largely responsible for the rise of Nazism." It made it possible for Hitler to "appear in the role of [a national] liberator," dismember Czechoslovakia, and create a German-dominated Europe.[5] The golem of nationalism rose against its creator, destroying Masaryk's work.

Popper held nationalism responsible for destroying the blissful world of his youth. The "currents [of immigrants] that flew from Czechia, Hungary and Germany to Vienna" included his own family.[6] "The shattering of dogmatic thinking, often a result of culture clash, especially in an expansive multinational empire,"[7] was most apparent in the Viennese Jewish intelligentsia. Within a generation, his father made a transition from a provincial ghetto to German urban culture, and in 1900 he renounced Judaism altogether. Such radical transformation of identity was a prime example of culture clash's effect. But clashes did not always have a desirable outcome. Acculturated Jews generally failed to gain acceptance as German Austrians, and antisemitism eventually pushed Popper himself into exile. He spoke little of the Jewish predicament, but the dilemmas of Jewish identity and assimilation informed his cosmopolitanism and shaped his political philosophy. He rejected all nationalism, German and Jewish alike. The Open Society offered a radical cosmopolitan alternative to Central European nationalism.

This essay explores the intimate relationship between Popper's cosmopolitanism and the dilemmas of ethnic identity among assimilated Viennese Jewish intellectuals. Exploring reality and dreams in Jewish assimilation and Viennese cosmopolitanism, I trace the formation of Popper's cosmopolitan ideas. My effort to restore his philosophy to its Viennese origins reflects more than historical interest. I seek to illuminate his cosmopolitanism in a manner that will posit it as an effective response to the poststructuralist critique of liberalism.

The Open Society established Popper as a foremost proponent of liberal cosmopolitanism. Recently, this cosmopolitanism has come under attack. Postmodern critics have directed their fire at Kant, the thinker who most inspired Popper. "After many revolutionary transformations," conjectured Kant, "nature's supreme aim, a universal cosmopolitan state-of-affairs [*Zustand*] ... will at last be realized."[8] His universal history assumed the convergence of separate national histories into a grand narrative issuing in a world federation, guaranteeing rights to all members—individuals and states alike. This vision has become the prime site for the postmodern critique of "modernity."[9] To critics, Kant's universalism prescribed suppression of particularity. Constructing the "individual" in the image of the male philosopher and the cosmopolitan state as a federation of republics, Kant's universal history enforced uniformity, excluding individuals and states not conforming to rational citizenship.

The enlightenment's emancipatory vision of unitary humanity, which the majority of German Jews, the European Jewish intelligentsia and Karl Popper enthusiastically adopted, appears to contemporary critics as pseudo-universal. They confront liberal pseudo-cosmopolitanism with true cosmopolitanism, founded in the unconditional postmodern acceptance of diversity.[10]

My discussion of Popper and Jewish cosmopolitanism suggests that the flight from enlightenment cosmopolitanism may be premature. To be sure, Popper's dilemmas of Jewish identity manifest tensions between particularity and universality. But, viewed from the perspective of Popper's cosmopolitanism, Kant's major problem seems to be not so much disingenuous universalism as a failure to negotiate between cosmopolitan and particular identities. Neither Kant nor Popper assumed that cultural differences would disappear from the cosmopolitan state, but they did not explain how universal and particular identities will co-exist. The gap left between the two resulted in an abstract and utopian cosmopolitan identity. The failure was due partly to their relegation of the particular to the non-essential, but, more importantly, to the resistance Central Europe offered to cosmopolitanism. The triumph of ethnonationalism, not disingenuous universalism, undid the promise of liberal cosmopolitanism.

I

Central European expatriates of Jewish origins have long imagined the late empire as a cosmopolitan golden age. Exiles who had been brought up in affluent bourgeois families in *fin-de-siècle* metropolitan centers recalled a thriving cosmopolitan culture. Stefan Zweig recounted their loss in *The World of Yesterday*.[11] Others who had grown up in the eastern provinces were nostalgic about vanished multiculturalism. Joseph Roth's *The Radetzky March* expressed their yearnings.[12] All wrote under the impression of the triumph of ethnonationalism and the collapse of Central Europe. They set forth two models of Austrian cosmopolitanism. The first emphasized the enlightenment heritage, universal humanity, and internationalism. The second stressed the imperial idea of supranational unity in multinational diversity. Both recognized that the Habsburg Empire advanced cosmopolitanism by mediating between universal humanity and cultural particularity.

The exiles' longing for the golden age conflicted with equally powerful testimonies to vicious ethnonational strife under the Habsburgs. In his diaries and correspondence, Franz Kafka frequently despaired at the political and cultural struggles among Czechs, Germans, and Jews in Prague. They created, he thought, an impossible situation for Jewish writers, caught in between. Czech Jews writing in German gained acceptance neither among Czechs nor among Germans. They often had an ambivalent relationship to the Jewish community.

> Most [Jewish writers] who began writing in German wanted to distance themselves from Jewishness ... but their hind legs were still stuck to their father's Jewishness and their forelegs found no new ground. Despair over [the situation] was their inspiration.... That in which their despair found an outlet could not be German literature, [although] outwardly it seemed to be. They existed among ... linguistic impossibilities.[13]

No national literary tradition left room for them. Their ethnocultural marginality gave rise to their cross-cultural endeavors, but also set the limits of their audience. The secret of late Habsburg cosmopolitanism was precisely its marginality.

Multinational networks of intellectual exchange gave tangible evidence to Central European cosmopolitanism during *fin-de-siècle* and interwar years. The Vienna Circle, for example, developed, during the interwar period, an organizational network in Central Europe's urban centers: Vienna, Berlin, Prague, Warsaw, Budapest, Lwów, Bratislava. The circle sought to apply recent advances in logic, mathematics and scientific theory to philosophy. Networks such as the Circle's, however, remained thin and fragile. Triumphant nationalism and ethnopolitics limited their influence everywhere. Pre–World War I ethnic minorities, turned interwar national majorities, sought to eliminate any transnational influence and construct an authentic indigenous culture. The networks' members were preponderantly of Jewish origins, everywhere suspect to the ethnic majority. German was their *lingua franca,* and they critically appropriated German cultural traditions. This limited their appeal to non-German intelligentsia, while making them anathema to German nationalists. When Moritz Schlick, the Vienna Circle's head, was murdered by a deranged student in 1936, a Viennese paper described him as representative of an alien Jewish philosophy.[14] (Schlick was Prussian, not Jewish, and a German patriot at that.) The legacy of the multinational networks was formidable. Many of their members emigrated West in the 1930s, and reshaped entire disciplines in Western academies. But, precisely on account of their supranationalism, they remained marginal in Central Europe.

Pronounced cosmopolitanism was rare in Central Europe. It echoed resoundingly among liberal Jews, but they too remained German nationalists. For Adolf Jellinek, Viennese chief rabbi, 1865–1891, Jews superseded national existence. Becoming exemplary citizens in their respective countries, they testified to cosmopolitanism's viability. But, in Austria, "exemplary citizenship" meant devotion to the ideas of enlightenment, emancipation, *Bildung* (culture), and German nationality all at the same time.[15] Liberal Jews were German cultural chauvinists. Opting for integration, and often making a rapid transition from traditional small-town Jewish life to German-speaking urban intelligentsia, liberal Jews could not understand the discrepancy between their dreams and those of other nationalities. Why would Czechs not be content with integration into German culture? They envisioned a civilizing mission for the Habsburg Empire: German culture overcame "regressive half-Asian cultures," both traditional-Jewish and Slavic ones. Confounding enlightenment and German culture, cosmopolitanism and nationality, liberal Jews espoused enlightenment universalism, but rejected multinational diversity.

Not all Jews concurred with the liberals. The ambiguity of Austrian nationality gave different Jewish communities broad space for negotiating Jewish and national identity. The Austrian imperial idea emphasized the blessings of imperial rule in a multinational empire. It offered dynastic patriotism whose underlying rationale was not ethnonational, but multinational, making Jewish participation unproblematic. Jews became the only ethnic group to adopt enthusiastically the Austrian imperial idea. Still, the politics of Jewish identity remained contentious. Traditional "Eastern" Jews regarded themselves as a separate people, united by observance of Jewish law, religious tradition, language (Yiddish) and common ancestry. They rejected acculturation on ideological grounds, but manifested various degrees of it in practice. In contrast, modern "Western" Jews—a majority in Vienna and the Czech crownlands—openly debated strategies for acculturation and national integration. Their leaders insisted that, in so far as Jews constituted a people, they were united by religion alone. They denied that Jews were a nation (*Volksstamm* or *Nationalität*). They read the German enlightenment into Judaism and spoke of Jews' universal mission: spreading monotheism, the golden rule, egalitarian citizenship and cosmopolitanism. Orthodox Jews charged that liberal acculturation meant assimilation; liberals urged the orthodox to relinquish ghettoized Judaism. All negotiated Jewish identity across cultures.

The liberal Jewish synthesis of cosmopolitanism and German nationalism came into a crisis with the emergence of pan-German antisemitism in the 1880s. As long as German nationality was defined culturally, liberal Jews could regard themselves as its messengers to the Eastern Jews and Slavs. Once it became racially defined, they faced exclusion from the nation. Liberals argued passionately that those advancing racial, as opposed to cultural, definitions of nationality would destroy the German cause: true German nationalism was enlightenment cosmopolitanism.[16] But most German Austrians opted instead for an exclusivist ethnonationalism. To worsen the liberal predicament, a growing vocal minority of Zionists and Diaspora-Nationalists responded to antisemitism by claiming that Jews were a nation like any other. Zionists strove to rebuild the Jewish community in Palestine; the Diaspora-Nationalists wished to guarantee cultural autonomy in Europe. Both orthodox and liberal Jews fought the nationalists, the former on account of their secularism, the latter their nationalism. Liberals were anxious lest the nationalists vindicate the antisemites' exclusionary platform, putting Jewish integration in jeopardy, but they could not be Germans in an age of ethnonationalism and had nowhere to turn politically. German cosmopolitanism represented the aspirations of ethnopolitics' prospective losers.

Popper's response to the predicament was to reject both German and Jewish nationalism in favor of uncompromising cosmopolitanism. This may have been the only logical answer, but it was an extremely rare one. It required one to give up both Jewish and German identity. Few intellectuals were willing to go this far. Popper's radicalism left him a permanent exile, a citizen only in a utopian Open Society. Central European intellectual networks may have given glimpses of such a cosmopolitan republic. But, in *fin-de-siècle* and interwar Central Europe, the conscious pursuit of cross-cultural exchange was limited by class, education, language, and ethnic origins to the Jewish intelligentsia. The supranational character of Habsburg Jewry and Jewish intellectuals' ethnic marginality gave rise to cosmopolitan visions that promised Jewish integration, and to cross-cultural efforts to realize them. They were noble, but failed miserably—everywhere. Neither in theory nor in practice was Central Europe ever cosmopolitan.

II

Karl Raimund Popper was born on 28 July 1902 in Vienna. He was a first-generation Viennese. His father, Simon Carl Siegmund (1856–1932), came from Bohemia, and his maternal grandparents from Silesia and Hungary. The abolition of imperial residence restrictions in 1848 resulted in massive migration of Czech and Hungarian Jews to the capital in the following decades.[17] Simon Popper's rise to the bourgeoisie reflected the remarkable success of many of them. Having earned a law degree, he became the legal partner of Vienna's last liberal mayor, Raimund Grübl. He married "up." Popper's mother, Jenny Schiff (1864–1938), was daughter to a family of the Viennese high bourgeoisie. In 1896 Simon Popper took over the legal firm and the family moved into a huge apartment with adjoining offices, across from St. Stephen's Cathedral at the city's center. The family embodied the ideals of property, law, and culture that were held in the highest esteem by Viennese liberals.[18]

In 1900 Simon and Jenny Popper renounced their membership in the Jewish community and converted to Lutheranism. (Their two daughters, Dora [1893–1932] and Annie [1898–1975], perfunctorily became Protestant, too.) Vienna was overwhelmingly Catholic, but Simon Popper, master of the leading masonic lodge *Humanität,* shared the anti-clericalism of Viennese progressives. He preferred Protestantism, the German enlightenment's religion. He was not alone. Vienna had the highest conversion rate of any European urban center, and Lutheranism was the religion of choice for upper-class Jewish converts. Assimilated Jews remained, however, a small minority. Jewish acculturation to German culture rarely led to assimilation. Both the Popper and Schiff grandparents remained Jewish, and the larger Popper family, apparently not quite as upwardly mobile as the Schiffs, seems also to have remained Jewish. In contrast, two or three of the Schiffs' children converted to Lutheranism. Religious affiliation seems to have made no difference in family relations, at least not among the Schiffs. All seemed to partake in family vacations, social events and the like.[19]

Simon Popper had close non-Jewish friends, but the family's social circle remained primarily Jewish. Assimilated and non-assimilated upper-class Jews belonged to the same social networks. Neither acculturation nor religious conversion overcame the barriers of ethnicity. Intermarriages were actually less common in Vienna than in other European cities.[20] The assimilated Jewish intelligentsia managed to construct bridges to progressive secular Austrians opposed to antisemitism. Together they formed the utopian visions of a secular commonwealth that became the mark of *fin-de-siècle* Viennese progressivism. In such a state, free of religious superstition and ethnic prejudice, the assimilated Jewish intelligentsia would finally find their home: no one would probe their ethnic origins, or challenge their claims to be German. But reality defied utopia. Secular progressive Germans were marginal to their ethnic group. The Poppers spent much of their life in company with other Jews.

The educational patterns of Viennese Jews militated against assimilation. Jews constituted about 9 percent of Vienna's population, but a quarter to a third of *gymnasia* and university students. (This may explain their preponderance in *fin-de-siècle* culture.)[21] Since Jews concentrated in three districts (the first, second, and ninth), Jewish students often constituted a majority in their schools. *Lycée*-educated Jewish girls, like Dora Popper, comprised almost half of Viennese *lycée* students, over two-thirds in progressive ones. From 1908 to 1912, Karl Popper went to the *Freie Schule,* a private school established in 1905 by progressives and socialists to provide an education free from clerical influence. Jewish children were probably a plurality. Almost half of the students in the three *gymnasia* he attended between 1912 and 1918 were Jewish. Scattered information about his companions from kindergarten to university suggests that he had non-Jewish friends—some, like Konrad Lorenz, life-long—but a majority were of Jewish origins. There was nothing Jewish about Karl's and Dora's education: it was progressive German education in the *Freie Schule* and *lycée;* and classical German, with a scientific bent, in the *Realgymnasium.* But "a certain separation of Gentiles and Jews into groups," recalled Arthur Schnitzler, "could be felt always and everywhere, also therefore in school."[22] Contrary to their aspirations, neither assimilated nor acculturated Viennese Jews became German Austrians. Much like their predecessors in nineteenth-century Germany, they constituted a German-Jewish community of their own, united by ethnic origins, social class, German education, the enlightenment's ethos, liberal politics and, of course, the antisemites' malice.[23]

Throughout his youth, Popper was surrounded by progressive intellectuals. They rebelled against the social conservatism of mainstream liberalism, and sought a dialogue with socialists. They organized a political party, the Sozialpolitische Partei, but it ran against the twin obstacles of Catholicism and antisemitism, and remained small. They increasingly channeled their efforts to a large network of associations for educational reform, social welfare, and economic planning.[24] One was the Monists, founded by Ernst Mach's disciples in 1911, dedicated to the "scientific" reform of philosophy, education, and law. Virtually all Viennese reformers belonged.[25] Arthur Arndt, a socialist family friend and the young Popper's personal guide, took him to the Monists' meetings.[26] Militantly secular, politically radical, trusting in social reform, popular education, and technological progress, this was the young Popper's social and intellectual milieu. It reflected, to use Friedrich Stadler's term, the late-enlightenment spirit (*Spätaufklärung*).[27]

Ethnonationalism was *Spätaufklärung's* greatest enemy, but the progressives underestimated its danger and responded ambivalently to it. Their ranks included pacifists and federalists, but also German nationalists. They fought antisemitism that offended their humanity and excluded their Jewish members from the nation, but they could see no harm in the expansion of the German cultural sphere in Central Europe. They regarded Slavic nationalism as reactionary. Ethnopolitics was, they thought, a passing frenzy. In contrast to the socialists, whose party structure forced recognition of multinationalism, the progressives drew no plan for imperial reform. They were content to "think of themselves as guardians of liberal values and as the intellectual elite of a huge state whose composition gave it the appearance of the international order of humankind in miniature."[28]

Both socialists and progressives denied that Jews were a nationality. In *Die Nationalitätenfrage und die Sozialdemokratie*, Bauer rejected the claims of Galician Jewish socialists for Jewish autonomy. Jews should, and will, assimilate to the majority nationality wherever they live.[29] Similarly, when a 1905 electoral reform in Bukovina, the center of Jewish Diaspora-Nationalism, established a Jewish curia, progressive Viennese Jews led the charge against the "electoral ghetto" (*Wahl-Ghetto*).[30] They felt that their own German identity was at issue. Striving for recognition as German Austrians, they sought to strip religion and ethnicity of significance—their own first and foremost. Their non-Jewish colleagues were happy to oblige. German nationality was a matter of culture, not race. The progressive intelligentsia represented a class that, to overcome the burden of its own ethnicity, needed to dissolve all ethnicity and recover universal humanity—Marx's universal class.[31]

The progressives' denial of ethnonationalism flew in the face of historical reality. Progressive culture remained marginal. It conflicted with the religious beliefs, nationalist values, and ethnic identity of most Germans. There was nothing essentially Jewish about it, and progressive Germans recognized it as their own. Almost every progressive circle had both Jewish and non-Jewish members. But there were relatively few progressive German Austrians, and the marginality of progressive culture cannot be over-emphasized. It made few inroads into the court, the civil service, and aristocratic circles. Class and education limited it to the intelligentsia. Even in the academy, where Jews were heavily represented, progressivism represented a minority. Virulent German nationalism dominated much of the student body, and conservative Catholic and nationalist traditions prevailed in the humanities and social sciences. Through their organizational network, the liberal professions and

Vienna's salons and coffee houses, the progressives contributed to Vienna 1900's legendary cultural intensity. But they remained a narrow segment of the German intelligentsia allied with a sub-group of an ethnic minority who posed for a short time as a social and cultural elite: Vienna's "non-Jewish Jews."

Popper would spend much of his life refashioning progressive philosophy and politics. He freed progressivism from ambivalence about nationalism. Regarding the dissolution of the Habsburg Empire as an unmitigated disaster and holding nationalism, especially German nationalism, responsible, he rejected German nationality and dissociated the enlightenment from Germany. He made good on enlightenment cosmopolitanism, but inherited also its dilemmas. He was just as impatient as the progressives with multicultural diversity. As an anti-nationalist, he defended it in the strongest terms, but its major benefit was that it created a culture clash that could open closed communities. He thought it a major advantage that immigrants to Vienna "had to learn German," thereby opening themselves to a new cultural tradition. But, precisely as Czech immigrants protested, German schools meant German hegemony and Czech assimilation. Popper would not budge. Discounting all national, ethnic, and religious identity as culturally primitive and politically reactionary, he posited a universalistic vision of the Open Society where none of them counted. His relentless hostility toward Zionism, his rejection of any and all religion (Judaism even more than Christianity), his passionate defense of liberalism and the enlightenment were a metamorphosis of Viennese progressivism. He remained an assimilated progressive Jew to the end of his life. Through his migration and exile, progressive philosophy, a product of marginal Viennese milieux, made cosmopolitan dreams and dilemmas part of mainstream Western culture.

III

"The breakdown of the Austrian Empire and the aftermath of the First World War ... destroyed the world in which I had grown up," wrote Popper in his autobiography, *Unended Quest*.[32] In the immediate post-war years, he experienced revolution, mass hunger, and cold. The runaway inflation almost reduced his family to poverty. His sheltered life as an upper-middle-class boy had come to an end.[33] But, beyond his personal misery, he felt that the war destroyed "the commonwealth of learning" he had known as a child. In the vicious ethnopolitics of interwar

Austria he could find no intellectual or political home. But in the Vienna Circle he saw—for all his life-long confrontation with it—guardians of the enlightenment legacy and descendants of *fin-de-siècle* progressives. The Circle's network represented a vestige of the lost commonwealth of learning. In 1934–36, his last years in Vienna, Popper became a member of the network, a "Central European intellectual."

But ethnonationalism shattered Central European culture once more and drove him to exile. As early as 1927, Popper was full of premonitions about the collapse of Austrian democracy.[34] After the attempted Nazi coup of 25 July 1934, he thought that a Nazi take-over and a German invasion were merely a matter of time. A close friend's letter from 1942 remembered his foreboding of the impending disaster: "[We] often recall your remarkable predictions of the catastrophe in its totality as well as in more detailed features."[35] By 1935, Popper was searching desperately for a way out of Austria. After much travail, he accepted an offer from Canterbury College in Christchurch, New Zealand. In January 1937, he left Austria forever, spending the Second World War in New Zealand and the postwar years in England. In exile, he shaped science and politics in the image of the lost "commonwealth of learning:" free cosmopolitan communities, engaged in critical debates. The progressive imagination recovered Central Europe as the Open Society.

Cosmopolitanism's promise was contingent on the triumph of enlightenment and the Open Society. This entailed the disappearance of German racism, but also the opening of the Jewish ghettoes. Herein lay the dilemmas of enlightenment cosmopolitanism. How did one open a closed community? Popper suggested that cross-cultural interaction in a multinational empire, such as the Roman or Habsburg Empire, could do so. Central Europe demonstrated that this was insufficient. Empire did not tame nationalism; nationalism undermined empire. Culture clash did not open ghettoes; it reinforced some, and destroyed others. Moreover, the possibilities for abuse of imperial hegemony—by nationalism, no less—were colossal. Assuming success, how multinational, or culturally diverse, would the cosmopolitan empire be? Would the triumph of enlightenment over the ghetto not imply a universal (progressive) German identity? Most Germans, Czechs, and Central European Jews identified the enlightenment (*Aufklärung*) with Germany. Was it not pseudo-universal? Popper denied this—and with good reason. All the same, his analyses of nationalism and the Jewish Question disclosed major problems of cosmopolitanism.

Already in 1927, in a seminar lecture on the idea of *Heimat* at the Vienna Pedagogic Institute, the young Popper expressed deep antipathies to nationalism. Originating with the German romantics, *Heimat,* a convergence of country and home, denoted patriotism and civic culture to nineteenth-century liberals; but, in interwar years, it became the Austrian fascists' leitmotif. They used it to express local patriotism, attachment to provincial customs, family, and religion, hatred of urban industrial society, parliamentary politics, and Viennese culture. In the 1930 elections, the paramilitary *Heimwehr* (Home Guard) groups ran a unified list under the banner of the *Heimatblock.* Popper felt threatened. Noting *Heimat's* amorphous character, he moved to purge the concept of its mystical nationalist meanings. He founded *Heimat* on individuals' psychological relationship to their environment, but remained suspicious even of this "native" environment. It connoted a rejection of the new and different as "foreign." It constituted a point of departure for education, but it should open to new experiences and ideas. Pedagogy, such as Plato's, that closed it to external influences, was counter-educational. *Heimat* existed, but it needed to be overcome.

Popper's argument was as much about political culture as about education. He recognized that individuals' psychological relationship to their environment established a "naturally given primitive cultural community" that supported larger cultural units, but he did not investigate the transformation of multiple local communities into a nation. Instead, he defined the nation as a legal association. Legal systems, not cultural heritage, set national boundaries. Popper insisted that a universal ethic must shape national legal codes, making good citizenship compatible with internationalism. Education should cultivate respect of law, a sense of justice, and a critical awareness of social inequities. It should not foster patriotism, though, or love of *Heimat.* Love is an aesthetic feeling, not a virtue, so there is no duty to love. Patriotic actions violating internationalism are unethical. Threatened by the fascist *Heimat,* Popper contained its political force and emotional appeal first by restricting it to individuals and their environment, then by transforming national collectives into legal associations protecting universal rights.

Popper's cosmopolitanism was already full-blown in this uneven early essay. So also were his difficulties in negotiating national identity. He recognized cultural-historical communities, but divorced nationality and citizenship from them: the latter were legal concepts. National differences appeared insignificant. All nations must conform to the legal code of a yet-to-come world federation. "From good Germans to good cosmopolitans," he quoted Eduard Burger, a noted socialist school-reformer. For socialists, the dictum justified a German national focus. For Popper, good Germans virtually ceased being German, becoming cosmopolitans. He heaped abuse on German epistemology and natural philosophy that reflected, in his view, something of a German national character. Their superstition, making truth relative to national circumstances, could bring philosophy down. Popper seemed to suggest, however, that education could change "national character" by transforming affective relationships and aesthetic feelings into legal relationships and ethical actions. Love of *Heimat* may develop into an appreciation of nature's beauty, anxieties about "bad" outsiders into ethical judgments, native art and music into high culture. His suggestions reflected not so much cultural elitism, or authoritarian universalism, as an assimilated Jew's mortal fear of German ethnonationalism. Excluded from *Heimat* on ethnic grounds, Popper responded by subjecting ethnic and national identities to a universal humanity.[36]

These were daring moves for a young student to make. Popper's radical cosmopolitanism was uncommon in Vienna. In his family's progressive milieu, only Bertha von Suttner (1843–1914), the pacifist leader of the Austrian Peace Movement, and a few freemasons and Monists articulated similar positions.[37] Conservative proponents of the Austrian idea from Hofmannsthal to Roth expressed similar anti-German sentiments and opposition to nationalism, but they were not progressive universalists. As for the socialists, German nationalism always tempered their internationalism. During the interwar period, they supported unification with Germany. The editor of *Die Quelle* may have gotten more than he bargained for when he requested Popper to open the *Heimat* seminar.

To be sure, Popper's cosmopolitanism involved limited conceptual innovation. His central ideas belonged to Kant: the state as a legal and political entity (not a cultural-historical one), the parallel between civil, national and cosmopolitan rights, the universality of the moral imperative and its expression in law, and the division between aesthetics and ethics (ruling out derivation of moral imperatives from aesthetic judgment).[38] Yet, political realism and government pressure had constrained Kant's cosmopolitanism. His republican government and international federation were a future prospect, a conjecture about historical progress that would lead humankind to enlightenment and cosmopolitanism, the descent of the Kingdom of Ends upon earth. In reality he faced an absolutist monarchy. There were many escape clauses for an absolutist monarch. The security of the state was a supreme imperative. Under no circumstances was resistance to the monarch permitted. Rebellion was "the greatest crime." A country in the midst of Europe (i.e., Prussia), subject to pressures from powerful neighbors, was exempted from a republican constitution.[39] The moral imperative was universal, but its political fulfillment was problematic and required caution.

Young Popper would have none of it. With typical single-mindedness—reflecting philosophical consistency, moral uprightness, and more than a touch of political naiveté—he collapsed Kant's future and present, conjecture and reality. He freed Kant's cosmopolitanism from its historical and political limits, daringly proclaiming its universal validity, here and now.

The triumph of National Socialism reinforced Popper's hostility to nationalism. He regarded Nazi racism as the highest stage of nationalism, its inevitable conclusion. Central European conceptions of nationality shaped his views. Imperial Austria made *Volksstamm* (tribe, race, or ethnicity) the basis of claims for nationality and cultural autonomy. Popper spoke therefore of "tribal nationalism" (in current parlance, "ethnonationalism").[40] But there were no good and bad nationalisms: he would not second cultural nationalism any more than ethnic nationalism. The only nation he recognized was a political one, founded on the French Revolution's concept of citizenship. Ethnic origins, religious affiliation, and cultural difference were irrelevant to it.

Alone among liberals of his generation Popper challenged the principles of national self-determination and the national state. Nationalities did not exist. German thinkers from Herder to Fichte to Hegel invented them to serve the interests of reactionary states.

> The idea that there exist natural units like nations or linguistic or racial groups is entirely fictitious.... The principle of the national state ... owes its popularity solely to the fact that it appeals to tribal instincts.[41] ... None of the theories which maintain that a nation is united by common origin, or a common language, or a common history, is acceptable, or applicable in practice. The principle of the national state ... is a myth. It is an irrational, a romantic and Utopian dream.[42]

Wilson's and Masaryk's "well meant" effort to apply national self-determination consistently throughout Central Europe—"one of the most mixed of all the thoroughly mixed regions of Europe"—was an incredible folly that brought about Versailles's failure. "An international federation in the Danube basin," argued Popper, "might have prevented much."[43] National Socialism was the culmination of the national state. So was Bosnia, he said in his 1994 Prague speech. If the principle of national self-determination did not lose its authority, post-Communist Central Europe could also fall prey to ethnic terrorism. The only remedy was abandoning self-determination, recognizing state boundaries as conventional, sanctioning the status quo, and establishing an armed international organization to guarantee peace. National identities were false, reactionary, and utopian. Individual, imperial, and cosmopolitan identities were true, progressive, and possible.[44]

Popper ingeniously deconstructed nationality, pointing out its complex historical formation and diffused character. Yet, he never extended this mode of questioning to imperialism. The nation-state was historicized and delegitimized; empires went unexamined and were vindicated. He glorified classical Athens as a democratic, progressive, and cosmopolitan empire, overlooking evidence of oppression and intolerance.[45] His recollection of historical episodes of imperialism was selective. He recalled Alexander's cosmopolitanism, the Napoleonic Code and Habsburg multinationalism, but not Spanish colonialism, the Middle Passage, and Nazi *Lebensraum*. Imperialism represented cosmopolitanism's possibility: this was enough. The historicity of imperial identities—past or future— never became an issue. They were divested of historical specificity. They did not emerge from historical identities, but overcame them.

Popper was convinced that if we deconstruct false collectives and get to the individual, we will have reached the truly universal, but cosmopolitan identity seemed abstract and unreal. Popper himself conceded that "concrete groups"—families, churches, voluntary associations, possibly even ethnic communities—would remain even in the Open Society. They would continue to fulfill some of the functions that kinship groups had in the "closed society." Indeed, they were essential: people, Popper said unsympathetically, will "try to satisfy their emotional social needs as well as they can."[46] But "emotional social needs" remained foreign to him, implicated with fascism. He never negotiated between the closed and the Open Society, ethnicity and cosmopolitanism, or showed their possible convergence in his future cosmopolitan federation.

There was no room for negotiation with fascism. Popper's uncompromising universalism, his categorical rejection of the claims of closed communities against the cosmopolitan Open Society, ought to be understood in the context of Central European ethnonationalism. Enlightenment universalism made his polemical rejection of particularity possible, but it did not require it. Central Europe did. Popper acknowledged "diversity" and—with the exception of Jewish religion and nationality which, he insisted, must be given up—assailed any effort to suppress difference. He defended minorities' rights. On one of his last public appearances, he acerbically suggested that Germany's and France's "homogeneous populations" were due to "political and educational means suppressing minorities or dialects."[47] To be sure, he thought that ethnic and religious differences were insignificant. Diversity existed, but, unlike universal humanity, it was no cause for celebration. His refusal to celebrate diversity, however, was not a reflection of a desire to eliminate difference, but rather of a determination to ensure it does not infringe on universal humanity. The first response to the racist argument that those who are different are inferior and cannot be members of the nation is *not* that we ought to respect difference; it is that we are all equally human and due equal rights as citizens. *The Open Society* defended this universalist vision eloquently. Central Europe ensured that it remained forever utopian. It made it impossible for Popper to close the gap between national communities and cosmopolitanism.

The gap between cosmopolitan dream and ethnonational realities came back to haunt Popper with a vengeance. He presented his views on the Jewish Question as following from his cosmopolitanism. He treated Jewish religion, nationality, and ethnicity as if they were interchangeable and reducible to race. Hearing as a young boy the biblical story of the Golden Calf, said Popper, he had recognized the roots of religious intolerance in Jewish monotheism. The Hebrew Bible was the fountainhead of tribal nationalism. Oppressed and persecuted, exilic Jews created the doctrine of the Chosen People, presaging modern visions of chosen class and race.[48] Then, they shut themselves off from the world for two millennia. The ghetto was the ultimate closed society, a "petrified form of Jewish tribalism."[49] Its inhabitants lived in misery, ignorance, and superstition, their separate existence evoking the suspicion and hatred of non-Jews and fueling antisemitism. Integration into non-Jewish society was the only solution to the Jewish problem. Zionism was a colossal mistake; Israel, a tragic error. Israeli treatment of Arabs elicited his harsh condemnation. Zionism, he argued, degenerated from nationalism to racism.

Many assimilated Viennese Jews shared Popper's anti-Jewish convictions. Liberal Jews' anti-Zionism was almost as fierce. Such discourses have prompted scholars to hypothesize about the prevalence of Jewish self-hatred among the *maskilim* (proponents of Jewish enlightenment) and the sinister implications of enlightenment pseudo-cosmopolitanism. Yet, Popper's rhetoric expressed not hatred of the self, but concern for it. He did not internalize antisemitic norms, trying to transform a despised Jewish self into a respectable one. He was anxious lest Jewishness and Zionism provoke ugly and contemptible antisemitism. His critique of Judaism and Zionism was not applied cosmopolitanism, either. His demand that Jews relinquish their identity outright and assimilate exceeded the requirements of the Open Society and violated its imperatives of religious tolerance and cultural diversity. Antisemitism and the hopelessness of the Jewish Question made it impossible for him to negotiate between Jewish identity and cosmopolitan principles. Jews, he knew, will not be accepted as such. They had to disappear as Jews. They could only become cosmopolitan citizens in a Kantian Kingdom of Ends. Central European reality intruded into cosmopolitan dreams.

His analysis of antisemitism explains both his effort to delegitimize Jewish identity and Jewish heritage, and his inability to negotiate between nationalism and cosmopolitanism.

> After much thought my father had decided that living in an overwhelmingly Christian society imposed the obligation to give as little offence as possible—to become assimilated. This, however, meant giving offence to organized Judaism.... But ... anti-Semitism was an evil, to be feared by Jews and non-Jews alike ... [and] the task of all people of Jewish origin [was] to do their best not to provoke it. ... It was most understandable that people who were despised for their racial origin should insist that they were proud of it. But racial pride is not only stupid but wrong, even if provoked by racial hatred. All nationalism or racialism is evil, and Jewish nationalism is no exception.

> I believe that before the First World War Austria, and even Germany, treated the Jews quite well. They were given almost all rights ... [and] treated as well as one could reasonably expect....

> Many Jews looked conspicuously different from the "autochthonous" population.... [S]ome of the rich ones were typically *nouveaux riches*.... [A]nti-Semitism was basically an expression of hostility towards those who were felt to be strangers....

> The situation improved legally with the dissolution of the Austrian Empire... but...it deteriorated socially: many Jews, feeling that freedom and full equality had now become a reality, understandably but not wisely entered politics and journalism.... The influx of the Jews into the parties of the left contributed to the downfall of these parties.[50]

Popper was aware that the Jewish Question was highly controversial. He was playing with fire, but he felt compelled to express his views, something he had never before done in print. A draft of the autobiography was even more polemical. His father's conversion, Popper said, met with "attacks" by "organized Judaism." The Jews were "guests" in Austria, and antisemitism reflected "resistance ... against infiltration from the outside." His paternal family looked "typically Austrian," but most Jews looked different, and some "behaved in a manner that made the rest blush." In imperial Austria, Jews were treated "as well, or better, than one could expect." In the republic, Jews "invaded politics and journalism." The logic of racial pride of both Jews and non-Jews led to racial war.[51]

These are staggering statements. Popper draws us back from cosmopolitan dreams to ethnopolitical realities. Antisemitism was to be feared at all times and places. Jews were not to expect fulfillment of cosmopolitanism's promise, but accommodate themselves to antisemitism. They were wrong to take advantage of openings in society and stupid to draw attention to their wealth and success. A separate Jewish community, however acculturated, endangered Jews. They had to assimilate to assuage antisemitism. This was not cosmopolitanism: a marginal community had to disappear, under threat, to appease a barbarous tribal movement, an embodiment of the closed society. Popper reversed the roles of persecutor and victim. Jews infiltrated Austria, invaded politics and journalism, attacked assimilationists, provoked antisemitism. By assuming leadership positions among the socialists, they contributed to the triumph of fascism. Retaining Jewish identity, they triggered a racial war that brought their own destruction. Popper's discourse descended from cosmopolitanism dangerously close to antisemitism.

Mortal fear of antisemitism accounts for Popper's willingness to tamper with cosmopolitanism. Jewish marginality first gave rise to cosmopolitan dreams, then made their realization impossible. Liberal and assimilationist Jews imagined a cosmopolitan community accepting them, but antisemitism constantly reminded them of the hopelessness of cosmopolitanism. Reality conflicted with dream. Antisemitism was a given, an immutable fact, a natural, if regrettable, response of a native population to strangers. Jewish identity, in contrast, seemed a variable, subject to change. Popper, like many progressives, thought the price of integration justified. Confusing assimilation with cosmopolitanism and pretending that humanity would remain intact if threats forced Jews to disappear, he gave up a tribal religion to join humanity. The refusal of most Jews to join seemed reactionary and treacherous, putting assimilation at risk by fueling antisemitism. Recalcitrant Jews, rather than antisemites, became the Jewish problem.

Ethnonationalism made reconciling German and Jewish, national and cosmopolitan identities impossible. The result was an indeterminate identity for assimilated Jews. If assimilation were possible, Popper would become a German Austrian. But neither would anyone but progressives accept him as German any time after 1880, nor would he, sworn enemy of nationalism, wish to become one. Enlightenment cosmopolitanism appealed to Popper and liberal Jews precisely because of their life in between cultures and their indeterminate identity. The German enlightenment may have been cosmopolitanism's source, yet Popper was *not* proffering a German vision. To suggest that would be to make German enlightenment, culture, and nationality interchangeable. Few Austrians secure in their German identity promoted universalism during the interwar period. Jewish intellectuals appropriated the enlightenment because it promised a home, an alternative to the ethnonational *Heimat.* Cosmopolitanism had a genuine universalist potential.

Claiming membership in an imagined cosmopolitan community, Popper rejected Jewish identity. "I do not consider myself 'an assimilated German Jew,'" he told a critic of *Unended Quest:* "this is how 'the *Führer'* would have considered me."[52] Could he be included in the Jewish Year Book, inquired an editor in 1969. No, answered Popper, "I am of Jewish descent, but ... I abhor any form of racialism or nationalism; and I never belonged to the Jewish faith. Thus I do not see on what grounds I could possibly consider myself a Jew."[53] He was right to refuse an ethnic reification of his identity. Living in-between Germans and Jews, assimilated Jews did not belong clearly to either. Their own profession of identity must be respected. The historian has the right, however, to interrogate Popper's claim to have overcome the conditions of "assimilated Jew." In an Open Society, those declining to belong to any nationality might be recognized as cosmopolitans. Popper did not live in such a society. From childhood to death, his closest friends were assimilated Jews. He grew up in an assimilated Jewish family. Progressive Viennese circles were essential to his intellectual formation and Central European networks to his intellectual growth. Both were preponderantly Jewish. His cosmopolitanism emerged from Jewish marginality and reflected the assimilated Jews' dilemma. Antisemitism drove him to exile. To call Popper "an assimilated Jew" is neither to follow "the *Führer's*" steps nor to deny cosmopolitanism. It is to recognize that the *Führer* and his cohorts created a world that set limits to cosmopolitanism.

Marginal and utopian, Popper's cosmopolitanism represented the vanished dreams of ethnopolitic's losers. He immortalized cosmopolitan dreams in the Open Society. His vision was not free of problems. Like most liberals, he was unable to negotiate effectively between nationalism and cosmopolitanism, communal diversity and universal humanity, the closed and the Open Society. He correctly emphasized critical dialogue that transforms identities, transgresses boundaries and changes communities, but he underestimated the difficulty in creating a situation that would make such a dialogue possible. Culture clash under conditions of unequal power does not always create dialogue, or advance cosmopolitanism. It may result in oppression. This happened to the Czechs and

Jews in Vienna, under Popper's eyes. All the same, Popper held fast to the emancipatory potential of culture clash. He had seen its wonderful effect, he thought, among German-acculturated Viennese Jews. They liberated themselves from traditional small-town Jewish life and became a cultural elite. Surely under the conditions of Western liberty such a result could be duplicated. Culture clash can expand horizons, open closed communities. It can advance recognition of rationality in relativity, unity in diversity, cosmopolitanism in multiculturalism. It may set humanity on the way to the Open Society.

Popper took it for granted that the conditions for cross-cultural dialogue already existed in Western societies. He was convinced that any culture clash would take place on a fairly level playing field. Freedom of expression, he believed, was necessary and sufficient for a productive clash. At times, he seemed aware that this was not quite the case. He noted that

> culture clash may lose some of its great value if one of the clashing cultures regards itself as universally superior, and even more so if it is so regarded by the other: this may destroy the greatest value of culture clash, [the development of] a critical attitude.... The critical attitude of trying to learn from the other will be replaced by a kind of blind acceptance.... Ontological relativity...can prove of immense value:... the partners in the clash may liberate themselves from the prejudices of which they are unconscious.... Such a liberation may be a result of criticism awakened by culture clash.[54]

Other than the moral injunction *not* to assume a superior attitude, however, he had no suggestion as to how to promote such ontological relativity. He himself was not free of superior attitudes toward closed communities, and Jewish and non-Western cultures. To be sure, dialogue can disabuse participants of superior attitudes. Self-criticism cannot be made a condition for exchange; it is its end. But the power of dialogue is limited. For optimal criticism, an ideal speech situation must be approximated. Popper and his students have not investigated the social and cultural conditions promoting critical exchange. They made it easy for critics of liberalism to deny the vital dialogue that opens closed communities one to another.

Critics of liberalism wish to create a protective environment for minorities where they are free to expand "their" culture without a challenge from the "hegemonic" one. But, to the extent that peremptory validation of "minority culture" prevents criticism, it hinders progress. The recent assault on the "enlightenment" and its Jewish proponents seeks to delegitimize the *maskilim*'s criticism of traditional Judaism and the ghetto. The underlying assumption seems to be an unconditional acceptance of an oppressed minority's culture. In contrast, efforts to improve, even transform a minority are held with great suspicion. The "enlightenment" is decried; the ghetto vindicated. But celebration of diversity of closed communities is a poor substitute to diversity in an Open Society: shifting boundaries, changing conventions, destabilized beliefs. Fascism, Popper thought, was fear of change. Culture clash is the salt of diversity.

The dilemmas of liberal cosmopolitanism may not lend themselves to easy solution, and yet the imperative of diversity provides no alternative. It derives, in the last analysis, from enlightenment universalism, the respect of humanity qua humanity. We are forever condemned to negotiating between unity and diversity, closed community and Open Society. Liberal universalism may threaten difference, but it has devised several ways of negotiating the threat. One of them is: reason about it. Enlightenment cosmopolitanism provided a vision of a home to refugees of the worst disaster that has befallen humanity this century. Critics have been interrogating this cosmopolitanism for too long. It is time we dedicate ourselves to resolving its dilemmas.

Notes

This is a revised version of lectures at the International Symposium, "Beyond Vienna 1900," Center for Austrian Studies, University of Minnesota, 1995, and the Annual Karl Popper Conference 1997, London School of Economics. An elaborated version of this essay, "Dilemmas of Cosmopolitanism: Karl Popper, Jewish Identity, and 'Central European Culture,'" appeared in *The Journal of Modern History* 71 (1999): 105–149.

I would like to thank Steven Beller for his invitation to the Symposium, critical readings, and intellectual support. Joseph Agassi, Anthony LaVopa, Julie Mell, and Ezra Mendelsohn read early drafts and made valuable suggestions. Mark Notturno drew my attention to the centrality of "culture clash" in the late Popper. The archivists at the Hoover Institute, Stanford, and the *Meldearchiv*, Wiener Stadt- und Landesarchiv, kindly helped with my research.

1. Karl Popper, "Epistemology and Industrialization" [1959; 1979], in *The Myth of the Framework* (London, 1994), 186.

2. Popper, "On Culture Clash" [1981], in *In Search of a Better World* (London, 1992), 124.

3. Popper, "Der wichtigste Beitrag seit Aristoteles," *Wissenschaft aktuell* 1 (September 1980). This is an interview with Popper on Kurt Gödel and the Vienna Circle, conducted by Peter Weibel in August 1978 in Alpbach. Translations are my own, unless otherwise indicated.

4. Popper, "On Culture Clash," 124.

5. Popper, "Epistemology and Industrialization," 186.

6. Popper, "Interview on Kurt Gödel and the Vienna Circle."

7. Ibid.

8. Immanuel Kant, "Idee zu einer allgemeinen Geschichte in weltbürgerlicher Absicht," *Gesammelte Schriften (Akademieausgabe)* (Berlin, 1912), vol. 8, 28, conclusion of the eighth thesis.

9. Jean-François Lyotard, *The Postmodern Condition* (Minneapolis, 1984); Michel Foucault, "What Is Enlightenment?" in *The Foucault Reader*, ed. Paul Rabinow (New York, 1984), 32–50.

10. Sygmunt Bauman, "Strangers: The Social Construction of Universality and Particularity," *New German Critique* 78 (1989): 7–42, collapses modernity, liberalism, and (Jewish) assimilation in his critique of universalism. Sander Gilman, *Jewish Self-Hatred* (Baltimore, 1985), focuses on the detrimental consequences of universalism's unfulfilled promises for assimilated Jews.

11. Stefan Zweig, *The World of Yesterday* (New York, 1943).

12. Joseph Roth, *Radetzkymarsch* (Berlin, 1932).

13. Franz Kafka to Max Brod, June 1921, *Briefe 1902–1924* (Frankfurt, 1966), 337.

14. Prof. Dr. Austriacus (Johann Sauter), "Der Fall des Wiener Professors Schlick—eine Mahnung zur Gewissenserforschung," *Schönere Zukunft*, 12 July 1936; reprinted in Friedrich Stadler, *Studien zum Wiener Kreis* (Frankfurt, 1997), 924–929.

15. For an overview of Jellinek's career and views, see Robert Wistrich, *The Jews of Vienna in the Age of Franz Joseph* (Oxford, 1988), chap. 5, 8.

16. Steven Beller, "Patriotism and the National Identity of Habsburg Jewry, 1860–1914," *Leo Baeck Institute Year Book* 41 (1996): 215–238.

17. Marsha Rozenblit, *The Jews of Vienna: Identity and Assimilation, 1867–1914* (Albany, 1983); Steven Beller, *Vienna and the Jews: A Cultural History, 1867–1938* (Cambridge, 1989).

18. Popper, *Unended Quest: An Intellectual Autobiography* (LaSalle, Il., 1976), 8–10, 53, 82; Popper, "Autobiography: Draft," Hoover Institute Archives, Popper Papers (134, 4, 9) (henceforth, Popper Archives); photos, Popper Archives (86039–10, A and BB); *Verlassenschaftsakt* of Max Schiff, *Meldearchiv*, Wiener Stadt- und Landesarchiv, Vienna. On Viennese liberal ideals: Carl Schorske, *Fin-de-Siècle Vienna: Politics and Culture* (New York, 1980).

19. Tax record for Simon Popper, IKG Archives, Central Archives for the History of the Jewish People, Hebrew University, Jerusalem (A/W 805, 23); *Verlassenschaftsakten* of Simon Popper and Max Schiff, *Meldearchiv*, Vienna; photo-negatives, Popper Archives (86039–10, BB). For conversion in Vienna, see Rozenblit, *Jews of Vienna*, chap. 6.

20. They required that one member of the couple convert to the other's religion, or declare himself/herself *konfessionslos* (without religious affiliation, i.e., atheist). Marsha Rozenblit, *Jews of Vienna*, esp. chap. 4.

21. Steven Beller, *Vienna and the Jews*.

22. Arthur Schnitzler, *My Youth in Vienna* (New York, 1970), 63.

23. Popper, *Unended Quest*, 12, 31–32, and "Draft," Popper Archives (134, 4, 9). For Jews in Viennese schools, see Marsha Rozenblit, *Jews of Vienna*, chap. 5. For the friendship with Lorenz, see Karl Popper, Konrad Lorenz, *Die Zukunft ist offen*, ed. by Franz Kreuzer (Vienna, Series Paper, 1985), esp. 13. (Joseph Agassi drew my

attention to their friendship.) David Sorkin, *The Transformation of German Jewry, 1770–1840* (Oxford, 1987).

24. Ingrid Belke, *Die sozialreformerischen Ideen von Joseph Popper-Lynkeus (1838–1921) in Zusammenhang mit allgemeinen Reformbestrebungen des Wiener Bürgertums um die Jahrhundertwende* (Tübingen, 1978), esp. 5–56; Albert Fuchs, *Geistige Strömungen in Österreich, 1867–1918* (Vienna, 1949), 133–162; John Boyer, "Freud, Marriage, and Late Viennese Liberalism: A Commentary from 1905," *Journal of Modern History* 50 (March 1978): 72–102.

25. Friedrich Stadler, *Vom Positivismus zur "Wissenschaftliche Weltauffassung"* (Vienna, 1982).

26. Popper, *Unended Quest*, 12–13.

27. Friedrich Stadler, "Spätaufklärung und Sozialdemokratie in Wien, 1918–1938," in *Aufbruch und Untergang: Österreichische Kultur zwischen 1918 und 1938*, ed. Franz Kadrnoska (Vienna, 1981), 441–473.

28. Paul Silverman, "Law and Economics in Interwar Vienna: Kelsen, Mises and the Regeneration of Austrian Liberalism" (Ph.D. diss., University of Chicago, 1984), 26.

29. Otto Bauer, *Die Nationalitätenfrage und die Sozialdemokratie* [1907] (Vienna, 1924), 366–381.

30. Gerald Stourzh, "Galten die Juden als Nationalität Altösterreichs?" in Anna Drabek, Mordechai Eliav, and Gerald Stourzh, *Prag-Czernowitz-Jerusalem* (Eisenstadt, 1984), 73–117.

31. Karl Marx, "Contribution to the Critique of Hegel's *Philosophy of Right:* Introduction," in *Selected Writings* (Indianapolis, 1994), 38.

32. Popper, *Unended Quest*, 32.

33. Ibid., 31–39.

34. Ibid., 104–105.

35. Frederick Dorian (Fritz Deutsch) to Popper, 10 April 1942, Popper Archives (28, 6, under Hellin). The "we" are Dorian and Fritz Hellin, Viennese youth friends of Popper.

36. Karl Popper, "Zur Philosophie des Heimatgedankens," *Die Quelle* 77 (1927): 899–908. Burger's quotation is on page 906.

37. Popper, *Unended Quest*, 11, 13–14; Richard Laurence, "Bertha von Suttner and the Peace Movement in Austria to World War I," *Austrian History Yearbook* 23 (1992): 181–201; Rainer Hubert, "Freimaurerei in Österreich 1871 bis 1938," in *Zirkel und Winkelmass* (Vienna, 1984), 31–46.

38. Immanuel Kant, "Über den Gemeinspruch: Das mag in der Theorie richtig sein, taugt aber nicht für die Praxis" [1793] and "Zum ewigen Frieden" [1795], in *Gesammelte Schriften*, vol. 8; idem, *Critique of Judgement* (Oxford, 1952), 2nd book, "Critique of Aesthetic Judgement."

39. Immanuel Kant, "Theorie [und] Praxis," esp. 297–300; "Zum ewigen Frieden," esp. 372–373; "Der Streit der Fakultäten" [1798], in *Gesammelte Schriften*, vol. 7, 79–94, esp. note on page 86.

40. Auriel Kolnai's use of "tribal egoism" in *The War Against the West* (London, 1938) may have first suggested the term "tribal nationalism" to Popper; but it seemed so fitting because it both connoted primitivism and conformed to official terminology.

41. Popper, *The Open Society* (London, 1945), vol. 1, chap. 9, note 7(1).

42. Ibid., vol. 2, page 49.

43. Ibid., vol. 2, chap. 12, note 53.

44. Ibid., vol. 2, chap. 5, note 13(2); chap. 6, note 44; chap. 9, note 7; vol. 2, 238; chap. 12, notes 19, 53; chap. 13, note 2(1); Popper, "Kant's Critique and Cosmology," in *Conjectures and Refutations* (New York, 1963), esp. 182; idem, *Unended Quest*, 10, 13–15, 32, 105–107; idem, "Epistemology and Industrialization," 185–187; idem, "On Culture Clash," 118–121; idem, "Prague Lecture," www.lf3.cuni.cz/aff/p2_e.html (access through the Karl Popper Web: www.eeng.dcu.ie/~tkpw/).

45. Malachi Hacohen, "Karl Popper in Exile: The Viennese Progressive Imagination and the Making of *The Open Society*," *Philosophy of the Social Sciences* 26 (December 1996): 473–475.

46. Popper, *The Open Society*, vol. 1, 175, 2nd and later English editions; (page 171 of the American edition, Princeton, 1950).

47. Popper, "Prague Lecture."

48. Popper, "Toleration and Intellectual Responsibility" [1982], in *In Search of a Better World*, 188–190; idem, *The Open Society*, vol. 1, 6–8, chap. 1, note 3; vol. 2, 21–22.

49. Popper, *The Open Society*, vol. 2, chap. 11, note 56.

50. Popper, *Unended Quest*, 105–107.

51. Popper, draft of autobiography, section 20 (later 21), Popper Archives (135,1). The holograph is 21 pages long. However, pages 140–141 of the typed version include most of the above. See also page 142 of the slightly later version (137, 3).

52. Popper to M. Smith, 7 August 1982, Popper Archives (407, 17).

53. Popper to Michael Wallach, 6 January 1969, Popper Archives (313, 10). He softened his stance in later years, agreeing to be included in Herlinde Koelbl's *Jüdische Portraits: Photographien und Interviews* (Frankfurt, 1989), 189–190.

54. Popper, "The Myth of the Framework," in *The Myth of the Framework*, 51.

Chapter 8

A MATTER OF PROFESSIONALISM

Marketing Identity in *Fin-de-Siècle* Vienna

Robert Jensen

Imagine this vignette of Viennese artistic culture in 1910. A young artist and two celebrated architects are sitting around a coffeehouse table, doing business. The artist, Egon Schiele, age 20, is selling a drawing to the older architect on the recommendation of his younger colleague. A nude, it belongs to a suite of large drawings Schiele made of his sister Gerti in the spring of 1910, from which he also produced two paintings.[1] His client is Otto Wagner, the dean of an extraordinary group of Viennese architects and designers. Wagner decides to capture the ritual flavor of the exchange—it does not matter when—with a carefully ruled inscription (as only an architect could write) in the large empty space on the drawing's left side. Here Wagner identifies Schiele's intermediary as Josef Hoffmann and notes that this is a study for the painting Schiele recently exhibited at the First International Hunting Exhibition. Let us take Schiele's drawing with its record of this seemingly casual commercial transaction as our guide to the network of personalities, institutions, and art works that constituted both the personal and professional identities of Viennese artists at the *Jahrhundertwende*, and as a way of approaching how Schiele, at such a remarkably early age, became an important player in Vienna, and also how, during the

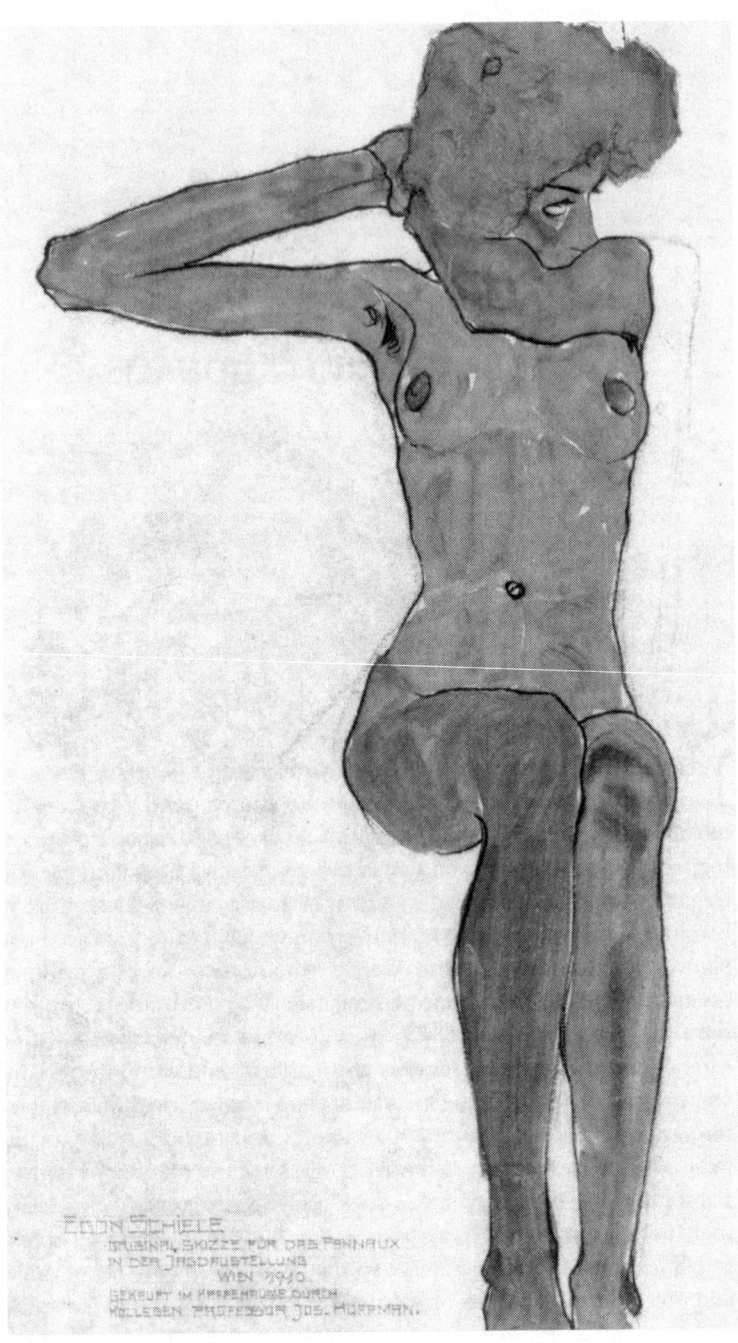

FIGURE 2 Egon Schiele, *Seated Female Nude with Raised Right Arm* (1910). Courtesy of Historisches Museum der Stadt Wien.

process of professionalization, his life became inextricably bound up with his art.

A Minor Art

The sudden prominence in 1909–10 of Schiele was made possible by the radical transformation of Vienna's art institutions. These changes may be measured by the general collapse of the Central European secessions in the face of an increasingly successful, and increasingly international, network of commercial galleries.[2] By collapse I do not mean the dissolution of these institutions; the Vienna Secession, to take only one, has had a long afterlife. What disintegrated was their sense of vitality, their commitment to non-commercial, even altruistic exhibitions, and especially their faith in their historical mission. Their ideological failure accompanied the general internationalization of the art market in the first years of this century, which brought French impressionism and postimpressionism into universal currency. French art became the standard by which Central European artists, whether they wished to or not, came to measure themselves. The market not only brought paintings and sculptures; Central European critics, historians, curators, and artists absorbed the theoretical paradigms that underpinned the Parisian avant-gardes. For example, German-language art history increasingly adopted the modernist conception of a necessarily evolutionary, and inevitably exclusionary history of modern art. These histories not only disposed of the academicians and most narrative art, they traced from Courbet's realism to Picasso's cubism the progressive disintegration of form and the freeing of color from its representational obligations in favor of a purely expressive function. What had been Central Europe's conservative, parochial, and slow-to-change artistic culture was suddenly caught up in the theories, the excitement, the publicity, and the altered institutional circumstances of an international modernism.

This internationalism occurred in roughly two waves, which though often confused must be carefully distinguished from one another.[3] The first took place in the 1890s with the international decorative arts movement. Central Europe's cultural elites embraced as equals the ideas and aesthetic vocabulary of such Arts and Crafts and Art Nouveau proponents as William Morris, Victor Horta, and Henri van de Velde. Latent, however, beneath these supremely visible activities in the decorative arts were the elements of dramatic changes to come. In defense of the modern in whatever form it took, *Jugendstill* art nouveau/secessionist artists, critics, and historians, their galleries and periodicals, became the primary conduits through which French modernism was introduced into Central Europe.[4] French impressionism, long suppressed in the international art market for complicated institutional reasons, suddenly emerged as the dominant style all over Europe at the very end of the century. Thus the second wave, coming immediately after 1900, was cast in terms of painting, and carried by the newly rediscovered postimpressionist generation of van Gogh, Gauguin, Seurat, and Cézanne. The supremacy of painting was abetted by considerable speculation in the market for contemporary art and by the discovery of new collectors, particularly in America and Russia, willing to pay very high prices for work by artists who, a generation before, had been reviled or unknown. This new high modernist culture, centered in the commercial galleries, challenged and in many places quickly overwhelmed the nearly equal footing the decorative arts had won in the prior decade. The success which French art enjoyed with collectors and museum curators naturally inspired local resistance. French modernism's opponents were very noisy, but largely ineffectual until abetted by nationalist fervor. Yet they are telling indicators of a culture under threat, now deeply uncertain of its equal stature with Parisian art.[5] In other words, Central European artists faced a general crisis of professional identity in the first decade of this century.[6]

The Vienna Secession, because it was comparatively late in forming and committed to the decorative arts more deeply than any other contemporary artist association, presents an anomalous situation. The prestige of Hoffmann's celebrated design studio, the *Wiener Werkstätte,* and the *Gesamtkunstwerk*-style of many of the Secession's exhibitions preserved in Vienna longer than anywhere else the appearance of an unproblematic alliance between the decorative arts and the high-culture painting tradition. Even with the arrival of the so-called Viennese "expressionists," such as Schiele and Oskar Kokoschka, Viennese art seemed to pursue a *Sonderweg.* Thus many historians have discerned a sudden, very late change in Viennese art between the 1908 *Kunstschau* and the second *Kunstschau* the following year. Carl Schorske once summarized this change as "an explosive reassertion of painting as the medium of instinctual truth."[7] Staged by Gustav Klimt and his friends, with elegant pavilions designed principally by Hoffmann, the first *Kunstschau* was an extraordinary celebration of Vienna's decorative arts movement.[8] The second proved to be a *de facto* international painting exhibition since, as the few critics who bothered to review the show outside Vienna observed, there was little that was new by way of decorative arts added to the pavilions.[9] Instead, the participation of the Kunstsalon Miethke in

Vienna, Paul Cassirer in Berlin, and the Parisian galleries of Bernheim Jeune and Émile Duret enabled the display of a small, but significant collection of French postimpressionist artists, which included the Nabis and some Fauves. Schorske's characterization of the second *Kunstschau* as a radical break from the secessionists in the 1890s also depended on the portrayal of artists such as Klimt as having "drained [their art] of its original function—to speak psychological truth—and adapted its visual language to purely decorative purposes."[10]

In one sense, the 1908 *Kunstschau* was indeed the swan-song of Vienna's extraordinary decorative arts movement (even though the *Werkstätte* remained a vital, influential institution until at least the First World War). Until 1908, the unification of the diverse arts still held out in Vienna its utopian possibilities, and painting, even that by Klimt, remained subordinate to its architectural setting. But in what sense did the 1909 *Kunstschau* mark a sudden collapse? Schorske has always argued that this "explosive reassertion of painting" was the product of a general psychic dissolution, for which artists such as Schiele served as lightning rods. The generation of 1910, in contrast to the Vienna Secession, initially possessed neither an aesthetic nor an ideological program. Schorske regarded this fact strictly as the consequence of a private, psychologically driven, rather than willed, art.[11] By taking expressionist rhetoric at face value, this reading obscures—like the accounts of the participants themselves—the evolution of Vienna's artistic culture.[12] From Schiele and Kokoschka's contemporary apologists (and the artists' own testimonials) to modern biographers, expressionist rhetoric sacrifices the artist's conscious agency to compulsive psychological forces. At the same time, it works to normalize the artist's relationships to his patrons and to the art institutions of the day under the mythology of genius. Thus Schorske once described Schiele (without attempting to distinguish the artist from his work) as exemplifying a "de-structured, de-cultured universe," while also betraying "a sense of total isolation and the hideous pressures of the insatiable id."[13]

In a parallel construction, by taking Klimt's increasingly decorative work and private commissions as a retreat from the premises that first informed the Secession, Schorske's model depends upon an idealization of these early, "public" years. Again, the rhetoric of the Secession's proponents has been taken too much at face value. In fact, from its inception the Secession was rich in contradiction. Consider Schorske's characterization of what he terms the three fundamental aspects of the Vienna Secession. First: "The Secession defined itself not as a mere *salon des réfusés*, but as a new Roman *secessio plebis*, in which the plebs, defiantly rejecting the misrule of the patricians, was withdrawing from the republic."[14] This assertion, which directly echoes Max Burckhard's introduction to the first issue of *Ver Sacrum*, is difficult to reconcile with the explicit tenets of the association.[15] As with the other Central European secessions, the first two organizational principles of the Secession declared the fundamentally elitist nature of the society. The secessions represented a European-wide response to pressures building within the art community over too many artists competing for too little exhibition space, too little patronage, and too few honors. So, as one German critic noted in 1896: "without question, the most important thing primarily owed to secessionism is the form of the small elite exhibition."[16] Every secession sought to exclude the mass, the true plebs, in an effort to shore up the quality of their fellow exhibitors. In reality, the *Kunstproletariat* always found its support among the aesthetically conservative, but sometimes more politically liberal older art associations, such as Vienna's Künstlerhaus.[17]

Every secession also professed a commitment to international art exhibitions. Behind this internationalism was a tacit faith in aesthetic heterogeneity, the desire to support "great" art, in whatever form it should take. Schorske's second criterion, the need to show "modern man his true face," from the very beginning had to be reconciled to the fact that this face could take a remarkable variety of forms. As Max Liebermann put it in one of his addresses to open the annual exhibition of the Berlin Secession, "there is no determined norm for what art is, taste alone decides; the continual reevaluation of art: what is today laughed at we see tomorrow as astonishing and admirable."[18] Liebermann rehearsed what already by 1900 was a very old cliché, that great artists, by virtue of being great, must inevitably be laughed at during their lives. He was perfectly serious, having experienced considerable controversy in his own youth, followed by universal admiration (save by the Kaiser and his artist henchman, the president of the Berlin Kunstakademie, Anton von Werner). In any case, such views led the secessionists to encourage the exhibition of artists whose work undermined the values even of the Vienna Secession. Cézanne, soon to be championed by the generation of 1910 who wished to supplant the secessions, debuted with much fanfare in Vienna at the Secession's important 1903 exhibition of French modernism, and even more remarkably, this took place before Cézanne had even been similarly acknowledged in Paris. The exclusionary teleology of the French avant-gardes that accompanied the exhibition of such artists as Cézanne and van Gogh provided a strong challenge from within the secessions to their doctrine of hetereogeneity.

The Secession's institutional elitism, internationalism, and commitment to aesthetic heterogeneity were the very elements that led the Secession to disintegrate in 1905.[19] Their elitism threatened, or at least appeared to threaten, the livelihood of the *Kunstproletariat* within their own ranks, while their aesthetic ideals (particularly their hope to incorporate painting into a general *Gesamtkunstwerk*, decorative environment) were challenged by the French modernist art they helped bring to Vienna. Moreover, this flourishing picture market was obviously explicitly commercial and everywhere superseded the decorative arts movement of the 1890s. So here was another paradox: Schorske's third guiding principle for the Secession, "that art should provide for modern man asylum from the pressure of modern life," was most often expressed as the non-commercial, essentially altruistic mission of the organization.[20] Yet the Secession worked far more successfully and extensively with art dealers in the management of their affairs than had their predecessors. The Secession's leadership developed close associations not only with Viennese galleries, but dealers abroad, enabling their impressive exhibition program that usually alternated between shows of local members and those devoted to an extraordinary array of internationally acclaimed artists.[21] After the Secession fissured in 1905, the emerging "Klimt-Gruppe's" involvement with commercial galleries naturally increased. The presence of the French postimpressionists at the 1909 *Kunstschau* paralleled the various exhibitions of the Galerie Miethke, whose artistic advisor, not incidentally, was the painter Carl Moll, long Klimt's right-hand man in the administration of the Secession.[22]

Here is also an example of the extraordinary centralization of power over Vienna's artistic affairs concentrated in Klimt's immediate circle and expressed in a subjacent manner by the activities of the *Werkstätte* (though not with the same hegemony over architecture, as Adolf Loos's career attests). It is hardly surprising that the Secession's rank and file, already troubled by the highly selective collection of secessionist art sent to the St. Louis World's Fair in 1904, rebelled the next year when Klimt and Moll proposed to bring the offices of Miethke into the Secession building itself.[23] In the contemporary histories of the Secession, written by journalists who were largely apologists for its leadership, such as Ludwig Hevesi and Bertha Zuckerkandl, the rebellion was described along aesthetic lines, pitting the majority, the "impressionist" painters, against the minority, the "decorative" artists, that is, Klimt and his allies.[24] These aesthetic oppositions merely blurred the economic realities that actually divided the Secession. Even in a small art world, getting access to the public, making a name for oneself, and thereby earning a living, was the driving force behind art politics. When Klimt and his friends walked out of the Secession, they not only destroyed its future aesthetic viability; by seceding directly into Miethke's, they unintentionally demonstrated the institutional paradigm of the future. Not only were the days of state commissions lost to artists such as Klimt, but their art would henceforth be displayed outside the publicly altruistic and ennobled spaces of state or artist-sponsored exhibitions.[25] In Vienna after 1905, a paternalistic patronage system, enabled by the centralization of power in Vienna's art circles and attested to by both Kokoschka and Schiele's careers, was essential for making one's way. Henceforth, however, a young artist's ultimate ambition would be to find a dealer to support his or her career.

Yet even as Central European artists turned from public institutions to the private arena of the commercial gallery, they were thrown into dramatic competition with Parisian modernism. It is useful at this point to invoke Gilles Deleuze and Félix Guatarri's concept of a minor literature, an idea they employ to describe the peculiar linguistic character of Kafka's work.[26] Kafka's "minor literature" is written in a language of sometimes unwilling dissonance set within and yet against what they call the major or "vehicular" language and literature of German. This concept provides a highly suggestive context in which to reinterpret what we call modernism in Central European visual arts, bracketing the *fin-de-siècle* crisis of identity among artists within the international art market.

Klimt's later work, the work which followed the University murals, should be seen as an effort to preserve the figurative tradition which informed his academic training, as well as the decorative tradition which had become the signature Viennese modernist manner over which Klimt so clearly presided. The increasingly elaborate ornamental surfaces of Klimt's paintings, combined with his often erotic subjects, could easily serve as virtual illustrations of the primitive sensuality Loos denounced when he wrote "Ornament and Crime."[27] (Loos, indeed, may very well have had Klimt more firmly in mind than any architect.) Klimt's paintings drew tightly together the strands of the decorative, the degenerate, the feminine, and a voyeuristic sexuality. Was this an unconscious act? I believe that Klimt worked this constellation of interests into his art precisely because he knew their sum to be *the* Viennese style, and as such, his art could confidently run an altogether distinct course from contemporary French art.

By treating Viennese modernism as a minor art, in Deleuze and Guatarri's non-valuative sense of the term, we can better examine its relations to the "major" artistic language of Parisian modernism. Klimt clearly did not suffer much from the comparison. Yet for younger artists such as

Schiele and Kokoschka, the example not only of such artists as van Gogh and Gauguin, but also Matisse and Picasso, redefined Viennese aesthetics; it also contributed to a redefinition of the very concept of what an artist is and does. Schiele, like Kafka, should be understood as a self-conscious, careful manipulator of the signs and institutions of the world in which he found himself, and, even more than Kafka, Schiele engaged in a career at once arrogant and, precisely because of that arrogance, insecure.[28] He understood intuitively, at the very least, how to make one's professional identity within the Viennese context. Yet, as he made personal and aesthetic allegiances, Schiele risked being swept aside by an art more potent, more seemingly sanctioned by the forces of "artistic progress" than his own. That Schiele was an obsessive self-portraitist—as were many of his Central European contemporaries—registers his personal and his professional crises of identity. Schiele was always in obvious need of shoring up his identity, for a politics of identity is the very substance of his art.

As postimpressionist painting poured into Central Europe (accompanied by its supporting theoretical discourses and habits of mind), artists everywhere developed a more polarized language for art. Already by 1912 in Germany a fundamental opposition between a "Germanic" expressionism and an international (but implicitly French) impressionism characterized much of the critical literature on contemporary painting. Nationalism obviously played an important role in politicizing the language of expressionism, which perhaps is also why in Germany, far more than in Austria-Hungary, expressionist rhetoric was characterized as not only a break with the immediate, secessionist, internationalist past, but also a return to the tradition of the great German art of the Renaissance.[29] Viennese art was spared that need for an absolute repudiation, but the relation to tradition and particularly to the decorative tradition represented by Klimt and the Secession was still deeply problematic. In Schiele's case, his work would always display a deep identification with, and yet a paradoxical effort to separate himself from, Klimt's art.

The Hunting Exhibition

Let us return to Schiele's contribution to the *Internationale Jagdausstellung,* the first of two to showcase hunting pictures in Vienna. Schiele's picture—like another large nude of Gerti, also painted against an undifferentiated white ground—has not survived; we know little about it beyond an installation photograph that appeared in the exhibition catalogue.[30] As for the exhibition, cultural historians have ignored it precisely because its theme is discordant with our modernist-inflected images of Vienna's cultural life. What was, then, the motivation behind holding an international hunting exhibition? To whom was such a show intended to appeal? And given its ostensibly conservative theme, why was Hoffmann charged with installing the exhibits?[31] Finally, how would Schiele's painting have been regarded as a "hunting picture?"

To begin with, we know that it was clearly important to Wagner that Schiele's drawing was a preparatory study for the exhibited painting. In citing its exhibition in his inscription, the architect may simply have wished to validate his purchase by referring to any public showing of an artist so young and still so little known. He might, however, just as well have identified with the values of the exhibition's sponsors—even if he, like others, might have dismissed the quality of most of the exhibits—for no other reason than because of Hoffmann's participation.[32] Austria's hunting culture has not been seriously studied. The existence of so many Alpine hunting lodges, familiar as a class to architectural historians, provides ample evidence that the empire's ruling elites shared the enthusiasms and the cultural orientations of their British contemporaries, about which we do have some recent, richly suggestive work. John MacKenzie especially has explored hunting as an agent within British imperialism.[33] He has shown not only how central a cultural formation hunting was, but also how socially complex were its meanings. During the nineteenth century, hunting became a significant marker of civilization and gentlemanly conduct, another expression perhaps of bourgeois fascination with aristocratic manners, modes of dress, and behavior codes. As the fashion for hunting descended the social ladder, it served to pass down aristocratic values and modes of behavior. One significant by-product of hunting culture was to divide further gender roles by creating a nearly all-male preserve. Hunting was upheld as an instrument of moral education, of physical training, and of scientific culture. For its proponents, hunting signified a culture of rationality and Western science; it was an important factor within the study of natural history, via specimen collection and classification. These rational, scientific values of the modern hunter were then upheld in opposition to the supposed behavior of so-called "primitive" societies, who merely hunted to eat. Yet for enthusiasts and opponents alike, the modern hunter equally embodied elemental passions. Nineteenth-century commentators often observed the relationship between hunting and sexuality, manifested in the fashion for trophies, popularly acknowledged emblems of sex and power. The modern (male) hunter mutually embraced reason and unreason, civilization and barbarism.

These general observations suggest that Schiele's and Hoffmann's involvement in an international hunting exhibition is less unlikely than it might appear today. In a peculiar way, the exhibition shared with Hoffmann and the *Wiener Werkstätte* the ambition to disseminate what they held to be positive cultural values and a particular way of life for the sophisticated, upwardly aspiring European male.[34] Underneath these aesthetic and behavioral prescriptions, the show also shared with Hoffmann those irrational elements that figured so prominently in the art and sensibilities of the Secession—at least insofar as we may identify Hoffmann with his friend, collaborator, and erstwhile leader of the Secession, Klimt. *Werkstätte* products shared Klimt's pleasure in ornament and richness of design and thereby suggested affinities with the irrational, sensual, and sometimes overtly sexual elements of Klimt's art. The celebration of hunting, aristocratic tastes, and sensuality can thus be cogently intertwined. More obviously, the exhibition's organizers brought Hoffmann in to provide the show with a *Werkstätte* look, to give it currency and cultural cachet. Even to the exhibition's jury, the conventional hunting picture may well have seemed conservative in 1910. Hoffmann modernized the show through its decor and made it distinctly Viennese. The installation photograph indicates that entrants were asked to submit to specific size restrictions, which created canvases of unusual rectilinearity. Their uniformity allowed Hoffmann to weld the disparate collection into a Secession-style *Gesamtkunstwerk*. Entries were then listed in the catalogue as "decorative panels."

The jury may have taken Schiele's submission to the exhibition to be an example of "decorative" art, fitting for a Hoffmann protégé and therefore consonant with the overall scheme for the show. They may also have found the overt sexuality of Schiele's picture reminiscent of Klimt's allegorical cycle recently installed in Hoffmann's celebrated Stoclet palace in Brussels. Yet Schiele's work is so stylistically dissonant in this company of sporting pictures that still more must have been needed to justify him to the committee. To include him, the jury had to forgive the artist's formal novelties, especially the painting's undifferentiated ground. Wagner himself was dissatisfied enough with this void in Schiele's study that he had no scruples filling in the area with his inscription. Being so emphatically empty, Schiele's picture could only be understood as decorative in the sense of contemporary poster art (ultimately derived from Japanese examples) and not in the sense of the richly ornamented surfaces of Klimt's work. Under such circumstances, to accept the painting, the jury had to be convinced that it belonged thematically to the exhibition.

Having no title, any answer as to the question of Schiele's subject must necessarily be provisional. But I believe the jury saw in it a modernist version of Ovid's story of Diana surprised at her bath. From the installation photograph it is clear that at least one other artist in the show chose the theme of Artemis at the hunt. Ovid's tale would have been quite suitable material. The figure of Diana/Artemis contains that mixture of sexuality and death with which Viennese audiences were so enamored, a subject in tune with the taste for the "decadent" in the theater, literature, and visual arts of the *Jahrhundertwende*. Moreover, the Greeks called Artemis a "lion unto women" for the quick and painless death she brought women in childbirth. She was thus oddly both a fertility *and* a virgin goddess, zealously guarding her chastity. The story of Diana surprised at her bath by Actaeon equally encompasses the goddess's chasteness and her penchant for violence. She transforms Actaeon into a stag, whereupon his own dogs pursue him to death. Schiele may even have had a specific precedent in mind: Titian's celebrated *Diana and Actaeon*, painted for Philip II (National Gallery of Scotland, Edinburgh). The two paintings share the motif of Diana's raised arm, shielding her gaze in an act of modesty while disclosing her body.

Schiele's choice of Diana/Artemis would have resonated with the many drawings he made in the spring of 1910. For these ground-breaking works, Schiele took as models poor female patients and their children treated at a clinic run by Erwin von Graff. These were not merely academic nudes, but explicitly erotic portrayals of pregnant women or mothers with their children, or the children alone. Both sexually charged and at least in some sense diseased, these women and children from the industrial suburbs of Vienna provided Schiele with ready, cost-free material to explore what would prove to be a life-long fascination for the apposition of sexuality and death. Schiele was probably no different from most of his contemporaries in seeing working-class women as inherently more sexual (as well as sexually more available) than their middle-class counterparts, and therefore willing to exploit their maternal identity as something fundamentally different from the bourgeois mother, belonging to an uncontrolled, perhaps uncontrollable, Other.[35] Certainly what characterizes Schiele's nude studies from 1909 onward is his deliberate attempt to depict the inherently transgressive body.

Graff, who was among Schiele's earliest patrons, not only purchased his pictures; he also involved himself in the artist's personal affairs, establishing an unusual interplay between the professional and private life of the artist within the artist-patron relationship. Significantly, this behavior was often reproduced in Schiele's subsequent relationships with other clients. Even as Schiele's painting was hanging at the Hunting Exhibition, Graff was treating one of the artist's models (and lover) for an unspecified reason. It could easily have been for a venereal disease, but an abortion is not altogether out of the question. The letter we have is extremely discreet, but in it Graff writes Schiele that the woman complained bitterly about the artist's faithlessness.[36] In this instance, Graff settled his messy affairs medically and personally. The Diana myth thus not only would have served public taste, it could have had considerable personal resonance for the artist. She was, after all, the dangerous goddess of sexual retribution, who had Actaeon torn apart merely for the crime of looking.

Institutions and Patronage

Schiele's participation in the Hunting Exhibition brought him no apparent notoriety; for his entire career he was to remain hungry for any kind of venue for his art, showing individually and as a member of various exhibition societies, and at both public and private exhibition locales. If he always struggled over his finances, it was less for want of money than for the freedom with which he spent it. What is most striking about Schiele's career is that by the age of 20, he had already discovered many of his most important and influential patrons. He had shown at the 1909 *Kunstschau* (although his four pictures were overshadowed by Kokoschka's entries that hung in the same room), and he had led a group of dissident students, unhappy with the pedagogy at Vienna's *Kunstakademie*, in a secession-like exhibition (at a commercial gallery, the Kunst salon Pisko) under the name *Neukunstgruppe*. Even if only modestly, Schiele had "arrived."

In this, as in so many other ways, Schiele's fortunes paralleled Kokoschka's.[37] Schiele was taken up by the Hoffmann/Klimt circle just as Kokoschka had received the patronage of another architect, Adolf Loos, who "discovered" Kokoschka at the first *Kunstschau*. Loos bought many of Kokoschka's early works, arranged for other commissions, accompanied the artist on his first trip outside Austria (to Switzerland), and brought him into the circle around Karl Kraus. How extraordinary this patronage was, especially for artists so young, may be more obvious if we consider that the most famous of twentieth-century artist prodigies, Picasso, was at the age of twenty laboring in relative obscurity in bohemian Paris. Therefore, before we concede their fortunes to talent alone, Schiele and Kokoschka's early success should be linked to Vienna's small, intimately interconnected art world.

At the same time such intimacy, in the absence of public patronage, meant a severely limited number of potential clients. Kokoschka, and to a lesser measure Schiele, used the international market for contemporary art as a vehicle to escape Vienna. With Kraus and Loos's help, Kokoschka came into contact with Herwarth Walden. At the time, Walden was running the Berlin office of Kraus's *Die Fackel;* within the year, he was to be Central Europe's most significant entrepreneur and provocateur for the avant-garde.[38] Walden arranged for Kokoschka to show in 1910 at the most important exhibition locale in Central Europe, Paul Cassirer's Berlin gallery. Soon Kokoschka entered into an exclusive contract with the dealer. Kokoschka's success probably inspired Schiele's efforts to discover a comparable German market for his art, but he was not so fortunate in his foreign contacts.[39] Instead of the internationally recognized figure of Karl Kraus, Schiele depended upon the more locally connected critic and entrepreneur Arthur Roessler. Schiele's initial attempts to develop a close relationship with the influential Munich print dealer Hans Goltz failed, and when Goltz finally did agree to take works on commission, only very modest sales and one small showing in his gallery ensued. On the other hand, no doubt through the influence of Hoffmann, Schiele was given his first one-man show at the Galerie Miethke in 1911. That same year he sold some watercolors to Karl Ernst Osthaus for the Folkwang Museum in Hagen. In 1912 he showed at the Secession, at Goltz's, and at Munich's preeminent contemporary picture gallery, Heinrich Thannhauser's, and most significantly, at the Cologne Sonderbund, the most important international showing of modern art in Europe before the First World War.

Kokoschka was notoriously jealous of his primary place among Vienna's modernist circles. In 1910, in a suite of letters to Walden, he made it clear how much he resented the success of Schiele's friend Max Oppenheimer, who showed at the Galerie Thannhauser in Munich.[40] Kokoschka accused "Mopp," as he was known, of plagiarizing his work, and used his allies at *Der Sturm* and *Die Fackel* to denounce Oppenheimer. Schiele's and Oppenheimer's work, it should be noted, closely resembled each other's (and therefore Kokoschka's as well). One can readily imagine the impression Kokoschka's diatribe and the support he marshaled against Mopp would have made on the 20-year-old artist. Kokoschka may even have played a role in keeping Schiele out of Cassirer's gallery in Berlin and off the pages of *Der Sturm.* Schiele became attached instead to the less aesthetically radical, but more politically committed Berlin journal, Franz Pfemfert's *Die Aktion,* a connection that might be owed to the fact that Roessler wrote for the Social Democratic *Arbeiter-Zeitung.* In any case, Schiele was caught between two institutional and aesthetic paradigms, represented on one side by Kokoschka and Loos and on the other by Klimt and Hoffmann. Whereas Kokoschka's German successes made him already a virtual émigré by 1911, Schiele's continued associations with the *Klimt-Gruppe* bound him forever to the cultural horizons of Vienna. Schiele's obsession with self-definition could only have been exacerbated by negotiating his mutual dependency on two dramatically opposed paradigms, while trying to assert his independence from each.

The Kokoschka influence is most evident in Schiele's art in the expressive distortion of limbs and hands, and most particularly, the placement of the figure against a generally blank background. At another level, Schiele's correspondence makes it abundantly clear that he never possessed Klimt-like ambitions to be a decorative artist. He expressly thought of his work as anti-decorative and of himself as very much the fine, rather than the applied, artist. In this he echoed Loos's attacks on the decorative arts and corresponding exaltation of the fine arts, particularly painting. Schiele's traditional academic training must also have played an important role in shaping his subsequent professional affinities. The many hours devoted to sketching from the model lies behind his precocious and extraordinary mastery of figure drawing. And because Schiele left the Vienna academy at an early age to pursue a more progressive artistic course, drawn by the example of the secessionists, as a painter he was largely self-taught. Consequently, Schiele came late to maturity in the medium and never achieved the kind of sophistication in oil that he obtained as a graphic artist.

To understand this "in-between" nature of Schiele's art, it is instructive to compare Schiele's relationship with Klimt to that of Picasso with his chosen master Cézanne. Between 1905 and 1910 Picasso internalized and then radically reconfigured Cézanne's work, first through the language of primitivism and then through cubism. Picasso eventually discarded the naturalist basis of Cézanne's art in favor of a constructed, essentially diagrammatic, pictorial language. The Viennese secessionist sensibility precluded such moments of crisis; the very word secessionism argues against the doctrine of radical rupture that characterized the Parisian avant-gardes. The secessionists seceded from a tradition no longer viable, but one nonetheless deserving respect and upon which one was entitled to build one's own art. In Vienna, no radical break with the academic tradition ever took place (the break upon which French modernism had grounded itself). Even in his most personal, late style, Klimt's paintings and drawings remain firmly within the traditions of his professional training. And this was true as well for Schiele's generation.

Schiele never questioned the value of figure drawing as the fundamental basis for art (a lesson instilled in every student at every European art academy in the nineteenth century). And in the "program" he wrote for the *Neukunstgruppe's* 1909 show, he declared that "Art always remains the same, art. Therefore, there is no new art, only new artists (*Neukünstler*)."[41] Consciously or not, Schiele's phrasing exactly reproduces the sensibilities of a Liebermann.

If we now return to our picture, Hoffmann's support for Schiele's admission to the Hunting Exhibition may be seen to mirror Loos's promotion of Kokoschka (whom Hoffmann through the *Werkstätte* had also fundamentally assisted at the beginning of his career). Loos rightly saw Kokoschka as an ally in his battle against *fin-de-siècle* aestheticism and the decorative. Hoffmann and Wagner, however, were deeply bound up with those values. By promoting Schiele, they must have knowingly supported an artist whom they took to be sympathetic with their horizon of beliefs. They would have found Schiele's art thematically and stylistically legible, a promising variation on the *Klimt-Gruppe* aesthetic. And why not? Schiele's subsequent identification with Klimt only underlines his deep connections to the *Werkstätte/Klimt-Gruppe*. His work for the Hunting Exhibition followed a long period in which the young artist had closely imitated Klimt's manner, imitations which naturally arose out of an art student's struggle toward a personal style, but also, I believe, out of a calculated identification with Klimt's aesthetics and reputation.

In 1912 Schiele commented on his relationship with Klimt—via a double portrait, "The Hermits" [Rudolf Leopold collection, Vienna], a painting in which Schiele depicts Klimt in a monk-like costume standing behind the similarly dressed young artist. Identifying both artists as prophets of a new vision, Schiele fantastically reversed his subservience to the older artist. While Schiele stares back at us, Klimt's eyes are closed; he leans on Schiele in an unmistakable attitude of physical and psychological dependence. Despite this continued need to foreground his relationship with Klimt, Schiele biographers have emphasized his development of an independent style, largely ignoring how Schiele carefully inserted his professional image within the career path laid out by Klimt. Schiele, in fact, replicated most of the genres favored by Klimt, their *oeuvres* differing only in two significant respects. Schiele never attempted the public, monumental narrative painting that occupied Klimt until his ill-fated University murals, while Klimt, always Vienna's darling despite the controversies, made only two, comparatively insignificant self-portraits.[42] In landscapes, portraiture, and nude studies (particularly the eroticized, female nude), their work neatly overlaps. Similarly, Schiele matures first

as a draftsman at a time when Klimt was deeply involved in figure drawing, creating a corpus that dwarfs even Schiele's in volume.[43] Klimt's
drawings are consistently voyeuristic in approach; at their most licen-
tious, they depict women masturbating or in each other's arms. Of
course, most of these "studies" never resulted in paintings.

This privileging of drawing owed much to the German exhibitions,
in 1905–06, of Rodin's erotic drawings.[44] For the German-speaking
world, Rodin recast the nature of the drawing enterprise, transforming
studio practice, life drawing, into an explicitly erotic encounter, something that used the private qualities of the drawing, but marketed that
intimacy for public consumption. Although Klimt did not show his
drawings, he could and did sell them. These transactions were of course
very discreet and provenances remain difficult to establish, yet there was
an unquestionable taste for Klimt's erotica that might be compared to
Peter Altenberg's now celebrated fetish-like collection of photographs
devoted particularly to images of girls and young women.[45] Schiele, too,
sought a public forum for erotic work; in 1911, for example, he approached Goltz, offering for consignment a portfolio of ten erotic drawings in print reproductions in an edition of 100.[46]

Marketing Identity

Let us return one last time to Schiele's painting at the Hunting Exhibition. If we can only guess at Schiele's subject, what we do know is that
Schiele's model was his sixteen-year-old sister Gerti. Whether either
Hoffmann or Wagner knew this, or even if they had met Gertrud
Schiele, is unknown. But anyone intimate with the drawings Schiele
made early in 1910 and who also knew Gerti would have had little difficulty recognizing his model. More to the point, we should ask whether
Schiele would have cared if Hoffmann and Wagner knew the identity of
the model. The answer is almost certainly no. We know that within a
year or two Schiele began the practice of having his models deliver the
erotic drawings he made of them to his clients. According to Alessandra
Comini, Wally Neuzil, Schiele's mistress and model for four years, complained that this activity "subjected her to occasional lewd interrogation
by some of the more curious customers and sent her back to Schiele in
tears."[47] In 1915, Edith Harms, whom Schiele had married the year
before, objected to any recognizable likeness in the nudes Schiele made
of her, since she too was very often put in the position of acting as an
intermediary for the artist. Schiele may have intended this simultaneous

display of model and art work as a demonstration of skill for his clients' benefit. For us, Schiele's strategy lays bare what is otherwise clothed. Whether or not Schiele took sadistic pleasure in this practice, he was ostentatiously untroubled by any connections that could be made between his pictures and the models who posed for them, no matter how intimately related to the artist. Or to put it more sharply, Schiele deliberately publicized his private relationships, because publicity as such was an important constant in his art; he wanted to blur the boundaries between his public and private lives.

Schiele's narcissism is a *topos* among his biographers. How could it be otherwise, when the artist himself clearly made a fetish out of the mirror that prominently stood in his studio, an artist who in a 1914 photo shoot posed in the contorted manner of his paintings, an artist who was a relentless self-portraitist? Such gestures defy any segregation of the work of art from the artist who produced it. Despite these deliberate displays of selfhood and even of self-mimicry, Schiele's biographers almost invariably present Schiele's narcissistic themes as products of an involuntary, intrinsically psychological excess, exemplifying the artist's status as an overwrought, but altogether typical "expressionist." They would also explain Schiele's excessive egoism by referring to his extraordinary youth. Certainly his early stylistic maturity was not matched by an emotional maturity and Schiele's narcissism unquestionably took the form of a remarkable megalomania. In a letter written in 1913, Schiele announced to his mother that "Without doubt I shall be the greatest, the most beautiful, the most precious [of your] fruit. Through my independent will all beautiful and noble effects are united in me—this also, no doubt, because of the male [principle]. I shall be the fruit which after its decay will still leave behind eternal life; therefore how great must be your joy—to have borne me?"[48] As much as such statements tell us about Schiele's personality, they tell us more about what he believed the artist to be. Schiele was hardly unique among Central European modernists in subscribing to the bohemian ideal of the artist's essential alienated otherness. The romantic ideal of the self-sacrificing artist had been powerfully underlined through the example of van Gogh, whose recently translated letters, along with numerous exhibitions in the region of his paintings (including a number of Viennese showings), made an impact on Central European cultural paradigms that can scarcely be exaggerated.[49] Schiele's early writings display the same rhetorical tropes as those Central Europeans discovered in van Gogh.[50] And again, Schiele's talent and immaturity were two interlocking, marketable commodities in a city that had always prided itself on its child prodigies. His narcissistic stance was consequently as much a commodity as a psychological condition, a fact made manifestly evident in the poster Schiele created to advertise his 1915 one-man exhibition at the second-best contemporary gallery in Vienna. Schiele measured his artistic triumph by his own presumed martyrdom, posing as a new St. Sebastian.

Schiele's work establishes a fundamental connection to Klimt while declaring its distance, resisting precisely those ornamental qualities that characterized Klimt's art. In the specific context of Klimt's work, the effect Schiele creates in the Hunting picture is precisely that of stripping away. Gerti is not only stripped of her clothes and made to strike a sexually provocative pose, she is simultaneously robbed of any context for her presence in the image, which of course is why we struggle to determine its subject. If she began as Diana, Gerti is reduced to a pin-up, defined by nothing but her sexuality. Here, Schiele's sensibility may be linked to Otto Weininger's notion of the egoless woman, his hysterical assertion that women are only concerned with and capable of sex.[51] Schiele's concentration on the unornamented body is all the more striking when compared to the work of Kokoschka and his other contemporaries. Despite the dramatic gestural qualities of most of his studies, Schiele had very little interest in the actions of his figures. Most importantly, he rarely allowed this gesturalism to contribute to a narrative. As his art matured, Schiele increasingly emphasized the lack of human agency through the body's inaction. Between 1913 and 1915, for example, Schiele often took to representing his figures as puppets, usually sprawling helplessly on the ground, as if their strings had just been cut. Similarly, Schiele registered artistic agency not in the acting but in the showing. The body was the drama, held up before a narcissistic mirror.

These are the signs of Schiele's modernity, his modernist style, that reflect the turn to the sort of non-narrative, and ultimately non-objective, painting flowing out of Paris through the international art trade. But by Picasso's standards, Schiele is implicitly conservative. In 1910 his knowledge of French modernism was neither deep nor theoretical.[52] Unlike the major art of Parisian modernism, the minor art of Central Europe, with its emphasis on the body, attempted to keep alive a tradition that for centuries had been devoted to making the body speak. Klimt and Schiele, by reimagining the body as a sexual entity, rather than a metonym for beauty, attempted to speak a truer speech than offered by the classical language of the body they inherited through the academies of art. But such efforts were made to appear backward-looking in an artistic atmosphere that was beginning to contemplate the throwing away of illusionistic representation altogether.

I am arguing that Schiele's professional self-definition was based on consciously pushing further the already taboo-driven art of Klimt. Schiele substituted children for the mature bodies of Klimt's women, and for Klimt's frankly voyeuristic art, he substituted an endless narcissism. So even as Schiele accepted in principle much of Klimt's sexual politics, albeit modified to encompass his own sense of pathetic sexual inadequacy, Schiele attempted to strip away the decorative surface of Klimt's *oeuvre*, whether understood as clothing, or as Klimt-like patterning. Both his awareness of the new traffic in pictures and his critique of the decorative are surprisingly in accord with that of his slightly older contemporary Kafka, whose ambition to find the truth, the "Holy of Holies," took on the metaphor of stripping away all one's clothes, then one's skin, to arrive finally at the inner soul.[53] Unlike Kafka, however, Schiele settled for truth-telling in the form of physical exposure. If we follow Michel Foucault's fundamental critique of the role of confession in the "science of sexuality," a "science" so integral to Viennese culture, Schiele's sexual truth-telling signified not opposition to society, despite his famous imprisonment in 1912 on the charges of kidnapping and obscenity, but was precisely oriented toward meeting a societal demand.[54] His work sustained rather than fundamentally criticized the social order. Intimate and direct, mythic yet shorn of narrative qualities, the art of the young Egon Schiele carefully restaged Klimt for a new sensibility, sustained by the marketplace.

Notes

1. Historisches Museum der Stadt Wien; Inv. 96030/2.
2. For a more extensive discussion of these and the subsequent arguments of this paper, see my *Marketing Modernism in Fin-de-Siècle Europe* (Princeton, 1994).
3. Historians have often linked the institutional phenomenon of secessionism to the aesthetic of impressionism—embracing not only the French masters, but also their Central European variants. These artists, however, could be as diverse as Max Liebermann and Edvard Munch. The confusion stems from the fact that what was called impressionism in the 1890s was actually an international salon art. Its internationally celebrated representatives were not Monet and Degas, but Albert Besnard and Charles Cottet. There was very little impressionist painting either practiced or purchased in Central Europe until after 1900.
4. There is no better example of this than the career of the German art critic and entrepreneur Julius Meier-Graefe. Caught up in the enthusiasm for the decorative arts in the 1890s, Meier-Graefe opened a gallery in Paris devoted to leading examples of French and German art nouveau production, but in the process was exposed to French postimpressionism. In 1900 Meier-Graefe wrote eloquently on behalf of German *Jugendstil*, but by 1904, he became almost completely committed to modernist French painting, writing some of the earliest German-language criticism on their behalf. See *Marketing Modernism*, 235–263.
5. The resistance to French modernism was loudest in Germany and deeply indebted to nationalist fervor. While there are many pamphlets, newspaper articles, and of course, the very public resistance of the Kaiser to all signs of modernism, the most revealing perhaps was the anthology of essays *Ein Protest deutscher Künstler*, ed. Carl Vinnen (Jena, 1911), which denounced the acquisition of French modernist painting by German museums as a Jewish dealer-led conspiracy and the reply, from many of French modernism's most ardent allies in Germany published as *Im Kampf um die Kunst: Die Antwort auf den Protest deutscher Künstler* (Munich, 1911).
6. The identity-crisis thesis has been most extensively argued by Jacques Le Rider in his *Modernity and Crises of Identity: Culture and Society in Fin-de-Siècle Vienna*, trans. Rosemary Morris (New York, 1993).
7. C. Schorske, "Cultural Hothouse," *New York Review of Books* (11 December 1975): 39–44, esp. 41.
8. In his underappreciated book on Klimt and the Secession, Werner Hofmann clearly lays out the differences between the 1908 and 1909 *Kunstschauen*. See his *Gustav Klimt*, trans. Inge Goodwin (London, 1972).
9. It was in just these terms that the second exhibition was brushed aside by the Vienna correspondent for *Die Kunst für Alle* 25:1 (1 October 1909): 20–22. These remarks are surprising for the journal that devoted considerable space to the various international exhibitions of contemporary art.
10. Schorske, *Fin-de-Siècle Vienna* (New York, 1978), 330.
11. See, for example, Schorske's contribution to the catalogue *Vienne 1880–1938. L'Apocalypse Joyeuse* (Paris, 1986), 72–81, in which he accepts the argument that Hoffmann's Stoclet palace was constructed for "homo psychologicus."
12. A thorough reexamination of expressionism, outside the literature and mentality that supported it, still needs to be done. From a theoretical viewpoint, Hal Foster's two essays "The Expressive Fallacy" in *Recodings* (Seattle, 1985), 59–73, and "Primitive Scenes," *Critical Inquiry* 20 (Autumn 1993): 69–102, provide a useful point of

departure. See also Helen Boorman, "Rethinking the Expressionist Era: Wilhelmine Cultural Debates and Prussian Elements in German Expressionism," *Oxford Art Journal* 9:2 (1986): 3–15.

13. C. Schorske, "Cultural Hothouse," 41.

14. Schorske, *Fin-de-Siècle Vienna*, 214.

15. M. Burckhard, introduction to *Ver Sacrum* (January 1898): 1–2.

16. Paul Schultze-Naumburg, "Die Internationale Ausstellung 1896 der Secession in München," *Die Kunst für Alle* 11 (1 July 1896): 289.

17. To take but one example, the secessions were far more likely to exclude women artists than their older counterparts.

18. M. Liebermann, "Rede zur Eröffnung von Ausstellung der Berliner Secession," (spring 1900), reprinted in *Die Phantasie in der Malerei*, ed. G. Busch (Frankfurt, 1978), 170–171.

19. The dissolution of the Secession in 1905 has never properly been studied. See, however, Wolfgang Hilger, "Geschichte der Vereinigung Bildender Künstler Österreichs. Secession 1897–1918," in *Die Wiener Secession: Die Vereinigung bildender Künstler 1897–1985* (Vienna, Cologne, Graz, 1986), 48–50; and Christian Nebehay, *Gustav Klimt: Dokumentation* (Vienna, 1969), 345–350. And see Jensen, *Marketing Modernism in Fin-de-Siècle Europe*, 163–200.

20. Schorske, *Fin-de-Siècle Vienna*, 117.

21. Virtually all of the Central European secessions worked in close cooperation with local, regional, or sometimes international galleries to bring at least a token display of French modernist art to their various exhibitions. The Berlin Secession, for example, was structured around its close relationship with Paul Cassirer, who was directly, sometimes contractually, connected to such Parisian firms as Durand-Ruel and Bernheim Jeune. And it was often through Berlin that other regional Central European exhibition societies received their collections of French art. The literature on these firms is growing. See especially the special issue, "Sammler der frühen Moderne in Berlin," *Zeitschrift des deutschen Vereins für Kunstwissenschaft* 42:3 (1988); Nicolaas Teeuwisse, *Vom Salon zur Secession* (Berlin, 1986); Josef Kern, *Impressionismus im Wilheminischen Deutschland* (Würzburg, 1989); and Jensen, *Marketing Modernism in Fin-de-Siècle Europe*. For a particularly illuminating account of the merchandising of one artist, see Walter Feilchenfeldt, *Vincent van Gogh and Paul Cassirer: The Reception of van Gogh in Germany from 1901 to 1914*, Cahier Vincent, vol. 2 (Zwolle, 1988).

22. Ludwig Hevesi once said of Moll that "his personal *rôle* in the modernising of the art life of Vienna consists in his restless energy in the service of a pet idea, and in the sociable, business-like and diplomatic qualities which are requisite in the struggle to maintain these interests. He was the very leaven of the new movement, a Minister of Fine Arts without a portfolio." See L. Hevesi, "Modern Painting in Austria," in *The Art-Revival in Austria*, special number of *The Studio* (summer 1906): section a (i–xvi), esp. viii.

23. See Bertha Zuckerkandl's account of the breakup in "Die Spaltung der Wiener Sezession," *Die Kunst für Alle* 20 (15 July 1905): 486–488.

24. See Zuckerkandl's report on the character of the two sides in her review, "Die XXIII. Ausstellung der Wiener Sezession," *Die Kunst für Alle* 20 (1 July 1905): 441. She describes the disputing parties as "eine Stil-Gruppe und eine realistische Gruppe. Die einen betrachten «Kunst» als Einheit, als großen dekorativen Zusammenhang architektonischer, bildnerischer und angewandter Gestaltungen, die anderen

wollen von der Unterordnung, von der Harmonisierung des Kunstwerkes mit dem Ganzen nichts wissen." For a brief but useful discussion of the role of the newspaper critics on behalf of the Secession, see Werner J. Schweiger, *Wiener Werkstätte* (New York, 1984), 13–15. Vienna's art critics were as concentrated and as exclusive a group as the Secession itself.

25. Klimt was explicit about this state of affairs in the address he gave in conjunction with the opening of the 1908 *Kunstschau*. He complained that "we know full well that the exhibition is in no way the ideal form for making contact between the artist and the public. The carrying out of large scale public art commissions, for example, would serve this purpose infinitely better for us." He attributed the absence of such patronage to the government's obsession with political and social matters. Klimt's address is reprinted in Nebehay, *Klimt: Dokumentation*, 394.

26. G. Deleuze and F. Guattari, *Kafka: Toward a Minor Literature*, trans. Dana Polan (Minneapolis, 1986).

27. Adolf Loos, "Ornament und Verbrechen," repr. in Loos, *Sämtliche Schriften*, vol. 1, ed. F. Glück (Vienna, 1962), 276–288.

28. Arthur Roessler even had to warn Schiele in 1911 to abandon his penchant for self-promotion and for exaggerating his ties to Gustav Klimt, Wagner, and other Viennese luminaries: "I must restrict my dealings with you until you bring to your behaviour—which I hope will become more adult—as much consideration and cultivation as you devote to your art. You should be less anxious to make capital by hawking around details of your relationship with Klimt and also less keen to try architect Wagner's patience or tactlessly to damage well-meaning friendships. I'm not bluffing." For the German original, see Christian Nebehay, *Egon Schiele, 1890–1918: Briefe, Dokumente, Gedichte* (Salzburg and Vienna, 1979), document #169, 163. This translation is from Frank Whitford, *Egon Schiele* (New York, 1980), 95.

29. Still the best discussion of the early literature on expressionist art and its underlying appeals to German nationalism and the German Renaissance past is Geoffrey Perkins, *Contemporary Theory of Expressionism* (Bern and Frankfurt, 1974).

30. The photograph has been frequently reproduced. See Jane Kallir, *Egon Schiele* (New York, 1994), 55.

31. The major monographs on Hoffmann do not treat this exhibition, a clear indication of how little regard modernist-informed sensibilities have had for such phenomena as "hunting exhibitions."

32. The only document beside the drawing to take note of Schiele's participation in the exhibition is a letter from Erwin Graff, one of Schiele's patrons, in which he notes that there was a general lack of quality to the exhibits—implying, of course, that Schiele's stood above all the others. See Nebehay, *Egon Schiele, 1890–1918*, document #102, 131.

33. J. M. MacKenzie, *The Empire of Nature: Hunting, Conservation, and British Imperialism* (Manchester, 1988).

34. Bertha Zuckerkandl, in a famous epithet, described Hoffmann as a leader in the "Aristokratisierung des Geschmacks, der Veredelung der Luxuswelt." For a reading of Hoffmann as a "conservative" modern, who refused to polarize industrial culture with hand-made goods, see Peter Gorsen, "Josef Hoffmann: Zur Modernität eines konservativen Baumeisters," in *Ornament und Askese*, ed. Alfred Pfabigan (Vienna, 1985), 69–92.

35. See Sander L. Gilman, in *Difference and Pathology: Stereotypes of Sexuality, Race, and Madness* (Ithaca, 1985), 15–35.

36. See Nebehay, *Egon Schiele, 1890–1918*, document #102, 131.

37. My discussion of Kokoschka and his patrons here and elsewhere in this essay is deeply indebted to Sherwin Simmon's important article, "Kitsch oder Kunst? Kokoschka's *Der Sturm* and Commerce in Art," *The Print Collector's Newsletter* 23:5 (November–December, 1992): 161–167. See also Patrick Werkner, *Austrian Expressionism: The Formative Years*, trans. Nicholas T. Parsons (Palo Alto, 1993), for his chapters on Kokoschka, Schiele, and their contemporaries.

38. For a discussion of and documents for these events, see *Oskar Kokoschka: der Sturm: die Berliner Jahre 1910–1916: eine Dokumentation* (Pöchlarn, 1986).

39. Schiele failed to land a similar contract or exhibition with Cassirer. See Roessler's card to Schiele dated 2 August 1911, in Nebehay, *Egon Schiele*, document #240, 179.

40. See Kokoschka, *Briefe*, vol. 1 (Düsseldorf, 1984).

41. This brief essay was republished with slight modifications under the title "Die Kunst—der Neukünstler," in *Die Aktion* 4:20 (1914): 428.

42. In an undated manuscript cited in Nebehay, *Klimt, Dokumentation*, 32, Klimt wrote that in fact "There is no self-portrait of me. I am not interested in myself as 'material for a picture,' rather in other people, especially women, and even more in other phenomena. I am convinced that as a person I am not particularly interesting."

43. Arthur Roessler, "Im memoriam Gustav Klimt," cited in Nebehay, *Klimt: Dokumentation*, 356.

44. See Albert Elsen, "Drawing and a New Sexual Intimacy: Rodin and Schiele," in *Egon Schiele: Art, Sexuality, and Viennese Modernism*, ed. Patrick Werkner (Stanford, 1994), 5–30.

45. Among the recent spate of literature on Altenberg's photograph collection, a representative essay is Leo A. Lensing, "Peter Altenberg's Fabricated Photographs: Literature and Photography in *Fin-de-Siècle* Vienna," in *Vienna 1900: From Altenberg to Wittgenstein*, ed. Edward Timms and Ritchie Robertson (Edinburgh, 1990), 47–72.

46. See Roessler's letter to Goltz cited in Nebehay, *Egon Schiele 1890–1918*, document #276, 186.

47. Without documentation, this is the story told by Alessandra Comini in *Egon Schiele: Portraits* (Berkeley and Los Angeles, 1974), 99.

48. Schiele's letter is dated 31 March 1913; this translation in A. Comini, *Egon Schiele*, 87.

49. See Ron Manheim, "The Germanic van Gogh: A Case Study of Cultural Annexation," *Simiolus* 19:4 (1989): 277–288.

50. For example, Manheim (ibid. 282) cites Gustav Pauli's pamphlet *Der Krieg und die deutsche Kunst: Vortrag gehalten am 20. November 1914 in der Reihe der "Deutsche Vorträge Hamburgischer Professoren"* (Hamburg, 1915), 13, to the effect that "alles, was wir als bezeichnend für den Genius unserer Rasse angesprochen haben, wohnte in seine [van Gogh's] Seele: die Selbstherrlichkeit, die den Saum verachtet, die Macht des Ausdrucks, die Ueberschwenglichkeit und die mystisch-schwärmerische Naturliebe." In a fragment cited by Roessler in an early essay on Schiele, reprinted as "Kritische Fragmente, 1909–1918," in *Egon Schiele in der Albertina*, ed. Erwin Mitsch (Vienna, 1990), 18, the artist writes: "Meine rohen Lehrer waren mir stets Feinde. Sie—und andere—verstanden es nicht, daß ich von Vornehmen der Vornehmste, von Rückgebern der Rückgiebigste bin; daß ich den Tod liebe und das Leben; daß ich alles zugleich bin, aber niemals alles zu gleicher Zeit tue. Ich bin kein zwiespältiges Wesen. Mensch und Künstler in einem bin ich. Und ich bin für mich und die, denen die durstige Trunksucht nach Freisein bei mir alles schenkt—und

für alle auch, weil alle ich auch liebe. In mir ist ein ewiges Träumen voll süßesten Lebensüberschusses. Rastlos, mit bangen Schmerzen innen in der Seele, lodert, brennt, wächst das Träumen zum Kampf, Herzenskrampf. Ich bin wahnwitzig rege mit aufgeregter Lust—denn nun kann ich endlich die spendende Sonne wiedersehen und frei sein. Die höchste Empfindung ist Religion und Kunst. Natur is Zweck—aber dort ist Gott, und ich empfinde ihn stark, sehr stark, am stärksten. Ich glaube, daß es keine, moderne' Kunst gibt, daß es nur eine Kunst gibt, und die ist immerwährend."

51. For a recent reading of Weininger as an extreme, but essential, mirror of male attitudes toward women at the *Jahrhundertwende*, see Slavoj Žižek, "Otto Weininger, or Woman Doesn't Exist," *New Formations* 23 (summer 1994): 97–113.

52. For instance, in a letter dating from November 1910, Schiele proposed to his friend Arthur Roessler that the *Künstlerhaus* (!) ought to arrange "a great international art show. I told this idea to Klimt." He then draws up a potential list of contributors: "Rodin, van Gogh, Gauguin, Minne, Klimt's work from the last ten years, Toorop, Stuck, Liebermann, Slevogt, Corinth, Meštrovič, and so on—only painting and sculpture. What a scream for Vienna!" Letter cited in Nebehay, *Egon Schiele*, document no. 144, 139. Meštrovič was a Croatian sculptor.

53. Schiele's love of dressing up and role playing, and his sense of fashion parallel in a striking way similar qualities of the life and work of Kafka. See Mark Anderson's brilliant analysis of Kafka's critique of ornament and fashion in *Kafka's Clothes: Ornament and Aestheticism in the Hapsburg Fin de Siècle* (Oxford, 1992). Anderson has shown the rich way in which the consciousness of trade, especially the trade in fashion, determined Kafka's orientation toward the idea of the decorative in *fin-de-siècle* aestheticism. Schiele's career shows a strikingly similar relationship both to commerce and to the decorative. Between these two readings, the strikingly idiosyncratic art of Kafka loses some of its exceptional qualities by reacquiring aspects of conscious agency, confined no longer to psychological and aesthetic matters, but one that acknowledges the intensely commercial world in which Kafka lived and his simultaneous struggle toward a literary and a personal identity.

54. See Michel Foucault, *The History of Sexuality*, vol. 1 (New York, 1980).

Chapter 9

THE IMAGE OF WOMEN IN PAINTING

Clichés and Reality in Austria-Hungary, 1895–1905

Ilona Sármány-Parsons

Ever since Carl Schorske's book *Fin-de-Siècle Vienna* first focused the attention of cultural and art history on Vienna, most references to Austro-Hungarian culture of the *fin de siècle* have tended to project the Viennese pattern onto the whole region. It is only local scholars who have attempted to correct this perspective when writing on Czech, Polish, or Hungarian culture, but they too have often narrowed the focus by discussing one nation only. Thus the publications of Czech, Polish, or Hungarian scholars tend to move within the framework of their own national discourse and neglect the comparative dimension with other cultural centers of the Monarchy. As a result of historically based attitudes, they prefer to stress the French connection with their individual national cultures. This attitude, which ultimately stems from the particularist preoccupations of alienated neighbors, is fairly widespread.

The present study is a first attempt at lifting the veil which has covered the visual culture of the region; that is, beyond the influence of Vienna. By using a specific theme—the representation of women—it attempts to map the attitudes and outlooks which were current in Prague, Cracow, and Budapest at the same time as Klimt's paintings were causing such a scandal in Vienna. It explores the question of whether the modern art of these centers reflected shared preoccupations, or rather expressed fundamental differences between national cultures, with distinct national and aesthetic priorities.

At the turn of the century Central Europe was relatively marginal to European culture as a whole. Culturally it looked to Germany, but also (and more importantly for the fine arts) to France for inspiration and models, absorbing many influences that originated in Paris.[1] The way in which the artists of the smaller nations selected from the pluralistic palette of the Western European art scene was decisively influenced by local artistic tradition and cultural heritage. In painting, not only the new stylistic experiments had to be learned, but also new ways of looking at familiar subjects, especially at women and femininity, although this latter task was not necessarily a conscious goal. Women provided the most popular subject matter, after landscapes, for the artists of modernism, and the one that offered the greatest potential for artistic experimentation. New approaches to art and a new aesthetic were phenomena parallel to the social developments of urban life, but there were also likely to be clashes between the two, in this age of the "new woman."[2]

In the four important art centers of the region (Vienna, Budapest, Prague, and Cracow), the breakthrough to modernism came simultaneously. The local (national) schools of art all attempted to be cosmopolitan and modern, but also to be unique, in the sense of producing art typical only of their own nation and its perception of itself.[3] This fundamentally similar *Kunstwollen* of the four art centers stimulated the leading masters to plough their own furrow strongly differentiated from their contemporaries, yet acting on similar impulses.

Fashionable Images of Woman in *Fin-de-Siècle* Painting

An amazingly rich variety of images of woman could be found in the painting of the 1890s. In traditional genres of painting, female figures were allegorical; this applied not only to traditional scenes with allusions to antiquity, but also to the representation of modernity, such as inventions and technology (e.g., electricity). Second, portraiture, especially the flattering portrayal of women, was still very much in fashion. Third, in genre painting, women from all classes of society were painted, from the poorest peasants through poverty-stricken working women (especially in Belgian painting), and all the layers of the middle class up to the highest ranks of society. Special attention was paid to domesticity as a characteristic of femininity. The Victorian "angel in the house" was a widespread ideal. Yet impressionism also depicted women in the public spaces characteristic of modern metropolitan life, and celebrated the contemporary fashionable types of "modern beauty" of a more liberated Western society.[4]

From the many novelties offered by the French painting of the 1870s and 1880s, two major shifts were influential as models that traveled far beyond the boundaries of the French art scene. First, there was the change in the painting of domestic interiors from one of narrative detail to one of atmosphere, focusing also on the emotional and intellectual state of the model. Second, there was the metamorphosis of traditional biblical and mythological subjects into misogynistic visions of woman, in which the female principle became demonized. These two different types of representations offered the artist two new ways of seeing womankind with a heightened psychological insight: painters now began to explore aspects of the autonomous individual behind the feminine façade. In the process they projected their own irrational fears and emotions onto the female model. The latter process has hitherto received more attention from art historians than the former because of its shocking images and its close connection to psychoanalysis.[5]

Every stylistic epoch creates its own dominant symbols of the female. The art of the *fin de siècle* from the 1890s onwards is particularly rich in representations of women, which, in contrast to the practice of realism, essentially drew on two opposed archetypes: the fertile, protective mother or pure virgin, and her opposite, the seductive courtesan, the mysterious female. One of the most important personifications of the sexual instincts was the wicked temptress—conceived as Eve, Salome, Nana, or similar biblical or literary figures. Freed from their traditional biblical and mythological contexts, as well as from religious significance, the *femmes fatales* of the nineteenth century became pervasive figures, the play of subjective fantasy.[6]

Although the male artists of the 1890s in the Dual Monarchy did not necessarily accept the hidden message concerning women in the works of the French impressionists as subsequently interpreted, they certainly perceived the difference between pictorial tradition of their native schools in the depiction of women, and the work of the modernists. The cultural climate of the Munich Secession and the strongly misogynistic streak in the German symbolists (well known in the art circles of the Monarchy) offered plenty of new clichés to be picked up and exploited.[7]

The Viennese Scene between 1897 and 1905

The artistic production of the period between 1897 and 1905 is so multifaceted, and its components influenced by so many political, social, and artistic factors, that it is impossible to offer a single, all-embracing theory to explain its protean character.[8] A great deal has been written about this *fin-de-siècle* Viennese art: important aspects of its genesis and the nature of its achievements have been analyzed in minute detail.[9] The inspiration of the philosophy of Schopenhauer and Nietzsche on the intellectuals and artists of the age has also been extensively examined. Nor is it surprising that psychoanalytic interpretations have proliferated in the analysis of an art that stemmed from the same milieu as Freud and Weininger.[10]

The outburst of creative energies, as shaped by the experimental phase of *Jugendstil*, created a specifically Viennese style in the visual arts. In painting, the dominant personality of the Secession, whose visual erudition supplied it with a new palette of images in the early years, was its charismatic first president, Gustav Klimt. All the decisive and remarkable artistic happenings, the great successes, failures, and scandals, revolve around his works. For this reason, I propose to limit discussion of the images of women in turn-of-the-century Viennese painting to the works of Klimt.[11]

Although far from being the only major theme or aspect to it, Klimt's fame was firmly established because of his art's openly erotic character. His whole *oeuvre* is indeed dominated by images of women. His drawings, in which he omits reference to the individual personality of the model, are likewise dominated by the image of "woman," of femaleness as such. However, his approach to femininity is by no means similar to the misogynistic depictions of some of the great symbolists (e.g., Gustave Moreau) or to those of popular contemporaries like Franz von Stuck. One reason for this difference may be that such literary or spiritual inspirations as stimulated this sort of view of women, like Decadence and satanism, were hardly present in Vienna, just as the Western European specter of the *femme fatale* was unable to flourish in Viennese culture.[12] Woman as the allegory of evil appeared only when she could be used as thematic material—for example by Klimt in his stern allegory of "Tragedy," in his oil painting *Judith* (1900), in the hostile forces of his *Beethoven frieze* (1902), or to indicate the inexorability of the Furies in his university painting *Jurisprudence* (1904).

Before the rise of the expressionist generation[13] (Schiele, Kokoschka), and apart from Alfred Kubin (who surely does not belong to the Viennese art world),[14] it is very difficult to detect earlier, in the circle of Klimt and his literary friends (Hermann Bahr, Ludwig Hevesi, Felix Salten, Hugo von Hofmannsthal, and even Arthur Schnitzler) an unrepentantly misogynistic attitude between 1890 and 1903; nor can we find much in the way of images of demonic women. The characterization of women in Schnitzler, the writer who created perhaps the richest gallery of them in his works, is always very acutely observed and realistic.[15] One could even say that he feels more sympathy for female characters than for men; his *süße Mädl* and trusting heroines inspire much more affection and pity in the reader than do the male protagonists. Typically they are more vulnerable and exploitable; their sins are the sins of the age. The archetypal evil heroines of mythology were all created later (e.g., Hofmannsthal's *Electra*, 1904). Even then these bewitching figures did not stand for the whole gender, rather constituting only one of several different types.

Whether the views on women of this generation of writers were really influenced by their everyday contact with Viennese feminists such as Rosa Mayreder, Marie Lang, or Grete Meisel-Hess, who were themselves literary personalities and whose critical attitude and views on the relationship between the sexes was by no means bitterly combatant, is an interesting question which merits further research.[16]

Although the theories of the "satanist" Przybyszewski were well known, they had no followers in Vienna, while the dramas of Strindberg and Wedekind made an impact only on the circle around Karl Kraus. The critics of the Secession—Loos and some of his hangers on—were the real representatives of the highly ambivalent and negative picture of woman.[17] Only after 1905 did they become influential among the young bohemians, while the realistic, and thus more understanding, representation of women was always present in the imperial capital.[18]

At the high point of their artistic careers, and before the time-bomb of Weininger's theories exploded in 1902–1903, there was little evidence that the vanguard of the Secession (Gustav Klimt, Kolo Moser, Carl Moll) suffered either as individuals or as philosophizing intellects from the sexual crisis of *fin-de-siècle* man which was the real source of the demonic image of woman.[19] Klimt never really focused on the issue of *Geschlechterkampf* as such. His allegory of love (*Love*, 1895) shows the woman as victim, whose tragic fate will inevitably follow the innocent self-abandonment of her first infatuation.[20] Contemporary woman never appears as a fearful, mesmerizing creature in Klimt's canvases. The demonic quality in his specific portrayals of powerful women is exclusively restricted to the goddesses and demonic figures of Greek mythology or to heroines from the Bible. The female element (femaleness) becomes frightful and menacing only if it represents something more than an individual woman, as when it stands for superhuman forces such as that of nature herself, or assumes the form of goddesses like Pallas Athena, of evil spirits like the Erinyes (Furies) or water nymphs. Their significance is closely tied to tradition, and thus to an historical representation of their specific roles; Klimt accepts this tradition, but nevertheless modernizes it by enriching its female depiction with disturbingly sensual and sexual qualities. In this way the female figures become the embodiments of eternal human instincts presented in a modern form.[21] The ambivalence of the power they represent in Greek mythology cannot be projected onto the larger canvas of Klimt's general statements about "woman." This is a point well made by Robert Goldwater, who writes: "… for Klimt the sexual is never the sinful: youth may suggest the sadness of old age, and birth an inevitable death, but the sensuous is not evil and woman is neither the incarnation of temptation, nor the image of all that is ideal."[22]

The most daring novelty of Klimt's representation of woman lay in the courage with which he broke the taboo of depicting pregnancy in the female nude (*Hope* I, 1903).[23] The artist's passionate interest in the female body was not an intellectual attempt to analyze the psyche of women, her fears, pains, sorrows or any powerful emotion, but an obsession with catching the individual moments of psycho-physical eroticism in the female body.[24] This is the obsession which drove him to draw hundreds of erotic sketches of his nude models. These drawings were not made for public consumption, nor were they loaded with the traditional visual codes of Western art. Thus they are deeply revealing of Klimt's preoccupations. Naturally every individual—and the artist is no exception—behaves and thinks according to social contexts and given situations. Klimt exploited his artistic knowledge of female physical eroticism in his symbolic "mankind" pictures, making them thus into powerful images of the victory of the life-principle over death. He was obsessed with catching and fixing the moment of sensual ecstasy. In the rapidly sketched drawings of models, no doubt voyeurism played a role, as well as the typical artistic obsession of catching each gesture, pose and feeling. But when such figures were included in his great symbolic canvases of life and death, Klimt certainly used them to symbolize and sensualize the anonymous miracle of love. Eros is portrayed as the only force on earth which can rescue life and beauty, even if only temporarily, from death and the shadow of mortality.

Nevertheless, Klimt cannot be regarded as the great "psychologist of women," since his psychological interest in his models—even in his portraiture—was very limited. Contemporaries saw these portraits, together with the great symbolic compositions, as the most bewitching novelties of the "Viennese Decadence," and they were quick to note the fact that, in most of the portraits, the ornamental dresses were evidently more the focus of the artist's attention than the models themselves.[25]

Klimt represented most aspects of life that interested him in the form of female figures; but this does not mean that he perceived the world as fundamentally the realm of the feminine. The female figure was a deliberate artistic device, but that did not imply that the artist was unaware of the other layers of reality which were not the province of the feminine. All the important decisions in turn-of-the-century Vienna were still made by men—it was only in the realm of sexuality that an awareness of tension between the sexes became a live issue in Vienna. No rational contemporary would have agreed that the entire multifaceted world could be represented only in terms of the figure of woman. By the same token, the *oeuvre* of Klimt cannot be interpreted only as homage to matriarchy, the supposed guiding force of modernism.[26]

One aspect of contemporary life, however—and an important one—did have an impact on Klimt's work, namely the change then taking place in the role of women, and the new discoveries of psychology, especially sexual psychology. Yet the vision of Viennese modernism cannot be reduced to this single aspect, nor forced into an artificially narrow frame of interpretation dependent upon it. The artist's individual psyche and intellect remain paramount. There is perhaps one very important point where a definite distinction has to be made between Klimt's erotica and the drawings of a Rops or a Schiele. There is no sign that Klimt despises women, desires to humiliate them, or regards them as hostile beings. To him, woman is part of the natural world, a fragment of the infinite continuum that is the stream of life, a passive element in nature. Thus women, in contrast to men, who are never represented as lost in the ecstatic moment, are much closer to nature itself. This reflected a widespread view at the time, and was by no means peculiar to Klimt. His attitude is that of the outsider, of the omnipotent but sympathetic voyeur, of the artistic genius who, through his intellect and talent is an observer of the woman's world but is not dominated by it. The *oeuvre* of Klimt, with its ultimately self-confident and calm attitude, reflects the standpoint of a generation of artists who had not experienced a sexual identity crisis, unlike the succeeding generation of expressionists.[27] This generation perceived and acknowledged the "otherness" of femininity, took joy in it and made it serve their art. Women were their models, muses, lovers, patrons, and even symbols, but were not feared as enemies or treated as equals.

Klimt's later pictures became more and more autonomous, and more distanced from any specific social reality. Their *Wirklichkeitsferne* (distance from reality) was heightened by sophisticated stylization and enigmatic allegorical content. It is exactly this solipsistic attitude, focusing on the inner world of the artist, which was carried further by the following generation of expressionists, and which differentiated the greatest achievements of the leading Viennese master from Czech, Polish, or Hungarian contemporaries. It is the sociohistorical component which, for understandable reasons, was missing from much of Viennese art around 1900. The other art centers, even if they were beginning to loosen the strong social ties between what the artists produced and what was expected of them, could never completely escape social reality to the same extent as the Austrians, especially Klimt, Schiele, and the young Kokoschka. In this respect, the expressionist generation, in spite of their generational revolt against the Klimt-generation, are faithful followers of the social pattern inherited from their fathers.

The attitude of this young generation toward women was fundamentally different from that of the fathers' generation, and not only because misogynistic theories arrived in Vienna later, after 1905. The sea-change in this respect was partly the result of the remarkable influence of Otto Weininger, but it was also the consequence of the fact, that the leading young painters such as Kokoschka and Schiele were psychologically unbalanced adolescents, yet already recognized as prodigies creating masterpieces. It was they who were exposed to fashionable sexual theories and whose artistic works were saturated with the then-popular misogyny.

These artists failed to develop a critical distance from the extremely negative attitude not only toward women, but also from the whole issue of sexuality. The Viennese artistic scene was not backward by comparison with Western-European art centers but it went its own individual way.

Images of Women in the Other Art Centers of Austria-Hungary

As mentioned above, the attention of artistic and social life in Vienna at 1900 was focused on the vanguard of the Secession, and especially on Klimt, although many other masters were active at that time. From the perspective of Prague, Cracow, or Budapest, the works exhibited in the

Secession represented the *Kunstwollen* (artistic will) of Vienna, from which local artists wished to be liberated.[28]

To begin with, opinions about the essential tasks of modern painting were quite different in the other artistic centers. Although the early 1890s were everywhere marked by an aesthetic revolt against the direct influence of politics in art, the patriotic themes of Czech, Polish, and Hungarian painting expected by the public were still deeply rooted in local cultures. When the local painters wanted to enrich their works with some profound significance, philosophical or mythical, they drew their inspiration from the traditional images of women already to hand in national mythology or history.[29] Thus, the personification of Prague, Hungary, or Poland goes back to earlier allegories incorporated in the figures of Libussa, Slavia, Hungaria, or Polonia. However, the way in which these mother-figures were represented could endow the image with a dramatically new meaning.

As already remarked, Greek mythology and the North German sagas provided appropriate models for treatment as *femmes fatales*, but now related to contemporary theories of religious history and anthropology. "Earth-mother" goddesses or progenitrisses could be represented as matriarchal powers ruling a city, a country or a whole region. Their symbolic potential made them especially beloved by the symbolists.

In Czech and Polish painting, symbolism and Decadence were the most important artistic tendencies in the 1890s; as a result, the national mythologies of these two nations were comprehensively reinterpreted by this artistic generation.[30] The situation was somewhat different in Hungary, where symbolism was not a dominant artistic trend, and its belated protagonists did not simultaneously absorb the most popular concepts of Decadence, which so often led to the demonizing of woman. In Hungary only a handful of such pictures were painted in the 1890s. Moreover, the figure of Hungaria, the iconographical type which had been crystallized by historicism, had a strongly positive significance which was widely accepted. There was no scope for artists to reevaluate her traditional attributes.

Another important reason why Hungarian *fin-de-siècle* painting is so lacking in images of demonic women is that the old patriarchal order of the family and the relationship between the sexes had hardly yet been challenged. There *was* a movement for women's emancipation in Hungary (mainly after 1904), but this found very little echo among Hungarian artists. The traditional roles of women were firmly defined, and even sensitive writers were hardly aware of the future danger posed by the emancipated woman to male hegemony.[31]

Poland

In Poland in the second part of the nineteenth century, female creativity was also much in evidence. There were several important and very popular female writers (e.g., Eliza Orzeszkowa [1841–1910], and Maria Konopicka [1842–1910] to mention the two most important). There were also several minor stars of the literary circles of Warsaw's and especially of Cracow's Bohemia—actresses, muses, or indeed writers. Perhaps the most plausible explanation for the relatively well-developed emancipation of Polish women has been given by Adam Zamoyski: "The frequent imprisonment or exile of the menfolk in a family left women in positions of great responsibility for its survival, and their participation in conspiratorial and even patriotic guerilla activity tended to place them on an equal footing with men. As a result, they were voicing views and demands on the subject of sexual equality and freedom that were not heard in England or France until after the First World War."[32] Polish modernist painting is rich in representing such figures. In portraiture, sharply observed and characterized pictures of fashionable ladies constitute a stunning gallery of emancipated femininity (for example, works by Konrad Krzyżanowski, Józef Mehoffer, and Stanisław Wyspiański); in religious and genre painting, peasant Madonnas populate the canvases (for instance, those by Kasimir Sichulsky, Vlastimir Hofman, and Władisław Jarocki).[33]

Unfortunately, one of the first symbolist paintings by the short-lived Polish impressionist painter Władisław Podkowiński was lost after it was shown at the Columbian Exhibition of 1893 in Chicago. We only know that it depicted nude women dancing in sinister abandon with skeletons. The old image of the *danse macabre* seemed to remain a popular theme with the Polish symbolists, since it occurs both in Wyspiański's dramatic *chef-d'oeuvre*, *The Wedding*, and in several paintings by Wojtech Weiss, the Cracow painter who was an enthusiastic follower of Stanisław Przybyszewski. *The Dance* (1899) and *The Obsession* (1899–1900), both by Weiss, represent male and female nudes in a Dionysian frenzy, totally abandoned to the instinct of lust. Although Przybyszewski's theories were well known and popular in Cracow for a time, his satanism did not find widespread reflection in pictorial representation, except for these few works by Wojtech Weiss.

All the great masters of Polish symbolism struggled with the intellectual and emotional trauma that arose from the partition of their homeland; they created symbolic compositions that were also a documentation of their artistic reaction to the tragic history of the Poles.[34] The works of two major artists, Malczewski and Wyspiański, demonstrate the different ways in which the female personification of Polonia was depicted in the 1890s.

The older master, Jacek Malczewski (1854–1929), was very prolific and throughout his career painted many compositions with powerful images of the *femme fatale* in different roles.[35] His highly enigmatic early work, the *Vicious Circle* (1895–97), concerns the workings of a distinctively Polish sensibility: the wheel of fortune whirls around the painter-acolyte, who sits at the top of a ladder. Among the wildly dancing nude or semi-nude figures are a young peasant couple and some peasant women. For the Polish intellectuals of the time, the role of these female peasant figures would have been an unmistakable reference to the nation, the earth-bound natural element of instincts which can turn destructive (as in the peasant riots), but which is also the potential future strength of the nation.

In all his work, Malczewski gave differing and ambiguous roles to women, depicting them as temptresses (*The Temptation of Fortune,* 1904), as harbingers of death, as harpies poisoning the source of life (*The Poisoned Well, Chimera,*1905), and as the personification of foreign oppressors such as Prussia and Austria (*The Year,* 1905). In 1897 he produced *The Painter's Inspiration,* where the vision of the eternal muse, Polonia, appears to the artist: "Like a sleep-walker, Polonia presents a disquieting rather than reassuring image, with a tattered army greatcoat falling from her shoulders, a straw crown hanging from her head, and a soap bubble borne carefully before her—the symbols of degradation, betrayal and illusion. She brings the painter not the benediction he might expect in better times, but the despair he is bound to feel in reconciling a pursuit of the goals of art with service to an enslaved nation."[36] This interpretation of the homeland, as a demanding lover who has to be served forever, is only one of the many projections of Malczewski's fertile imagination.

As his career progressed, Malczewski increasingly subjectivized his enigmatic allegories of tragic Polish history. He himself became the central hero of these symbolic compositions of life's wanderers, lonely men whose fate is determined by the irrational whimsies and moods of all-knowing evil—the female spirits. The general image of the martyred nation—so common since the Romantic period in Polish literature—was in Malczewski's art turned into the martyrdom of the lonely artist, the isolated Polish male genius.

No matter which were the evil powers that had to be confronted, foreign states, cruel lovers or death itself, they were all turned into appealing

Figure 3 Jacek Malczewski, *The Vicious Circle* (1895–97). Courtesy of: National Museum in Poznan.

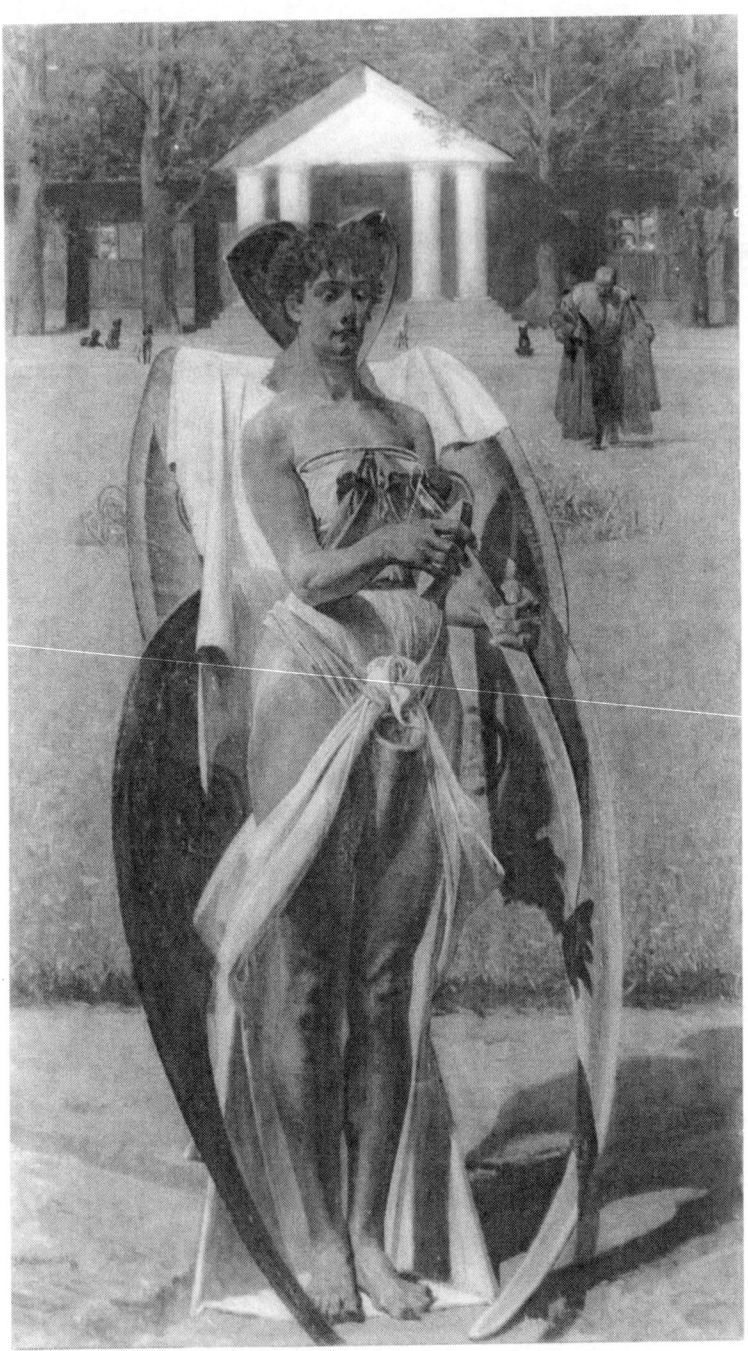

FIGURE 4 Jacek Malczewski, *Thanatos I* (1898). Courtesy of National Museum in Poznan.

sensual female bodies, ultimately all the expression of the same female principle. In this, Malczewski is the true disciple of Decadence and can be regarded as a Polish example of the artist who chose to demonize women. This was not surprising, as he lived long in Cracow and was familiar with the theories of Przybyszewski; nevertheless, his painting is too enigmatic and intellectual to be identified with the writer's crude satanism. Przybyszewski's demonic world is predicated on the statement "in the beginning there was lust."[37] Woman is the personification of all that is evil, the embodiment of an obscene nature, the predatory heroine who enslaves and ruins man. Malczewski sees the world around him as one dominated by female power; however, unlike Klimt, he is keen to portray himself as the long-suffering martyr and eternal victim. Narcissistically, he portrays himself as John the Baptist in his picture of *Salome* (1911), or even as Christ (*Christ and the Woman of Samaria*, 1909, 1910).

Malczewski, who all his life had contact with the German art world, certainly acquired misogynistic inclinations from German painters like Stuck, Slevogt, or Corinth. His special contribution to the gallery of artistic opportunities presented by the *femme fatale* was his way of polonizing the image: he created a strongly built, rather masculine, yet sensual and manipulative peasant woman, a type that would be recognized by Polish readers of Reymont's Nobel Prize winning novel *The Peasants* (1904–1909).[38] In this respect Malczewski differed markedly from his greatest Polish contemporary, Wyspiański, who idealized peasant women and who indeed married one.

Malczewski's urge to generalize the image of the opposite sex was missing from the works of the polymath genius Stanisław Wyspiański (1869–1907), who was a painter and a playwright, as well as a stage and book designer. He was the greatest Polish dramatist of his age, a reformer of the art of the theater, who concentrated mainly on literature after 1898. His art in all genres has a strongly expressive visionary quality, a typical example being his cartoon for a stained glass window for the cathedral of Lvov entitled *Polonia* (1894). It shows a delicate and melancholy lady falling into unconsciousness, a symbol of the tragic fate of the betrayed homeland. Wyspiański's favorite medium was pastel. In his sophisticated calligraphic portraits he depicted the personalities of the Cracovian cultural world, the individual personalities being brilliantly caught, whether men or women, but chiefly the former (*Portrait of Irene Solskij*, 1904).

The most popular images of womanhood created by Wyspiański are the pastel drawings made of his wife and son. Here we have the decorative and still intimate peasant Madonna figure, onto which are loaded all the

FIGURE 5 Stanisław Wyspiański, *Polonia* (1892–94). Courtesy of National Museum in Cracow.

FIGURE 6 Stanisław Wyspiański, *Motherhood* (1905). Courtesy of National Museum in Cracow.

earth-mother associations of comfort and warmth. Nevertheless, for Wyspiański's Polish contemporaries, these pictures symbolized something more: an alliance between the sophisticated, decadent artistic intelligentsia of Cracow and the genuine, natural and instinctive world of the Polish peasantry. Several leading members of Cracow's Bohemia married simple but well-off peasant girls from the neighboring villages "to refresh the tired blood of the gentry," but also had another motive: to strengthen the alliance between different social classes against the common enemy of foreign oppression. Despite Przybyszewski's satanism, the cherished images of modernism in Cracow are the Madonnas and children of Wyspiański.[39]

Prague

The erotic obsession of the coming generation of the 1890s in Prague was given fresh impetus by the enormous influence of French literature; however, the ground was well prepared for the reception of the latter since, from the Romantic period onwards, a heightened sensuality, closely bound up with *"Angst"* about mortality, had been a continuing source of inspiration for Czech artists.

The original source of this, *Máchas Mai*, was frequently reprinted and became the cult book of the decadent neo-Romantics. The local tradition and the general European fashion for the occult ensured that Prague's turn-of-the-century culture, especially its art, reflected the menacing but seductive world of mystical visions, of alienation and hopelessness. The fact that such "modern obsessions," which became characteristic of life in the great metropolises of the twentieth century, had their origin in the literature of a Gothic and Baroque city, shows how much they were psychically determined by the aesthetic environment to which their authors were exposed.

The year 1895 is often regarded as a turning-point in Czech literature, for it was in that year that the monthly *Moderní revue* began publication, and it was also the year of the manifesto of *Česká moderna* (Czech Modernism).[40] The *Moderní revue's* circle included very different sorts of writers, most of whom regarded themselves as Decadents. At least at the beginning, however, they shared three characteristics: they were rebels against the realistic stream in Czech literature; they had a penchant for philosophical lyricism and they were interested in the fine and applied arts.[41]

One of the most charismatic personalities among them was Karel Hlaváček (1874–1898), the poet and graphic artist who died at age twenty-three from tuberculosis after only three years of artistic activity. Hlaváček was an unrestrained experimenter who was not afraid to expose his hidden sexual complexes. He corresponded with the Pole Stanisław Przybyszewski, whose sexual theories hostile to women were well known in Prague. Indeed, on the eve of the birth of psychoanalysis, every kind of pseudo-scientific sexual theory was common currency in the city; they combined with the influence of Schopenhauer and Nietzsche to form the extremely pessimistic view of mankind and the world that the young artists shared.[42]

The significance of Hlaváček's graphics lies in the way in which they combined general symbols with personal feelings and passions, so that the medium attained a new emotional and expressive power. For example, in the drawing entitled *Phantom* (1897), the theme is that of woman and her erotic and emotional disillusion. She bends over the world like a blind, unfathomable, and obscure being, covering it with her dark hair; she is a bringer of misfortune, yet herself unfortunate. The sulphurous sky and the sickly yellow of the moon, rising behind her like the parody of a halo, suggest with their unnaturalness the fear abroad in the world, which is made more threatening by the fire burning on the horizon. An ancient and traditional allegory of despair is here greatly expanded and thereby achieves a greater significance. Hlaváček, the dying, marginalized Bohemian, projects his fear of death onto the woman and

FIGURE 7 Karel Hlaváček, *Phantom* (1897).

the world. In his poems and letters he described his personal Calvary in terms of cruel fantasies that recall Ensor or Kubin: "You will certainly perceive the sad inner process that I illuminate. A feeling of brutality, a sense of the terrible and monstrous, this is what I wanted to evoke, something that lurks always behind one's shoulder, which one is always trying to escape, yet which one is compelled eternally to serve."[43]

He used the medieval atmosphere of nocturnal Prague and especially the Prague ghetto, as a backcloth for these internalized visions; but this eerie, magical, and decaying world is itself transformed into a nightmare, or rather into a hostile, living being, the incarnation of unknown horrors. This transmutation is clearly described in Hlaváček's letter: "I see monsters everywhere, but they are actually in me, they are psychic, because I love fear. I love fear for its own sake. I often stay out after it gets dark; in the black night I walk through the dead, dark streets of Prague, in order to experience the fear of an unexpected, violent attack, that could come at any minute."[44] Nevertheless Hlaváček was an exception for the generation of the 1890s. The majority of his contemporaries were passionate Czech nationalists deeply rooted in national culture.

In Czech painting and graphics, in contrast to those of the Vienna school and of Hungary, the *magna mater* figure from the prehistory of the Slavs had been deeply embedded in the national psyche since the Romantic period. Princess Libussa, the legendary founder of Prague, wife of the mythical first Premysl, "the Ploughman," and female antecedent of the royal Premyslid line, was portrayed as the wise and just ruler. Her figure is closely bound up with the cult of the Slav origins of the city, for Libussa was the prophetess who, according to legend, foresaw on the eve of her death the foundation, the future glory and indestructibility of Prague. Even though the interest in the mist-enshrouded early history of the Slavs diminished somewhat in the period of realism in Czech literature, a number of authors such as Alois Jirásek, or neo-Romantic poets like Julius Zeyer and especially Smetana's opera *Lybussa*, revived the significance of the sibylline figure.[45] Historicist painting reproduces her idealized portrait repeatedly in the context of allegorical royal depictions, always against a background of the Hradčany.

From this it may be seen that an important source for omnipotent female figures in Czech art of the 1890s was the national myth; such figures, so far from representing a revolt against historicism, can more accurately be described as its metamorphosis, or its refinement.[46] In Karel Mašek's painting *The Seer—Libussa* (1893), the figure of Libussa is reinterpreted in terms of occult symbolism, appearing at night on the plateau of Vyšehrad above the Moldau as a powerful,

FIGURE 8 Karel Mašek, *The Seer—Libussa* (1893). Courtesy of Musée d'Orsay, Paris.

intimidating pagan priestess. Her ceremonial robe is decorated with the emblem of the Egyptian goddess of love, Hathor, and she holds a lime-tree branch from the holy tree of the ur-Slavs in her outstretched hand. She has become a *femme fatale,* ancestor of the race and goddess of love in one person, the sister of Astarte and Isis. The Vyšehrad legends included a group of apocryphal sagas which alluded to the evil, man-hating element in Libussa's nature, but which had been suppressed in the course of the national-Romantic revival. A saga about Czech Amazons who fought the Premysl men under the leadership of Vlasta kept the memory of the matriarchy of the pre-history of the Slavs alive, and thereby also the concept of the powerful woman. The figure of the beautiful Šárka, who enticed the hero, Ctirad, into a fatal trap, was a favorite theme of the neo-Romantics. She is especially prevalent in the sculpture of the 1890s. One of the most beautiful of these is by Quido Kocián, executed in alabaster and variegated marble, a sophisticated attempt to capture the ambivalence of Šárka's character.

Evil beauty that brought great misfortune was an important leitmotiv of Czech *Jugendstil* and was so deeply embedded in the contemporary international artistic repertoire of archetypes that critics and the public tended to take a negative interpretation of the male and female relationship, even when there was no convincing literary explanation of any particular scene. This emotional dissonance, the double isolation of man and woman, is particularly evident in the pictures of Jan Preisler (for example, the illustration to Julius Zeyer's poems *Píseň o hoři dobrého juna Romana Vasiliče* [1899] and the *Spring Triptych* of 1900). Even the Pre-Raphaelite-like popular picture by Max Švabinský, *The Communion of Souls* (1896), in spite of its title, does not embody the promised harmony of the muse and the artist. It reveals much more the discrepancy between male and female emotions and attitudes, according to which male genius cannot be bound by ties of gentle love, his vocation being the quest for the deeper significance of the universe. The sensitivity of Czech *Jugendstil* and symbolism to a type of painting that is laden with "philosophical" content was an inheritance of the 1880s.[47] The teachers of the younger generation who were active in Prague, such as Maximilian Pirner (1854–1924) and Vojtěch Hynais (1854–1925), undertook allegorical cycles of themes such as *Demon and Love* (Pirner) or a new interpretation of the traditional *Judgement of Paris* (Hynais), the focus of which were existential questions of life, love, and death. The red-haired modern Venus was equally a bringer of misfortune and danger, like Olympia or Nana. Generally, all traditional and sensual nudes could be interpreted as dangerously seductive creatures.

The typology and analysis of woman as presented in the work of Alfons Mucha would require a chapter of its own. It is only possible to indicate briefly that Mucha's world view was principally influenced by theosophy and gnosticism. His art is associated world-wide with the posters for Sarah Bernhardt, for which he developed an individual, yet very easily imitated, virtuoso calligraphic style.[48]

The *femme fatale* roles of this great actress, who liked to play the part of an irresistibly fascinating woman even in her own life, were immortalized for posterity with the help of Mucha's seductive art. Her poster image is one of the most popular icons of women at the turn of the century. Notwithstanding this, the Bernhardt Medeas and Toscas that Mucha depicted are scarcely more threatening or mysterious than the images in his biscuit or cigarette advertisements. Much more interesting are the less well-known early oil paintings and sketches, often depicting

FIGURE 9 Jan Preisler, *Spring* (1900)—central panel of a triptych. Courtesy of Gallery of West Bohemia, Plzen.

FIGURE 10 Max Švabinský, *The Communion of Souls* (1896). Courtesy of National Gallery, Prague.

dying women, or women who embody destructive passions (for instance, *The Absinthe Drinker*, circa 1900). Unfortunately an apparently key work for the metamorphosis of his *Weltanschauung* exhibited at the Salon des Cent in 1897, the cycle of *Sedm hlavních hříchu* (The Seven Deadly Sins), was lost. Contemporaries describe it as a philosophical work depicting the miserable state of mankind with all its sins, passions, and moral or psychological wounds.

However, when Mucha turned to Czech themes, his women figures gradually became idealized girls, pretty young peasants or priestesses who radiated purity and wisdom, as, for example, in his *Slavia* of 1908. These priestesses are no longer menacing, their magical aura being on the contrary comforting and protective, and above all full of hope for the future. His great late work, the monumental picture cycle entitled *Slav Epos* (1909–1930), incorporates these qualities.[49] The ur-Slav figures are here without exception positively portrayed and stand for such concepts as love, youth, mother-earth, and so on. The mysterious heathen priestesses have become blooming, innocent maidens of humble origin, and they are often wearing snow-white robes like those of the priestesses of Vesta. The patriotic feelings of the artist did not permit him to depict the daughters of the nation as sensual *femmes fatales*. Mucha's self-censorship was complete and incorruptible.

Women, whose traditional social and family roles, in both the preindustrial and industrial period, ensured stability, continuity, increase, and development, were seen by Czech artists and intellectuals as "indestructible sources of life, the life force." Whether this recognition of women arose from a bitter feeling of male inadequacy and frustration in the face of Czech history and politics, or was associated with a modern psychological and moral understanding arrived at through personal experience, depended on the character and position in society of the individual Czech artist or intellectual. The most important example of the modern, positive attitude was that of Thomas Masaryk, who stood against unthinking acceptance of social tradition.[50] Out of the confrontation of these two fundamentally opposed attitudes to women in Prague at the turn of the century, the supporters of tolerance and emancipation emerged victorious, at least in intellectual circles, where the influence of the "Realistic Party" under Masaryk's leadership was decisive.[51]

In Czech literature, there were also several leading authors, such as Julius Zeyer or František Xaver Šalda, who supported emancipation. Likewise, a number of painters showed little inclination to demonize women in their works. Jakub Schikaneder, for instance, painted women with great empathy. His female figures are always isolated, radiating loneliness and deep but ill-defined melancholy. His first great work, which was conceived in the Zola tradition of realism, depicted a tragedy in the slums of Prague (*The Murder in the House*, 1887–1890) and is uncompromisingly stark. Not surprisingly it was rejected by critics and publics alike, on the basis that the subject was not appropriate to painting. In the general artistic climate of Czech aestheticism and symbolism that was born out of the rebellion against realism, women were usually depicted either as fairies, ethereal virgins or tempting and menacing *femmes fatales* (see, for example, K. V. Mašek's *Spring* [1888] or his *The Seer—Libussa* [1893]).

While the protagonists of Decadence in the Czech 1890s turned away from reality and created its mythical opposite, the powerful, mystical woman who mastered man's fate, Schikaneder changed his style and painted the victims of life. His canvases show poetic, dreamlike interiors or the picturesquely crumbling streets of old Prague, winter scenes where lonely figures hurry along on unknown errands. These women are largely indefinable: what we perceive of them is their loneliness, a melancholy that radiates from their manner and gestures, and which become the hallmark of Schikaneder's work.

The only Czech painter who emphasized the peasant genre in the 1890s was the popular Joža Úprka, who concentrated on the decorative effect of colorful peasant costumes. In the pleasing decorativeness of his compositions, such as *Going to the Baptism* (1896) and *The Day of the Dead* (1897), something was retained of the Romantic idealization of peasantry. The peasant women stand for the moral purity of the nation and symbolize a genuine life close to nature. They are the storehouse of the nation's lost values, degraded by industrialization and urbanization. Although the Czech painters were mainly townspeople living in Prague, most of them, in common with their writer colleagues, stressed this dualistic concept of Czech culture. When the Czechs wanted to represent themselves to the outside world, they chose rural figures, such as pretty and "unspoiled" peasant girls in folk costume, to do so. A poster for the Paris World Exhibition of 1900 is a not untypical example; and when Rodin came to Prague for the opening of his exhibition in 1902, his hosts took him to a rural region of Moravia where the folkloristic traditions of the peasants were still alive.[52]

The art and literature of *fin-de-siècle* Prague was rich in *femme fatale* images because the city's creative artists were convinced that they were living under the spell of magical Prague (an ancient Slav Sorceress) and her unpredictable charm, in a city that embodied the principle of a powerful woman, mother and lover in one, a being who could bring her sons and lovers deliverance or damnation.[53] But Prague, the beautiful, mystical woman remained also the eternal muse, in whose heartbeat the artists recognized the rhythm of their dreams and their visions, precisely as Max Švabinský had depicted Prague on the poster for the Rodin exhibition.

Budapest

What seemed self-evident to the Prague symbolists at the turn of the century—namely, that without a muse there could be no great art, and without Eros no creativity—seemed to have less importance for Hungarian artists. At least it was evidently not something they thought worth discussing. The Czech and Hungarian painter generations of the 1890s were not only embedded in quite different political and social circumstances, but also drew on very different kinds of national mythology, not to mention traditions of literature and art.[54]

The world of Hungarian myth and legend lacks the destiny-determining demonic figure of the woman; here are no Ortruds or Krimhilden. The Hungarians do not look back to prophetess progenitors. In the cultural inheritance of medieval Hungary, there are few female figures that survive in the collective national memory. Those that do are chiefly pious, deferential daughters of the Arpad kings (Saint Elizabeth and Saint Margaret). The positive heroines of Hungarian prose and poetry were the female patriots of the Turkish wars, who courageously fought for their country.[55]

As for the private sphere of love life, Hungarian literature was traditionally extremely reserved, a characteristic that continued to the beginning of the twentieth century. Contemporary observers identified this strict self-censorship as a national characteristic of Hungarian men. Up to the First World War, it constituted a moral-aesthetic canon, especially for conservatives. Indeed, the modern poets of the *fin de siècle* were in rebellion against just this kind of prudery. Psychological realism and description of the real world were so deeply embedded in Hungarian prose that writers were scarcely able to depict women as demonic figures without some degree of irony or satire, an approach that fatally undermined the magical aura of these beings (as, for example, in Ferenc Molnár's comedies). Women played no powerful role in society; in contrast to Prague and Vienna, there were no literary salons or male supporters of female emancipation in the Budapest of the 1890s.[56]

The only poet who had the courage to deal openly with erotic passion and to unveil the power of the sexual instinct was Endre Ady, the greatest of the Hungarian symbolist poets.[57] In his famous (and also notorious) *Songs for Léda,* he wrote of joy and suffering, the torture of confusing feelings, and the merciless struggle between woman and man that ends in a murderous dance of death. Ady alone was capable of evoking the *femme fatale* as goddess; sometimes it appears as if his lover Léda herself was cast in this role. Yet a closer reading reveals that for Ady the individual woman is not a determining force; having no power over him, she becomes merely a (sometimes reluctant) means for reaching the state of ecstasy. Ady reflects only on himself, on his own passion, yearning, and misery. He is in love with love, or, more precisely, he loves only himself in the reflection of the beloved. The logic of this situation was that women were interchangeable and expendable. For the soul of the Hungarian male, as Ady discovered, the mortal danger lay in his own instincts, his greed, his lust for power, his apathy and yearning for death, the "inherited sins brought from the mythical east" which he shared with the nation as a whole. It was a nation in which (from a social point of view) only the men were truly visible.

Notwithstanding this basic situation, Hungarian *fin-de-siècle* painting is very rich in representations of women, although they are mainly featured in a very traditional way.[58]

Painting

The first Hungarian representation of the seductive, modern, and mysterious woman who clearly possessed intellectual power and the capacity to exercise it, was painted in Paris. In 1892 József Rippl-Rónai (1867–1927)[59] portrayed a slim young lady dressed in black with a glowing white skin. She is, however, no *femme fatale,* but rather an intriguing woman about whom the painter reveals very little. *The Woman with a Black Hat* (1894), however, painted two years later by János Vaszary (1867–1939),[60] is already a challenging and fascinating Parisienne, full of energy and vitality. She has something unsettling in her look, which reminds one of a highly strung animal, a cat that is tensed with energy, a dangerous, moody Nana. With its broad, generalized brush-stokes and its bold decorativeness, its glowing color contrasted with the jet-black hair and hat, this picture stands out as unique in the *oeuvre* of Vaszary. He was a relentless experimenter who was prepared to try out each new technique, style or fashionable subject; however, once he had solved a new formal problem with his usual élan, he turned to other inspirations or tasks and never repeated himself.

FIGURE 11 János Vaszary, *The Woman with a Black Hat* (1894). Courtesy of Hungarian National Gallery, Budapest.

His supple *Red-Haired Female Nude* is typical of the caprices he tossed off with such ease, a paraphrase in fiery colors of Franz Stuck's *Sin*. However, while Stuck's work is threatening and demonic, Vaszary's is more frivolous and modern. The seductive, sensual power of attraction of the red-haired model, with skin that gleams like mother-of-pearl, is enhanced by the starkly contrasting colors; she clearly represents something that is psychologically threatening, but is by no means the overblown, implausible allegory of the Stuck painting.

There is a particular group of pictures among Vaszary's works, painted between 1900–1904, which focus on women in interior settings. Some of these are somewhat enigmatic scenes, where two women (usually one of them nude) seem to be sharing an intense erotic intimacy. One such picture shows a girl combing her hair, while her companion sits to one side, scrutinizing this activity. In another scene, both women are looking into a small mirror, again one of them dressed, the other not. The soft, pleasingly sensual forms of these nudes are veiled in a half-light. The dim boudoir corners are only vaguely indicated, and the close focus concentrates on the human epidermis, intensifying the hot-house atmosphere of these scenes and suggesting an element of voyeurism.

About the same time, Vaszary painted some monumental portraits of old peasant women, which are perhaps the most striking in Hungarian painting (*Going to Church*, 1903). These black-robed women, with hardship and poverty written on their faces, display a profound human dignity and dogged perseverance in the face of fate.

Rippl-Rónai, the Hungarian recorder of feminine beauty *par excellence*, treated another Parisienne as a *femme fatale* when he painted *Mme Mazet* in 1896. The enchantingly beautiful and elegant woman in her black robe and luxurious taste in hats has something challenging and disturbing about her, which nevertheless remains puzzling and out of focus, perhaps because of her extreme elegance.

After resettling in Hungary, Rippl-Rónai followed in the impressionists' steps by painting women—mostly the members of his family circle—in traditional genre-scenes of the life of a provincial middle-class family, going about their everyday domestic activities. The women in these paintings thus form an organic part of the painter's life and environment. How they are objectified has nothing to do with misogynist attitudes; on the contrary, they are handled quite naturally, as pleasant human companions in all stages of their life, from childhood to old age. Especially the elderly are painted with compassion and deep understanding of the innate melancholy of old age (see, for instance, *When One Lives from Memories*, 1903).

FIGURE 12 János Vaszary, *Going to Church* (1903). Courtesy of Hungarian National Gallery, Budapest.

Like the majority of Hungarian painters in the early 1890s, István Csók (1865–1961)[61] was an enthusiastic follower of the fine naturalism of Jules Bastien-Lepage, and painted tender, emotionally moving scenes (*Holy Communion*, 1890, or *The Orphans*, 1893) in the naturalistic manner. It was nevertheless Csók who, of all the artists of his generation, produced the most sensual depictions of women, not flinching from such rare themes in the Hungarian context as sexual aberration. But his artistic output was very uneven, and occasionally he was not free from a type of vulgar sentimentality bordering on kitsch. He has given us one

FIGURE 13 István Csók, *Holy Communion* (1890). Courtesy of Hungarian National Gallery, Budapest.

unique depiction of *Salome*, which is perhaps the least threatening image of Herodias's daughter produced at the *fin de siècle*, when she was such a fashionable subject. Salome lies belly-down on a bed, with a few roses scattered around her; she looks out of the picture into our eyes without the slightest hint of emotional tension, despite the alarming fact that she is holding in her hands the head of John the Baptist. Indeed, she displays sublime indifference to the object, which might as well be a cushion for all the emotional drama involved. The challenge of a psychological depiction seems to have been beyond the painter, or perhaps it would be more accurate to say that it did not, in this case, interest him. Perhaps the other version of the same composition, in which the beautiful young girl embraces a heap of roses with an identical gesture, offers an explanation for this strangely inappropriate depiction. For Csók, conveying the sensuality of the nude model was the important artistic task, and he may have simply changed the props according to the wishes of the commissioner, from roses to the head of John the Baptist. Similarly, all his huge symbolic compositions were, without exception, artistic failures, although he tried desperately to paint subjects with complicated religious and philosophical messages, for example, *Christ and Venus* (1898).

His innate sensualism and materialism, which were totally inappropriate impulses for creating mystical visions of esoteric subjects, prevented him from painting a persuasive version of any symbolical or metaphysical subject. Of his failed attempts, only those have survived that he did not himself destroy (including *Christ and Venus*), to bear witness to his clumsy attempts to choose fashionable subjects, which were then treated without any inner conviction. In Paris, Csók painted several compositions of sensual nudes, sometimes using biblical subjects (for example, *Thamar*, 1906), or else in depictions of scenes of modern life *(The Corner of the Studio,* 1905). These pictures became very popular among contemporary Hungarian collectors, who appreciated their sensual quality, which perfectly matched the conservative concept of female sensuality. The women in Csók's pictures display their charms in a way that recalls languorous odalisques, seemingly oblivious of the male gaze. From 1901 onwards, he also devoted himself to the subject of vampires and painted a number of variations on this theme while he was in Paris. Even so, none of these ugly women corresponded to the model of the *femme fatale.* Csók's real strength lay in the painting of naturally sensual and attractively unsophisticated peasant girls in decorative costumes.

The young Lajos Gulácsy (1882–1932)[62] is fascinated by a very different world of feeling and fantasy. A psychologically unstable creative artist who was both painter and poet, Gulácsy was sunk in a "romantic-neurotic" world of the senses during his rather short period of activity. The motifs and ideas of beauty he adopted were borrowed from the Pre-Raphaelites. A stylized cult of love similar to that of Rossetti inspired Gulácsy's finest pictures, which are poetic visions of a dream world in which the unhappy lovers are eternally forced to part. Nevertheless, underneath the lyrical scenes of melancholy, where a certain harmony between man and woman prevails, lurks the impression of an intoxicating and confused encounter in the magic garden of love, which is also the source of knowledge. In *The Magician's Garden* (1904), it is the beautiful

FIGURE 14 Lajos Gulácsy, *Paolo and Francesca* (1903). Courtesy of Hungarian National Gallery, Budapest.

Vivien who casts a bewitching gaze on Merlin, her master. In the painting titled *Ecstasy* (1908) a naked girl embraces a youth with an awkward
passion that gives a flash of insight into the depth of the instincts. Perhaps this is the first painting that radiates a genuine anxiety in the projection of the Dionysian side of love in Hungarian painting.

These very few examples of the *femme fatale*, or more simply of "dangerous women," may paradoxically be seen as evidence for the fact that,
in Hungarian *fin-de-siècle* painting, the then extremely fashionable
theme of the "struggle between the sexes" was hardly exploited by the
best masters. Most of the depictions of women at that time belong to the
type of the *femme fragile*, enigmatic, lonely and gentle souls, who can
only ever be victims, not victors in the war of love. The general approach adopted both by minor and leading artists—even when, from a
stylistic point of view, they were highly experimental—was that of a
painstaking realism in the depiction of human relations. The very few
painters not belonging to this tradition were those rare and exalted individuals (Csontváry or Gulácsy) whose images of women (if they were
decisive at all, as in the case of Csontváry) were not so much shaped by
the real circumstances of Hungarian society, as by an individual history
of pathological obsessions.

It can thus broadly be said that, in Hungarian *fin-de-siècle* painting,
women were hardly ever demonized. Instead, it is the traditionally
feminine aspects of women (such as fragility, ethereal purity, melan-
cholic pensiveness, or more frequently, maternal warmth and traditional domestic virtues) which characterize the majority of the portraits,
domestic interiors and genre scenes painted at this time. Old-fash-
ioned self-censorship functioned even more rigorously in painting than
in literature.

There is, however, one picture in which a pregnant woman is portrayed, and although the work is not of high quality, it makes a significant
and startling comparison with Klimt's *Hope*, which was coincidentally
painted in the same year (1903). The Hungarian master, Sándor Nagy (a
minor painter, but a very good designer and a follower of both the
French *Rose et Croix* ideals and those of the Pre-Raphaelites)[63] painted
The Blessed Condition, a double portrait of his pregnant wife and himself
in front of his studio window. She is of course fully dressed and leans
against her husband, their bodies and profiles in a harmonious parallel,
suggesting an ideal unity of soul and body. Both gaze out of the window,
through which can be seen an angel-like apparition holding an equally
wraith-like baby, the expected, unborn child. There is an air of prepos-
terous piety and naivety about the scene, which, in spite of the painter's

best efforts, is embarrassingly childish, if also childlike. The art colony to which this couple belonged—the only one following the arts and crafts workshop ideal of William Morris and cultivating utopian ideas of socialism—of course rejected the sensuality of Viennese art on moral grounds, and aimed to restore the nobly moral quality of life of the Hungarian peasants. The Gödöllö artists' most lasting contribution to the visual arts was their rediscovery of folk art and the integration of its ornament into applied art nouveau; but these works lack any individualizing element.[64]

Pretty peasant girls and women in their decorative folk costumes, radiating good health, happiness and contentment with their station in life, were the favorite models of genre painting since the onset of romanticism in Hungarian art. Although—as in literature—some realist painters around 1900 (for example, Adolf Fényes)[65] occasionally chose to depict the pariahs of rural life (in a manner similar to German *Arme Leute Malerei*), the majority of the peasant models of the time belonged to an idealized world where man and woman still lived in harmony with nature and with each other. After 1900, depictions of peasant women became more and more idealized, biblical and doctrinal symbols placed in a context where genuine or normative human values are still intact and powerful. The ultimate artistic expression of this tendency is to be found in the peasant Madonna of József Koszta[66] (*The Three Magi*, 1906).

If there was a dominant visual representation of women in Hungarian painting between 1890 and 1905, it is that of women depicted in nature—in a garden or park, working in the fields or in a picturesque landscape. In most of these paintings the relationship between nature and the human figure is perfectly balanced. The women are seen as in perfect harmony with their natural surroundings, like plants or flowers. They are therefore not individualized, still less demonized, but rather idealized. The overwhelming number of these paintings show that this interpretation of women as natural beings, belonging more to nature than to the world of man, was not simply a reflection of the complacent attitude of male painters toward the other sex, but was one also happily accepted by the public. It seems clear that the public shared the view of women reflected in such works, or was happy to be convinced by it, as a comforting vision of the unchanging order of things.

The dream of an ideal symbiosis between woman and nature was a wishfully selective view of the world, but it contained a great residual power of suggestion and was capable of inspiring great masterpieces, for example, some of the pictures of Károly Ferenczy,[67] the most poetical of which is *The Painter and the Model* (1901).

FIGURE 15 József Koszta, *The Three Magi* (1906). Courtesy of Hungarian National Gallery, Budapest.

Conclusion

The aim of this study has been to trace the connections between the clichés of womanhood in painting, with a side-glance at the socio-cultural structure of the relations between the sexes at the turn of the century. These connections are sometimes very direct, at other times indirect or nonexistent.

When comparing national schools, certain preferences are easy to explain. For example, in the strongly metropolitan painting of Vienna, peasant women are hardly featured. (The exception is the work of Andri, with his market figures). However, in all the other schools in Central Europe, we find that the representation of the peasantry, and especially of peasant women, was not only popular, but had strong ideological support: it offered the alternative of a rural utopia to the modern world

FIGURE 16 Károly Ferenczy, *The Painter and the Model* (1901). Courtesy of Hungarian National Gallery, Budapest.

of industrialization. Naturally, such attitudes precluded demonization of peasant women.

National mythologies that served as the golden store of artistic capital for nations which were not yet independent, like the Czechs or the Poles, were the carriers of positive values, even if, for the rebelliously Decadent generation, the omnipotent protectress of the glorious past could also become an ambivalent evocation of female power. Such cases were rare, however, and the phase of demonizing the sacred figures of national mythology was very short. There was soon a return to traditional idealization.

For nations where the influence of symbolism and Decadence was strong and profound, woman became a mysterious and enigmatic being, one from whom man was alienated, although he could not escape an anguished emotional dependence on her (see for example, the works of the Czech Jan Preisler and Karel Hlavácek, or the Poles, Jacek Malczewski and Wojciech Weiss). If the influence of Decadence was weak and the local literary tradition was dominated by realism, as in Hungary, decadent images of woman (*femmes fatales*) or the element of the *Geschlechterkampf* were more or less missing from painting. The few examples to be found were evidently "imports," stylistic exercises painted abroad (János Vaszary, István Csók).

Before the birth of expressionism, the concept of the *femme fragile* was much more popular all over the Dual Monarchy, including Vienna, than the demonic woman; if so-called "modern types" were represented, the painters preferred the gently feminine wife-figures (Carl Moll, Rippl-Rónai), the *süßes Mädl* type (Felician von Myrbach) or the pretty cocotte (Luděk Marold), to the sensual *demi-mondaines* with "symbolic souls" (e.g., Wyspiański's *The Portrait of Irene Solskij*, 1900).

Although the celebration of sensuality was not confined to Vienna, it was most common in Viennese art. The virtuoso protagonist of erotic painting (Klimt) was obsessed with evoking the sexual attraction of women, but in the other art centers of the Monarchy, the intellectual climate still demanded pure and worthy subjects from the painters of the nation. From their formative years on, those artists were continuously under pressure to create something noble and sublime, to dedicate their creative powers to the national cause. Their self-censorship was more effective than that of masters in the much more metropolitan and cosmopolitan Vienna. Here, the *genius loci* encapsulated in the slogan "*Wein, Weib und Gesang,*" worked also at the level of everyday behavior to stress the sensual elements in life and to make easier the social acceptance of a more open and more "modern" art and a less restrictive metropolitan life for women.

An additional factor in the individual painter's choice of what type of woman to paint, was, of course, the presence (or absence) of the emancipated woman in his immediate environment. A life embedded in well-preserved patriarchal norms did not stimulate the imagination to demonize women, as can be seen from the case of Hungary. In this context, it is perhaps of importance that the majority of Hungarian modern painters worked in the country, in provincial small towns with conservative mores, and were determined to remain close to nature. There was a steadily growing animosity toward the "cosmopolitan" capital of Budapest, which was neither aesthetic nor "national" enough to be worthy of the painter's brush. That is why Hungarian painting of this period entirely lacks modern cityscapes of Budapest. By contrast, in a town like the beloved Prague, where artistic life was open to many creative and emancipated women, even if they were mostly active in fields other than the fine arts, the view of women was more complex and ranged more widely between appreciation and fear (e.g., Max Švabinský, Jan Preisler, Luděk Marold and Karel Hlaváček).

In the hothouse of Cracow's Bohemia where, from 1897 onwards, the charismatic Przybyszewski focused attention on the sinister world of instincts, there existed a suitable microclimate for the demonization of women. The fact that, in spite of this, only a few pictures were inspired by these theories, reveals that for most Polish intellectuals the issue of national destiny and the controversies surrounding the concepts of Christian faith and hope were considered more worthy subjects for the arts (for example, the works of Wyspiański).

Although many examples of sensual female figures can be found in the *oeuvres* of Hungarian, Czech and Polish painters, sensual aestheticism in its most liberated version, which included the possibility of ornamentation for its own sake or as veiled eroticism, was ultimately the prerogative of Vienna. The other three art centers of the Dual Monarchy followed different paths, the local image of woman being dictated by the locally determined national, cultural and psychological considerations that this study has sought to define and explicate.

The hallmark of the first generation of Viennese modernism in literature was the hegemony of the inner life of the psyche over that of quotidian reality. This narrow focus—which was concentrated on the ego of the author himself in various guises—was interwoven with a sensitive concern for language *per se*, and a desire to exploit its potential for decorative ornamentation and the creation of style (as in the case of Hofmannsthal). The painting of this generation followed a similar pattern. The mood (*Stimmung*) of the soul projected onto nature and the external world was a fundamental preoccupation; stylized role-play, *inter alia*, in the context of male eroticism, was adopted as a form of self-expression.

This ambivalent role-play itself involved a certain amount of legerdemain (it concealed, for example, a desire to exert power over the viewer, to manipulate and impress him with the force of the artistic achievement); but it also could involve self-deception, a self-conscious determination to be modern at any cost. The artists exploited social patterns, artistic clichés, and finally non-organic stylistic solutions, as quotations or formulas not integrated organically into the composition. The thirst to create something new led to the invention of a symbolic code-language for eroticism. It can be interpreted as an unconscious self-defense of the male artist against the dangerous power of femininity. But the highly stylized and sophisticated angular-geometric system of the Viennese Secession became too enigmatic and too much of a closed system to allow the free flow of emotional expression. The "golden Style" of Klimt became an obstacle to creative freedom itself; because it allowed only an indirect expression of emotion, it had to be abandoned. The demands put upon such devices proved to be too great for the next generation. The result was an artistic or intellectual crisis, as in the careers of Hofmannsthal and Ernst Stöhr, which might even lead to the disintegration of the work and psychological disintegration of the artist, in the tragic case of Richard Gerstl to his self-destruction.

Those artists who kept themselves apart from social and artistic role-playing of this kind were equally able to withstand the impact of fashionable clichés in the social realm or the exaggerated utopian pessimism of the Kraus circle. They were thus able to maintain a balance between male self-respect and the newly discovered power of the *anima*, the mystical female force. The ultimate artistic embodiment of this delicate and highly individual balance is the art of Gustav Klimt.

The situation changed when the generation of expressionists entered the art scene. The mesmerizing influence of Otto Weininger and other misogynist authors was decisive for the child prodigies, Schiele and Kokoschka. Especially in the early years of their creativity, they focused on the tortured, neurotic images of carnal love; they demonized women not so much because of their own social experiences, but because of their tortured and problematic psychological attitude toward sexuality. Social reality is largely excluded from their early works—it is the obsession with their own traumas and fantasies that determines their vision of mankind.

In the other art centers of the Dual Monarchy, the creative female powers were everywhere differently perceived and the reaction to them was also varied.

In Prague, recognition of these powers came through the important role of Czech feminism, which sensitized not only modernists to the issue of women's emancipation, but also representatives of the previous generation of realists. While some young modernists indulged in the demonization of women for a while, the realists worked out a solution to the problem of integration, recognizing the immense potential of the feminist contribution to the cultural struggle of the Czech nation against the Germans.

In Poland, although the "New Woman" was a live issue, acknowledged among intellectuals, the situation was similar to that in Prague. Apart from a few decadent modernists, the majority of artists represented national heroines and earth-mother figures, thus the protectress rather than the inner enemy.

Before 1905 in Hungary, the issue of the discovery of the "New Woman" did not play an important role in the artistic sphere, and feminism did not constitute a challenge to artistic perception. Writers and painters seemed to be rather unaware of the coming storm in the relations between the sexes. After 1905, artists and intellectuals were not to be spared this shock even in Hungary. Nonetheless, other factors, such as political crises and an accumulation of serious social tensions, meant that the issue of women's emancipation never became central, in either literature or the fine arts. Hungarian culture and history in the twentieth century has been dominated not so much by the *femme fatale* as by the *homme fatal.* It is, however, by no means certain that the situation was markedly different anywhere else in the region.

Notes

1. There is no concise comparative study on the art of Central Europe at the turn of the century. Works on the art of the individual nations or cultural centers are available, but they focus on the art contacts with Western countries only, especially on French influences. Selected comprehensive monographs and catalogues on the local national schools of painting of this age are: Peter Vergo, *Art in Vienna 1898–1918* (London, 1972); *Traum und Wirklichkeit* (Vienna, 1985); *Tschechische Kunst 1878–1914: Aus dem Weg in die Moderne*, Catalogue (Darmstadt, 1984); Petr Wittlich, *Prague Fin-de-Siècle* (Paris, 1992); *Symbolism in Polish Painting 1890–1914*, Catalogue (Detroit, 1984); Jan K. Ostrowski, *Die polnische Malerei* (Munich, 1989); Julia Szabadi, *Art Nouveau in Hungary* (Budapest, 1989); *A Golden Age*, Catalogue (London, 1989).

2. Timothy J. Clark, *The Painting of Modern Life: Paris in the Art of Manet and His Followers* (London, 1985); J. Rose, *Sexuality in the Field of Vision* (London, 1986); Tamar Garb, "Gender and Representation," in Francis Frascina et al., eds., *Modernity and Modernism: French Painting in the Nineteenth Century* (New Haven, London, 1993).

3. Ilona Sármány-Parsons, "Malerei 1890–1900: Aufbruch in die Moderne—Vienna, Prague, Budapest," in Richard G. Plaschka and Horst Haselsteiner, eds., *Mitteleuropa: Idee, Wissenschaft und Kultur im 19. und 20. Jahrhundert* (Vienna, 1997), 175–186.

4. Griselda Pollock, "Modernity and the Spaces of Femininity," in Pollock, *Vision and Difference* (London, New York, 1988), 50–90.

5. H. J. Schickedanz, *Femme fatale: Ein Mythos wird entblättert* (Dortmund, 1983); Elaine Showalter, *Sexual Anarchy* (London, 1990); Barbara Eschenburg, ed., *Der Kampf der Geschlechter: Der neue Mythos in der Kunst 1850–1930* (Munich, Cologne, 1995).

6. Werner Hoffmann, *Das irdische Paradies: Motive und Ideen des 19. Jahrhunderts* (Munich, 1960), 146–163, and 202–289.

7. Maria Makela, *The Munich Secession* (Princeton, 1990).

8. William M. Johnston, *The Austrian Mind* (Berkeley, 1972); Allan Janik and Stephen Toulmin, *Wittgenstein's Vienna* (New York, 1973); Carl E. Schorske, *Fin-de-Siècle Vienna* (New York, 1980); James Shedel, *Art and Society: The New Art Movement in Vienna, 1897–1914* (Palo Alto, 1981); Jacques Le Rider, *Das Ende der Illusion: Zur Kritik der Moderne* (Vienna, 1990).

9. Peter Vergo, *Art in Vienna, 1890–1918* (London, 1975); Wolfgang Hilger et al., *Die Wiener Secession* (Vienna, 1986); Gottfried Fliedl, *Gustav Klimt* (Cologne, 1989).

10. Alfred Pfabigan, ed., *Ornament und Askese* (Vienna, 1985).

11. Fritz Novotny and Johannes Dobai, *Gustav Klimt* (Salzburg, 1967); Werner Hoffmann, *Gustav Klimt und die Wiener Jahrhundertwende* (Salzburg, 1970); Alice Strobl, *Gustav Klimt: Die Zeichnungen*, vols. 1–3 (Salzburg, 1980–84); Frank Whitford, *Gustav Klimt* (London, 1990).

12. Hans Bizanz, *Vienna 1900* (Bristol, 1990), 14.

13. Patrick Werkner, *Physis and Psyche: Der Österreichische Frühexpressionismus* (Vienna, Munich, 1986).

14. Alfred Kubin spent his formative years in Munich at the turn of the century and was much more under the influence of the occultism and pseudo-science that was so popular with the French and Belgian symbolists, than that of the Viennese art scene. See Hans Bizanz, *Alfred Kubin* (Munich, 1877).

15. Rudolf Peter Janz and Klaus Laermann, *Arthur Schnitzler: Zur Diagnose des Wiener Bürgertums im Fin de Siècle* (Stuttgart, 1977).

16. Harriet Anderson, *Utopian Feminism: Women's Movements in Fin-de-Siècle Vienna* (New Haven, 1992), 246–248.

17. Nike Wagner, *Geist und Geschlecht* (Frankfurt, 1982); Edward Timms, *Karl Kraus: Apocalyptic Satirist* (New Haven, London, 1986); Lisa Fischer, *Lina Loos* (Vienna, 1994).

18. See works of Carl Moll, Max Kurzweil, Wilhelm List, Wilhelm Gause.

19. The only unequivocal depiction of the *Geschlechterkampf* in Vienna was published in *Ver Sacrum* in 1899 by Ernst Stöhr, and is an illustration to his own poem (*Ver Sacrum* 2, no. 12 [1899]: 8). It demonstrates the victory of the liberated woman over man. The artist, who was multitalented (a poet, a musician and a painter), left only a few works behind; deep depression blocked his creativity. See Christian M. Nebehay, *Ver Sacrum 1898–1903* (Vienna, 1975), 184–188; Michael Pabst, *Wiener Grafik um 1900* (Munich, 1984), 154, 156, 158.

20. Ilona Sármány-Parsons, *Viennese Painting at the Turn of the Century* (Budapest, 1991): text for page 17.

21. Werner Hofmann, "Das Fleisch erkennen," in Pfabigan, *Ornament und Askese*, 122.

22. Robert Goldwater, *Symbolism* (New York, 1979), 247–248.

23. Gottfried Fliedl, *Gustav Klimt* (Cologne, 1989), 127–132.

24. Ilona Sármány-Parsons, *Gustav Klimt* (New York, 1987), 83–87.

25. Max Eisler, *Gustav Klimt* (Vienna, 1920), 22; Angelica Bäumler, *Gustav Klimt's Women* (London, 1986).

26. Gottfried Fliedl offers a different opinion about this issue in his book (op. cit., 200–206).

27. Jacques Le Rider, "Modernismus—Feminismus, Modernität—Virilität: Otto Weininger und die asketische Moderne," in Pfabigan, *Ornament und Askese*, 242–260.

28. Roman Prahl, "Anfänge der Modernen Galerie in Prag," *Stifter Jahrbuch*, New Series, 7 (Munich, 1993): 115–125; Ilona Sármány-Parsons, "Entfremdete Nachbarn," in Eugen Thurnher, Walter Weiss et al., eds., *"Kakanien"* (Vienna, 1991), 415–437.

29. It was everywhere, above all through national Romanticism in literature, that the image-making of the nation and national heroes or heroines occurred. The visual arts relied heavily on the patterns given by native poetry or prose. Under the influence of Herder, Central European artists began to construct a national mythology out of the folklore of the peasants.

30. Robert B. Pynsent, "The Decadent Self," in Pynsent, *Questions of Identity—Czech and Slovak Ideas of Nationality and Personality* (London, 1994), 101–146; Agnieszka Morawinska, *Polnische Malerei* (Warsaw, 1984), 40–47.

31. Aladár Schöpflin, *A magyar irodalom története a XX. században* (Budapest, 1937/1990), 42–112.

32. Adam Zamoyski, *The Polish Way* (London, 1989), 318.

33. Wieslaw Juszczak, *Malarstvo Polskie: Modernism* (Warsaw, 1977); Agnieszka Mora vinska, ed., *Symbolism in Polish Painting, 1890–1914*, Catalogue (Detroit, 1984), 129–137.

34. Jan K. Ostrowski, *Die polnische Malerei vom Ende des 18. Jahrhunderts bis zum Beginn der Moderne* (Munich, 1989), 103–146.

35. Agnieszka Lawniczakowa, ed., *Malczewski: A Vision of Poland*, Catalogue (London, 1990).

36. Ibid., 16.

37. Stanisław Przybyszewski, *Totenmesse* (Berlin, 1893); Stanisław Eile, "The Prophet of the 'Naked Soul': Stanisław Przybyszewski," in László Péter and Robert B. Pynsent, eds., *Intellectuals and the Future in the Habsburg Monarchy 1890–1914* (London, 1988), 173–190.

38. Czesław Miłosz, *The History of Polish Literature* (Berkeley, Los Angeles, London, 1983), 369–371.

39. Ibid., 351–358.

40. The Manifesto of Czech Modernism demanded absolute individualism in the arts. It was published in October 1895 in the journal *Rozhledy* in Prague and signed by the most important Czech writers and critics of the time, e.g., Josef Svatopluk Machar, Otokar Březina, Antonín Sova, the critic František Václav Krejčí, and František Xaver Šalda.

41. Otto M. Urban, ed., *Moderny Revue* (Prague, 1995).

42. Robert B. Pynsent, "Decadence, Decay, Innovation," in Pynsent, ed., *Decadence and Innovation* (London, 1989), 111–248.

43. The author's own translation from the German of *Tschechische Kunst 1878–1914* (Darmstadt, 1984), 74–75.

44. Ibid., 74.

45. The legend of Libussa was very popular among German writers: Gottfried Herder, Clemens Brentano and Franz Grillparzer wrote versions of it and the last named, in his drama *Libussa*, made something like a modern, Green feminist of the mythical matriarch. The apotheosis of Libussa is to be found in the opera by Smetana. See John Tyrell, *Czech Opera* (Cambridge, 1988), 41–44, 135–141.

46. Bedřich Loewenstein, "Theatralik, Historismus, Bürgerliche Repräsentation," in *Bohemia* 29, no. 1 (1988): 33.

47. Thomas Vlček, "Natural Sensualism, Czech *Fin-de-Siècle* Art," in László Péter and Robert B. Pynsent, eds., *Intellectuals and the Future in the Habsburg Monarchy 1890–1914* (London, 1988), 107–126.

48. Jiří Mucha, *Alphonse Mucha, His Life and Art* (London, 1966).

49. Karel Srp, ed., *Das Slawische Epos*, Catalogue (Krems, 1994).

50. Katherine David, "Czech Feminists and Nationalism in the Habsburg Monarchy: 'The First in Austria,'" *Journal of Women's History* 2 (1991): 24–45; Helena Vollet-Jeanneret, *La Femme Bourgeoise à Prague, 1860–1895* (Ph.D. thesis, Lausanne, 1988).

51. Marie Neudorfl, "Masaryk and the Woman Question," in Stanley B. Winters, ed., *Thomas G. Masaryk (1850–1937): Thinker and Politician* (London, 1990).

52. *Tschechische Kunst 1878–1914*, Catalogue (Darmstadt, 1984), vol. 1, 64–65.

53. Ilona Sármány-Parsons, "The Image of the City in Turn-of-the-Century Painting in Central Europe," in *Central European University History Department Yearbook* (Budapest, 1996).

54. On Hungarian literature and culture, see Lóránt Czigány, *The Oxford History of Hungarian Literature* (Oxford, 1984); John Lukács, *Budapest 1900* (London, 1988); Peter Hanák, *Der Garten und der Werkstatt* (Vienna, 1992); Thomas Bender and Carl E. Schorske, *Budapest and New York* (New York, 1994).

55. Hungarian history painting features many heroines fighting against foreign oppressors. Examples include *Women of Eger* (1867) by Bertalan Székely, in which the enemy are the Turks, or *Ilona Zrinyi* (1859) by Viktor Madarász, in which they are the Habsburgs.

56. A book on Hungarian women writers published recently does not change the overall picture in this respect. See Anna Fábri, *"A szép tiltott táj felé"—A magyar írónök története két századforduló között, 1795–1905* (Budapest, 1996).

57. Loránd Czigány, *The Oxford History of Hungarian Literature* (Oxford, 1984), 290–297; John Lukács, *Budapest 1900*, 164–167.

58. Gyöngyi Eri and Zsuzsa Jobbágyi, eds., *A Golden Age*, Catalogue (London, Miami 1989), 143–174.

59. Mária Bernáth, *Rippl-Rónai* (Budapest, 1976).

60. Lenke Haulisch, *Vaszary János* (Budapest, 1982).

61. András Székely, *Csók István* (Budapest, 1977).

62. Judith Szabadi, *Gulácsy Lajos* (Budapest, 1983).

63. Katalin Gellér, *Nagy Sándor* (Budapest, 1978).

64. Katalin Gellér and Katalin Keserü, *A gödöllöi müvésztelep* (The Gödöllö Art Colony) (Budapest, 1987).

65. Nóra Aradi, *Fényes Adolf* (Budapest, 1979).

66. László Bényi, *Koszta József* (Budapest, 1979).

67. István Genthon, *Ferenczy Károly* (Budapest, 1963).

AFTERTHOUGHTS ABOUT
FIN-DE-SIÈCLE VIENNA

The Problem of Aesthetic Culture in Central Europe

Mary Gluck

*F*in-de-siècle Vienna" conjures up a complicated set of images. It is, first of all, a famous book of essays that reinterpreted Viennese cultural life at the turn of the century. But it is also an academic phenomenon that was inspired and generated by those essays. On the most abstract level, however, we have to see "*fin-de-siècle* Vienna" as a generalized vision of modernist culture, based on a particular theory about the relationship between aesthetics and politics.

Undoubtedly, the most immediate association of the term is with Carl Schorske's *Fin-de-Siècle Vienna: Politics and Culture*, first published as a book in 1980, though well-known as individual essays years earlier than that. *Fin-de-Siècle Vienna* succeeded in capturing both scholarly and popular imagination as few academic books have done in recent times. Through an elegantly written, cogently argued, and powerfully conceived hypothesis, it linked the political and social developments of Habsburg Vienna with a flourishing aesthetic culture, whose defining characteristics were a retreat from politics, extreme sensitivity to subjective states, and a systematic interest in psychic phenomena.

A testimony to the fertility of Schorske's conception is the endless flow of articles, dissertations, popular books, conferences, seminars, art exhibitions, and undergraduate courses that *Fin-de-Siècle Vienna* has inspired since its publication. Thanks to these activities, older stereotypes of Vienna, the city of waltzes, operettas and coffeehouses, have given way to a new myth of Vienna, the habitat of aesthetes, connoisseurs and psychoanalysts. Vienna has been transformed, according to a witty parody, into "a city vibrant with intellect and sex ... [where] Freud, seizing his unique opportunity, used the first to explode the second."[1]

The tremendous resonance of Schorske's work is not accidental. For his book is far more than a case history of a local aesthetic culture. Though undoubtedly intended strictly as a historical reconstruction of certain aspects of Viennese aestheticism, Schorske's vision, nevertheless, implicitly presents a paradigmatic case for the historical understanding of all modernist cultures. Perhaps the central accomplishment of this historical theory is the link it forges between the modernist self and *fin-de-siècle* politics. According to its argument, the rise of Psychological Man and the internalization of modernist culture were a direct response to a political world in disarray, which had rejected the norms of enlightened liberalism and had turned to the irrational, collectivist values of mass politics. Through this theory, Schorske became, as one commentator put it, the "historian of de-historicization," the scholar who accomplished the paradoxical task of "weaving a history around the modern retreat from the historical."[2]

But the very conception of modernism as a cultural retreat from history, which lies at the heart of Schorske's work, is an unexamined theoretical construct. As an axiomatic assumption that links Schorske's historical hypothesis with academic and popular public opinion, it represents the third, perhaps most general, dimension of the "*fin-de-siècle* Vienna" phenomenon.

This particular conception of modernism has deep theoretical and ideological roots in twentieth-century liberal culture. It was formalized into a coherent aesthetic philosophy during the interwar years by critics such as Theodor Adorno, Clement Greenberg, Meyer Schapiro, Joseph Frank, and others. But it quickly acquired the status of an ideology of modernism among the general public. According to its tenets, the work of art constitutes an autonomous, organic, self-referential universe, free from the contaminations of history; the true artist is a radical iconoclast, divorced from social, political, and professional affiliations; and aesthetic creation is a subjective act, fundamentally incompatible with the market place and popular culture.

How do these different components, implicit in the Vienna 1900 idea, coexist with each other? What do the popular myth, the historical theory and the aesthetic philosophy contribute toward our understanding of the cultural world of the Habsburg Monarchy and its successor states? Does "*fin-de-siècle* Vienna" continue to have validity as an analytic tool for further research? These were some of the overarching questions posed by the conference, "Beyond Vienna 1900: Rethinking Culture in Central Europe," hosted by the Center for Austrian Studies at the University of Minnesota in October 1995.

No simple or unambiguous answer emerged to these questions in the course of the two-day conference, which brought together over twenty scholars from the United States, England, Austria and Hungary. Based on the high quality of the presentations, many of which are being published in this volume, there is little doubt that Viennese and Habsburg cultural history is a vibrant field that continues to generate innovative and sophisticated scholarship. However, the relationship of this new scholarship to the idea of "*fin-de-siècle* Vienna" is a deeply ambiguous one. The very notion of "*fin-de-siècle* Vienna" as a cultural paradigm with multiple sites of interpretation is a point of contention among scholars active in the field.

Schorske's students and admirers are, perhaps, the most critical of the "*fin-de-siècle* Vienna" idea. Protective of the integrity of Schorske's individual achievement, they have been eager to extricate his book from both popular images of Vienna 1900, as well as from generalized theoretical conceptions of aesthetic modernism. As Michael Roth recently pointed out in the introduction to a collection of essays honoring the distinguished historian, "Schorske proposes no meta-narrative to provide closure," in *Fin-de-Siècle Vienna*. His collage-like, fragmented strategies were indebted, Roth insists, "to the aesthetic sensibility of the moderns," rather than to the ideological narratives of theorists of modernism.[3]

Understandable as such arguments are, they are ultimately contradictory, since they are forced to deny the very elements that lend broader significance to Schorske's individual scholarship. The attempt to restrict the meaning of *Fin-de-Siècle Vienna* to a particular historical achievement and to separate it off from the aesthetic philosophy on which it is grounded and the popular myth which it helped create is misconceived. Vienna 1900 has become a cultural paradigm precisely because of its complexity. For this reason, the real question is not whether it constitutes a paradigm or not, but rather, how we can understand the nature of the implicit relationship between its different component elements.

It is this latter issue that forms the subtext of the essays that have been brought together in this volume. The authors of these essays are implicitly agreed that there exist irreconcilable conflicts, both between and within the historical and aesthetic hypothesis, that constitute the interpretative ground for the Vienna 1900 phenomenon. Empirically, the authors have thematized these conflicts around two separate, though obviously interrelated, issues. The first has to do with the fate of liberalism and its relationship to Austro-Hungarian political culture at the turn of the century. The second revolves around the interpretation of modernism as an ahistorical, apolitical enterprise that exists in isolation not only from the political realm, but also from commerce and popular culture.

Austro-Hungarian political culture, according to these accounts, was considerably more complex, more fluid, and more differentiated than the Vienna 1900 model implies. Schorske's portrait of an individualistic, rational Austrian liberalism, which, after a brief moment of flowering, was overshadowed by nationalist mass movements, has been challenged in a number of ways. Austrian liberalism has been reinterpreted as a movement not necessarily in conflict with chauvinistic nationalism, but rather as a prelude to such politics. From this vantage point, there was no decline of Austrian liberalism in the strict sense of the word, but rather a logical extension or playing out of its innermost tendencies. On the other side of the picture, the politics of ethnic nationalism has also been shown to be less homogeneous and less single-mindedly opposed to classic liberal agendas and identities than previously imagined. Finally, even the centrality of liberalism to Austro-Hungarian political culture has been questioned by some who have shifted attention to the dynastic traditions of the Habsburg state as the defining factor in Austrian politics and public life.

What is noteworthy about these recent reassessments of Austrian politics at the turn of the century is their silence on the question of culture and aesthetics. However the nature of Viennese liberalism is interpreted, its fate does not seem to point unambiguously toward a particular type of aesthetic development. The links between politics and psyche have proven to be unexpectedly hard to demonstrate on the empirical plane.

The aesthetic vision implicit within the Vienna 1900 idea has turned out to be equally at odds with the empirical findings of recent scholarship. At the heart of these new approaches to aesthetic modernism has been a growing skepticism about the supposed ahistoricity of the modernist project, especially as expressed through the metaphor of the retreat into the garden or the psyche. Art historians and literary scholars have pointed out that aesthetic culture at the turn of the century was not necessarily synonymous with individual passivity, narcissism and the negation of the political and economic realms of modern life. On the contrary, aesthetic self-fashioning could be a politically charged, aggressively self-assertive project whose impact was not necessarily restricted to the garden of aestheticism. Moreover, aesthetic production itself did not take place in a vacuum, but was an integral part of the commercial art market that increasingly defined the fate of avant-garde art at the *fin de siècle*. Far from being above history, the modernist aesthetic project has come to appear as deeply implicated in the political values, commercial relations, and social practices of the world of bourgeois modernity that it denounced.

These empirical reinterpretations of Viennese modernist culture and politics have undeniably opened up new perspectives for further research. They have deepened and made more complex our understanding of liberal ideologies and institutions in this part of the world. They have also redirected our attention from the autonomous work of art and artist to the multiple contexts—political, institutional, commercial—which have defined modernist aesthetics at the turn of the century. This more nuanced picture of the world of *fin-de-siècle* Vienna has come at a price, however. It has resulted in the unraveling of the theoretical and methodological assumptions at the root of the Vienna 1900 idea and the inevitable collapse of the generalized model of aesthetic modernism that has dominated the field for over two decades. The big losers have been intellectual historians of modernism, who have implicitly relied on this model in their efforts to conceptualize the meaning of modernist high culture as a general historical phenomenon. What role remains for intellectual historians, in the absence of a synthetic theory establishing the place of aesthetics within the field of modern politics and social experience?

The answer to this question cannot be given with certainty at this point. What seems clear, however, is that the concept of culture as a general integrating factor will play an increasingly important role in the analytic strategies of intellectual historians. Culture is, of course, one of the most elusive and overused ideas in contemporary academic debates. It can refer to canonical high art, as created by exceptional individuals with supposedly privileged insights into the nature of the self and society. It can just as frequently imply popular cultural expressions, reflecting the social, ethnic and class identities of particular groups. It can also mean, however, the everyday practices and habitual customs of an entire society, conceived as a symbolic unit. The need to clarify and make permeable the boundaries between these different versions of culture is a precondition for a viable model of the cultural history of modernism.

This is not a new agenda. Since the 1980s, thoughtful practitioners in the field of intellectual history and cultural studies have been calling for the clarification of the relationship between high and popular cultures and the bridging of the "Great Divide" between the two realms.[4] As Andreas Huyssen, who coined the phrase, has pointed out, the fragmentation of the idea of culture into hierarchically defined realms, with elite culture occupying the highest status, and popular and everyday cultures relegated to lesser forms of expression, was a historical development whose roots were in the late nineteenth and early twentieth centuries.[5] It has produced not only philosophic distinctions, but also methodological divisions between analysts of high art and popular cultures. In Roger Chartier's words, there grew up a sharp differentiation "between the culture of the greatest number, which calls for an external, collective and quantitative approach, and the intellectuality of the highest form of thought, which requires internal analysis to individualize the irreducible originality of their ideas."[6]

The call for a new model of cultural history that could heal "the discursive separation of art from culture" has not had tangible results yet.[7] There has not emerged a generalized theory of culture or a new methodology for students of modernism. Yet, as the essays in the present volume indicate, the cumulative impact of empirical research has substantially changed our inherited paradigms of modernism. They have not only deepened our understanding of the inner dynamics of high culture, but have also expanded our knowledge of what lies outside the aesthetic realm. What needs to follow now is a growing theoretical clarification of the implications of this new vision of cultural production beyond the dualistic spaces of the "Great Divide." Such a theory would no longer talk of high art or popular culture, but rather of different human responses to the problem of creating values and meaning in an unprecedented modern world, where such values and meanings are no longer given in existing social and religious structures.

Notes

1. Peter Gay, *Freud, Jews and Other Germans: Masters and Victims in Modernist Culture* (New York, 1978), 30.
2. Michael S. Roth, "Performing History: Modernist Contextualism in Carl Schorske's *Fin-de-Siècle Vienna,*" *The American Historical Review* 99 (June 1994): 735–736.
3. Michael S. Roth, ed., *Rediscovering History: Culture, Politics, and the Psyche* (Palo Alto, 1994), 3.
4. Cf. Fred Inglis, *Cultural Studies* (Oxford, 1993).
5. Andreas Huyssen, *After the Great Divide: Modernism, Mass Culture, Postmodernism* (Bloomington, 1986).
6. Roger Chartier, "Intellectual History and the History of *Mentalités*: A Dual Re-evaluation," in *Cultural History: Between Practices and Representations*, trans. L. G. Cochrane (Ithaca, 1988), 37.
7. George E. Marcus and Fred R. Myers, "The Traffic in Art and Culture: An Introduction," in *The Traffic in Culture: Refiguring Art and Anthropology* (Berkeley, 1995), 6.

SELECTED BIBLIOGRAPHY

Adler, Max. *Der Sozialismus und die Intellektuellen* (Vienna, 1910).

Adorno, Theodor W. "Meditationen zur Metaphysik," in *Negative Dialektik* (Frankfurt, 1990), 354–400.

———. "The Essay as Form," trans. Bob Hullot-Kentor and Frederic Will, *New German Critique* 32 (1984): 151–71.

Amann, Klaus, and Hubert Lengauer, eds. *Österreich und der große Krieg, 1914–1918* (Vienna, 1989).

Anderson, Harriet. *Utopian Feminism: Women's Movements in Fin-de-Siècle Vienna* (New Haven, 1992).

Anderson, Mark, ed. *Reading Kafka: Prague, Politics, and the Fin de Siècle* (New York, 1989).

Anderson, Mark. *Kafka's Clothes: Ornament and Aestheticism in the Hapsburg Fin de Siècle* (Oxford, 1992).

Apollonio, U., ed. *Futurist Manifestos,* trans. R. Brain (New York, 1973).

Aradi, Nóra. *Fényes Adolf* (Budapest, 1979).

Assoun, Paul-Laurent. *Freud et Nietzsche* (Paris, 1980).

Auernheimer, Raoul. "Beard of the Prophet," *Herzl Year Book* 6 (1964–65).

Bäumler, Angelica. *Gustav Klimt's Women* (London, 1986).

Bahr, Hermann. *Secession* (Vienna, 1900).

———. *Prophet der Moderne: Tagebücher, 1888–1904,* ed. Reinhard Farkas (Vienna, 1987).

———. "Die Überwindung des Naturalismus," reprinted in Gotthart Wunberg, ed., *Die Wiener Moderne. Literatur, Kunst und Musik zwischen 1890 und 1910* (Stuttgart, 1980).

Bauer, Otto. *Die Nationalitätenfrage und die Sozialdemokratie* [1907] (Vienna, 1924).

Bauman, Sygmunt. "Strangers: The Social Construction of Universality and Particularity," *New German Critique* 78 (1989): 7–42.

Bein, Alex. *Theodore Herzl,* trans. Maurice Samuel (Philadelphia, 1941).

———. *Theodor Herzl* (Vienna, 1934).

Belke, Ingrid. *Die sozialreformerischen Ideen von Joseph Popper-Lynkeus (1838–1921) in Zusammenhang mit allgemeinen Reformbestrebungen des Wiener Bürgertums um die Jahrhundertwende* (Tübingen, 1978).

Beller, Steven. *Vienna and the Jews, 1867–1938: A Cultural History* (Cambridge, 1989).

———. *Herzl* (London, 1991).

———. "Herzl's Tannhäuser: The Redemption of the Artist as Politician," in Robert S. Wistrich, ed., *Austrians and Jews in the Twentieth Century: From Franz Joseph to Waldheim* (New York, 1992), 38–57.

———. "Patriotism and the National Identity of Habsburg Jewry, 1860–1914," *Leo Baeck Institute Year Book* 41 (1996): 215–238.

Bender, Thomas, and Carl E. Schorske. *Budapest and New York* (New York, 1994).

Bensmaïa, Réda. *The Barthes Effect: The Essay as Reflective Text* (Minneapolis, 1987).

Bényi, László. *Koszta József* (Budapest, 1979).

Berger, Christian-Paul. "Kritischer Katholizismus versus kritische Theorie. Der Brennerkreis und die ältere Frankfurter Schule," *Mitteilungen aus dem Brenner Archiv* 10 (1991): 72–92.

Berger, Johann N. "Die Pressefreiheit und das Pressegesetz" (Vienna, 1848), 1, in *Oberösterreichische Landesarchiv, Flugschriftenversammlung*, A, Vol. 24.

Berkley, George E. *Vienna and its Jews: The Tragedy of Success, 1880–1980s* (Cambridge, Mass., 1988).

Berkowitz, Michael. *Zionist Culture and West European Jewry before the First World War* (Cambridge, 1993).

Bernáth, Mária. *Rippl-Rónai* (Budapest, 1976).

Bernays, Jakob. *Zwei Abhandlungen über die Aristotelische Theorie des Drama* (Berlin, 1880).

Berner, P., et al. *Wien um 1900: Aufbruch in die Moderne* (Vienna 1986).

Bizanz, Hans. *Alfred Kubin* (Munich, 1977).

———. *Vienna 1900* (Bristol, 1990).

Blackbourn, David, and Geoff Eley. *The Peculiarities of German History: Bourgeois Society and Politics in Nineteenth-Century Germany* (Oxford, 1984).

Blackbourn, David. "The Discreet Charm of the German Bourgeoisie," in *Populists and Patricians: Essays in Modern German History* (London, 1987).

Blei, Franz. "Drei Briefe an einen jungen Mann," in *Hyperion* 1 (2 vols.) (1907).

Bloom, Allan. *The Closing of the American Mind* (London, 1988).

Boorman, Helen. "Rethinking the Expressionist Era; Wilhelmine Cultural Debates and Prussian Elements in German Expressionism," *Oxford Art Journal* 9:2 (1986): 3–15.

Botstein, Leon. "Egon Schiele and Arnold Schoenberg: The Cultural Politics of Aesthetic Innovation in Vienna, 1890–1918," in Patrick Werkner, ed., *Egon Schiele: Art, Sexuality, and Viennese Modernism* (Palo Alto, Calif., 1994), 101–18.

Bourdieu, Pierre. *The Logic of Practice*, trans. Richard Nice (Cambridge, 1990).

Boyer, John. "Freud, Marriage, and Late Viennese Liberalism: A Commentary from 1905," *Journal of Modern History*, 50 (March 1978): 72–102.

Boyer, John W. *Political Radicalism in Late Imperial Vienna* (Chicago, 1981).

———. *Culture and Political Crisis: Christian Socialism in Power, 1897–1918* (Chicago, 1995).

Broch, Hermann. *Hofmannsthal and his Times*, trans. Michael Steinberg (Chicago, 1984).

———. "Hofmannsthal und seine Zeit," in P. M. Lützeler, ed., *Schriften zur Literatur 1*, (Frankfurt, 1975), 111–284.

Bronner, Stephen E., and F. Peter Wagner. *Vienna: The World of Yesterday, 1889–1914* (Atlantic Highlands, N.J., 1997).

Burke, Peter. *Venice and Amsterdam* (Cambridge, 1994).

Chartier, Roger. "Intellectual History and the History of Mentalités: A Dual Re-evaluation," in *Cultural History: Between Practices and Representations,* trans. L. G. Cochrane (Ithaca, 1988).

Clair, Jean, ed. *Vienne 1880–1938: L'apocalypse joyeuse* (Paris, 1986).

Clare, George. *Last Waltz in Vienna* (London, 1983).

Clark, Timothy J. *The Painting of Modern Life: Paris in the Art of Manet and his Followers* (London, 1985).

Comini, Alessandra. *Egon Schiele's Portraits* (Berkeley, 1974).

———. *Gustav Klimt* (New York, 1975).

Coreth, Anna. "'Pietas Austriaca': Wesen und Bedeutung habsburgischer Frömmigkeit der Barockzeit," *Mitteilungen des Österreichischen Staatsarchivs 7* (Offprint, 1954).

Corngold, Stanley. "Kafka and the Dialect of Minor Literature," *College Literature* 21, no. 1 (1994): 89–101.

Czigány, Lóránt. *The Oxford History of Hungarian Literature* (Oxford, 1984).

Dahrendorf, Ralf. *Society and Democracy in Germany* (New York, 1967).

Daviau, Donald G. *Der Mann von Übermorgen: Hermann Bahr 1863–1934* (Vienna, 1984).

———. *Hermann Bahr* (Boston, 1985).

David, Katherine. "Czech Feminists and Nationalism in the Habsburg Monarchy: 'The First in Austria,'" *Journal of Women's History,* no. 2 (1991): 24–45.

De La Grange, Henry-Louis. *Mahler,* 3 vols. (Paris, 1979–84).

Deleuze, Gilles, and Félix Guattari. *Kafka: Pour une littérature mineure* (Paris, 1975), trans. Dana Polan, *Kafka: Toward a Minor Literature* (Minneapolis, 1986).

Dethloff, Klaus. *Theodor Herzl oder Der Moses des Fin de Siècle* (Vienna, 1986).

Devereux, Georges. *From Anxiety to Method in the Behavioral Sciences* (The Hague, 1968).

Doderer, Heimito von. *Die Strudlhofstiege oder Melzer und die Tiefe der Jahre* (1951; reprint, Vienna, 1993).

Eckstein, Freidrich. *Alte unnennbare Tage* (Vienna, 1988).

Ehalt, Hubert Ch., et al., eds. *Glücklich ist, wer vergisst ...? Das andere Wien um 1900* (Vienna, 1986).

Eisler, Max. *Gustav Klimt* (Vienna, 1920).

Elon, Amos. *Herzl* (New York, 1975).

Elsen, Albert. "Drawing and a New Sexual Intimacy: Rodin and Schiele," in Patrick Werkner, ed., *Egon Schiele. Art, Sexuality, and Viennese Modernism* (Palo Alto, 1994).

Eri, Gyöngyi, and Zsuzsa Jobbágyi, eds. *A Golden Age,* Catalogue (London, 1989).

Eschenburg, Barbara, ed. *Der Kampf der Geschlechter: Der neue Mythos in der Kunst 1850–1930* (Munich, Cologne, 1995).

Evans, R. J. W. *The Making of the Habsburg Monarchy, 1550–1700* (Oxford, 1979).

Falk, Avner. "Freud and Herzl," *Midstream* 23, no. 1 (1977): 3–24.

Feilchenfeldt, Walter. *Vincent van Gogh and Paul Cassirer: The Reception of van Gogh in Germany from 1901 to 1914,* Cahier Vincent, vol. 2 (Zwolle, 1988).

Field, Frank. *The Last Days of Mankind* (London, 1967).

Fischer, Lisa. *Lina Loos oder wenn die Muse sich selbst küßt* (Vienna, 1994).

Fleischer, Ludwig. *Österreichischer Bürgerkunde: Ein Lehr- und Hilfsbuch für Bürgerschulen und die mit denselben verbundenen Einjährigen Lehrkurse* [4th edition] (Vienna, 1908).

Fliedl, Gottfried. *Gustav Klimt* (Cologne, 1989).

Foster, Hal. "The Expressive Fallacy," in *Recodings* (Seattle, 1985).

———. "Primitive Scenes," *Critical Inquiry* 20 (Autumn 1993): 69–102.

Foucault, Michel. *The History of Sexuality* (New York, 1980).

———. "What is Enlightenment?" in Paul Rabinow, ed., *The Foucault Reader* (New York, 1984), 32–50.

Francis, Mark, ed. *The Viennese Enlightenment* (Beckenham, 1985).

Franz, Georg. *Liberalismus: Die deutschliberale Bewegung in der habsburgischen Monarchie* (Munich, 1955).

Freud, Sigmund. *Der Humor*, in *Studienausgabe*, vol. 4 (Frankfurt, 1970).

———. *Der Wahn und die Träume in W. Jensens, "Gradiva,"* (Frankfurt, 1973).

———. *An Autobiographical Study*, trans. J. Strachey (London, 1935).

———. *The Complete Letters of Sigmund Freud to Wilhelm Fliess, 1887–1904*, ed. J. M. Masson (Cambridge, Mass., 1985).

———. *The Letters of Sigmund Freud*, ed. Ernst L. Freud, trans. T. and J. Stern (New York, 1975).

Friedell, Egon. *Kulturgeschichte der Neuzeit*, 2 vols. (Munich, 1979).

Friedmann, B. *Die Wohnungsnot in Wien* (Vienna, 1857).

Fuchs, Albert. *Geistige Strömungen in Österreich, 1867–1918* (Vienna, 1949).

Gaisbauer, Adolf. *Davidstern und Doppeladler. Zionismus und jüdischer Nationalismus in Österreich 1882–1918* (Vienna, 1988).

Garb, Tamar. "Gender and Representation," in Francis Frascina et al., eds., *Modernity and Modernism: French Painting in the Nineteenth Century* (New Haven, 1993).

Gay, Peter. *Freud: A Life for Our Time* (New York, 1988).

———. *Freud, Jews and Other Germans: Masters and Victims in Modernist Culture* (New York, 1978).

Gellér, Katalin. *Nagy Sándor* (Budapest, 1978).

Genthon, István. *Ferenczy Károly* (Budapest, 1963).

Giampieri, Patrizia. "Freud und die österreichische Philosophie," in Nagl Vetter and Leupold Löwenthal, eds., *Philosophie und Psychoanalyse* (Frankfurt, 1990), 41–54.

Gilman, Sander L. *Jewish Self-Hatred* (Baltimore, 1986).

———. *Difference and Pathology: Stereotypes of Sexuality, Race, and Madness* (Ithaca, 1985).

———. "Opera, Homosexuality, and Models of Disease: Richard Strauss's *Salome* in the Context of Images of Disease in the Fin de Siècle," in *Disease and Representation: Images of Illness from Madness to AIDS* (Ithaca, 1988), 155–81.

Giskra, Carl. *Wahlrede des Dr. C. Giskra für die Landtagscandidaten des II. Bezirks in Brünn* (Brünn, 1861).

Glettler, Monika. *Die Wiener Tschechen um 1900* (Munich, 1972).

Gluck, Mary. *Georg Lukács and his Generation 1900–1918* (Cambridge, Mass., 1985).

Godsey, William D., Jr. "The Nobility, Jewish Assimilation, and the Austro-Hungarian Foreign Service in the Late Imperial Era," *Austrian History Yearbook* 27 (1996): 155–80.

Goffman, Erving. *The Presentation of Self in Everyday Life* (New York, 1959).

Goldhammer, Leo. "Theodor Herzl and Sigmund Freud," *Theodor Herzl Jahrbuch* (Vienna) 1937.

Goldinger, Walter. "Geschichte der Organisation des Handelsministeriums," in *100 Jahre im Dienste der Wirtschaft*, ed. Bundesministerium für Handel und Wiederaufbau (Vienna, 1961).

Goldwater, Robert. *Symbolism* (New York, 1979).

Good, David F. *The Economic Rise of the Habsburg Empire, 1750–1914* (Berkeley, 1984).

Habermas, Jürgen. *Strukturwandel der Öffentlichkeit* (Neuwied, 1962).

Hacohen, Malachi. "Karl Popper in Exile: The Viennese Progressive Imagination and the Making of *The Open Society,*" *Philosophy of the Social Sciences* 26 (December 1996).

Hanák, Peter. *Der Garten und der Werkstatt* (Vienna, 1992).

———. *The Garden and the Workshop* (Princeton, 1998).

Handler, Andrew. *Dori: The Life and Times of Theodor Herzl in Budapest (1860–1878)* (Univ. of Alabama, 1983).

Hanisch, Ernst, and Ulrike Fleischer. *Im Schatten berühmter Zeiten. Salzburg in den Jahren Georg Trakls (1887–1914)* (Salzburg, 1986).

Hantsch, Hugo. *Geschichte Österreichs 1648–1918,* 2 vols. (Graz, 1968).

Harrison, Thomas. *Essayism: Conrad, Musil, and Pirandello* (Baltimore, 1992).

Hasiba, Gernot D. *Das Notverordnungsrecht in Österreich (1848–1917): Notwendigkeit und Mißbrauch eines Staatserhaltenden Instrumentes* (Vienna, 1985).

Haulisch, Lenke. *Vaszary János* (Budapest, 1982).

Heer, Friedrich. *Der Kampf um die österreichische Identität* (Vienna, 1981).

Heerde, Jeroen Bastiaan van. *Staat und Kunst: Staatliche Kunstförderung 1895 bis 1918* (Vienna, 1993).

Hegel, G. W. F. *The Philosophy of Fine Art,* trans. F. P. B. Osmaston, 4 vols. (1920; reprint, New York, 1975).

Heindl, Waltraud. *Gehorsame Rebellen: Bürokratie und Beamte in Österreich 1780 bis 1848* (Vienna, 1991).

Hermand, Jost. "Gralsmotive um die Jahrhundertwende," in *Von Mainz nach Weimar (1793–1919)* (Stuttgart, 1969), 269–297.

Herzl, Theodor. *Briefe und Tagebücher,* ed. Alex Bein et al., 5 vols. (Berlin, 1983).

———. *Der Judenstaat: Theodor Herzl oder der Moses des Fin de Siècle,* ed. Klaus Dethloff (Vienna, 1986).

———. "Compagniearbeit: Lustspiel in einem Act," *Wallishausser'scher Theater-Katalog* 10 (1880).

Hesse, Eva. *Die Achse Avantgarde—Faschismus: Reflexionen über Filipo Tommaso Marinetti und Ezra Pound* (Zürich, n.d.).

Hilger, Wolfgang, et al. *Die Wiener Secession* (Vienna, 1986).

Hirsch, Waltraud. *Eine unbescheidene Charakterologie: Geistige Differenz vom Judentum und Christentum als Lehre vom bestimmten Charakter bei Otto Weininger* (D.Phil. diss., University of Tübingen, 1995).

Höbelt, Lothar. *Kornblume und Kaiseradler: Die deutschfreiheitlichen Parteien Altösterreichs 1882–1918* (Vienna, 1993).

Hoffmann, Robert. "Bürgerliche Kommunikationsstrategien zu Beginn der liberalen Ära: Das Beispiel Salzburg," in Hannes Stekl et al., eds. *"Durch Arbeit, Besitz, Wissen und Gerechtigkeit": Bürgertum in der Habsburgermonarchie II* (Vienna, 1992).

Hoffmann, Werner. *Gustav Klimt und die Wiener Jahrhundertwende* (Salzburg, 1970).

———. *Gustav Klimt,* trans. Inge Goodwin (London, 1972).

———. *Das irdische Paradies: Motive und Ideen des 19. Jahrhunderts* (Munich, 1960).

Hofstadter, Richard. *Anti-Intellectualism in American Life* (New York, 1967).

Hubert, Rainer. "Freimaurerei in Österreich 1871 bis 1938," in *Zirkel und Winkelmass* (Vienna, 1984), 31–46.

Hull, Isabel V. *Sexuality, State, and Civil Society in Germany, 1700–1815* (Ithaca, 1996).

Huyssen, Andreas. *After the Great Divide: Modernism, Mass Culture, Postmodernism* (Bloomington, 1986).

Inglis, Fred. *Cultural Studies* (Oxford, 1993).

Jacoby, Russell. *The Repression of Psychoanalysis* (New York, 1983).

Janik, Allan. *Essays on Wittgenstein and Weininger* (Amsterdam, 1985).

————. *How Not to Interpret a Culture: Essays on the Problem of Method in the Geisteswissenschaften* (University of Bergen Philosophy Department Stencil Series, no. 73; Bergen, Norway, 1986).

————. "Ebner contra Wagner. Erkenntnistheorie, Ästhetik und Erlösung in Wien um 1900," in Emil Brix and Allan Janik, eds., *Kreatives Milieu Wien um 1900* (Vienna, 1993), 224–241.

————. "Georg Trakl und die Zerstörung des habsburgischen Mythos," in Fausto Cercignani, ed., *Studia Trakliana* (Milan, 1989), 51–62.

Janik, Allan, and Stephen Toulmin. *Wittgenstein's Vienna* (New York, 1973).

Janz, Rudolf Peter, and Klaus Laermann. *Arthur Schnitzler: Zur Diagnose des Wiener Bürgertums im Fin de Siècle* (Stuttgart, 1977).

Jászi, Oscar. *The Dissolution of the Habsburg Monarchy* (Chicago, 1966).

Jensen, Robert. *Marketing Modernism in Fin-de-Siècle Europe* (Princeton, 1994).

Johnston, William M. *The Austrian Mind: An Intellectual and Social History 1848–1938* (Berkeley, 1972).

Jones, Ernest. *The Life and Work of Sigmund Freud*, 3 vols. (New York, 1953).

Judson, Pieter M. *Exclusive Revolutionaries: Liberal Politics, Social Experience and National Identity in the Austrian Empire, 1848–1914* (Ann Arbor, 1996).

————. "'Whether Race or Conviction Should Be the Standard': National Identity and Liberal Politics in Nineteenth-Century Austria," in *Austrian History Yearbook* 22 (1991).

————. "Inventing Germans: Class, Nationality and Colonial Fantasy at the Margins of the Hapsburg Monarchy," in *Nations, Metropoles, Colonies*, ed. Daniel Segal and Richard Handler, *Social Analysis* 33 (1993).

————. "Deutschnationale Politik und Geschlecht in Österreich 1880–1900," in David F. Good, Margarethe Grandner, and Mary Jo Maynes, eds., *Frauen in Österreich* (Vienna, 1994).

————. "'Not Another Square Foot!': German Liberalism and the Rhetoric of National Ownership in 19th-Century Austria," *Austrian History Yearbook* 26 (1995).

Kafka, Franz. *Briefe 1902–1924* (Frankfurt, 1966).

————. *Letters to Friends, Family, and Editors*, ed. Max Brod (New York, 1977).

Kallir, Jane. *Egon Schiele* (New York, 1994).

Kammerhofer, Leopold, ed. *Studien zum Deutschliberalismus in Zisleithanien 1873–1879* (Vienna, 1992)

Kann, Robert A. *A History of the Habsburg Empire 1526–1918* (Berkeley, 1977).

————. *The Multinational Empire: Nationalism and National Reform in the Habsburg Monarchy 1848–1918*, 2 vols. (New York, 1977).

Kann, Robert A. *A Study in Austrian Intellectual History: From Late Baroque to Romanticism* (New York, 1960).

Kant, Immanuel. *Gesammelte Schriften (Akademieausgabe)*, vols. 7–8 (Berlin, 1912).

————. *Critique of Judgement* (Oxford, 1952).

Karpfen, Fritz. *Literarisches Verbrecheralbum* (Vienna, 1918).

Kern, Josef. *Impressionismus im Wilheminischen Deutschland* (Würzburg, 1989).

Kerr, John. *A Most Dangerous Method: The Story of Freud, Jung und Sabina Spielrein* (New York, 1993).

Knoll, Philipp. *Das Deutschthum in Böhmen* (Dresden, 1885).

———. *Vortrag über die Prager Universitätsfrage* (Vienna, 1881).

Koelbl, Herlinde. *Jüdische Portraits: Photographien und Interviews* (Frankfurt, 1989).

Kokoschka, Oskar. *Briefe*, vol. 1 (Düsseldorf, 1984).

Kolnai, Auriel. *The War Against the West* (London, 1938).

Komlos, John. *Nutrition and Economic Development in the Eighteenth Century Habsburg Monarchy:An Anthropometric History* (Princeton, 1989).

Kornberg, Jacques. *Theodor Herzl: From Assimilation to Zionism* (Bloomington, 1993).

Koshar, Rudy. *Social Life, Local Politics and Nazism* (Chapel Hill, 1986).

Kraus, Karl. "Eine Krone für Zion," in Joh. J. Braakenburg, ed., *Frühe Schriften*, 2 vols. (Munich, 1979).

———. *Die Fackel* (Vienna, 1899–1936).

———. *Nachts* (Vienna, 1924).

Krieger, Leonard. *The German Idea of Freedom* (Chicago, 1972).

Kuhn, Thomas S. *The Structure of Scientific Revolutions*, 2nd ed. (Chicago, 1970).

Kundera, Milan. "The Tragedy of Central Europe," in *New York Review of Books*, April 26, 1984, 33–38.

LaCapra, Dominick. *Rethinking Intellectual History: Texts, Contexts, Language* (Ithaca, 1983).

———. *History and Criticism* (Ithaca, 1985).

Laurence, Richard. "Bertha von Suttner and the Peace Movement in Austria to World War I," *Austrian History Yearbook* 23 (1992): 181–201.

Lawniczakowa, Agnieszka, ed. *Malczewski: A Vision of Poland*, Catalogue (London, 1990).

Lensing, Leo A. "Peter Altenberg's Fabricated Photographs: Literature and Photography in *Fin-de-Siècle* Vienna," in Edward Timms and Ritchie Robertson, eds., *Vienna 1900: From Altenberg to Wittgenstein* (Edinburgh, 1990), 47–72.

Le Rider, Jacques. *Modernité viennoise et crises de l'identité* (Paris, 1990). In English as *Modernity and Crises of Identity: Culture and Society in Fin-de-Siècle Vienna*, trans. Rosemary Morris (Cambridge, 1993).

Leroy, Robert. "*Der Gral*: Aus den Anfängen einer katholischen Literaturzeitschrift," *Tijdschrift voor Levende Talen/Revue des Langues Vivantes* 25, no. 1 (1979): 29–53.

Leser, Norbert. *Zwischen Reformismus und Bolschewismus: Der Austromarxismus als politische Theorie und Praxis* (Vienna, 1968).

Lesky, Erna. *The Vienna Medical School of the Nineteenth Century*, trans. J. Levij (Baltimore, 1976).

Liebermann, Max. "Rede zur Eröffnung von Ausstellung der Berliner Secession," (spring 1900). repr. in G. Busch, ed., *Die Phantasie in der Malerei* (Frankfurt, 1978).

Locke, John. *Two Treatises of Government* (New York, 1965).

Loewenberg, Peter. "Theodor Herzl: Nationalism and Politics," in idem, *Decoding the Past* (New York, 1983), 101–135.

Loos, Adolf. "Ornament und Verbrechen," repr. in Loos, *Sämtliche Schriften*, vol. 1, ed. F. Glück (Vienna, 1962), 276–288.

Lorenz, Konrad. *Die Zukunft ist offen*, ed. Franz Kreuzer (Vienna: Series Paper, 1985).

Luft, David. *Robert Musil and the Crisis of European Culture* (Berkeley, 1980).

Lukács, Georg. *Die Seele und die Formen* (Neuwied and Berlin, 1971), trans. Anna Bostock, *Soul and Form* (London, 1974).

Lukács, John. *Budapest 1900* (London, 1988).

Lyotard, Jean-François. *The Postmodern Condition* (Minneapolis, 1984).

Macartney, C. A. *The Habsburg Empire, 1790–1918* (New York, 1969).

MacKenzie, J. M. *The Empire of Nature: Hunting, Conservation, and British Imperialism* (Manchester, 1988).

Magris, Claudio. *Il mito absburgico nella letteratura austriaca moderna* (Turin, 1963).

———. *Danube* (London, 1989).

Makela, Maria. *The Munich Secession* (Princeton, 1990).

Manheim, Ron. "The Germanic van Gogh: A Case Study of Cultural Annexation," *Simiolus* 19:4 (1989): 277–288.

Marchetti, Maria, ed. *Le Arti a Vienna* (Venice, 1984).

Marcus, George E., and Fred R. Myers. *The Traffic in Culture: Refiguring Art and Anthropology* (Berkeley, 1995).

Marquard, Odo. *Schwierigkeiten mit der Geschichtsphilosophie* (Frankfurt, 1973).

Marx, Karl. "Contribution to the Critique of Hegel's *Philosophy of Right:* Introduction," in idem, *Selected Writings* (Indianapolis, 1994).

May, Arthur J. *The Habsburg Monarchy, 1867–1914* (New York, 1968).

———. *Vienna in the Age of Franz Josef* (Norman, 1966).

Mayer, Arno J. *The Persistence of the Old Regime* (New York, 1981).

Mayer, Hans. *Outsiders: A Study in Life and Letters,* trans. Denis M. Sweet (Cambridge, Mass., 1982).

McCagg, William O., Jr. *Jewish Nobles and Geniuses in Modern Hungary* (Boulder, Colo., 1972).

———. *A History of Habsburg Jews, 1670–1918* (Bloomington, 1989).

McCarthy, John A. *Crossing Boundaries: A Theory and History of Essay Writing in German, 1680–1815* (Philadelphia, 1989).

McGrath, William. *Dionysian Art and Populist Politics in Austria* (New Haven, 1974).

Merkel, Reinhard. *Strafrecht und Satire im Werk von Karl Kraus* (Baden-Baden, 1994).

Methlagl, Walter. "Nietzsche und Trakl," in Gerald Stieg and Remy Colombat, eds., *Frühling der Seele* (Innsbruck, 1995), 83–123.

Methlagl, Walter. "Der schlafende Sohn des Pans," in Fausto Cercignani, ed., *Studia Trakliana*, (Milan, 1989), 63–80.

Methlagl, Walter. "'*Der Brenner*'—Beispiel eines Durchbruchs zur Moderne!'" *Mitteilungen aus dem Brenner Archiv* 2 (1983): 11–12.

Mill, John Stuart. *On Liberty* (Garden City, N.Y., 1973).

Miłosz, Czesław. *The History of Polish Literature* (Berkeley, Los Angeles, London, 1983).

Morawinska, Agnieszka. *Polnische Malerei* (Warsaw, 1984).

———, ed. *Symbolism in Polish Painting, 1890–1914,* Catalogue (Detroit, 1984).

Morton, Frederic. *A Nervous Splendor* (New York, 1980).

Mosse, George L. *Nationalism and Sexuality: Respectability and Abnormal Sexuality in Modern Europe* (Madison, 1985).

Mosse, George L. *The Image of Man: The Creation of Modern Masculinity,* Studies in the History of Sexuality Series (New York, 1996).

Mucha, Jiří. *Alphonse Mucha, His Life and Art* (London, 1966).

Musil, Robert. *Precision and Soul,* ed. and trans. Burton Pike and David S. Luft (Chicago, 1990).

Musil, Robert. "Der deutsche Mensch als Symptom" [1923], in idem, *Gesammelte Werke* 8, ed. Adolf Frisé (Reinbek bei Hamburg, 1978), 1353–1400.

———. "The German Personality as Symptom," in J. C. Nyíri, ed., *Austrian Philosophy* (Munich, 1981), 173–200.

Nadler, Josef. *Literaturgeschichte Österreichs* (Linz, 1948).

Nägele, Rainer. *Theater, Theory, Speculation: Walter Benjamin and the Scenes of Modernity* (Baltimore, 1991).

Nebehay, Christian M. *Gustav Klimt: Dokumentation* (Vienna, 1969).

———. *Egon Schiele, 1890–1918: Briefe; Dokumente; Gedichte* (Salzburg and Vienna, 1979).

———. *Ver Sacrum 1898–1903* (Vienna, 1975).

Nipperdey, Thomas. "Verein als soziale Struktur in Deutschland im späten 18. und frühen 19. Jahrhundert: Eine Fallstudie zur Modernisierung," in *Gesellschaft, Kultur, Theorie: Gesammelte Aufsätze zur neueren Geschichte* (Göttingen, 1976).

Novotny, Fritz, and Johannes Dobai. *Gustav Klimt* (Salzburg, 1967).

Östreich, Gerhard. *Geist und Gestalt des frühmodernen Staats* (Berlin, 1969).

Offermann, Alfred Freiherr von. *Die Bedingungen des Constitutionellen Österreichs* (Vienna, 1900).

Ostrowski, Jan K. *Die polnische Malerei* (Munich, 1989).

Oxaal, Ivar. *The Jews of Pre-1914 Vienna: Two Working Papers* (Hull, 1981).

Oxaal, Ivar, et al., eds. *Jews, Antisemitism and Culture in Vienna* (London, 1987).

Pabst, Michael. *Wiener Grafik um 1900* (Munich, 1984).

Paret, Peter. *The Berlin Secession: Modernism and Its Enemies in Imperial Germany* (Cambridge, MA, 1980).

Pauley, Bruce. *From Prejudice to Persecution: A History of Austrian Antisemitism* (Chapel Hill, N.C., 1992).

Pawel, Ernst. *The Labyrinth of Exile: A Life of Theodor Herzl* (New York, 1989).

Perkins, Geoffrey. *Contemporary Theory of Expressionism* (Bern, 1974).

Péter, László, and Robert B. Pynsent, eds. *Intellectuals and the Future in the Habsburg Monarchy 1890–1914* (London, 1988).

Pfabigan, Alfred. *Geistesgegenwart: Essays zur österreichischen Moderne* (Vienna, 1991).

———, ed. *Ornament und Askese im Zeitgeist des Wien der Jahrhundertwende* (Vienna, 1985).

Plener, Ernst von. *Erinnerungen*, 2 vols. (Stuttgart/Leipzig, 1911–1921).

Pock, Friedrich. *Grenzwacht im Südosten, ein halbes Jahrhundert Südmarck* (Graz, 1940).

Pollak, Michael. *Vienne 1900: Une identité blessée* (Paris, 1984).

Pollock, Griselda. "Modernity and the Spaces of Feminity," in idem, *Vision and Difference* (New York, 1988).

Popper, Karl. *The Open Society* (London, 1945).

———. *Unended Quest: An Intellectual Autobiography* (LaSalle, 1976).

———. *In Search of a Better World* (London, 1992).

———. *The Myth of the Framework* (London, 1994).

———. "Zur Philosophie des Heimatgedankens," *Die Quelle* 77 (1927): 899–908.

———. "Kant's Critique and Cosmology," in idem, *Conjectures and Refutations* (New York, 1963).

———. "Der wichtigste Beitrag seit Aristoteles," *Wissenschaft aktuell* 1 (September 1980). ["Interview on Kurt Gödel and the Vienna Circle."]

———. "Autobiography: Draft," Hoover Institute Archives, Popper Papers (134, 4, 9) [Popper Archives].

Prestel, Claudia T. "Frauen und die Zionistische Bewegung (1897–1933): Tradition oder Revolution?" *Historische Zeitschrift* 258 (1994).

Przybyszewski, Stanisław. *Totenmesse* (Berlin, 1893).

Pynsent, Robert B. *Questions of Identity: Czech and Slovak Ideas of Nationality and Personality* (London, 1994).

Pynsent, Robert B., ed. *Decadence and Innovation* (London, 1989).

Raeff, Mark. *The Well-Ordered Police State: Social and Institutional Change through Law in the Germanies and Russia, 1600–1800* (New Haven, 1983).

Redlich, Josef. *Das österreichische Staats- und Reichsproblem: Geschichtliche Darstellung der inneren Politik der Habsburgischen Monarchie 1848 bis zum Untergang des Reiches*, 2 vols. (Leipzig, 1926).

——. *Emperor Francis Joseph of Austria* (New York, 1928).

——. *Schicksalsjahre Österreichs 1908–1919: Das politische Tagebuch Josef Redlichs*, ed. Fritz Fellner, 2 vols. (Graz, 1953).

Reik, Theodor. *Arthur Schnitzler als Psycholog*, ed. Bernd Urban (Frankfurt, 1993).

Ritter, Harry. "Austro-German Liberalism and the Modern Liberal Tradition," in *German Studies Review* 7 (1984): 227–247.

Robertson, Ritchie. "The Problem of 'Jewish Self-Hatred' in Herzl, Kraus and Kafka," *Oxford German Studies* 16 (1985).

Rose, J. *Sexuality in the Field of Vision* (London, 1986).

Rossbacher, Karlheinz. *Literatur und Liberalismus: Zur Kultur der Ringstraßenzeit in Wien* (Vienna, 1992).

Roth, Joseph. *Radetzkymarsch* (Berlin, 1932).

Roth, Michael S. "Performing History: Modernist Contextualism in Carl Schorske's *Fin-de-Siècle Vienna*," *American Historical Review* 94 (June 1994): 729–745.

——, ed. *Rediscovering History: Culture, Politics, and the Psyche* (Palo Alto, 1994).

Rozenblit, Marsha. *The Jews of Vienna 1867–1914: Assimilation and Identity* (Albany, 1983).

Said, Edward. *Culture and Imperialism* (New York, 1993).

Sármány-Parsons, Ilona. *Gustav Klimt* (New York, 1987).

——. *Viennese Painting at the Turn of the Century* (Budapest, 1991).

——. "Malerei 1890–1900: Aufbruch in die Moderne—Vienna, Prague, Budapest," in Richard G. Plaschka and Horst Haselsteiner, eds., *Mitteleuropa: Idee, Wissenschaft und Kultur im 19. und 20. Jahrhundert* (Vienna, 1997), 175–186.

——. "The Image of the City in Turn of the Century Painting in Central Europe," in *Central European University History Department Yearbook, 1996* (Budapest, 1996).

Schaukal, Richard. *Meine Gärten* (Berlin, 1897).

——. *Sehnsucht* (Munich, 1900).

——. *Intérieurs aus dem Leben der Zwanzigjährigen* (Leipzig, 1901).

——. *Das Buch der Tage und Träume*, rev. ed. (1899; Leipzig, 1902).

——. *Ausgewählte Gedichte* (Leipzig, 1904).

——. *Leben und Meinungen des Herrn Andreas von Balthesser eines Dandy und Dilettanten* (Munich, 1907).

——. *Vom Geschmack: Zeitgemässe Laienpredigten über das Thema Kultur* (Munich, 1910).

Schaukal, Richard, and Arthur Schnitzler. *Briefwechsel* (1900–1902), ed. Reinhard Urbach, *Modern Austrian Literature* 8, no. 3/4 (1975).

Schaukal, Richard von. *Beiträge zu einer Selbstdarstellung* (1929; reprint Vienna, 1934).

————. "Selbstdarstellung," in *Um die Jahrhundertwende* (1928/29; reprint, Munich, 1966).

Schickedanz, H.J. *Femme fatale: Ein Mythos wird entblättert* (Dortmund, 1983).

Schnitzler, Arthur. *Das weite Land*, in idem, *Das dramatische Werk*, 2 vols. (Frankfurt, 1962), 2:217–320.

————. *Der Weg ins Freie* (Frankfurt, 1978), in English as *The Road to the Open*, trans. H. Samuel (Evanston, 1991).

————. *Undiscovered Country*, trans. Tom Stoppard (London, 1980).

————. *My Youth in Vienna* (New York, 1970).

Schorske, Carl E. *Fin-de-Siècle Vienna: Politics and Culture* (New York, 1980).

————. *Thinking with History: Explorations in the Passage to Modernism* (Princeton, 1998).

————. "Politics and Psyche in *fin-de-siècle* Vienna: Schnitzler and Hofmannsthal," in *The American Historical Review* 66 (July 1961): 930–946.

Schultze-Naumburg, Paul. "Die Internationale Ausstellung 1896 der Secession in München," *Die Kunst für Alle* 11 (1 July 1896).

Schwarz, Egon. "Arthur Schnitzler und die Aristokratie," in Hartmut Scheible, ed., *Arthur Schnitzler in neuer Sicht* (Munich, 1981), 54–70.

Schwarzer, Ernst. *Geld und Gut in Neuösterreich* (Vienna, 1857).

Schweiger, Werner J. *Wiener Werkstätte* (New York, 1984).

Seton-Watson, Hugh, and Christopher Seton-Watson. *The Making of a New Europe: R. W. Seton-Watson and the Last Years of Austria-Hungary* (Seattle, 1981).

Shedel, James. *Art and Society: The New Art Movement in Vienna, 1897–1914* (Palo Alto, 1981).

————. "Emperor, Church, and People: Religion and Dynastic Loyalty During the Golden Jubilee of Franz Joseph," *The Catholic Historical Review* 76 (January 1990).

Showalter, Elaine. *Sexual Anarchy* (London, 1990).

Silverman, Paul. "Law and Economics in Interwar Vienna: Kelsen, Mises and the Regeneration of Austrian Liberalism" (Ph.D. diss.: University of Chicago, 1984).

Simenauer, Erich. *Rainer Maria Rilke: Legende und Mythos* (Frankfurt, 1953).

Simmons, Sherwin. "Kitsch oder Kunst? Kokoschka's *Der Sturm* and Commerce in Art," *The Print Collector's Newsletter* 23:5 (November–December, 1992): 161–167.

Simon, Walter. *Rainer Maria Rilke: Die Weise von Liebe und Tod: Texte und Dokumente* (Frankfurt, 1974).

Sked, Alan. *The Decline and Fall of the Habsburg Empire, 1815–1918* (London, 1989).

Sokel, Walter. "Two Views of 'Minority' Literature: Deleuze, Kafka, and the German-Jewish Enclave of Prague," *Quarterly World Report* 6 (1983): 5–8.

Sonnleitner, Johann. "Eherne Sonette 1914: Richard von Schaukal und der Erste Weltkrieg," in Klaus Amann and Hubert Lengauer, eds., *Österreich und der große Krieg, 1914–1918*, (Vienna, 1989), 152–158.

Sorkin, David. *The Transformation of German Jewry, 1770–1840* (Oxford, 1987).

————. "From Context to Comparison: The German Haskalah and Reform Catholicism," *Tel Aviver Jahrbuch für deutsche Geschichte* 22 (1991): 23–58.

Spiel, Hilde. *Vienna's Golden Autumn* (London, 1987).

————, ed. *Wien: Spektrum einer Stadt* (Munich, 1971).

Srp, Karel, ed. *Das Slawische Epos*, Catalogue (Krems, 1994).

Stadler, Friedrich. *Vom Positivismus zur "Wissenschaftliche Weltauffassung"* (Vienna, 1982).

——. *Studien zum Wiener Kreis* (Frankfurt, 1997).

——. "Spätaufklärung und Sozialdemokratie in Wien, 1918–1938," in Franz Kadrnoska, ed., *Aufbruch und Untergang: Österreichische Kultur zwischen 1918 und 1938* (Vienna, 1981), 441–473.

Steed, Henry Wickham. *The Hapsburg Monarchy* (New York, 1969).

Steinberg, Michael P. *The Meaning of the Salzburg Festival: Austria as Theater and Ideology 1890–1938* (Ithaca, 1990).

——. " 'Fin-de-siècle Vienna' Ten Years Later: 'Viel Traum, Wenig Wirklichkeit,'" *Austrian History Yearbook* 22 (1991): 151–162.

Steiner, George. "Le langage et l'inhumain," *Revue d'esthétique*, new series, 9 (1985): 65–66.

Stekl, Hannes, et al., eds. *Bürgertum in der Habsburgermonarchie I* (Vienna 1990).

——. *"Durch Arbeit, Besitz, Wissen und Gerechtigkeit": Bürgertum in der Habsburgermonarchie II* (Vienna, 1992).

Stewart, Desmond. *Theodor Herzl: Artist and Politician* (New York, 1974).

Stieg, Gerald. *Der Brenner und Die Fackel* (Salzburg, 1977).

——. "Ferdinand Ebners Kulturkritik. Am Beispiel der Salzburger Festspiele," in Christoph König et al., eds., *Gegen den Traum vom Geist* (Salzburg, 1985).

Stölzl, Christoph. *Kafkas böses Böhmen* (Munich, 1975).

Stone, Norman. *Europe Transformed* (Glasgow, 1983).

Stourzh, Gerald. "Galten die Juden als Nationalität Altösterreichs?" in Anna Drabek, Mordechai Eliav, and Gerald Stourzh, eds., *Prag-Czernowitz-Jerusalem* (Eisenstadt, 1984), 73–117.

Strobl, Alice. *Gustav Klimt: Die Zeichnungen*, vols. 1–3 (Salzburg, 1980–84).

Suchy, Viktor. " Die 'österreichische Idee' als konservative Staatsidee bei Hugo von Hofmannsthal, Richard von Schaukal und Anton Wildgans," in Friedbert Aspetsberger, ed., *Staat und Gesellschaft in der modernen österreichischen Literatur* (Vienna, 1977).

Sulloway, Frank L. *Freud—Biologist of the Mind: Beyond the Psychoanalytic Legend* (Cambridge, Mass., 1992).

Szabadi, Julia. *Gulácsy Lajos* (Budapest, 1983).

——. *Art Nouveau in Hungary* (Budapest, 1989).

Székely, András. *Csók István* (Budapest, 1977).

Taylor, A. J. P. *The Habsburg Monarchy, 1809–1918: A History of the Austrian Empire and Austria Hungary* (Chicago, 1976).

Teeuwisse, Nicolaas. *Vom Salon zur Secession* (Berlin, 1986).

Teich, Mikuláš, and Roy Porter. *Fin de Siècle and Its Legacy* (Cambridge, 1990).

Tezner, Friedrich. *Der Kaiser* (Vienna, 1909).

Thurnher, Eugen, Walter Weiss et al., eds. *"Kakanien"* (Vienna, 1991).

Timms, Edward. *Karl Kraus: Apocalyptic Satirist* (New Haven, 1986).

Tögel, Christfried. *"und gedenke die Wissenschaft auszubeuten." Sigmund Freuds Weg zur Psychoanalyse* (Tübingen, 1989).

Trommler, Frank. "The Creation of a Culture of *Sachlichkeit*," in Geoff Eley, ed., *Society, Culture, and the State in Germany, 1870–1930* (Ann Arbor, 1996), 465–485.

Trommler, Frank. "Sachlichkeit statt Bürgerlichkeit," in Christian Jansen, Lutz Niethammer, and Bernd Weisbrod, eds., *Von der Aufgabe der Freiheit: Politische*

Verantwortung und bürgerliche Gesellschaft im 19. und 20. Jahrhundert (Berlin, 1995), 635–646.

Tschechische Kunst 1878–1914, Catalogue (Darmstadt, 1984).

Tyrell, John. *Czech Opera* (Cambridge, 1988).

Ucakar, Karl. "Demokratie und Wahlrecht in Österreich: Zur Entwicklung von politischer Partizipation und staatliche Legitimationspolitik" (Habilitationsschrift, University of Vienna, 1984).

Varnedoe, Kirk. *Vienna 1900: Art, Architecture and Design* (New York, 1986).

Vergo, Peter. *Art in Vienna, 1898–1918* (London, 1975).

———. *Vienna 1900: Vienna, Scotland and the European Avant-Garde* (Edinburgh, 1983).

Vodopivec, Peter. "Die sozialen und wirtschaftlichen Ansichten des deutschen Bürgertums in Krain vom Ende des sechziger bis zum Beginn der achtziger Jahre des 19. Jahrhunderts," in H. Rumpler and A. Suppan, eds., *Geschichte der Deutschen im Bereich des heutigen Slowenien 1848–1941* (Vienna, 1988).

Wadl, Wilhelm. *Liberalismus und soziale Frage in Österreich* (Vienna, 1987).

Wagner, Nike. *Geist und Geschlecht* (Frankfurt, 1982).

Waissenberger, Robert, ed. *Traum und Wirklichkeit: Wien 1870–1930* (Vienna, 1985).

Wallas, Armin A. "Ort des paradiesischen Lebens und Ort der Verwüstung: Das Bild des Gartens in der österreichischen Literatur der Jahrhundertwende," in *Protokolle* 1 (1991): 73–94.

Wassermann, Jakob. *Mein Weg als Deutscher und Jude* (Berlin, 1921).

Weininger, Otto. *Geschlecht und Charakter* (Vienna, 1903).

———. *Eros und Psyche: Studien und Briefe,* ed. Hannelore Rodlauer (Vienna, 1990).

Weltsch, Felix. "The Rise and Fall of the Jewish-German Symbiosis: The Case of Franz Kafka," *Leo Baeck Institute Yearbook* 1 (1956).

Werfel, Franz. "Brief an einen Staatsmann," in idem, *Zwischen Oben und Unten: Prosa-Tagebücher-Aphorismen-Literarische Nachträge,* ed. Adolf Klarmann (Munich, 1975), 210–215.

Werkner, Patrick. *Physis and Psyche: Der Österreichische Frühexpressionismus* (Vienna, 1986).

———. *Austrian Expressionism: The Formative Years,* trans. Nicholas T. Parsons (Palo Alto, 1993).

White, Hayden. *Metahistory: The Historical Imagination in Nineteenth-Century Europe* (Baltimore, 1973).

———. *Tropics of Discourse: Essays in Cultural Criticism* (Baltimore, 1978).

Whitford, Frank. *Egon Schiele* (New York, 1980).

———. *Gustav Klimt* (London, 1990).

Winters, Stanley B., ed. *Thomas G. Masaryk (1850–1937): Thinker and Politician* (London, 1990).

Wistrich, Robert S. *The Jews of Vienna in the Age of Franz Joseph* (Oxford, 1989).

Wistrich, Robert S. "Karl Kraus: Jewish Prophet or Renegade?" *European Judaism* 9, no. 2 (1975).

Wittels, Fritz. *Freud and the Child Woman: The Memoirs of Fritz Wittels,* ed. Edward Timms (New Haven, 1995).

Wittlich, Petr. *Prague Fin-de-Siècle* (Paris, 1992).

Wollstonecraft, Mary. *A Vindication of the Rights of Woman* (New York, 1975).

Zamoyski, Adam. *The Polish Way* (London, 1989).

Zizek, Slavoj. "Otto Weininger, or, Woman Doesn't Exist," *New Formations* 23 (summer 1994): 97–113.

Zöllner, Erich. *Geschichte Österreichs: Von den Anfängen bis zur Gegenwart* (Munich, 1979).

Zohn, Harry. *Karl Kraus* (New York, 1972).

Zweig, Arnold. "The Emergence of Theodor Herzl," in Meyer W. Weisgal, ed., *Theodor Herzl: A Memorial* (New York, 1929).

Zweig, Stefan. *The World of Yesterday* (New York, 1943).

———. "King of the Jews," *Herzl Year Book* 3 (1960).

INDEX

Lightning Source UK Ltd.
Milton Keynes UK
UKOW031857220313

208049UK00004B/24/P